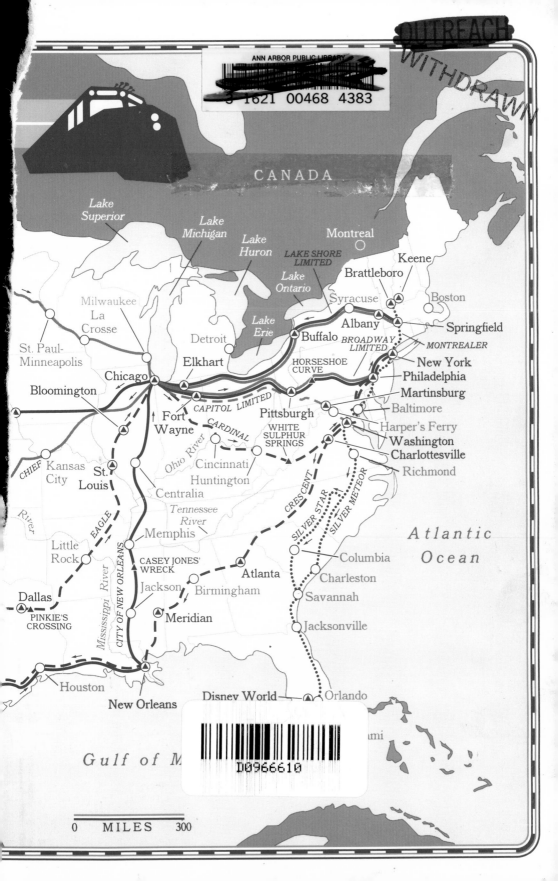

CANADA

Lake Superior

Lake Michigan

Lake Huron

LAKE SHORE LIMITED

Lake Ontario

Montreal

Keene

Brattleboro

Syracuse

Lake Erie

Buffalo

Albany

Boston

Springfield

BROADWAY LIMITED

Milwaukee
La Crosse

Detroit

MONTREALER

St. Paul-
Minneapolis

Elkhart

Chicago

HORSESHOE
CURVE

New York

Philadelphia

Bloomington

CAPITOL LIMITED

Pittsburgh

Martinsburg

Fort
Wayne

CARDINAL

WHITE
SULPHUR
SPRINGS

Baltimore

Harper's Ferry

Ohio River

Cincinnati

Washington

Charlottesville

CHIEF

Kansas
City

St.
Louis

Huntington

Richmond

River

Centralia

*Tennessee
River*

CRESCENT

EAGLE

Memphis

SILVER STAR

SILVER METEOR

*Atlantic
Ocean*

Little
Rock

CASEY JONES'
WRECK

Columbia

Dallas

Mississippi River

Jackson

Birmingham

Atlanta

Charleston

PINKIE'S
CROSSING

CITY OF NEW ORLEANS

Meridian

Savannah

Jacksonville

Houston

New Orleans

Disney World

Orlando

Gulf of M

mi

0   MILES   300

MAKING TRACKS

MAKING TRACKS

An American Rail Odyssey

TERRY PINDELL

GROVE WEIDENFELD
NEW YORK

Published by Grove Weidenfeld
A division of Wheatland Corporation
841 Broadway
New York, NY 10003-4793

Published in Canada by General Publishing Company, Ltd.

Excerpt from "They Call the Wind Maria" (Alan J. Lerner / Frederick Loewe)
© 1980 Chappell & Co., Inc. All Rights Reserved. Used by Permission.

Library of Congress Cataloging-in-Publication Data

Pindell, Terry.
Making tracks: an American rail odyssey / Terry Pindell.—1st ed.
p.   cm.
1. United States—Description and travel—1981-   2. Railroad
travel—United States.   3. Pindell, Terry—Journeys—United States.
4. Amtrak.   I. Title.
E169.04.P56   1990
917.304′927—dc20   89-77973
                                                            CIP
ISBN 0-8021-1279-X

Manufactured in the United States of America

This book is printed on acid-free paper

Designed by Irving Perkins Associates

Maps by Arnold Bombay

First Edition 1990

1   3   5   7   9   10   8   6   4   2

*For my father, whose untimely passing
set this journey in motion.*

Acknowledgments

I would like to thank the following people for helping to make this book possible:

—Dayton Duncan, writer and sometime-presidential-campaign press secretary, whose book *Out West* inspired this one and whose encouragement and tutelage moved it from fantasy to reality.

—Steve Hall, English department chairman at Keene High School, whose early proofreading and good sense suggestions kept the book on track.

—Ernest Hebert, author of the Darby novels of Cheshire County, whose experience and tough wisdom taught me that it takes work and suffering to write a book, even one like this.

—Connie Sayre, formerly of Weidenfeld and Nicolson, who found the book an audience.

—Clifford Black, director of public relations at Amtrak, whose cheerful and intelligent assistance opened a lot of doors.

Acknowledgments

—My colleagues in the Keene School District, whose support in my former career gave me the confidence to pursue this one.

—Jane Perlungher, the staff of the Keene Public Library, and nameless heroes who invented the inter-library loan system which enabled me to do virtually all of my historical research in the comfort of my small New England city.

—William Strachan, formerly of Grove Weidenfeld, whose gentle editing made this a better book than it was when he took it up. Of all the horrors in publishing which writer friends warned me about, difficult relationships with an editor is one I have yet to encounter.

—Ted Johnson, my copy editor, who patiently waded through the morass of conflicting rail usage and my habitual inconsistency.

—Amtrak employees named throughout the book, who, while carrying out some of the most demanding and sometimes thankless jobs in America, still found time and grace enough to enrich my story with theirs.

—Proprietors and employees of various trackside establishments also named throughout the book, who risked a "bad review" to allow me to portray another less well-known travelers' America.

—The scores of fellow travelers who willingly shared so much of themselves to provide the drama of continental rail travel. With a few exceptions who wished to have their real names used, I have changed names to protect their privacy.

—My mother, Arlene, whose gift of a turbocharged portable IBM computer allowed me to overcome the last obstacle (my klutziness with pen and paper) to my becoming a writer—just as she prophesied twenty-five years ago.

—My children, Molly and Katie, who endured nightmares about far-away train crashes and a year of having a part-time father.

—And most of all, my wife, Nancy, who despite unspoken misgivings, gave me the latitude and support needed to pursue this project to completion—and whose idea the whole thing was to begin with.

Contents

Contents

Prologue

I SPENT most of 1988 riding long-distance passenger trains throughout America. I traveled them all—all twenty-one Amtrak routes,
thirty thousand miles—through all but three states, with debarcations
in virtually every major city in the country and special visits to some
smaller towns with strong memories of a bygone era.

When I first began this odyssey, I had no idea what I was looking for.
I wanted to see the country from a vantage point that today is not well
known, to immerse myself in the mode of travel that dominated the
greatest eras of the country's growth, to see if the rail routes would lead
me to integration of past and present, of history and headlines, of mind
and memory.

I wanted to travel the entire country without ever eating in a fast-
food restaurant, spending money in a mall, driving on an interstate, or
waiting in an airport. I was inspired by William Least Heat Moon, who
discovered America by following the blue highways, and by Dayton
Duncan, who rediscovered the west by following the route of Lewis and
Clark in a VW camper. I aspired to extend their explorations by riding
the steel rails.

The object of my quest emerged as I traveled. The view of the American landscape from the rails invokes the theory that history progresses through revolutionary leaps rather than slow evolution. Once people left the shores of the Atlantic, it was the routes of the railroad that radically shaped the face and drew the map of America that became, for a time, a reference point, a platform for the next leap. Since the heyday of the railroad, we have leaped again; but the routes of the railroads delineate the shape of America at the last still point before we embarked on our current trajectory. I discovered in my travels that I was seeking the remnants of this platform, like looking for the germinal railroad station in a city where all travel now runs through the airport and interstates outside of town. I finally found what I didn't know I was looking for—a lost grail of our American selves that sobered me with the price we have paid for our success.

I also found something I wasn't looking for: the people who travel by train. The decision to take the extra time to travel by train implies a certain set of worldviews and priorities that indeed define a subculture. Only a small proportion of these people are what one would call rail buffs. Rather the steel-riders represent a colorful spectrum of American life united by a common willingness to slow the pace of their lives, to defy modern travel convention, to see their country by taking "the road less traveled." Take the lounge-car testimony of one steel-rider over that of a herd of travelers by air or concrete—he has seen the country and he has something to say about it.

So here are two stories: one of the historical American landscape defined by the passenger rail routes that shaped it; the other of the people who travel those lines today. I might have written two books, but for the delightful surprise that, so often, the two tell the same tale.

The true history of America is the history of transportation—in which the names of railroad presidents are more significant than the names of Presidents of the United States.

—PHILIP GUEDALLA

MAKING TRACKS

Introduction

THE MONTREALER AND THE SILVER STAR

. . . Trains cross the continent in a swirl of dust and thunder, the leaves fly down the tracks behind them: the great trains cleave through gulch and gully, they rumble with spoked thunder on the bridges over the powerful brown wash of mighty rivers, they toil through hills, they skirt the rough brown stubble of shorn fields, they whip past empty stations in the little towns and their great stride pounds its even pulse across America.

—THOMAS WOLFE

IT'S 2:00 A.M. down by the single-track line of the Boston & Maine in Brattleboro, Vermont. The sodium-vapor lights of the warehouse lot across the tracks cast grim shadows from two small figures huddled by the rails. One puts her head on the rail and writhes around while the other rummages through the stones between the ties. A handful of people lean against a cinder-block wall and watch them while a man in a blue coat paces the platform pavement and checks his watch.

There are traces of crusted snow along the ends of the ties, and fickle April clouds drift across the thin old moon. The air hangs silent except for the passing of an occasional auto down Main Street. A police cruiser slows and turns into the alley by the tracks, and the man in the blue coat goes to confer with its driver while the radio crackles and sputters.

The officer has brought a cup of coffee from the Dunkin' Donuts over on Main Street.

My seven-year-old daughter, Molly, calls out, "I'm listening for the train like the Indians, Daddy." Her younger sister, Katie, holds up a cinder and shouts, "There are lots of these, Daddy." Their excited voices rupture the somnolence of the nighttime hour and seem to cause each of the leaners on the wall to stir. For the man in the blue coat and the faceless cops in the cruiser, the hour is an interlude in their work shift. For the other adults on the platform, it's a slightly unreal, inconvenient interruption of sleep. For my kids, who have never before been up and about at this hour, never mind waiting for a train to take them to Florida, the night buzzes with the magic of anticipation and freedom. I can feel it too, looking south down the tracks toward some blue lights gleaming like ice in crystal moonlight. I swear you can see forever.

The Boston & Maine tracks run along the Connecticut River behind the commercial blocks of downtown Brattleboro. The quaint station, once a major junction for travelers in this part of the country, has been made into a museum. Today's station consists of a small waiting room and a bathroom in the backside basement of the museum. Skip, the stationmaster, arrives an hour before the southbound train to open up and turn on the lights. He will stay till the arrival and departure of the northbound at 4:00 and then will close up and go home for a few hours of sleep before going to work at his job as a security guard at 9:00.

He explains that the train is often several hours late. "Guilford Industries, the parent company of the Boston & Maine, don't care about railroading. They want to sell this line to developers buying up property for malls and condos up the Connecticut River valley. So they let the track go to hell in hopes that Amtrak will give up on the route."

But tonight's southbound train is almost on time. A distant whine of the dissonant horns rouses Skip to action checking tickets and reminding folks to stay behind the yellow line on the platform. When he checks our ticket, he mumbles, "*Montrealer* to New York and *Silver Star* to Florida. Boy, yer gonna ride the worst and the best."

The horn blares closer now and a headlight beam suddenly flashes down the tracks as the *Montrealer* rumbles into the Brattleboro station. I can feel it in the pavement underfoot, and the last blast of the horn sends Molly scurrying toward the station wall. The waiters are beyond wakefulness now, as if the arrival of the train somehow casts a workaday sunlight over the scene. Attendants pop off the train with their portable metal steps and with gestures and shouts guide the waiting passengers to the correct cars. With a fury of fumbling, my wife, Nancy, and I drag our bags behind our bouncing kids into a coach for the nighttime ride to New York.

Inside, dimly lit bodies sprawl in a variety of contorted positions on the reclining seats. My kids hush as if walking into church. They slide quietly into their seats and cuddle up with their stuffed animals and blankets; after a few excited giggles, they are not heard from again. My wife is able to resume the sleeping position she had in the car while waiting for the train.

Not me. Sleep is out of the question. Shortly past Brattleboro, the train stops in the middle of nowhere. A talk with the conductor reveals that a freight car has been spotted sitting on the main-line tracks. No one knows how or why it got there. The train has to wait for it to be removed by a switch engine from down the line. The conductor shakes his head and says that the *Montrealer* is cursed. "Whatever can go wrong does go wrong on this line."

At 3:00 near Hadley, Massachusetts, the train stops again at a lonesome spot far from a station. I hook up with the conductor in the vestibule between cars, where he has the top half of the Dutch door open. We are on a siding waiting for the northbound *Montrealer* to pass. He tells me when to look and puts his hand on my shoulder to make sure I get my head back in time as the northbound roars by with a tremendous blast.

Later the train backs into the Springfield station, which is located on an east-west line that intersects with our route. From my window I can see the lifeless neon of late-night downtown streets, the silent police cruisers, and the anonymous figure striding to wherever he goes at 4:00 A.M. in center city.

In New Haven, the diesel engines are decoupled and replaced by electric engines for the remainder of the run down Long Island Sound to New York. Strings of bare light bulbs cast their derelict glow over a railroading ritual that has continued uninterrupted here for nearly a century.

The run from New Haven down the Connecticut coast is schizophrenic. We roll through industrial centers, patrician enclaves, ghettos, and substantial middle-class suburbs with mechanical indifference—the railroad links them all. Sunrise catches commuters waiting for their Metro runs over these same tracks, and the *Montrealer* rattles over Hell Gate Bridge into Queens with the new day, the towers of Manhattan glowing pink in the morning light. The train plunges into the tunnel under the East River and stops at Penn Station in Manhattan. Nancy and the kids wake up disoriented, hungry for breakfast. Though I don't know it at the time, this nighttime coach ride on the *Montrealer* will turn out to be the first step of a very long journey.

After the night ride to New York, we change trains at New York's dismal Penn Station to the *Silver Star*, which runs through the tunnel under the Hudson and emerges into the meadowlands and many of the familiar images I've seen driving I-95 through New Jersey dozens of times before. Snug in our sleeping compartment, we begin to marvel at how fast the train flashes from the refineries of Jersey City to the truck farms of Princeton, along the Delaware River across from the gingerbread designs of the rowing club boathouses and into the bustling downtown of Philadelphia.

There's a real dining car on this train, and the vegetable soup and hot sandwiches are especially tasty as we pass the wide vistas of ships working the lower Delaware on our left. It reminds the kids of how food always tastes better on camping vacations. After lunch they set up camp with their dolls in the lowered upper bunk of our compartment while I watch the inlets of Chesapeake Bay roll by. Fishermen in their skiffs wave to the train as we rumble over the heavy steel bridges. My wife has struck up a conversation with the couple in the next room, and, after my sleepless night on the *Montrealer*, I doze to the combined sleepy hum of the tracks, the kids' soft chatter, and the voices in the next compartment.

By midafternoon, as the old row houses of Baltimore glide by our window, I am feeling refreshed. Near Washington, approaching that hour when I habitually experience an excruciating exhausted tension when driving, the service attendant arrives at our compartment with a box of ice and two small bottles of wine. I catch myself in the act of declining as I realize that I don't have to drive. I drink a little bottle of wine and then another before dinner, putting my feet up with a good pack in my pipe and watching Maryland whiz by at 110 miles an hour.

I time our speed by the mileposts and say to the kids several times, "We're really humming." The kids pick up on the phrase, recognizing in it and its moment a quality of satisfaction and genuine ease that is rare and precious. Ever since, when they want to know if life at the moment is right, they ask me, "Are we humming, Daddy?"

The electrified high-speed corridor between New York and Washington is a real surprise to first-time riders. The tracks are jointless welded ribbon rail laid on spring-loaded concrete ties. The engines are modern electrics powered by seventeen thousand volts pumped through an overhead catenary where the blue spark blazes as the engine's pantographs flash by. All grade crossings have been eliminated—one misses the familiar Doppler clanging of crossing signals. There is no clickety-clack at 120 miles an hour over welded ribbon rail, just a low hum that resonates in the bones.

But just a few feet beyond the roadbed itself, the metropolitan corridor shows its true colors of decay and dereliction. It is ironic that in rebuilding the northeast-corridor tracks on an existing infrastructure of the old Pennsylvania Railroad, Amtrak has run its flagship route through a landscape otherwise characterized by aggressive neglect. It seems almost sinful to be riding to Florida just a few feet from slums where people can't even afford the ticket out of the neighborhood. And yet in an instant the view can evolve from rusted bedsprings, abandoned refrigerators, garbage, and ghetto streets to the green lawns of thriving New Jersey industries, the graceful walks of Philadelphia parks, or the clean stone of Washington monuments; America has grown up haphazardly along its rail routes.

South of Washington, where diesel engines take over, there are still grade-level road crossings whose clanging signals evoke mythic nostalgia. The train attendants joke about the occasional good old boy in a pickup truck whose race with the train to a crossing would end in a disastrous tie. Here the train rolls at seventy-five to ninety miles an hour through greening Virginia countryside on the tracks of the Richmond, Fredericksburg & Potomac. We pass freights carrying autos and trucks to the south and others with refrigerator cars full of oranges heading north.

In the small town of Ashland, Virginia, the tracks run through a green separating the two lanes of Main Street in the center of the village. Folks sitting on the front steps of the Ashland Pharmacy wave as the train passes at the reduced speed of forty miles an hour. A family picnics on the green, and an old black couple rocks in the swing on the porch of what looks like a small mansion, complete with Doric columns.

South of Richmond we have dinner riding the tracks of the old Seaboard Air Line Railroad, now part of the CSX conglomerate. We are seated at a booth with a blue plastic tablecloth, real stainless dinnerware, and yellow silk roses in stainless-steel bud vases. But the dominant ambience is provided by the North Carolina sunset over the tobacco fields and forests of southern pine.

The dinner is served on plastic platters, but there any resemblance to airline meals ends. My sirloin steak with mushrooms is cooked to order with touches of the flame still smoking as it is served by a waiter who tells jokes and fusses over the kids. They delight in the traditional railroad cheesecake and carrot cake.

Later, with the kids tucked securely in bed, Nancy and I visit the lounge car, better known to train travelers as the bar car. This is the heart of the train, where on overnight runs the conductor, service chief, and assistants camp out, count money, check manifests, make announcements, and hold court. Here passengers gather to smoke, drink, flirt, find friends, and tell stories.

Tonight a college girl who rolls her own cigarettes describes her quest by train for spirituality as she seduces a young traveling salesman. An insurance company executive works out of his briefcase and explains that these days he travels to U.S. meetings almost exclusively by train because he considers airlines to be the travel equivalent of fast food—"same quality, same service, same body hangover." Here he can "catch my breath, get off the clock, and get real again." He has made himself valuable enough to his employer that if the company wants him in Miami by Wednesday, it gives him enough time to get there by train.

A middle-aged conductor grumbles that real railroad men like himself who have learned the trade by working up through the ranks are today passed over for guys with MBAs who "don't know a fishplate from a fishhook." But it's not as bad on the railroad as in some walks of life. He recalls a passenger's story about being passed over for a promotion at a bank because a handwriting analyst interpreted his signature as too timid, lacking in boldness.

When we return to our bedroom, the beds have been prepared, the sheets turned down, and bedtime snacks left on the fluffy pillows. "Is this real?" asks Nancy as we snuggle in to the clickety-clack underneath the floor. The day has indeed had a quality of remoteness from the familiar that feels like the enchantment of childhood memory.

Walt Disney, a rail fan himself, created Mickey Mouse during a train ride on the old Santa Fe, and Disney World today is crisscrossed by various kinds of trains. But the one ride I would like to see is missing— an old-time passenger train with full luxury service running from Disney World to some real place, like Orlando or Tampa.

In the beer emporiums, visitors enchanted with the spell of illusion discuss the proposition that the Disney people should be hired to run places like New York City. "People management" is a phrase used loosely here by folks who aren't trying to be funny. Its fundamental proposition is that fantasy makes people docile, malleable, conforming. In the sunbaked central Florida desert, this kind of talk is taken with philosophical seriousness.

Introduction

The trip to Disney World makes philosophers of my children at a very young age. Early in the first day I lean against a boulder along one of the paths that gives ever so slightly under my weight. My children rap on it; it is plastic and hollow.

When we return to our hotel that night, we discover that the rocks in the gardens are plastic and hollow like those in Disney World. So are those in the courtyard outside the restaurant across the highway. For the remainder of the trip my children rap on things and ask the age-old question "What is real?"

This first family train trip leads to others. There is a trip to historic Williamsburg, lovingly restored with authentic materials, and Busch Gardens, which consists of "re-creations" of European settings through which violently careen a variety of high-tech amusement-park rides. The advertising for the place invites visitors to experience Europe without the hazards and hassles of travel to Europe itself.

In Denver at the Casa Bonita you eat Mexican fast food in a plastic re-creation of the wild west. The whole place is located inside a shopping mall; not even the weather need intrude. Literally hundreds of people per hour are run through the restaurant and then treated to a "shoot-out" in which the victim falls fifty feet into a pool (with real water—I checked). Action and illusion, violence and lies—prime-time TV imprinted on the American landscape.

What a relief, after each of these excursions, to return to the passenger trains. I believe part of that feeling is due to the fact that in the jet age, we think of trains as Disney rides. To board a train and discover it running fast and carrying real people long distances to real places is like a splash in the face with cool water on a nauseatingly hot day.

After Disney World, I began to dream of riding trains in search of a real America. I dreamed for four years, with an occasional family train trip here and there and rail history books cluttering the house, and then, at age forty, I knew that I had to do it all the way.

I woke up one day that year, having just lost an election for mayor of my small city in New Hampshire, on leave from my teaching job, dissatisfied, restless, and still mourning the untimely passing of my father a year earlier. Steinbeck's title *The Winter of Our Discontent* kept creeping into my thoughts, and it was only November.

They call it midlife crisis, a rite of passage. I inventoried my assets: leave of absence, understanding spouse, maps, rail histories, timetables, and a recurring vision that somewhere down my grandfather's tracks, I might learn something that would help me get on with the business of living in America in the twilight of the twentieth century. What better route than the web of American rails, historical symbol of national unity and synthesis of time and place? What better conveyance than coaches, dining cars, and sleepers inhabited by folks avoiding airports, fast-food chains, shopping malls, and interstate highways? By February, like generations of seekers for America before me, I was making tracks.

PART ONE

Winter West

This is the way to India!

—THOMAS DURANT

Winter West

Chapter One

Passages

THE *LAKE SHORE LIMITED*

W HILE most Americans across the land are settling down with their popcorn and soft drinks, hero sandwiches, or pizza and beer in warm little gatherings before the flickering glow of the video hearth for the Super Bowl, I am waiting for a train to Chicago in the drafty hole in the wall that passes for the Amtrak station in Springfield, Massachusetts. When the cavernous old station was abandoned during Amtrak's 1981 budget cuts, the new station was literally carved into the Boston & Albany's east-west granite overpass at street level. Though the station serves a growing class of business commuters to New York, inside I still have to ask the ticket agent behind the wired-glass partition to release the electrically operated lock to the rest room.

A freight thunders overhead and the waiting travelers stir in their plastic airport-style bucket seats. There are two black mothers with children crawling over them, a trio of professorial types intensely declaiming in tweed, two college girls gushing in whispers, an elderly black man behind a *New York Post*, an irritable bearded father with his wife and two docile small girls, a nervous teenage couple huddling conspiratorially, and a friendly husky fellow listening to the Super

Bowl on a Sony Walkman who once a month takes the train from Buffalo to visit his girlfriend in Hartford. "If I can wait a month to get it," he says, "I can sure as hell wait out a train ride and save some bucks over airfare." Earlier on a weekday, there would be more of the brief-case set commuting to New York, but at this hour on Sunday evening, these are long-distance passengers.

The station resembles nothing so much as an inner-city bus station, but to rural central New Englanders, it is a gateway to America. Springfield is the northernmost extension of Megalopolis, the supercity that runs northeastward from Washington. Here there are buildings over six stories, an international airport, an intersection of interstates, the NBA Hall of Fame, big-city crime, and, best of all, an Amtrak station that connects with west and south. Springfield today is still a frontier crossing, just as it was three hundred years ago when the first expedition went up the Connecticut River to scout the area that became Keene.

I see the ticket agent take the call alerting him to the imminent arrival of our train and head up the stairs to the platform ahead of the announcement. Outside the frigid February air contends with the warm grumble of an idling locomotive with a few passenger cars at-tached to it, a scene that often greets the traveler at even the smaller stations on the line. That train is never the one you're going on, but it whets the appetite. On the siding two tracks away from the platform a Conrail diesel releases its air with a gasp and begins backing toward a line of empty flatcars while two trainmen chug coffee straight from the thermos on its front platform.

The teenage couple has followed me outside and neck joylessly in the shadows. I can hear the girl sobbing and asking if she can call her mother from Chicago. The boy is good to her: of course she can call; she can call right now and they can go back home if she wants to. But she rallies: "No, we're goin' for it—California—aren't we? Can't go back now."

I scan the nearest track to see if anyone has left a penny to be flattened as a souvenir for a subsequent traveler as we used to do on the tracks of my grandfather's Gulf, Mobile & Ohio in Bloomington, Illi-nois, but find only bare track and the usual scattering of candy wrap-pers, soda cans, odd twisted pieces of metal, hanks of cable, bolts, and nondescript lumpy detritus on the scummy ties. I place a penny on the rail, and then feel the burst of excitement I have been waiting for. As if in response to my invocation of the charm on the rail, a headlight gleams over a rise a mile away and slowly grows as the Boston section of the *Lake Shore Limited* drifts in.

For nearly a century, crossing the continent by rail served as a prerequisite rite of initiation before one could earn the title of "well-traveled American." That tradition was inaugurated on May 23, 1870, when members of the Boston Board of Trade made the first transcontinental rail passage in George Pullman's *Hotel Express,* a year after the driving of the golden spike which finally linked the coasts with steel. The trip was recorded by journalist W. R. Steele, who printed twelve issues of the *Trans-Continental* during the journey on a printing press carried in the baggage car. Editor Steele reported that a crowd of thousands gathered at South Station for the train's departure. In a flight of eloquence, he compared the conductor's "All aboard for San Francisco" to the "Yes" of Helen of Troy, to the "nod of a Belgian peasant to Napoleon" and the opening dots of the first transatlantic cablegram.

Tonight, a far more modest occasion, my goal is California too, over much of the same route as that first passage of steel-riders. Just two years ago this night I saw my father conscious for the last time as we watched the Super Bowl in the intensive-care room at the Lahey Clinic near Boston. In my own flight of fancy, I imagine him twenty years earlier boarding this train's forebear to journey by rail to his home town, Bloomington, Illinois, one last time after the death of his father. Already I feel part of something that generations of Americans have shared since early pioneers realized that they were possessed of a continent for a country. But I'm not going to stop with Bloomington or San Francisco; I mean to ride until I've seen it all.

On board, the *Lake Shore Limited* is crowded, and warm and stuffy, despite the cold outside. I notice a number of passengers fiddling with radios and earphones trying vainly to pick up the Super Bowl inside the stainless-steel car. Once we are underway, the conductor comes on the PA to announce that the *Lake Shore Limited* is on time for Albany, Buffalo, Cleveland, Toledo, and Chicago. He continues with a commentary on the progress of the game, which he has tuned in on the train's radio; he will update his report periodically.

As the train picks up speed in the yards of West Springfield, I spot the teenage runaways across the aisle from my seat. The boy has just finished spiking a can of Coke with a little bottle of rum he carries hidden in his pack and sees that I have caught him in the act. "Gimme a break—it's a long train ride," he says.

It takes several tries at conversation before I can convince them that

I'm not bent on hassling them, but finally Tom Grover and Jane De-maris share with me a few pieces of their story. They're both sixteen and have been dating since their first year in high school. Tom's parents are divorced, and he's lived with a friend's family for a year. "Nobody's going to miss me—it's Jane's family that's the problem." They want eventually to get married, but her father doesn't approve.

"We're not eloping," she urges. "We're going to California, where Tom's gonna work and we'll get our own start. Then we'll come back and get married after we've shown my dad that we can make it."

Jane's dad has been outspoken about his disdain for Tom: "You'll never earn what my daughter deserves . . . you aren't half the man I planned to give her to." Tom explains that in southern California he'll get a good construction job and Jane will work at a McDonald's or something. People have told them that you can do that in America today—just split and head for a new place to work.

I ask them why they are taking the train. Jane answers that it's pretty cheap, they don't have much money, and her dad happens to be a train buff. This is how he would do it.

They've never been on a train before, so they join me for a stroll to check it out. The Boston section of the *Lake Shore Limited* is a short train; when it meets and is joined to the New York section at Albany it will be a long one. At this point the consist—that is, the collection of engines and cars that forms a train—includes one F-40 engine, a baggage car, a sleeper, two coaches, and the lounge or bar car. We sit down in the lounge car—beer for me, unspiked Coke for the kids—and I survey the patrons' destinations: Syracuse, Buffalo, Cleveland, De-troit, several to Chicago, and one to Denver. "Looks like we're the long hitters here," I tell the kids.

"Yeah. Our friends think we're crazy, and there's something about how I could get in trouble because of Jane's age, but it doesn't matter. We just gotta do it," says Tom. "Where you headed?"

"Home to New Hampshire—by way of San Francisco, Los Angeles, and New Orleans."

"You're crazy too. Why don't you fly?"

"Because I want to see America."

It may be that television, with events like the Super Bowl, is the bond that unites and defines America today. The jury is still out on whether or not this is a positive expression of a great nation's identity, but there is no question that the thing that begat and bonded a new kind of national community on this continent was the railroad.

True, America didn't invent the railroad, and her early history was shaped more by her seafaring exploits than by the tentative experiments with rails out of Charleston and Baltimore and between Albany and Schenectady. When, in the 1830s, the prototypical Baltimore & Ohio established regular railroad service as a viable form of transportation, the railroad was still subordinate to water transport. Those early short roads linked seaports to nearby rivers, and even the great Pennsylvania Railroad began merely as a series of links over the ridges of the mountains to connect the network of canals in the Alleghenies.

But the steel link between America's railroads and her destiny and identity was inevitable. Here was a nation expanding to a three-thousand-mile width and populated by a people bound and determined to subdue and make use of every mile of it. The sea routes were expensive and slow and could link only the coastal edges. The canals and rivers could not leap mountain ranges and ultimately lost their continental promise when the dream of a Northwest Passage died. Americans saw their future in the great overland trails: the Cumberland, the Santa Fe, the Oregon, the California. These links were tenuous and frail as long as they depended on beast-drawn Conestoga wagons and Concord stagecoaches. But the iron horse would require much the same necessities as the flesh-and-blood steed: water, attainable grades, outposts for service, and a reason for taking people and freight to a particular place. Only when trains began to run on tracks laid on the routes of those trails could the nation begin to achieve its passage to maturity.

By the Civil War, railroads were fixtures in the east, so much so that they were partly responsible for making that war the first of the world's devastating modern conflicts. It wasn't just that American sectional rivalry demanded more hate and bloodshed; it was also the railroads' ability to bring larger numbers of troops to the field of battle in less time: more guns and more bodies to fall.

Despite damages to tracks and delays in building programs it caused, the Civil War ultimately assisted the progress of the railroads. Railroading changed the face of the land, the towns and cities, the business world, and the life-style of people as no other invention had since the wheel. Folks who were oblivious to ways in which other aspects of the industrial revolution were changing their world seized upon the highly visible railroad as the object of righteous outrage. It was largely the Civil War's demonstration of the national need for physical union that overcame this opposition, because the railroads were the one entity that could fulfill that need.

The railroads created the melting pot, too. It wasn't just that waves of immigrants worked for the railroad; the railroads actively recruited homesteaders throughout the world and brought them to settle the vast spaces they served. So the railroads also created the west. The generations that responded to Horace Greeley's "Go west, young man" did so on the steel rails to the sunset.

No other entity so united the frontier and the industrial revolution, pluralism and mobility, freedom and unity. No other symbol so concretely embodied the national Manifest Destiny during America's rush into her century. And yet today, within one generation, the memory fades into a curious obscurity, like the rusted tracks one stumbles upon with surprise amid weeds and brush behind abandoned warehouses on the forgotten side of town.

As the squealing rails announce the tight curves of the Massachusetts Berkshires, the Super Bowl is already history around the orange Formica tables of the bar car, and the kids have gone back to snuggle in their coach seats. At the booth nearest the bar, three young men with the look of a trendy rock band have been asking questions about the game; they don't seem to know what it is. One has his hair cropped burrishly short and wears a weathered green leather jacket; the other two sport spiked hair and T-shirts with obscure logos.

All three have that slightly strange look of foreigners, and indeed Joe Fitzpatrick, Michael Moynihan, and Gary O'Leary are illegal aliens. They are the last of a group of seven that came to America from Ireland last year. "There's no work in Ireland," explains Joe. "All the young people back there want to come here for work, even the rock stars," he adds in reference to U-2, a popular rock group whose leader hails from Joe's hometown of Bray.

It's apparently easy if you don't mind being illegal. All you need is a letter from family or employers saying you're on vacation for three weeks. Joe claims that 160,000 applied for such visas last year; only forty-nine were turned down. He's been hassled a few times by immigration officials. "But I show the lady at the office a new letter from home. She shakes her head and says she sees letters like this all the time but always gives me an extension."

Despite the $8 an hour they could earn installing Sheetrock in Boston versus the $3.80 they'd earn back home if they could find a job, four of their group got homesick and returned to Ireland. "But not me," says Joe. "I'm never goin' back—not as long as I can send my mother more in a month than I could earn altogether in Bray." The remaining three are traveling to Albany to meet up with some friends who came over a couple of years ago.

After a few beers I become accustomed to the strong Irish accent and a barroom intimacy prevails. Joe has mixed feelings about his extra-legal status in America. On the one hand, he gets an adolescent charge out of being "a bit of an outlaw." That status has already netted him certain social benefits, including a shocking sexual offer from the first girl he met in a Boston nightclub, who delivered on the promise in somebody's unlocked car and then disappeared into the night wishing him, "Welcome to America." "But it's not fair really. The immigration quotas favor Hispanics over Irish, but I speak English. I work hard, I have dozens of American relatives, and I won't end up on welfare. I just don't get it."

Yet, restrictive immigration quotas or no, Joe has no doubt that he will someday be a legal U.S. citizen one way or another. "Back home everybody has relatives who came to America. You take it for granted—it's an option that's just there when things don't work out well at home. Isn't that how this whole country was built?"

Joe wants to introduce me to another young European he met boarding the train in Boston. We make our way to the next coach, where we find Franz, staring out the window of the darkened car. Franz is an Austrian rock guitarist, though in his blue serge suit and Reaganesque pompadour he looks more like a Young Republican. He played in night-clubs in Vienna and Budapest till a friend told him about America's current fascination with foreign musicians. He says he was tired of Europe anyway, so he bought a plane ticket and never looked back. But New York felt too much like Europe, "claustrophobic." Someone told him L.A. was different, so he purchased a train ticket.

As the train rolls down into the Hudson River Valley, Franz explains his quest in a soft, halting Germanic accent. "My family is musical—they trained me as classical guitarist from the time I was little boy. But once I first heard rock sound and knew that it came from electric guitars, I learned how to do it. Now—here I am."

Franz is enchanted with how easy it is to travel long distances in America without anxious border crossings. "The worst thing about Europe, let me tell you how bad."

Franz and his girlfriend were visiting Budapest last year. One day a man bumped into her on a busy city street and snatched her purse. Franz chased the man for several blocks and retrieved the discarded

19

purse, expecting to find it empty of valuables. Surprisingly, his girl-friend's money and some jewelry were still there; they concluded that the chase had thwarted the robber's intent and soon forgot the incident.

But at the border stop on the train returning to Vienna, when the Hungarian authorities demanded passports, Franz discovered what the thief had been after. "It's common in eastern Europe—valid pass-ports are valuable on black market. So stupid not to think of that." Without passports, Franz and his girlfriend were taken off the train and detained at gunpoint in the cold outside a desolate border guard-post until an inbound train could take them back to Budapest under arrest. There they had to wait a week till the Austrian consulate rescued them with new passports.

"We took night train to Vienna, clutching our passports . . . just wanted out and never come back." But at the border stop, they encoun-tered the same customs guard who had stopped them before. Though their passports were in order, the guard vaguely remembered them and, associating them with trouble, put them off the train again, per-haps thinking that the passports were forged. For six hours they waited again under guard outside that miserable frontier hut. Tele-phone calls were made, and they were finally allowed to leave on the next train.

Franz has never been able to cross a European border without fear ever since, but in America the dread is transformed into a thrill every time he crosses a state line.

I will discover in the next six months that the melting pot still bubbles, especially on trains. Accustomed to shorter traveling dis-tances and unaccustomed to the preeminence of auto travel massively subsidized by government-built highways, foreigners in America take the train as a matter of course, just as they do at home, where railroads are still promoted, rather than neglected, by their governments.

At Albany, Franz and I detrain to stretch our legs and say farewell to our Irish friends, who are greeted lustily at trackside by their waiting compatriots. One of the group has brought a six-pack of Budweiser in a paper bag and pops one for each of us right on the platform. Ignoring the disapproving glances from the stationmaster on duty, I feel a sense of initiation into an American ritual normally outside the experience of natives. When the rowdy young Irishmen disappear into the night and Franz and I reboard the train, I hear one of them shout out a line from a U-2 song, ". . . into the arms of America."

Now the Boston section is clunked onto the New York section and I am finally able to settle into my sleeping compartment, which had originated in New York. This is one of the pleasurable moments for which there is no equivalent in other kinds of travel. For this ride I am in Amtrak's cheapest sleeping accommodation, a slumbercoach room. With incredible economy of space it contains a small but comfortable cushioned seat; a bed that folds down from the opposing walls in two halves that meet; pillows, sheets, and blankets; a flush toilet; a sink with running hot and cold water that folds down over the toilet; a mirror and shelf with washcloths, towels, and soap; adjustable lighting fixtures; heat and air-conditioning controls; a 120-volt electrical outlet; a tiny closet; and, most important, a large window on the passing world with a pull-down shade. For $34 additional to Chicago, not bad, not bad at all.

When we think of comfortable sleeping cars on trains, we think of George Pullman—the words "Pullman" and "sleeper" have become almost interchangeable. According to the myth, George Pullman suffered an excruciating ride on this route from New York to Chicago in 1858 which prompted him to a burst of inventiveness resulting in the Pullman Palace Car. The comforts of the Palace Car were so attractive that by the end of the Civil War every American railroad with overnight runs placed orders, creating a spontaneous monopoly for Pullman's company. Europeans flocked to America to copy these wonders of American ingenuity, and thus Pullman established luxury rail travel worldwide.

The true history of passenger sleeping railcars is a skewed variant. Indeed George Pullman was invited in 1858 to assist the Field brothers of Chicago in designing a sleeping car specifically for the Chicago & Alton Railroad, running to St. Louis. The comfort and functional design of the cars were abominable. Beds were formed simply by dropping the seatbacks of hard wooden coach seats, there were no partitions or compartments, lighting was by candle, heat was from woodstoves at each end of the car and the wheel trucks were taken directly from freight cars with heavy, stiff springs. But Pullman was an early practitioner of packaging and promotion. He created the illusion of luxury in these cars with such accoutrements as cherrywood paneling, heavy tapestries, and white linen.

By the end of the Civil War, Pullman was ready to revolutionize the railroading world with the Pioneer, the forerunner of his famous Palace Car, but it was too big for the rights-of-way of most railroads' tracks. Pullman saw his opportunity in Lincoln's assassination when he managed to convince Mrs. Lincoln that the Pioneer was the only fitting carriage for the body of the beloved President in its cross-country funeral procession. In deference to Mrs. Lincoln's grief, railroads along the route made the necessary enlargements to their rights-of-way. Thus in one stroke Pullman was able to recover from an engineering blunder while accomplishing one of the truly remarkable promotional stunts of that or any century. All along the route people gazed not only at the body of the slain President but also at Pullman's revolutionary railroad car. The orders began to roll in.

That first transcontinental *Pullman Hotel Express* of 1870 was another characteristic promotional coup. Pullman's genius for publicity is evident in the brilliant device of publishing editor Steele's newspaper on the train en route. Distributed at stations along the way and carried into posterity after the trip by the illustrious passengers on board, the paper guaranteed the association of the Pullman name with both luxury and long-distance travel. The elaborate masthead portrayed a brooding Indian on a rock ledge in the foreground watching a great train steam across the plains toward distant mountains. On each car in clearly legible letters appeared the words "Pullman Pacific Car Company."

Within a decade, Pullman was able to ruthlessly buy out, drive out, or swindle competitors till, with one notable exception, he had achieved a virtual monopoly of sleeping-car travel. To cement that monopoly he insisted on contracts with the railroads stipulating that Pullman cars would be manned only by Pullman personnel. Thus came about the one Pullman innovation which would make a concrete contribution to the comfort of travelers: the through car, which afforded continuous service, making it unnecessary for passengers to make connections as they traveled over long routes involving several railroads.

The one rail system Pullman would not conquer in the nineteenth century was the Vanderbilt system, including the Lake Shore & Michigan Southern, over whose route today's Amtrak *Lake Shore Limited* travels. Commodore Vanderbilt personally insisted on contracts with Pullman's only surviving rival, the Wagner Company. It wasn't that the Wagner cars were more comfortable—though they were—but that the great rail monopolist could not abide being the victim of another monopolist in his own business.

Testimony is ample that nineteenth-century travel in Pullman's Palace sleepers and diners provided something less than luxurious comfort. Concerning the dining service, Mark Twain wrote in 1866 of "flabby rolls, muddy coffee, questionable eggs, gutta-percha beef, and pies whose conception and execution are a dark and bloody mystery."

Concerning the highly touted sleeping cars, Twain commented that their only advantage over European coaches was that they were at least intended as sleeping cars. Frequent complaints of other travelers, including Robert Louis Stevenson and Charles Dickens, included the low backs of the hard seats, excessive heat or cold, dim lighting, sleeping berths so crowded that one usually slept with someone's feet in one's face, lack of privacy and provision for undressing, and questionable cleanliness of blankets.

The evolution of modern sleeping cars with private compartments happened in Europe, and Pullman was only incidentally involved. Spurned in love, one Georges Nagelmackers, the man ultimately credited with luxury long-distance travel in Europe, came to America in 1866 to bury his hurt and investigate this marvelous American invention, the long-distance luxury train. He returned to Europe disappointed by Pullman's open berth design but convinced that the through car was the key. In the meantime, the American confidence man Colonel William d'Alton Mann, who had made his fortune selling bogus Pennsylvania oil wells, brought his concept of "Boudoir Cars," sleeping cars with partitions and separate compartments, to Europe after being locked out of the American market by Pullman. In 1868 he took up with Nagelmackers and formed the Compagnie Internationale, which established the first long-distance luxury railroad routes across Europe. By 1869, Pullman wanted a piece of this action, but Mann was able to repay Pullman for his kindness in America with a clever campaign warning Europeans of the licentiousness and debauchery promoted by the Pullman cars' open-concept berths. Ironically the privacy afforded by the European closed compartments made them very quickly a popular spot for trysts and even the place of business for rail ladies of the night. But the ruse worked, and with its European monopoly firmly established, the Compagnie Internationale was able to provide Europeans with truly luxurious long-distance travel from 1870 on.

Americans would not see this quality of accommodations until the next century. The train was the New York Central's *20th Century Limited*, forerunner of today's *Lake Shore Limited*. The cars, built in my family's hometown, Bloomington, Illinois, would be provided by the Pullman-Standard Company. The date was 1904, and a new generation of managers ran both concerns.

Sleep comes slowly on the first night of a train ride. The slumbercoach bed is not very wide and runs lengthwise in the car; my usual drifting-off position on my side doesn't work because of the rocking motion. I finally decide to adjust and sleep on my back, and apparently succeed, because after Syracuse and Rochester, I miss the stops at Buffalo and Erie and don't wake up till Cleveland. This is the last night I will have trouble falling asleep for the next nine thousand miles.

I awake to the clatter of George, our car attendant, making up beds in adjacent compartments. George is an attractive and striking buxom, thirtyish black woman with a wide smile and a gold upper front tooth. "Ah hate these eastern trains, slave work here. Ah got two dozens bedrooms to deal with in one car. Ah like the western trains better. It's easier. But Ah'm quittin' it altogether after this run." She smiles too much to be a woman who takes her own complaints very seriously. Despite her oath, somehow I think I just might meet her again somewhere down the tracks.

I have breakfast, eggs over, sausage, fried potatoes, toast, tomato juice, and two refills of coffee, with Tom and Jane, and their new friend, Suzie Picharski. Suzie, a pretty curly-haired blonde of twenty, is running away to California too. The three met at the pay phones in the Albany station last night, where the two girls were calling their mothers. Suzie's mom cried and asked about what Suzie had had to eat on the train. "I don't eat, see," she says. "My mom drives me crazy about it. That's why I'm going to California to live with my sister, so I can do what I want."

Suzie loved high school, has pictures of herself on prom night, youthfully glamorous but a little heavier in a red dress. She passes them around the table, and tears appear in Jane's eyes while Tom clenches his fists. This is what they have missed by running away.

Suzie was a Polish dancer, has toured, danced in Macy's parade, and appeared on television with her high school dance group. But graduation was like a death. "Nothing ever happened after that. Everything was boring." She moved to New York with a friend and went to work as a teller at Citibank. She was too afraid of the city to go out much and spent most of her free time listening to the likes of Mötley Crüe and Ozzy Osbourne on her Walkman. "So I decided to get thin. It makes me feel good." Then last week she quit her job and called her sister in California.

My runaway companions remind me of an incident that happened at my old fishing cabin in the woods back in New Hampshire. One morning I found a broken window and a dead partridge (called grouse outside of New England) amid the glass on the floor. My knowledgeable fishing buddy explained that this is a common thing. At the age of one year, the equivalent of human adolescence, the young partridge is possessed of what is called "the crazy flight"—it leaves the nest in a sudden spasm of wild flight. If it survives the crazy flight, the bird finds itself in the territory where it will make its nest. If it doesn't . . .

Back in my slumbercoach compartment watching the icy shores of Lake Erie drift by, I search for perspective. Tom and Jane riding west to escape dysfunctional families, Suzie pursuing her anorexia to the sunset—are these the personal tales behind the "crazy flight" romanticized as the urge to go west in our national mythology? The stories of the young foreigners I have already met more nearly fit the myth, yet we all began as foreigners at some time on this continent; and, in a sense, both my young friends and I are sojourning aliens today—they toward a future they can't conceive, I toward a past scarcely remembered.

At Toledo the train pauses for a refueling and servicing stop and I get off to take pictures. It is rainy, misty, murky. The Toledo station is emblematic of the recent history of American passenger rail travel. The tracks have been pulled up from several now abandoned platforms, but the crumbling platforms themselves have not yet been removed, testimony to a nation's continuing indecisiveness about the future of its heritage. Meanwhile the platform at which our train has stopped buzzes and clatters with activity and bustle.

The full consist of the *Lake Shore Limited* is now pretty impressive after the junction at Albany. There are two F-40 engines, three mail cars (I'm told that rail mail sorted en route is still faster than air mail between big cities), the Boston sleeper, the two Boston coaches, a lounge (bar car), a diner, three New York coaches, a New York slumbercoach (my car), two New York sleepers, and a trailing baggage car—two engines and fifteen cars, all full. When the New York Central discontinued this train's predecessor, the *20th Century Limited*, in 1967, the *Limited* was limping along with one failing engine and two ragged coaches of mostly empty seats.

Cornelius Vanderbilt—the Commodore—boasted that he never built a railroad in his life. Instead he bought existing railroads. He had already made his fortune as a young man with ferries and steamboats operating in the harbor of New York, but at the age of sixty, when most men would be content to enjoy the fruits of success, he risked his fortune and reputation on the new-fangled transportation technology. He began his march toward a railroad empire by buying two rickety roads, the New York & Harlem and the Hudson River, which, when combined, yielded a through route all the way to Albany.

Erastus Corning had established the precedent in 1853 when he welded a series of small upstate routes into the old Central to provide competition for the Erie Canal. Corning was never paid a penny for his management of the road but made a fortune anyway by making his ironmongery business its sole supplier. This was the era one historian has called the "age of bare knuckles." There were few rules governing private enterprise, and there was an enormous opportunity. The Erie Railroad, hailed as the "work of the age," already provided a rail link, via the southern tier of the state, to the Great Lakes, but it quickly became the financial football of men like Daniel Drew, Jay Gould, and Jim Fisk who plundered it regularly in a series of infamous corners and short-selling operations.

Its moribund condition left plenty of room for another well-run railroad to the Great Lakes when the Commodore's Harlem and Hudson lines built a bridge over the river to connect with the Central lines at Albany. Corning's Central continued for some time to transfer its freight and passengers to riverboats for the trip down to New York. Vanderbilt got a piece of the action only when the rivers froze and his riverside rails were the sole option for continuing passage to the city. But in the icy winter of 1867, Vanderbilt refused to send his trains across the bridge to make connections with the Central.

Passengers trudged through the snow across the bridge, and freight piled up. Legislators in Albany called upon Vanderbilt to know why his trains wouldn't make the connection. He produced an old forgotten law, instigated by the canal people, forbidding his trains from crossing the river. He shrugged and the legislators departed. The price of Central stock plummeted, and Vanderbilt began buying. Soon he had control. He united the Central lines to his own and, taking their name, improved the route with major infusions of capital. Thus was born the New York Central of modern times. With the additional acquisition of the Lake Shore & Michigan Southern and the Boston & Albany, the Vanderbilts had put together the line over which runs today's *Lake Shore Limited*.

The *Pullman Hotel Express* of 1870 was a harbinger of great things to come in passenger railroading. In addition to the baggage car carrying W. R. Steele's printing press and five ice closets, it included a smoking car with a wine-tasting room, a shaving salon, a card room with mahogany euchre tables, and an office for editor Steele. There followed two hotel cars, each containing a library, a Burdett organ, and a drawing room. Then there were two sleeping cars and finally the commissary and dining cars. All were finished with extravagant hangings, plush upholstery, and dark polished woodwork. But that train was a one-shot spectacular. It wasn't until the turn of the century that American passengers on scheduled runs would see anything like that kind of luxury.

Ironically it was Vanderbilt's great failure to purchase the competing Erie Railroad in the 1870s which led to the grand service the New York Central would provide on the *20th Century Limited* in the next century. Convinced of the necessity of monopoly, Vanderbilt tried again and again to purchase a controlling percentage of Erie Railroad stock and was thwarted each time by the Erie's simple expedient of printing more stock. When Vanderbilt enlisted the aid of injunctions from a friendly New York City judge, Drew, Gould, and Fisk fled across the river to New Jersey with such haste that they literally left a paper trail of documents which had been desperately stuffed into their pockets. Vanderbilt eventually accepted the defeat with stoicism, saying that he had enough money to buy all the stock and injunctions he needed, but he could never get enough money to buy the Erie's printing press.

Disorderly as it was, the episode affirmed limits to monopoly and firmly established that competition over routes serving the same terminal points was possible. It forever changed the assumptions in the railroad game. And down along the rivers, canals, and ridges of Pennsylvania, a far greater threat than the Erie was taking shape in what would become the Pennsylvania Railroad. Out of the clash of these two rail behemoths, the next century would see the classic textbook argument for the advantages to the consumer of American capitalist philosophy.

By 1900 there were twelve competing trunk routes from the urban east to Chicago, but the dominant players were the Pennsylvania and the New York Central. The NYC had already made its first luxury run with the *Exposition Flyer* over the route for the Chicago Columbian Exposition in 1893. The consist included three Wagner sleeping cars, a library/smoker car, a luxury diner, a parlor car, and an observation car with an open platform. Various versions of the train made the run in twenty hours over the next nine years and received such good press that the railroad inaugurated the first *20th Century Limited* on June 15, 1902. The name was a stroke of genius, playing as it did on the hoopla hailing the new century as America's. By 1904 the Pullman-Standard Company had taken over the sleeping accommodations, and the intense competition with the Pennsylvania's rival *Broadway Limited* established the service of these two trains as the class of the world.

In 1914 the schedule of the two routes was down to eighteen hours.

The *20th Century* at this time offered the first all-steel cars (some feared these would attract lightning), aboard which were a barber, a manicurist, a stenographer, valets, lady's maids, bathrooms with fresh and salt water, and a stock-market ticker. In 1926, for safety reasons, the two railroads negotiated a mutual twenty-hour schedule.

In 1938, Pullman finally dropped its open berth cars (the kind one sees in old movies in which only a curtain separates the sleeper from the corridor) in favor of the European-style compartments one finds on Amtrak today. In this year the schedule reached its all-time fastest, sixteen hours from Grand Central Station in New York to Union Station in Chicago (the *Broadway Limited* matched it).

After World War II, the NYC bravely struggled, as did most American railroads, to promote a new era of rail travel. But the federal subsidy of highways and airports for the auto and aviation industries, along with the clear preference of the new American traveler for the freedom and speed those industries promised, was already creating an environment in which passenger service would become increasingly unprofitable. There is some question today whether American passenger travel ever really made money for the railroads. The New York Central, the Pennsylvania, and others had always fostered the illusion of profitable passenger service, but the real money was in freight, and passenger trains existed primarily to promote a corporate image and to generate freight business along the routes. Current evaluation of accounting methods of those times shows all sorts of expenses not included in the ledgers of passenger service. By today's accounting standards, it is quite possible that America's most lucrative passenger train never showed a profit.

In the late forties and early fifties, the New York Central introduced through cars with the Union Pacific to San Francisco—lightweight stainless-steel cars with modern conveniences—and a host of special programs and incentives to attract riders. But ridership continually declined until, in 1958, the *20th Century* stopped carrying sleeping cars and luxury accommodations. The publicists put a brave face on it by announcing that the great train had been brought within the reach of the common man, but the end was in sight. In 1967 the *20th Century Limited* was dropped from service.

As the train rattles westward over the flat farmland of northern Indiana, five watchers sip Cokes and munch potato chips in the lounge car. Tom, Jane, Suzie, Franz, and I have coalesced into a group of travel companions in which I am the senior member. By now I have told my story and my young friends are helping me to look for my roots as we approach Elkhart, where I lived as a small child.

The landscape is impossibly nondescript, so much so that Suzie begins to yawn, fidget, and chain-smoke her Tareytons. It is Franz who first mentions the windmills that rise in an infinite variety of postures. Here is one that is overgrown with ivy, a steel-and-vegetation sculpture of surprising beauty. There is another broken and falling over like a neglected metal scarecrow, looking as though the next breeze will bring it down. And finally a working windmill, all of its blades intact, whirls and pumps with well-oiled productivity.

The same variety of existential conditions appears in the farms. They range from the overgrown to the merely derelict to the white-fenced, manicured and scrubbed, prosperous and proud Stark Farm, its name and founding date, 1926, in bold black on a brilliantly white-washed barn. This is encouraging, since I'm looking for something from only as far back as the early fifties.

Soon we enter Elkhart, where thirty-five years ago on my way to kindergarten I would wait with my lunchbox for New York Central freights to cross Division Street. Somewhere near the tracks there is a duplex house where Lionel electric trains raced around a Christmas tree, and hoboes off the line could count on my mother's handout sandwiches at the back door. There are also memories of a dog and a treehouse my father built, of a terrible fire in the shacks across the river where "the bums" lived, and of one glorious Easter with visiting grandparents when the joy of being a small boy on a sunny Indiana spring morning was so intense that it hurt forever.

Today there are residential streets with duplex houses, but we roll through without my seeing anything but a quickly passing town that looks like any other. There the McDonald's arch triumphs, and there sprawls a parking lot and its mall. Only at the downtown crossing is there a hint of this town's past and uniqueness—in the brick train station and block building housing the original establishment of Florsheim Shoes. But the station has been converted to retail shopping, and Florsheim has become a national chain. The train pulls on past the downtown crossing to stop at a tarmac platform behind a cinder-block warehouse. Memory is too feeble, change is too formidable.

After Elkhart, the services chief announces that there will be no lunch served on this train. I find this unusual and irritating. Other Amtrak trains squeeze in one last meal before arrival at the end of the line, and since we have crossed a time zone, that means that my stomach will interpret our arrival time of 1:15 as 2:15. I eat a piece of the wretched microwave pizza you can buy in the lounge car and ride through Gary, Indiana, sullen and sulking while the youngsters play cards. This wouldn't have happened on the *20th Century Limited*.

But the *Lake Shore Limited* does arrive in Union Station on time, eighteen and a half hours out of New York, two and a half hours slower than the *20th Century* at its zenith, three hours faster than Amtrak ran it when it took over in the early seventies, two days faster than the *Pullman Hotel Express*. Editor Steele described an immense crowd of dignitaries and curious common folk who greeted the first transcontinental at the station. Speeches were made on the platform as passengers hung listening out of their open windows. Later the Chicago Board of Trade celebrated their Boston counterparts' successful passage of one-third of the continent with feasts and more speeches.

As the *Lake Shore Limited* backs into the station today there are no dignitaries on hand to toast my passage, and I play travel guide for my young companions. To the right looms the huge Great Lakes Warehouse and ahead towers the post office, under which arriving and departing trains have passed in my memory since the beginning of time when I would wait for my grandfather's train at the end of the platform. Inside, the train sheds are just as dark as they have always been, and the train makes a safety stop and then a final stop short of the track-end bumper just as my grandfather explained it would eons ago. I show the kids the spot on the platform where I would stand waiting for his train to pull in from Bloomington, where even now another small boy wearing a St. Louis Cardinals cap waves at this train.

Chapter Two

Conquering a Continent

THE *CALIFORNIA ZEPHYR*

E V E N before the Civil War, there was a vision of the railroad as the national bond. In 1832 a Michigan editor promoted the building of a railroad from New York to Oregon. He was proposing a three-thousand-mile road at a time when the total of rails in the country extended only 229 miles and when the operations on those miles were highly experimental. The challenge surpasses President John F. Kennedy's proposal to put a man on the moon within a decade. Kennedy had much of the technology in place and an organized space research establishment with millions of dollars of federal support. In 1832, the manufacture of a rail was still a highly questionable experiment with wood and iron strapping, and the engineering of engines, tunnels, cuts, fills, and mountain grades and the design of a support system across a continent would be pioneered as the voyage of construction proceeded.

Furthermore, the expanse of land running west of the Mississippi to the fertile valleys of Oregon and California was viewed as the Great American Desert, a desert with a terrible mountain range, the Rockies, running down its middle. As late as 1843, Senator George Duffie of South Carolina blasted Jefferson and his captains, Lewis and

31

Clark, for cursing America with a territory "which no American citizen should be compelled to inhabit unless as a punishment for crime. . . . I would not give a pinch of snuff for the whole territory. . . . I wish to God we did not own it." The vision of railroads uniting the continent faced trials not only of geography and untried technology, but also of politics.

One man, Asa Whitney of California, deserves credit for finally establishing the national commitment to a transcontinental railroad. It was the combination of his experience with truly functional but short railroads in England and his travels to China which convinced him that the railroad was the key to the nation's becoming a world power. His message was simple: if a railroad could be built connecting the seaports of both coasts, America would link Europe and Asia and become the center of the world. When Whitney presented his first petition to Congress in 1844, the established eastern railroads were far more interested in maintaining and expanding their own regional monopolies than becoming involved with a pipedream in the Great American Desert. By 1850, the westward movement had helped Whitney's crusade mature from the visionary to the seriously practical; by 1853, the approaching rumble of disunity promoted the idea to the level of urgent national necessity. Whitney died in disgrace, but history validated his dream.

For two hours I doze in and out of dreamland on a couch in Amtrak's bland first-class lounge in Chicago's Union Station. The floor is carpeted, and potted plants adorn the corners of the room; a Chicago Bulls basketball game flickers on the television hanging high on the papered wall beneath the suspended acoustic ceiling. People didn't wait for trains this way in the heyday of the railroad. The cavernous old Main Hall still echoes out past the ticket windows, but its hard benches don't encourage napping. Amtrak has here taken a page from airport design—comfort over aesthetics.

I catch bits and snatches of conversations about train schedules, relatives waiting at other stations, the weather, surly attendants, helpful attendants, the weather, a good meal had somewhere, how bad the food was somewhere else, the weather. This habit of weather speculation in travel terminals seems a carryover from nervous waits in airports where foul weather has potentially mortal significance. I hope it snows like crazy.

Then comes the call to board; and after farewells to Tom, Jane, and Suzie, who are waiting for a later train to L.A., I board the *California*

Zephyr, bound for San Francisco 2,400 miles away, and we pull out into the labyrinthine Chicago yards amid a gathering snow squall.

Undistracted by personal reminiscence now, I am more aware of the hopeless Chicago slums which border the elevated tracks than I was coming in on the *Lake Shore Limited.* It's Monday, a workday; young men hang about the street corners drinking quarts of beer as if it were a weekend, but no one plays basketball in the playgrounds, where the snowflakes melt on contact with the trash-fouled pavement. There are no rims on most of the backboards anyway. The snow blurs the ever-present husks of derelict autos and the illegible but highly stylized graffiti on nearly every vertical surface.

The people here do not smile and wave at the train as it passes. It's too cruel that they should have the horizons of their world bounded by conveyances taking other people to other places. "The people keep a-comin', but the train done gone." Here the train goes every day. Those without a ticket no longer care even to watch.

Once we are out of the city I turn my attention to my surroundings inside the train. Since the Superliners of Amtrak's western trains have no singles, the economy bedroom serves as either a rather tight double or a fairly spacious single for the same price. There are two wide seats facing each other that collapse into a bed at night, a closet, a glass door with curtains (which is nice if the neighbor across the hall keeps his curtains open), a huge window, and a bunk up top. There is no sink or toilet as in the Heritage sleepers of the eastern trains; on the Superliners, only the deluxe accommodations have these (plus a shower!). There is one communal bathroom upstairs and several downstairs. The window in the upstairs bathroom is a real treat for those who like to sit awhile.

Amtrak's western trains provide a radically different experience from eastern trains in two respects. First there are the Superliner cars themselves. Since they are sixteen feet tall, these cars will not fit through the tunnels under cities on the eastern routes and thus are relegated to the open spaces of the west. Placed in service in 1979, the Superliners have two levels in every car and are the heaviest passenger cars in the world. The result is a heightened sense of space and vision and a ride that does not feel like that of a train. One can travel two days and two nights in these cars without the same sense of confinement and bodily wear and tear that might be expected in a ride this long in the old Heritage cars of the eastern trains. But some of the equipment on these cars, particularly the seats and beds, is already in a worse state of repair after only ten years than is similar equipment on the thirty-to-forty-year-old Heritage cars. Says one Amtrak employee, "Superliners sure were nice to work in when they were new. But they're all mobile-home construction. They'll fall apart and be replaced by something new while Heritage cars keep on rattling along."

The second difference between eastern and western trains is that most of Amtrak's western trains, especially the *California Zephyr*, make no pretense of being fast. They travel far greater distances than eastern trains and generally at slower speeds, reminding one of the sardonic football coach who says of his team, "We're not very big, but we're slow." This is usually the result of having to cross mountain ranges, but in some cases it is simply due to bad track and the overextended maintenance operations of the giant western railroad systems.

Amtrak puts the best face on it by referring to these trains as "Long Distance Cruise trains"—an apt description, considering the spaciousness and ride of the Superliner cars and the fact that even fast trains could not begin to compete with air travel over these distances. Most of the people on these trains are indeed along for the cruise and in nowhere near the same hurry as riders of eastern trains. "They get on to scratch an itch as old as the pioneer's urge to see what's out there on the western half of the continent," says conductor D. R. Burand, who has stopped by my room to chat after collecting tickets.

D.R. grew up on a poor farm in northern Illinois, where he felt that itch. His father wanted him to take over the farm, but D.R. saw his future in the Burlington Route tracks that ran right through their cornfield. "Graduated from high school on a Thursday and went to work for the railroad on Monday. It really hurt my father, but there just wasn't much of a living on that farm." He never regretted the choice, but still feels the pain. "It's too bad—you gotta walk away from somebody to be able to make your own life."

Today he is one of the first to take advantage of a new program offering the opportunity to cross over from a freight railroad to Amtrak. "It's a cut in pay but it gets you in out of the cold and gives you a break in seniority." I will hear of this job-swap scheme all across the country. Previously the train crew, engineers and conductors, were employees of the railroads over which Amtrak's routes ran. Amtrak's contracts with those roads covered the wages of these employees. The job-swap scheme gives employees of the railroads an opportunity to become permanent employees of Amtrak. The pay cut saves Amtrak money and gives it full control of its own trains, and the railroads are happy to be able to cut their work force without having to lay people off. The deal seems to have something for everyone.

We are joined by assistant conductor Howard Prevette, who lives in Bloomington, Illinois, just a few blocks from the house where my father grew up and walked away from the railroading life of his father for a different future in medical school. Howard is "a railroad man through and through," but likes working in a suit and tie. He says that those who did not make the change to Amtrak are folks who don't like working with people. "They want to move freight that doesn't complain, that doesn't ask questions and doesn't need to be kept warm and comfortable—you know, freight that you can kick and curse with no backtalk."

I ask both D.R. and Howard about what happens if the government abandons Amtrak, as President Reagan urged Congress to do in every budget throughout the 1980s. Though their contracts guarantee them railroad jobs of some sort, somewhere, I am mystified by their sublime faith. "There will always be an Amtrak," says Howard. They view my question as hypothetical in the same way an Englishman might if one asked him, "What happens if an earthquake submerges your island?"

Howard explains his view: "The President only talked about canceling Amtrak because he knew he had no shot. If he thought there was a chance that Congress would really do it, he wouldn't have said a word. He's a man of history—he knows the railroads conquered the continent."

D.R. calls my attention to the Mississippi crossing. The river is a bit disappointing; it's hard to picture Huck Finn and Jim getting lost here where the water is less than half a mile wide and there are no islands. Of course the Chicago, Burlington & Quincy Railroad, whose route we are following to Denver, chose this spot for the bridge precisely because the river is not so mighty here.

Though the railroad histories dwell on the New York Central and Pennsylvania, the Union Pacific and the Great Northern, the Santa Fe and the Southern Pacific, it seems that there has always been a Burlington Route, treated as a sidebar, often a pawn in the gamesmanship of the rail barons. This and the other railroads built throughout Illinois, Iowa, Missouri, and Wisconsin were called "granger" roads. They were the first great railroads, aside from the anthracite coal roads in Pennsylvania and West Virginia, whose original purpose was seen as providing freight and passenger service primarily for the developing places along the route rather than as linking widely separated strategic locations. Thus the fertile farms of the great American breadbasket between Chicago and the Missouri River and the granger roads flourished together.

But in 1848, the city fathers and premier merchants of Chicago were doing their best to prevent the city from becoming the rail center of the nation. While the trunk lines from the east were well established, the prevailing wisdom held that rails would never be profitable in the great open expanses west of the city. Instead the city's profitable trade with the farms to the west was based on the plank roads and their beast-drawn wagons. Merchants, hotelkeepers, restaurateurs, and teamsters alike simply couldn't conceive of trade more thriving and prosperous than that generated by the plank roads. Even the prostitutes with their red lanterns and the gambling kingpins with their loaded roulette wheels participated in the antirailroad stance. It was believed that if farmers could ship their goods into Chicago by train, they would not come to spend money themselves.

Much of the romance of the American rails is due to the fact that so many of its great chapters were shaped by the efforts of individual men. Such was the case with the granger roads out of Chicago. One man, William Butler Ogden, initiated the Galena & Chicago Union Railroad by going out and talking it up among the farmers it would serve. Meanwhile the Chicago powers enacted an ordinance to prevent any western railroad from setting up a depot along the waterfront, or anywhere in the city limits for that matter. Ogden quietly began running trains over his ten-mile run into wheat country and started stockpiling carloads of wheat just outside the city limits. When Chicago's laggard merchants beheld that pile of potential profits, they rescinded their ordinance and hailed Ogden as a great man. The Illinois Central was chartered and the granger route building spree was on. In thirty years, Illinois would have more track mileage than any other state in the Union.

Enter another of the individuals who would shape rail history, John Murray Forbes of Boston. After a successful start building lines in the east, Forbes arrived in Chicago and began duplicating Vanderbilt's modus operandi by acquiring a series of short lines west of the city and linking them to form a route which in 1855 reached the Mississippi at a narrow point opposite Burlington, Iowa. Thus began the greatest of the granger roads, the Chicago, Burlington & Quincy.

The line was extended across Iowa toward Council Bluffs, where it would eventually link up with the transcontinental route, the Union Pacific, and southwest over a route through Missouri with acquisition of the Hannibal & St. Joseph. In 1859, long before there was any bridge across the Missouri, engines appeared on the west bank opposite St. Joseph. Temporary tracks were laid on the ice. An engineer on the east side would start the engine onto the ice and jump off. The engine would continue unmanned across the ice and another engineer on the opposite shore would board and take control. When the great national project of the Pacific railroad was finally commenced from Omaha westward, there was the Burlington, already established as the key link with Chicago.

Forbes made the Burlington a coveted prize in the western rail empire-building to come in the latter years of the century with two policies. One was the shrewd location of routes. Time and again, more powerful transcontinental lines would find the location of existing Burlington routes to be critical for their connections east to Chicago. The other was the public-spirited cultivation of mutually beneficial economic relations with places along its routes. Throughout the "gilded age," when most railroads garnered a reputation for duplicity, rapaciousness, and corruption, the Burlington stood nearly alone as an exception to that record of infamy. It was a rare case in railroad history in which sheer virtue proved profitable. Ralph Waldo Emerson said of Forbes, "How little this man suspects, with his sympathy for men . . . that he is not likely, in any company, to meet a man superior to himself."

By the twentieth century, the Burlington would reach westward to Denver, northwest to connect with the James Hill lines in Montana, and southward through St. Louis and Kansas City all the way to the Gulf. The invading Burlington brought real competition to the Union Pacific in Nebraska, Colorado, and Wyoming, spreading growth and prosperity throughout the plains states as a result. It would become the key point of contention in the titanic struggles between Harriman's Union Pacific and Hill's Great Northern empires, neither of which could reach Chicago without it.

The Burlington also became an engine of technological innovation. Westinghouse's first air brakes were tested on a Burlington train in 1887, and the railroad pioneered the first U.S. Railway Post Office, Vista Dome cars, and the use of stainless-steel streamlining. In 1934, a sleek, silvery snake of a train whined its way from Denver to Chicago in eighteen hours. It was the original *Zephyr*, the world's first diesel-powered train, which demonstrated overnight that at least for passenger travel, the steam engine was dead. When most passenger routes collapsed in 1970, Amtrak's route to San Francisco originally followed the Union Pacific from Omaha to Salt Lake with a dip down to Denver. But when the Denver & Rio Grand Western finally threw in the towel on its passenger route from Denver through the Rockies to Salt Lake,

Amtrak inaugurated today's *California Zephyr* over the Burlington Route to Denver and then the scenic DRG route to Salt Lake.

Finally, through its merger with the Great Northern and Northern Pacific in 1970, the Burlington Northern became one of the largest railroads in the world, with thirty thousand miles of track in a network radiating from Chicago to the Gulf, and to the Colorado Rockies and over the northern Rockies to Portland and Seattle on the West Coast. The small Illinois granger road operated from the start primarily for the benefit of little folks in the whistle-stop towns along single-track midwestern rural routes eventually became more than just the midlink in the conquering of the continent; it became the greatest transcontinental of them all.

The best way to travel through Iowa is while having dinner on a Superliner. The upper-level dining room is so open and has so much glass that you feel almost as if you were riding out in the open. The scenic features of Iowa are not demanding enough to distract from the enjoyment of dinner but rather, with the continual images of food production, stimulate the appetite as does a fine apéritif. The widely separated clusters of individual farm structures with their silos, barns, farmhouses, and outbuildings further urge one to settle in, relax, and eat while this fecund landscape rolls by.

I order the regional specialty and am served two pork tenderloins, an inch and a half thick, cooked tender and almost flaky in a wine-sweet sauce. The broccoli is hot and crisp, the cheesecake homemade and delicious. The golden Iowa sunset over snow-dusted soybean fields, the winking red crossing signals, lamps in the windows of farmhouses, headlights of automobiles on the nearby highway, and two glasses of decent California rosé season a mellow hour to perfection.

Over coffee I talk with Michelle LeFebvre, an Amtrak project manager, and Roger Stark, the chief of on-board services.* Michelle, dressed more like a bank executive than a railroad employee, describes herself as "an idea person. I look for ways to make the trains more attractive to the average traveler." She claims responsibility for on-board service innovations such as the showing of full-length feature movies (on VCR), activities such as "Amtrak Trivia," and the live organ music on the *Montrealer.*

She says that today the great battle is with hostile administrations

* I have changed the names of these two Amtrak employees.

and tight budgets rather than a hostile continent. Maintenance costs are 90 percent of Amtrak's budget, and the cuts have hit hardest there. "We've been stripping equipment off of some cars to repair others," she says.

Roger believes that Amtrak has to get itself free of politics by becoming independently profitable. I suggest that passenger rail travel may be inherently unprofitable. Michelle rolls her eyes. "That was the old railroad. It's just a matter of getting the product and service right." Roger expands on the potential in high-speed lines, intercity monorails, pneumatic-tube trains capable of airline speed, and other dizzying innovations that will get the political monkey off Amtrak's back.

When Roger gets up to welcome passengers at the station stop in Creston and Michelle returns to her reports in her room, I wonder at their lack of the profound faith I saw in the conductors, D.R. and Howard. And then it strikes me that Michelle and Roger are not really railroad people, as are the conductors. Their world is product development, customer service, and marketing. It is a shifting, elusive world, much less firmly founded than that of the rails themselves, stretching to the horizon in a firm line that has run unbroken for generations.

Returning to my compartment, I pass through the beautiful all-glass lounge car where the drinkers, smokers, and socializers have all been shooed out for tonight's showing of *Spaceballs*. A handful of teenagers and two elderly couples have settled before the video screens mounted in the walls at either end of the car. Their eyes are glazed and their mouths are lifeless except for the chewing of gum. The conversation with Michelle and Roger has given me indigestion. The profitable Amtrak they envision is one I may not care to ride.

In my room with the lights turned out I try to shake the sourness that hangs on my mood by soaking up nighttime images of the passing continent outside. A full moon has risen over Iowa and the weather has turned, the smoke from farmhouse chimneys swinging around before a severe north wind. We are approaching the Missouri River, and I want to see the crossing which was so much greater a conquest than the Mississippi.

The rails squeal as we roll through the curves leading down from the level Iowa plain into the gullies and washes approaching the river valley. The farms and their clusters of huddling buildings are fewer here and the spectral shapes of trees begin to multiply, coalescing into glades, then groves, and finally deep woods. There I see a swath between the trees—a deserted road or a creek? Here a glimmer in a glen, and slow-moving shapes casting dim shadows—hunters jacking deer, or old women performing unspeakable rites? Finally there are no lights to be seen at all, only the increasingly dense shadows of what by day would be cottonwoods in the mucky Missouri bottomland. But now they are like ghosts of the toilers who built the railroad—*Spaceballs*, trivia, and monorail tubes, how will they ever forgive us?

With a metallic rumble we cross a small bridge, and then another. The moonlight glints off surfaces that could be ice, water, pavement, metal, or even flame, then is muted in clumps of cattails, reeds, and more woods. A furious rush of motion amid the cottonwood shadows— have we disturbed some deer? There rises a glowing miasma behind the passing trees—marsh gas or more spirits? Another bridge and mud flats appear, but still no expanse of the river itself. We pass over several more bridges—I've lost count now—and mud flats and lunar flashes off tilting silver surfaces. Huge irregular black shapes pass underneath— boats? junkheaps? Now plumes of smoke or steam boil past the window. The train slows into a creaking and groaning tight curve, wheel flanges screaming against the bending rails, and suddenly lights, thousands of blazing lights, electrify the sky. Brakes whine the train to a stop, ascending an agonizing musical scale, and a thunderous roar shakes the metallic body of the car. Somewhere a distant voice is chanting, "Oh my-gawd, Oh my-gawd," amid the earsplitting crescendo, and then the rumble subsides into an eerie white silence of whirring ventilators.

I hear footsteps in the corridor: "Om-a-ha, this station stop is Omaha."

Omaha, a refueling stop. I step off the train to the roar of a SAC bomber taking off from the nearby Air Force base. I know that there are dozens of intercontinental nuclear missiles buried in silos all around here. Omaha, on the day of Armageddon, will be the first cinder.

A fierce blast of cold pierces the light jacket I began the trip with back in the January thaw. I should have heeded the chimney smoke I saw in Iowa.

I have crossed another frontier, only the second really since Springfield. The Mississippi crossing, with the friendly Iowa farms awaiting on the west bank, is hardly comparable. There is a more epic dimension to this passage; in times past there would be no sure sustenance or safety until the deadly desert was crossed to a better world by Pacific shores. Today it is the hidden weapons of the holocaust lurking just beneath modern consciousness that makes the crossing so strange and foreboding. And if the day ever comes, even the railroads will have a part to play.

As of this writing, the final decision to place intercontinental ballistic missiles on railcars has not yet been made, but the plan is far enough along that the military already has designed a "Rail Garrison" logo featuring a train superimposed on a missile, an American flag, and two strands of Nebraska wheat with the inscription "Peacekeeper." The impetus for the plan is the fear of a possible enemy first strike that might disable the 1,054 missiles located in fixed concrete silos.

The missile trains' consist begins with a production-model engine equipped with bulletproof glass, armor plating, and flash curtains, manned by military-trained crews with railroad employees as pilots. Following the engine, a windowless security car, bristling with antennae, cameras, and firepower, protects the train from saboteurs. Inside, the security crew lives in quarters tighter even than in submarines, surrounded by weapons, gas, radiation, and biological warfare survival gear, and surveillance and communications devices designed for the horrific reality of WWIII.

The third car, mounted on telltale eight-wheel trucks, contains an MX missile with its ten independently targeted warheads, each capable of destroying a city and a significant chunk of surrounding countryside. When a launch order is received from the President, the train can stop in three minutes. It takes an additional five minutes to reorient the missile's guidance system. During this time the car's roof doors open and the missile is raised into firing position. With a blast of steam, the missile is ejected from its canister and then fires its engines above the train and begins its flight.

The fourth car houses the command center, a compact version of those attached deep underground to silo missiles. Here two pistol-packing officers, upon receipt of the coded message from the President, would simultaneously insert keys, kept in double-locked safes, into switches that activate the launch sequence. Nearby the senior command officer's console maintains contact, through a variety of fail-safe communications links, with the President, SAC headquarters, the locomotive crew, the security crew, and the other cars in the train.

The fifth car is another missile car, the sixth a spare supplies car, and the seventh a second security car. The train may carry up to seven additional camouflaging boxcars to complete the consist.

Because of the possibility of sabotage, harassment by antiwar activists, and massive satellite-guided first strikes against even moving missile trains, the Air Force envisions camouflaging the trains to resemble ordinary freight trains as much as possible. Some of the missile trains would be dummies, thus creating a mobile shell game. The trains would be housed in concrete bunkers with hinged roofs through which the missiles could be fired on short notice, like those in silos, in the event of a surprise launch by an enemy. In what the Air Force considers the more likely scenario of a period of rising international tensions, the trains would move out and begin cruising the lines of the Burlington Northern, the Union Pacific, and other roads with far-flung rail networks. Eventually the trains could disperse over the 150,000 miles of track crisscrossing the country. At full dispersal, the system would introduce an awesome new force into the volatile chemistry of an international crisis.

I approached Omaha looking only for the Missouri bridge which played such a key role in the conquering of the continent, but instead I was confronted with the fundamental specter that haunts all thought and action in our age. No search for modern America can proceed without this confrontation. No future for the continent can be conceived without the hope that these images themselves may become things of the past, like the buffalo, the steam engines, and the Great American Desert.

So I have missed the Missouri bridge. There was some question in 1867 whether it ever would be built. Here the granger roads from the east would meet the Union Pacific; here would be the rail gateway that would provide safe crossing to the newest of the New World. But well after the mountains had been subdued, the badlands traversed, and the Indians pacified, the bridge linking the UP on the west bank to the Burlington on the east was the very last segment of the route to be completed because of the interminable squabbles about the route of the line. Omaha—a place of unfinished business in the building of a better world in 1867 just as it is today.

While the first great transcontinental railroad is deservedly a symbol of national will and accomplishment, the story of its building is not a pretty one. It involves deception, greed, corruption, disillusionment, violence, disease, death, and the extermination of an animal species and a human race.

By the 1850s the transcontinental railroad was an idea whose time had truly come. Whitney's crusade had taken root beyond his death, and John C. Frémont's expedition to Oregon in 1842 kindled visions of a northwest empire confirmed by the treaty acquisition of Oregon in 1846. Brigham Young and his prosperous Mormons at Salt Lake City were ready to be reenfolded into the national embrace—at a distance— by rail. Defenders of the Union who foresaw the coming conflagration looked to the Pacific railroad as a desperate means of holding the Union together or, at least, of strengthening the northern half of it. All that remained was to find a method of financing the road and to determine its route.

When Congress chartered the fulfillment of Asa Whitney's dream twelve years after he died poor and disgraced, everyone knew that the Pacific railroad would generate fortunes and empires. But from the start, politicians and entrepreneurs alike labored under two disastrous delusions. First was the belief that the real fortunes to be made would accrue from the building of the road rather than the subsequent running of it. Second was the misconception that a project so massive would be done only once, that there would be only one Pacific route, and thus before the Civil War its location was almost as hot a topic as the issue of new slave versus free states. The chaotic feeding at the trough which followed was inevitable.

The financing debate sounds so familiar. Conservatives railed that the federal government had no business getting mixed up in the building of railroads, while liberals worried that only through federal control could the Pacific road be free of the machinations of the robber barons already building monopolies in the east. The solution was, of course, a public-private cooperative venture, with the government providing subsidy and regulation of standards of construction performance while the actual building was carried out by private enterprise. The Pacific Railroad Act of 1862 provided for outright grants of the odd-numbered sections of land, forming a ten-mile checkerboard strip along the right-of-way, which was also guaranteed by the government. The dollar portion of the subsidy would consist of U.S. bonds at the rate of $16,000 per mile in the plains, $32,000 per mile in the plateau, and $48,000 per mile in the mountains. The bonds were to be sold for terms of thirty years and pay 6 percent interest. This would turn out to be a witch's brew of potential abuse for power and profit which would cost the taxpayer untold dollars, some of the honest entrepreneurs their reputations, and others even their lives.

The chief officer of the company, the ever-scheming Thomas (Doctor) Durant, operating on the assumption that the money to be made was in the building, arranged for the creation of two companies. One would be the Union Pacific Railroad, which could not take profits directly out of the government bonds paid to it. The other was the construction company Crédit Mobilier of America, which could take profits from payments for construction by the railroad. Ironically, the heart of the famous Crédit Mobilier scandal was less about this patently shady arrangement than it was about the buying of Crédit Mobilier stock by congressmen, who were then deemed to be compromised (despite the fact that they had actually paid for their stock). Some surely were corrupted, but recent research suggests that more honest men were ruined and, further, that the investigation never did identify a significant number of influential congressmen who had bought Crédit Mobilier stock.

Despite, or perhaps because of, the serpentine financial arrangements, the railroad was continually short of cash during its construction. Subsidy bonds were paid on the basis of completion of twenty-mile sections of the railroad. It became common practice for construction engineers to falsely sign off on the supposed completion of sections ahead of time to keep the subsidy money rolling in. In 1864, engineer O. A. Talcott refused such a request. When Crédit Mobilier vicepresident Sam Hallett had Talcott's signature forged and the paperwork sent to Washington, Talcott persisted in his righteousness and wrote a letter to President Lincoln blowing the whistle on the company and causing a hold in the payment of the subsidy. Hallett was so enraged that he ordered his brother, Thomas, to teach the whistleblower a lesson; Thomas sought Talcott out and beat him to a bloody pulp. Talcott was not heard from again until the day Sam Hallett returned to the west from Washington. Talcott was waiting and shot him dead outside the station in Wyandotte. The finance question drew the first blood.

The controversy over routes avoided bloodshed but was tangled—as larger issues loomed. Before the Civil War, there was intense regional competition. Southern states argued, correctly, that the shortest and fastest route with the easiest crossing of the continental divide ran from New Orleans to southern California. Oregonian-oriented interests in Wisconsin and Minnesota urged a northern route through the passages found by Lewis and Clark. Among proponents of a central route, there was intense competition between an Iowa-Nebraska faction and a Missouri-Kansas group. And there were Texas cattlemen allied with traders in Santa Fe who pushed a south-central route over the Santa Fe Trail. Five routes were given preliminary surveys in 1859, but the outbreak of the Civil War settled the issue. The superior southern routes were eliminated, as was the far-northerly route because of its remoteness from the heart of the Union. It came down to Iowa versus Kansas.

In 1859 a young lawyer from Illinois met with general manager Grenville Dodge and others of the Iowa faction, some of whom would be

Iowa delegates to the Republican nominating convention in Chicago the next year. Dodge presented the advantages of the Iowa-Nebraska route. The young lawyer was impressed. At the 1860 convention, the Iowa delegation was a solid block for Lincoln, and by 1863, the Iowa route was firmly established with Omaha as the eastern terminus by presidential executive order. No one has ever suggested any impropriety on Lincoln's part, but there is no question that the members of the Iowa delegation who flocked to Washington following Lincoln's election were greeted with open doors, receptive hearings, and cushy appointments in the Pacific railroad organization. Many of the practices whose consequences fell on President Grant's head during the Crédit Mobilier scandal were begun as early as 1863.

But Lincoln's directive of 1863 was vague about whether Omaha, on the west bank of the Missouri, or Council Bluffs, on the east bank, was to be the eastern terminus of the route. Omaha wanted the transfer for passengers and freight from the granger railroads to occur on its side of the river; thus it wanted one of the Iowa granger roads, preferably the Burlington, to build and run over the bridge. Council Bluffs, of course, wanted the opposite. Further, the granger roads through Iowa were poised to arrive at the Missouri at several different points, some of which involved neither Omaha nor Council Bluffs.

While the debate raged, passengers and freight were transferred twice: from the Burlington to barges at Council Bluffs for the river crossing and again from the barges to the UP at Omaha. When the bridge was finally built in 1871, the Iowa railroads refused to cross it; Omaha threatened eternal enmity if the UP crossed the span and the profitable transfers took place in Council Bluffs. Thus resulted the infamous Omaha Bridge Transfer. Transfers took places at both ends of the bridge with the short run over the bridge treated as a separate shuttle rail. For years, the Missouri bridge remained the major bottleneck in the transcontinental route, just as if it had never been built.

Today the Burlington has its own tracks west of the bridge all the way to Denver. After leaving the maze of the Omaha freight yards and stockyards, we run more or less parallel to the UP tracks to the capital of Nebraska, founded by the UP and named, of course, Lincoln. But since Amtrak does not follow the UP route to Salt Lake today, I watch the UP tracks bend off to the northwest as we pull out of Lincoln. A Union Pacific freight rolls by right beside us; and as the two routes diverge, there on the rear of the freight rides a private deluxe passenger car with an open balcony observation deck and white-jacketed attendants bustling about. There are probably politicians aboard.

In the lounge car of the *California Zephyr*, *Spaceballs* has finished. Nonetheless most of the action is downstairs in the cramped lower lounge; the magnificent dark-glassed upper lounge is now deserted. One descends a narrow spiral stairway to the lower lounge, which is dense with cigarette smoke. Since it's not on a walk-through corridor, the room has a dead-end atmosphere about it, down between the wheel trucks in the very bowels of the train. I much prefer the lounges in eastern bar cars; everybody passes through them on a level above the wheels.

Through the clouds of smoke I watch a lean, wiry man playing king's corner with two ten-year-old boys. He keeps showing them how to spot their opportunities in the game. They keep missing them, every single one. He has the patience of Sisyphus, they the initiative of the stone. He says, "Ya know what it means if you see three engines on one of these trains?" The boys don't. "It means that they're expecting a serious snowstorm and the third engine is insurance against getting stuck. Ya know what it means if one of the engines is a freight engine rather than Amtrak?" I guess that it means that an Amtrak engine has broken down and been temporarily replaced by one from the contracting railroad. "Nope," he says. "It means you're being hijacked or something else terrible has happened. Amtrak don't let no other engines ever pull its trains." He buys me several beers while I play straight man to more rhetorical questions with unlikely answers. Finally the kids head off to bed and I take their place in the game, missing opportunities with increasing frequency as the suds flow.

An intense, rotund, thirtyish-looking fellow with owl spectacles enters the lounge and announces loudly, "Any chess players here?" He has a chessboard and box of pieces in hand. The king's corner player responds to his challenge, the chess master sits down, and I watch.

Chess master opens with the sucker opening and the king bites. He just barely avoids checkmate in four moves with the queen-bishop gambit. Chess master is intense, grandiose as he sits Buddhalike, his hands gripping the corners of the table, shoulders pressed back against the wall and stomach rolling ever so slightly up and over the edge of the table. He never smiles. The king has finally met his match and concedes as chess master is aligned for mate with the queen rook. "Anyone else?" asks chess master.

An aloof-looking fellow in his upper twenties with a sweatshirt that says "Sweden" and a ski hat perched on his head has been writing on a yellow pad, smoking Camels, and frowning during the chess game. I instinctively don't like him; if I were the type and a little more drunk, he's the man in the bar I would pick my fight with. It's the air of condescension and disdain that pushes my button. Instead, I try to talk to him. He says he's an actor and a playwright. I tell him about my mini-career as a stage technical director. "God bless techies," he says. After several rounds of beer we finally join forces to denounce the use of green lighting and electronic sound effects in theater. But he's still a horse's ass, holds his cigarette like one, and thinks I should have flown part of my route to the west.

"I want to see America," I say. "Without any gaps in it."

Chess master is about to leave and Sweden can't resist. "I gotta beat the guy."

After an initial slaughter resulting in a more or less even exchange of pieces, the board now looks rather like the kind of classical encounter one sees diagrammed in the chess books about games between great masters where each side has four or five strategic pieces left and the battle will now go on for hours with stalemate a real possibility.

Suddenly I experience a wave of a feeling I have seldom felt since late-night booze bashes in college. I eye the pyramid of dead aluminum soldiers which king has been stacking against the window, check my watch, and realize that I'm about to ruin my morning. Without waiting to see the outcome of the game, I stumble up the steps from the lower lounge to find my compartment. At least I don't have to drive.

When Robert Louis Stevenson crossed America in 1879 on the Union Pacific, just a few miles north of our Burlington route, he wrote, "We were at sea—there's no other adequate expression—on the great plains of Nebraska." The Scottish writer Ludovic Kennedy, traveling the route in 1981, described "a great green and golden sea." Even by day both writers felt a vertiginous doubt, like swimmers in the middle of the ocean, too puny to imagine ever reaching a safe shore. Now it is after midnight in Nebraska.

In the darkened upper lounge I am overwhelmed by moonlight on the endless snow-dusted Nebraska stubble. At night this is a prospect that is neither sea nor land but some other world prowled by purgatorial ghosts. Small dense clouds drift south and periodically blot out hunks of the moonlight, casting monstrous black holes across the landscape. There are no roads, no houses here. The landscape isn't quite flat, but tilts and slants with every roll of the car. The floor is less steady than by day as I bump my way to my bedroom. I fall into bed, oppressed by a sense of the train hurtling headlong into a featureless abyss while bombers from Omaha trace the black sky, and I whirl off to sleep dreaming of watching my father die, missing opportunities at the card game of life, and searching through the cottonwood shadows and black holes for the Missouri River.

Morning in eastern Colorado brings a cotton mouth and a headache —hungover, dammit. I have forty-five minutes to pull myself together in time to meet a dear aunt at the Denver station who is going to lend me her car so that I can drive to Cheyenne to see the Union Pacific division headquarters. Over breakfast and lots of coffee, I watch our passage through a large stockyard. I hear a small boy ask, "Is that where Big Macs and pot roast and steak come from?" "Yes it is, Johnny," says Dad. "And see those men, those are reeeeal cowboys." This is called penance.

At the Denver station I meet Sweden and the king on the platform. Sweden turns out to be not such a bad fellow after all; he's an academic, thus the haughtiness. "I beat him, but it took two hours." King confirms that it's true. Chess master took it badly apparently, claiming that smoke in the lounge distracted him.

Sweden slaps me on the back and says, "You had a rough night, didn't you? We considered checking to see if you ever made it to your room." Though my headache throbs, I am grateful to Sweden for the thought; nothing like companionship to banish evil spirits. It's a lesson not lost on this neophyte solo traveler. Eventually I will make finding a friendly companion the first task of each train ride.

"So how did you sleep?" I ask.

"Lousy. I kept imagining I was hearing bombers taking off all night. I'd look out the window to shake it off, and you should've seen the creepy shadows across that god-awful Nebraska landscape—like the night after World War III. Thought we'd never get back to civilization."

First there are the planned community developments, condos, shopping malls, and service stations, sprawling north from Denver, one after another. Layer upon layer of new-built suburbs, coalescing around the now-dwarfed core of urban Denver: Murphy's Law in wide-open spaces, clutter expanding to occupy unobstructed available space. Then there are oil wells, dozens of them on the barren high plains, and the occasional beef ranch, its clientele gathered in this season around the water wellheads. Finally, near the Wyoming border, there is nothing but a moonscape, even the semiagricultural stubble of Nebraska erased from the face of the earth.

I am driving north on I-25. To the left rises the Front Range of the

Rockies, slowly receding westward as I speed northward. Closer on the left and paralleling the interstate is the UP route from Cheyenne to Denver, the UP's concession to the booming Rocky Mountain gateway after the railroad had made the decision to cross the Rockies through the easier route in Wyoming.

To the right is the moonscape, crossed here and there by barbed-wire fences whose purpose is difficult to fathom. In some places hunks and shreds of a fabriclike material flap from the top wire of the fences in the steady northwest breeze. I learn later that these are the skins of antelope and deer that have become tangled in the barbed wire.

I have been told in Denver that I won't need directions to find the UP in Cheyenne, and sure enough, the interstate crosses a bridge where there is no water and there it is, stretching arrow-straight to horizons east and west—the awesome Cheyenne yards of the Union Pacific Railroad.

On the day Lincoln was shot in 1865, the first rail of the road that owed so much to his patronage had not yet been laid, because of squabbles about routing, financing, and company leadership. It was the entry into the fray of the wealthy and respectable New Englanders Oakes and Oliver Ames that got the project off the ground. While the rest of the country was dusting itself off and counting its dead in the aftermath of the Civil War, the surveyors of the Union Pacific, under the direction of general superintendent Grenville Dodge, were engaged in their own epic struggle against a wilderness and a native people, neither of which would yield the long-sought rail line from Omaha to Salt Lake without a fight.

Through Nebraska the line was relatively easy to lay, aside from the Indian attacks; the Platte River provided a natural thoroughfare as far west as Julesburg, where a decision about which fork to take would have to be made. Then came Wyoming.

Typical of the exertions required was the thirteen-day journey made by surveyor Sam Reed in hired stagecoaches across untracked wilderness. With meals of nothing but hardtack and dried bacon, Reed and his men crisscrossed the dusty barren wastes in search of water and level grades. Rarely could both be found in the same place. Indian attacks hampered the work, as did outbreaks of illness from drinking alkaline water. Worst of all were the dust storms of pure alkali that would burn and scar the throat and lungs.

One obstacle in particular was the Wyoming Black Hills, today called the Laramie Mountains to avoid confusion with the Black Hills of South

Dakota. They weren't particularly high or rugged, but they were crawling with hostile Indians, and a reasonable grade on their eastern slope eluded the surveyors. Grenville Dodge himself and his party had spent nearly as much time fighting off repeated Indian attacks as they had marking the line, and they little suspected that the Indians would hold the solution to their problem. But as they were considering declaring the route impossible, they were assaulted by a war party on the eastern slopes. After they had succeeded in fending off one attack, Dodge was surprised at how quickly his attackers had been able to disappear, since his position on high ground seemingly commanded a view of all approaches. Upon following the trail of the retreating Indians, he found a narrow ridge that wound down in a gentle grade to the eastern plain. A lone tree midway down the ridge provided a landmark—the eastern approach to the Black Hills had been found.

Preliminary surveys going back as far as 1859 had long suggested that the easiest route to Salt Lake would cross through Wyoming and thus miss Denver. The discovery of the Lone Tree route confirmed this, especially since the Black Hills were designated as mountainous territory in the subsidy rate. The Lone Tree route would be extremely cheap to build and thus provide the company with a real windfall. In the Crédit Mobilier scandal it would be suggested that government and company officials were aware of the cheapness of the Lone Tree route when the subsidy designations were made. The issue was not settled in the scandal trials, but subsequent research has established beyond a doubt that the route was well known by both parties when the rates were set. The branch line which would connect Denver to the UP was a further windfall, because of the discovery of valuable coal and iron deposits near its route.

Meanwhile, to the rear of the surveyors, Jack Casement and his Irish construction crews were pushing into the wastes beyond the Platte River. The graders would come first, moving millions of tons of earth from cuts through rises into fills over depressions and then shaping the roadbed, all with hand shovels. Then came wagons with the ties to be laid and fixed in place with stone ballast, again shoveled by hand. More wagons carrying forty rails each followed. Five men lifted each 560-pound rail, pulled it on rollers into place, and at the cry of "Down!" dropped it into the steel chairs, on the ties. Then the gaugers adjusted the width of the rails and pairs of spikers finished the job with three blows to each spike, ten spikes to the rail, four hundred rails per mile for two thousand miles. This was the feat of the Irish toilers who built the railroad.

It is small wonder that the work spawned the infamous "Hell on Wheels" that established itself at each succeeding townsite along the construction end of the line. Julesburg was typical. Booze, gambling, and prostitution were the mainstays of the local economy, but horse thieving, cattle rustling, and profiteering in goods stolen from the railroad were common as well. Julesburg was known as "the wickedest city in America." Reed called it a place where "vice and crime stalk unblushingly in the midday sun." Visiting dignitaries, intrigued at the prospect of visits to "lively western dance halls," were aghast when they beheld the indecencies performed upon the tables and benches. For the most part the railroad was tolerant, but when an aggressive group of gamblers took possession of UP lands without paying for them, Jack Casement hired an outfit of soldiers and brought them to town to clean up. When the gamblers "spat contempt" at him, he ordered his men to open fire and mowed down those who didn't flee fast enough. When Dodge visited Julesburg later, all lands had been paid for. Pointing to a hill of fresh graves, Casement told Dodge, "They all died with their boots on and Julesburg has been quiet since."

A surveying party headed by Grenville Dodge himself located the townsite for the main division point of the line from Omaha to Salt Lake in 1867. Situated on high, gently rolling ground near the base of the Rockies, the site had water and was directly north of Denver, thus allowing the shortest possible branch to that city. Despite the continual harassment by Indian attackers, Dodge named the site Cheyenne, out of respect, if not love, for his great nemesis. On the Fourth of July a grand celebration was held. Its mood lasted until the next day, when a war party of Indians attacked an approaching Mormon wagon train. After the attackers had been driven off, the dead were buried, Cheyenne's first permanent inhabitants. Cheyenne soon became the next hell on wheels.

The Plains Indians seemed to understand from the start that the railroads threatened their existence. Even before the railroads cut up the buffalo herding grounds and brought in the hunters who pursued the Indians' source of sustenance to extinction, tribes that had previously been peaceful made raids upon the surveying and construction gangs. Initially the Indians pursued tactics developed out of tribal warfare which made little impression on the white men. They would swoop down, drive off or steal the livestock, and then withdraw. It took a few years before they learned that the white men were dependent on their machines in the same way that Indians were dependent on their beasts. They learned to cut telegraph wires, derail trains, and attack, loot, and burn the things of the white men. Now it became a truly bitter struggle as the railroad men fought back with aggressive cavalry detachments whose operations were often far from defensive in nature. Even the trainmen viewed themselves as combatants in the struggle and reveled in stories of heroism such as that of the engineer who was shot, clubbed, stabbed in the neck, and scalped yet managed to fight off his tormenters and even retrieve his own scalp.

As early as 1865, surveyor James A. Evans wrote, "Until they are exterminated, or so far reduced in numbers as to make their power contemptible, no safety will be found. . . ." Even the abolitionist New Englander Oliver Ames had this to say in 1878: "I see nothing but the extermination of the Indians as the result of their thieving disposition, and we shall probably come to that before we can run the road safely." But there was also this from General John Pope, a man who would command operations in that extermination, "The Indian . . . no longer has a country. He is reduced to starvation or to warring to the death. . . . The Indians' first demand is that the white man shall not drive off his game and dispossess him of his lands. How can we promise this unless we prohibit emigration and settlement? . . . No [such] promise can be fulfilled. . . . Whatever may be the abstract right or wrong of it, the result must inevitably be the dispossession of all his lands and their occupation by civilized white men. The only practical question is how this can be done with the least inhumanity. . . . The end is sure and dreadful to contemplate."

But by the end of the 1880s the Indian situation began to ease, much to everyone's surprise. More and more tribes opted for a kind of peaceful coexistence and moved their home bases to locations along the North Platte near the railroad. The Indians had "chosen" an alternative which Pope had respected them too much to consider—surrender, dependency, and subservience.

The wounds and scars of those days are not apparent in Cheyenne today, though Wounded Knee is just a day's drive over the horizon. Cheyenne, though still a far cry from Boston's Back Bay, is tamed. The main drag is Lincolnway, and most of the other streets are named after men who played major roles in the building of the line: Dillon, Ames, Dodge, and Snyder. Though Lincolnway is lined with neon and glitz, diners, motels, bars, loan companies, and other accoutrements of an economy based on a traveling work force, the street, despite cowboy pretensions, is bourgeois blue-collar, almost gentrified since the days of Hell on Wheels. The locals drive pickups with no roll bars or roof lights, no fat tires or racing stripes. Their talk in the diner at lunch is hearty and real: kids, house, work, weather, politics.

The rail yards one block away are never out of sight, and their presence dominates the tone of the downtown even though a power company is just as big an employer these days as the railroad. The skyline is low and has a temporary look about it, even more so than in most young American towns. In the heart of downtown the five-story Plains Hotel is the tallest commercial structure.

Then there is Capitol Street with the capitol building to the left, but to the right, larger and more substantial in its granite-and-red-sandstone Victorian architecture, looms the churchlike Union Pacific station and division headquarters. It faces down its governmental neighbor opposite, as if to prevent Wyoming legislators from forgetting the reason for Wyoming's existence. Without the UP, Wyoming might yet be a white space on the American map—or an Indian nation.

The station doesn't fit Cheyenne's throwaway architecture, but does seem to act as an anchor to keep the city from being blown away by the Chinook winds. Inside, the old passenger concourse is preserved just as on the last day Amtrak ran passenger service through here before the Denver & Rio Grande Western route became available. The heavy oak benches have been polished, as has the brass filigree at the ticket windows. The slate floor has been waxed, and there are no cobwebs in the corners above the tall windows. Only the computer-generated "Printshop" signs on office doors suggest that this is a company headquarters rather than a public edifice currently serving passengers. DON'T COME INTO THIS OFFICE WITH GREASE ON YOUR FEET; EMPLOYEE TOWN MEETING, 7:00 P.M., FEBRUARY 25; SIGN-UPS FOR THE LAS VEGAS EXCURSION IN ROOM 303; THINK SAFETY—CONTINUE OUR JANUARY RECORD; NO WE DON'T HAVE RAFFLE TICKETS IN THIS OFFICE!

Jack Kates, a UP employee at division headquarters, takes me under his wing and shows me around. We walk across the tracks of the main line out behind the station; he says, "Just don't step on the tracks." Then I notice the sign reading, "All employees will use the underground walkway in crossing the main line." The tracks are wired, and a footstep sets off a safety alarm.

Jack narrates the approach of a huge mixed freight from North Platte. The mile-long train slows to a stop just behind the station. The engine crew jump down and exchange surprisingly few words with the new crew, waiting with lunchboxes and travel satchels in hand. Jack tells me that a split of cars is being added to the train somewhere nearly a mile east of where we stand. Then the new crew are up into the engine, and with a roar of the diesels, the freight pulls out to the west. It takes longer for the train to pass than it has for the division stop.

The yard of UP's central division headquarters has been cut back. Three-quarters of the engine maintenance building has been removed and more than half of the tracks have been torn up. But there isn't a sense of decline here, rather of productive leanness. The facilities remaining are all in top shape and are actively used. No indecisiveness here as in the Toledo station.

In the engine maintenance building, there are three GP-40 freight engines (a recent design) undergoing routine repairs and a magnificent freshly painted passenger steam engine, a 4-6-4 (four pilot wheels, six driver wheels, and four trailing wheels) with eighty-inch drivers. It is taking on water for an excursion run to Las Vegas. The shop is noisy, brightly lit, well organized, and very busy. Bright yellow lines delineate hard-hat areas (nobody offers me one). I am struck by how orderly and clean the place is, not like my corner service station. The mechanics and hostlers seem very much at ease around an intruder with a camera.

Jack says that most of the diesel work involves pistons and cylinders. Unlike an automobile engine, which has a solid block, a railroad diesel engine has removable cylinders. He shows me a row of them lined up on a bench beside a temporarily gelded engine. "It's easier on the knuckles to work on one of these babies with the guts all lined up nice on a bench than it is twisting yourself into knots to work under the hood of your car."

Inside one of the engines I'm shown the simple flick switch which is used to start it. I ask, "If it's so simple, then why do you always see diesels sitting around running when they're not being used?" I always thought that was because the things must be hard to start.

Jack explains, "It's because you can't let them cool down, especially in cold weather. The engine is so big that when it cools down, different parts shrink differently, so that things don't fit right anymore and everything leaks—oil, coolant, fuel. A cold diesel in the winter makes a god-awful puddle where it's left standing. Also you get moisture condensing in the cylinders, which then has to be blown off. An idling diesel burns five gallons of fuel an hour, but they've found out that a cold one costs even more just sitting there piddling."

Jack asks if I'd like to peek inside the steam barn. In contrast to the maintenance barn, the steam barn is dark and silent, and we are alone with ghosts. But lined up in immaculate condition and ready for active duty are four steam engines: a 4-6-6-4 mallet (two sets of power wheels), a 2-10-4 freight monster, a 4-8-4 passenger engine with smoke lifters that look like a racehorse's blinders (Jack says it's a frequent pattern for HO-scale models), and an antique 4-6-0. Almost as an afterthought, the barn also houses an E-9 diesel and a 6,600-horsepower EMD Centennial diesel, the largest ever built. I scurry about trying to get pictures that will fit into my 50mm lens, while Jack delivers a low reverent monologue.

He says that the most frequent visitors to this barn are Union Pacific brass and politicians who commonly stop here after martini lunches or cocktail socials. They giggle and tell jokes inspired by the sexual symbolism of the well-hung steam engines. A standard joke involves the automatic coal stoker of the tender to the 4-6-6-4, a twenty-foot-long shaft containing a huge screw which rams pea coal into the orifice of the firebox in the belly of the engine. Once the screw was broken and had to be repaired with massive welds. The brass retell this story with guffaws and expressions of mock pain every time they come here. Jack regards their visits as a defilement of this sanctuary. "They get their rocks off joking about the iron they own here."

Finally Jack shows me the huge snowblower, which he says used to be critical in keeping the line over the continental divide open in bad winters. I bite: "Why isn't it needed anymore?"

"Traffic. Today there're so many freights, and they're so regular, that the snow can't pile up. You've seen the plows on the front of the engines. When you got 'em coming through every couple of hours, that does the job." So what Grenville Dodge needed back in 1873 was simply more traffic. And today, in the railroad's supposed sunset days, the Union Pacific traffic is so heavy as to void the curse of winter weather that brought the mighty road to its knees in better days.

"Sunset days, hell," says Jack. "You tear up that track right out there and you can kiss California goodbye. You can't put enough trucks on the interstate to carry what rolls through here every day. This is the main line of America, right here."

Writer Ludovic Kennedy regretted the auto side trip he made to Cheyenne in 1980. He wrote that the place was "as dull and bleak as any place I had ever visited." I can't argue with that, but I wasn't disappointed in my visit to this outpost along the line of progress. Here you can see what it means to conquer a continent. I suppose from a little distance in space, all you would see looking down on Cheyenne would be the rail line, the low-built city blending into the sagebrush waste just as it did back in 1873. But here is a place that matters, whose purpose and function can never be in doubt—nothing less than a welded joint that binds San Francisco to Chicago, California to the midwest, coast to coast, past, present, and future.

Chapter Three

Jackalopes and Golden Spikes

The California Zephyr

I'm back in Denver's Union Station, waiting for the next westbound edition of the *California Zephyr*, where a good crowd of camera-toting tourists and fashionably attired skiers gathers to ride one of the world's most scenic train routes. Aside from continental rail travelers like myself, many sight-seekers fly to Denver just to ride the daylight stretch over the Rocky Mountains to Salt Lake City. The atmosphere here is different from that in many old stations where towering concourse rooms seem deliberately designed to generate a cool darkness; here the tall windows of all four walls flood the air, the benches, the floor with golden Colorado light. Yet the high-backed oak benches are arranged almost like church pews, providing a paradoxical sense of intimacy amid the wide-open space that celebrates the distinctive quality of life in the west.

Aboard today's edition of the *California Zephyr*, I meet Terry North over breakfast in the diner as the train wends its way through the sprawling Denver suburbs. Terry's Irish ancestors settled in upstate New York around Troy in the 1830s, and each generation worked on the railroads as they built their way west. Terry lives in Oakland and is among the first generation of his family not to work on the railroad. He also doesn't look very Irish with his graying blond hair, blue eyes, and tanned, chiseled features.

But Terry did service on a railroad during the armistice at the end of the Korean War—he rode shotgun for the Army on supply trains out of Inchon. One long climb in particular was so slow that the thieves would just casually unload stuff as the train inched along. In keeping with armistice rules, he could only load his shotgun with rock salt, but the few times he had to use it convinced him that lead shot might have been more humane. He says the sounds and sensations of the mountain route we will travel today take him back to Korea the way helicopter imagery does Vietnam vets.

"Why don't you fly?"

"Well, my grandfather laid rail on this line. It's a kind of family heirloom. All the Norths ride this train when they come west—like a pilgrimage. It's expected. Where did you get on?"

"Springfield."

"Illinois?"

"No, Massachusetts."

"Why don't you fly?"

"I want to see America."

He smiles and shakes my hand. We're traveling companions for the duration of the trip.

The sensation of pressure in my ears alerts me that the climb up the Front Range has begun. We move to the lounge car, and Terry narrates the route he knows like family history. Already we have been crawling up a rolling ridge, known as Leyden Ramp, which conveniently extends eastward of the face of the foothills. The 2 percent grade is definitely noticeable inside the train, and the slow speed combined with the sound of squealing flanges on curving rails suggests the struggle with gravity. On one especially tight curve I look out the window and see a Denver & Rio Grande freight engine leading a second Amtrak engine on the head end of the train and remember the card king's warning: "It means big trouble. Amtrak don't allow no other engines to pull its trains."

Terry says, "You've been fed a jackalope."

"What's a jackalope?"

"Well, they're a kind of cross between a jack rabbit and an antelope. Supposedly they appear most often when there's alcohol around. Westerners lure them out with a bait of bourbon, beer, and baloney. But only easterners ever get to actually see them."

At one time the idea of a rail line up this mountain face was thought to be a jackalope. What made it plausible was the surveyors' strategy of gaining as much altitude as soon as possible, even before taking on the mountains proper, since the line must climb from Denver's 5,200 feet to the nearly 10,000 feet of the tunnel through the continental divide. As the crow flies the distance is twenty-eight miles, but it takes sixty-two miles of horseshoe curves, loops, and canyon contours to cover that distance.

About forty-five minutes out of Denver there is a particularly spectacular stretch. Here the train is climbing bald foothills with a series of horseshoe curves where you can look out the window and see the engine grinding in the opposite direction. The route turns south for one especially tight bend known as Big Ten (for its ten-degree curve) and we pass a row of stationary coal cars filled with rocks sitting on a siding. These are here to protect the passing trains from Chinook winds that blast down the mountainside at sixty to eighty miles per hour, enough to blow the train right off the edge. Then the train turns north again and climbs across the sheer eastern face of the tallest part of the Front Range wall. We turn westward into Coal Creek Canyon and claw our way to its head, cross on a high bridge, continue back eastward on the canyon's north side, higher now, and emerge back on the open face. Finally, after Plainview, where I can see a hundred miles to the east, we enter a tunnel and plunge westward through a gap in the wall into the forested South Boulder Canyon.

Here the tracks cling to the clifflike slopes of ravines and gulfs, piercing the rock periodically with short tunnels; now the expanse of the plains is out of sight. The sense of incline does not abate, however, and my ears continue to pop. Higher and higher we climb through dense stands of lodgepole pines and Douglas firs, along icy cliffs and past rushing streams. It is a world where the vertical dimension overwhelms the horizontal.

And then we enter a high valley where a road appears and with it log houses, little ranches, a schoolhouse, and a store or two. It strikes me that until this point we have been riding through country accessible only by the rail route. Up on a ridge there are several expensive contemporary mountain houses with huge expanses of glass. A real estate agent has told Terry that these places were built by the hundreds during the late seventies and early eighties and are now selling for fractions of their original appraisals. I guess that the romance of living high on a Rocky Mountain ridge wears a little thin in the isolation of the long winters and the hot dry summers.

"No, the shale-oil boom went bust," explains Terry.

Finally there is an actual village, East Portal, and then the blackness of the seven-mile-long Moffat Tunnel under the continental divide. The engineer sounds the horn periodically in the tunnel to chase out any animals that have ventured in. People at the portals frequently see antelopes, deer, and occasionally even a mountain lion bounding out of the tunnel just ahead of the train.

Here the route reaches 9,239 feet, the highest elevation of any railroad in the United States. I can't feel the altitude till a deliberate jog down the corridors of two adjoining bedroom cars makes my head light and my heart rapid. In Peru there is a railroad that, at sixteen thousand feet, requires the distribution of oxygen in balloons to prevent debilitating altitude sickness. Here the effect is simply a bit of "Rocky Mountain high," but the thought of Terry North's grandfather's toil at this altitude is sobering.

With its claim, even before the Civil War, to being the only city of significance between the Missouri River and the Pacific Ocean, Denver fully expected to be a major station on any central transcontinental line that might be built. The gold fever which brought settlers and miners by the thousands into the mountains west of the city only confirmed that presupposition. When Grenville Dodge settled on the Wyoming route for the UP, which left Denver a hundred miles off the main line, it amounted to an act of war for which no branch line from Cheyenne could ever compensate. Denver interests began building their own railroads with a pugnaciousness and belligerence that in cases actually led to pitched battles and bloodshed.

The most significant of Denver's rail ventures was the Denver & Rio Grande. As the name suggests, the road was initially conceived as a link to the southern Colorado River, New Mexico, and Texas. It also built into the mountain mining country, frequently on narrow-gauge track because of the tight curves needed in the rugged terrain. In the "Bloody Angle" of southeastern Colorado, the DRG clashed with another westward-building transcontinental, the Santa Fe.

In 1878 the two railroads recognized the spectacular, narrow Royal Gorge as being the critical passage through the southern Colorado mountains, both for access to the mining country and as an opening to a possible southern Colorado route to Salt Lake. When the DRG, which ran all of Colorado's telegraph lines, intercepted a Santa Fe directive ordering its men to seize and hold the canyon, a trainload of a hundred armed men was dispatched to the gorge. The Santa Fe brought in its hired guns and erected fortresslike barricades—this was war. At one point where the DRG route along the upper canyon wall looked down on the Santa Fe route on the gorge floor, rock slides wiped out each new Santa Fe encroachment. The Santa Fe people retaliated with dynamite charges that brought down the underpinnings of the DRG's tracks above. Former Colorado governor A. C. Hunt led a two-hundred man army to take over the Santa Fe route leading from Pueblo to Canyon City at the mouth of the gorge; the Santa Fe countered with no less a figure than Bat Masterson. There were pitched battles. Train crews were attacked and beaten, families were threatened, stations and yard installations were sabotaged, and public officials were kidnapped. Colorado was near open insurrection when the Supreme Court ended the mayhem in 1880 with a verdict awarding the DRG rights to the gorge and first option to purchase all Santa Fe track that had been built from Pueblo to the gorge. Score one for the DRG.

But meanwhile another race was shaping up with the Santa Fe for the crucial crossing of the old Santa Fe Trail over Raton Pass into New Mexico. The Santa Fe Railroad's intent to reach the West Coast and the DRG's plan to follow the Rio Grande to Texas clashed in the high pass where an old toll road owner, Dick Wooten, held the key to success. The DRG was caught napping this time (actually it was busy building a superfluous spur to a townsite where the DRG held real estate development rights), and the Santa Fe and Dick Wooten were waiting, their pact already made, when the DRG surveyors arrived in Raton. Score one for the Santa Fe.

The DRG would content itself with its narrow-gauge routes in the mining country and, by 1890, a route to Salt Lake through the southern Rockies nearly as far south of Denver as the Union Pacific was north of the city. Meanwhile Denver had acquired two links to the east, aside from the hated UP, in the Burlington to Chicago and the Kansas Pacific to St. Louis. But still the direct route west, ever more like a jackalope, failed to materialize.

It was another one-man initiative that would finally make the ambition a reality and rectify the situation to Denverites' satisfaction. For forty years, David Moffat, banker, merchant, real estate tycoon, and civic leader, nourished a dream of finding a main-line route over the Front Range. In 1902, he initiated the project with surveyor H. A. Sumner. The keys to Sumner's route were three: gain as much altitude as possible before climbing across the face of the range; follow the contours of larger canyons to their heads and back again on the opposite wall rather than bridge them; and, most important, tunnel under the continental divide. Such a tunnel had never been built before, and when the project was begun, the necessary technology didn't even exist. For twenty-five years the route had to rely on temporary tracks climbing an awesome series of switchbacks called the Giant's Ladder at the rarefied altitude of 11,600 feet over Corona Pass, just above today's tunnel location. With the completion of the Moffat Tunnel in 1928, the five-hour climb and the severe limitations on the size of trains over this route ended. Now the same distance could be covered in ten minutes.

Moffat originally called his line to Salt Lake the Denver, Northwestern & Pacific; meanwhile the Union Pacific used all of its considerable influence to keep Moffat's route out of the station in his own city. The direct main-line connection to Salt Lake was finally established when the well-connected Denver & Rio Grande took over the line and linked it to the Burlington's eastern connection at Denver.

Now the DRG, which could stand for Denver's Revenge and Glory, settled the longstanding score with the UP as the Burlington–DRG route became in the twentieth century the premier passenger route to San Francisco because of the spectacular mountain scenery. Despite its highly touted *Overland Limited*, the UP was increasingly relegated to freight duty, though of course there was probably little sorrow in Omaha and Cheyenne, since that's where the profits always have been anyway. Amtrak's initial San Francisco route followed the UP only because the DRG was able to hang on until 1983 as the last privately operated passenger route in America. Since 1983, Amtrak's *California Zephyr* follows the DRG route and the UP passenger station in Cheyenne stands polished and empty—waiting.

We emerge from the Moffat Tunnel to the sight of ski lifts, packed open slopes, and brightly clad skiers just to the left of the train. Like a slap in the face, the sight reorients me to an age where the mortal toils of previous generations are now commemorated by the installment of playthings. Winter Park is a celebration of man's seemingly total conquest of nature; and, as if to underscore the point, a waving snowmobiler outside my bedroom window races the train to the stop at Frazier and wins.

For some time, Frazier, Colorado, has been vying with International Falls, Minnesota, for the title Icebox of America. I have pictured Frazier as a settlement of log houses huddled amid tall firs in a box canyon between towering peaks; instead, Frazier is a modern, affluent community of split-level homes with two-car garages and well-plowed streets sprawling on a broad open basin rimmed by the mountains. I can see four-wheel-drive Jeep Wagoneers and Audi Quattros in drive-ways, and everyone seems to be wearing fashionable ski clothes. The tourist trade has been good to Frazier, that and a little cattle ranching on the high pastures.

The afternoon glides by as we wind down through the canyons of the Colorado River. Here there are towering redstone cliffs and places where the railroad clings to sheer rock over the stream. Rock-slide fences have been installed to warn the engineer with a radio signal if there are rocks on the tracks. "But what happens if the slide occurs as the train is passing?" I ask Terry North. He shrugs and makes a thumbs-down gesture that suggests limits to man's ability to take precautions.

After a while the continual barrage of verticality numbs the senses and I am consciously looking for something to disrupt the soporific mood. The service chief comes on the PA inviting passengers to a trivia game in the lounge and a contest for who can be the first to spot the rare jackalope.

Amid the general rowdy cheer generated by the games, Terry directs my attention to the construction of Interstate 80 through Glenwood Canyon.

Environmentalists have fought the feds on this for years. Everyone agrees that Glenwood Canyon is both a geological and biological national treasure. Opponents of the road have argued that with the railroad already established on the south wall, an interstate dynamited into the north side would destroy this natural wonder. The engineers of the feds pulled the rug out from under the environmentalists by designing a road which required no blasting, no cut into the north wall. Instead the interstate is built out from the wall and in some places literally hangs from the wall by cables. It's hard to see how this is any less disruptive to the geology, ecology, and aesthetics of the canyon, but since opposition has been based so much on the issue of dynamiting and cutting, the project forges ahead.

The DRG isn't enthusiastic about sharing the canyon with the entity that is a leading cause of the hard times railroads have faced nationwide, but has lain low, knowing that it can only compromise the cause of the environmentalists. There was a time when this railroad would have gone to war to keep a competitor out of a canyon. Now, with two lanes of the road open over most of the stretch, tandem trucks roll along at sixty miles an hour on the north wall hauling the same trailer rigs that ride piggyback on the flatcars of the DRG at forty miles an hour along the south wall. Add the railroad to the species endangered by the project.

By dinnertime the spectacular vertical scenery has finally leveled out into the sunset-pink eastern Utah desert. The swordfish is delicious, broiled and smothered in a wine sauce of red and green peppers, onions, garlic, and cayenne. My dinner companions are a retired couple from Grand Junction traveling to Las Vegas "to lose all our money." They aren't kidding. Garry and Gina Selznik make the trip twice a year, when interest on a few bonds and some stock dividends accumulates to make the bankroll fat enough, and return home when it's gone.

"Why?" I ask.

He says, "It's something to do—we can do it together. We don't really have a whole lot of use for our money, you know. Kids are off on their own, doing okay. But it's action and it's real life. Sure as hell beats watching soap operas for the rest of our days. And then, you know, we just might really hit the jackpot one of these years!"

"What would you do with it?"

"Go to Atlantic City. Change of scene and play for bigger stakes."

Gina explains, "You get to be our age and you want some glamour, just a little, some real glamour out of life."

"But not if I have to fly," insists Garry. They always take the train ever since he dropped five thousand feet in a sheer downdraft on a flight to Texas. He vowed he would never fly again. She talked him into it once for one of these trips to Reno. He kept his eyes closed the whole flight and bought an Amtrak return ticket when he arrived in Reno. "I'm no wimp, you understand. I can make a hundred-dollar bet on a long-shot number at the roulette wheel without flinching or even sweating. But you plunge five thousand feet in an airplane . . . it's a feeling that gets under your skin, and once it's happened, it's with you every time you get on an airplane. I don't need it. Besides, isn't this a whole lot more fun anyway?"

They're delighted when the PA announcer names them as winners in the afternoon trivia contest. "Sure we play. We play everything." There has also apparently been one person who has seen a jackalope. "They get at least one sucker every time."

After dinner in the upstairs lounge, the glazed-eyes set has settled in in front of *Beverly Hills Cop*. Downstairs in the lower bar, conductor Melvin Holyoak introduces himself and sits down with me. "I hear you're from New England. You know, you've got a city up there named after me," he says. Jackalopes, rail hijacking, and now a guy who lays claim to the naming of venerable Holyoke—my ability to discriminate fact from fiction is going to be tested in these travels.

"There was a poor, illiterate preacher in England in the early nineteenth century who didn't even have a church; he preached the gospel under a huge oak tree. Well, there was a baby born. The mother died in childbirth, and some Mormon missionaries urged the family to leave England and come to Salt Lake. The father only got as far as Massachusetts, where he founded a town. The grandparents brought the baby to Salt Lake, and I am descended from that baby. The town in Massachusetts, Holyoke, is misspelled, probably because of the father's lack of education. Most of the family is still Mormon, though some have fallen away. The story is family legend. You're supposed to be able to tell it like a myth or a Bible story, but I never had the knack."

Melvin grew up on a poor farm in Arizona. His brother went to telegraph school and worked for the Southern Pacific. Melvin never had the schooling but was hired anyway because of his brother's tutelage. He went over from telegraph to train service with the Santa Fe in 1968.

Now he is one of the pioneers taking advantage of the Amtrak job-swap deal. "I'd rather be working here in air-conditioned cars than out there hanging on the side of a boxcar." He believes this is a revolutionary development in railroad management-labor relations and feels sympathy for the senior folks on the freight lines who didn't make the jump. "The precedent is set. They're going to take the pay cut eventually anyway. As the Bible says, there's going to be weeping and wailing and gnashing of teeth." From Melvin's perspective, the deal means that ultimately the freight railroads will train railroad men and employ them during their younger years. Then, at some point in their careers, most will make the transition to Amtrak passenger service for their later working years. Eventually it won't involve a pay cut because Amtrak's rates will become the standard; everyone will have taken the pay cut from what the railroads and Amtrak believe is a currently inflated rate.

Melvin sees it in eschatological, utopian terms, proof of a design in the universe right down to the level of government-railroad-union negotiations. "These things don't happen by accident, you know."

Weeks later back in Keene, I contact the Holyoke public library to confirm that I've encountered a Mormon jackalope, since most of the major towns of central New England were founded in the eighteenth century, long before Melvin's mid-nineteenth-century tale begins. After a few days the helpful librarian returns my call. Holyoke was founded by Eleazar Holyoke, a Mormon, in 1850. Melvin's story is no jackalope, but a little golden spike, like those in the rails themselves, binding time and widely separated places together.

It's midnight in Salt Lake. Here the *California Zephyr* is split in three with the main section going on to San Francisco, the *Pioneer* heading northwest to Portland and the *Desert Wind* southwest to Las Vegas and Los Angeles. There are goodbyes on the platform between folks who have come this far together and who have ritually detrained for this long stop even though this is not their final destination. Melvin gets off and goes home to bed. The five small children of a couple headed for Portland ask for autographs in quintuplicate from the train crew. The Selzniks receive wishes of good luck at the gaming tables. New dining- and lounge-car crews arrive for the *Pioneer* and *Desert Wind*. Terry North and I, aboard the *California Zephyr* section, pull out first for San Francisco.

West of Salt Lake, I am finally on Union Pacific track for the short stretch south of Salt Lake and into the salt desert, where the Southern Pacific will take over. The moonlight sparkles on this strange inland body, and across the water I can see the peaks of Promontory, where the Union Pacific and Central Pacific met for the famous Golden Spike ceremony in 1869.

Any new teller of the story of the Golden Spike has to pause in humility before a tale told so often. What strikes me after my readings of the history is how the Union Pacific must have staggered toward that supposedly triumphant meeting. It wasn't just the continual bleeding from conflict with the Indians, nor the debilitating struggle with the continental divide, which turned out to be two divides separated by a deadly alkali basin, nor the blizzards that buried tracks under twenty feet of wind-packed snow, nor even the necessity for that final mad dash in competition with the Central Pacific's Chinese workers racing across the flats of Nevada. What must have sapped the strength of the great enterprise the most was the continual organic bleeding: the struggles for control of routing, funding, contracting, and paying of dividends involving men who still labored under the notion that the fortunes were to be made during the construction and that the party would be over when the line was done. Here was a great beast straining toward a noble goal while wolves and vultures chewed at its flanks and parasites ravaged it internally.

The race with the Central Pacific building eastward from California resulted from the simple fact that the Pacific railroad legislation had never specified the meeting point. Each railroad assumed that its power and profits would depend upon having as much of the mileage under its domain as possible, and both regarded the Salt Lake region as a prize which neither was interested in sharing with the other. At one point Central Pacific surveyors were scouting lines as far into supposed Union Pacific territory as Wyoming while Union Pacific surveyors worked well into western Nevada. The situation reached absurdity when road graders for each railroad worked right past each other running parallel grades in opposite directions. Shortly the track layers would be doing the same. Both roads had cheated by skipping over critical stretches which would have to be constructed later. Bridges were unfinished and track quality in many places was substandard. Negotiations were in order.

In the spring of 1869, the agreement was reached which fixed the meeting point at Promontory, the mountainous peninsula protruding into the north end of Salt Lake. The Union Pacific held on to Salt Lake and Ogden, but would sell some of its route west of the arbitrary terminus point to the Central Pacific. The key to the bargain was the erroneous belief that a major junction town would spring up at the connecting point.

Once the agreement was made, the competition to fill in the last gaps in both routes became more sporting, though it never had truly involved bloodshed as some have maintained. After Jack Casement showed with pride the six miles of track his Irish terriers had laid in one day, the Central Pacific's Charles Crocker carefully prepared material for a greater feat. On April 28, with Union Pacific officials in attendance, the Chinese workers laid ten miles of track in one day, a feat not duplicated since. But there was still tension. Casement set his crews to work building eastward from the proposed meeting point to guarantee the meeting point with steel, rather than just paper. In a final act of territorial behavior, Casement had his workers toil all night to build a siding at the meeting point before the arrival of the Central Pacific's work train. He was leaving no stone unturned.

May 10, 1869, dawned sunny and briskly cold at Promontory. Strangely there were no Washington politicians on hand for the long-awaited ceremony. Dodge was there, and Casement and Durant, as well as Stanford, representing the Central Pacific. The Ames brothers were not present, nor were the other three of the big four from California. What was well represented was the media, in a form that was prophetic of the future: three photographers, C. R. Savage, A. J. Russell, and A. A. Hart, found immortality that day. Their shots of the two engines meeting amid champagne toasts would become ingrained in American pictorial history. The telegrapher, W. N. Shilling, who wired the hammer and spike to his set so that the waiting nation could electrically experience the blow that united the hemisphere likely had no inkling of just how much of a paradigm of the future his stunt would turn out to be. Newsmen and public officials from New York to San Francisco huddled over telegraph sets to hear Shilling's commemorative dot. The publicists who orchestrated the formal ceremony in a nation not known for its sense of public ritual had mined just the tip of a vein of wealth and power which would become a dominant feature of American life a hundred years later—the contrived media event.

Bands played, patriotic speeches were made, and a Chinese crew dropped the last rail in place. There was a prayer, and then silence as telegraph operators across the country awaited the three dots that would mean that the next dot transmitted would be the first blow to the spike. At half past noon the three dots were sent. Stanford swung the hammer—and missed the spike entirely but hit the rail squarely enough to transmit the dot over the telegraph. The nation cheered. Then Durant took his turn, saying, "This is the way to India." Extra editions of newspapers across the continent carried cryptic headlines: LAST RAIL LAID! THE SPIKE IS DRIVEN. DONE! Everyone knew what it meant.

There were celebrations in every major city. The American century was still thirty-one years away, but the feat and the way it was commemorated heralded the global village which Americans would come to dominate in another age.

But there were debts to be paid. A week later, when he had had a chance to review the staggering cost of the final push, the respectable Bostonian Oliver Ames told Dodge, "I am so thoroughly sick of my connection with the Road that I propose to get out of it just as soon as I can. If I could go out today, I would be a happier man." A year later, Crédit Mobilier began to unravel.

It is morning in Nevada, not a tree in sight as we parallel the Humboldt River. The river goes nowhere—it just sinks into the sponge of the Nevada basin. The Donner Party followed this route, and the spongy footing of the basin floor contributed to their deadly tardiness in arriving at the Sierra foothills. I see the steam geysers that with their false promise of fresh water were such a tease to pioneers. The Humboldt itself becomes increasingly brackish as it approaches the sink area.

At Sparks, a servicing stop, Terry North and I get off and wander toward the head end of the train. The engineer going off duty accosts us and, seeing my camera, says, "You're not going to take a picture of the head end, are you?" That assures it, of course, so he accompanies us to soften the blow. The first thing I notice is a stomach, hanging from the coupler, then I realize that I am looking at entrails, skin, and bone matted all over the plow and hood of the engine. And something I take for mud is caked on the forward wheel truck and splattered as high as the windshield—it's not mud, it's feces.

"Sheep. Happens every once in a while," says the engineer. "You can see, we got about fifteen of 'em last night. They just pop like balloons."

"More like shit grenades," says his assistant, whose job includes removing the stuff from the windshield. "They're always full of shit, just goddam shitbags."

"What happened to the old cowcatchers?" I wonder.

"Speed," says Terry, and the engineer agrees. The cowcatcher, which never caught on in Europe, was the distinguishing feature of American steam engines for nearly a century. At low speeds, the device enabled engines to shoulder their way even through large herds straddling the tracks with no more damage to the animals than occasional broken legs. But at high speeds, "it doesn't matter what you have on the front of the train, the animals are hamburger." Ironically, the original cowcatchers were pointed spikes to spear animals, which later would be divided up for meat among the crew.

Farmers in Michigan once fought a little war with the railroads over the issue of killed livestock. They tore up track, derailed engines, and burned down stations. Today the issue is settled in courts. The engineer explains, "The sheep farmers figure what they lose this way is less cost to 'em than proper fencing. They usually try to sue the railroad. Sometimes the railroad has to pay, sometimes it doesn't. Today both sides figure it as just another cost of doing business."

Just before Reno the service chief points out the famous Mustang Ranch, a high-class brothel in the Nevada desert that recently became the object of a well-publicized stock takeover. It specializes in "fantasy fulfillment—a sexual Disney World." Wealthy men fly to Reno from all over the country to order a particular fantasy, and the Mustang Ranch serves it up hot. If you want to be an Arab sheik, an appropriate set complete with authentic props is created. White pioneer meets nubile Indian maiden is a particularly popular entree on the regular menu. Says the chief, "You can even take a jackalope to bed here, and it ain't no stuffed animal neither." The engineer lets out several salutes with the horn as we pass. From the train the place looks very modest—built of pink brick and surrounded by a parking lot with a dozen cars sporting various state licenses, it looks like any garden-variety desert motel.

Just beyond Reno, I see trees for the first time since yesterday—in fact, discounting the forests of the Rockies' Front Range, I haven't seen trees since the Missouri crossing. These are not weedy cottonwoods or mesquite bushes, but real pines, firs, and even hardwoods. Robert Louis Stevenson wrote while riding this very stretch in 1879, "I had come from unsightly deserts to the green and habitable corners of the earth." He reported on a man from Maine who burst out at this point in the trip, "By God, I smell pitch again." In those days, they would have been riding for a week since they left Chicago.

Today I can't smell the pitch inside this air-conditioned train and I've been riding only twenty-nine hours since Denver, but the visual images of the climb up the Truckee Canyon into the Sierra Nevadas stir anticipation and excitement. The climax is the crossing of the pass high above Donner Lake where, in 1846, the Donner Party succumbed to cannibalism, depravity, and murder fifty miles short of the place they had traveled two thousand miles to find. The water today is ice-free and the cheery resorts along the shores repeat the pattern of today's recreation centering on places of yesterday's struggle or tragedy.

The Golden Spike at Promontory is the most literal of connections in the dream of uniting the continent. The Moffat Tunnel is another, as is Cheyenne and the Missouri and Burlington bridges. But there are other earlier symbolic golden spikes. The Donner Party disaster has obscured the story of one of them.

The sad tale of the Donner Party has been told often enough. They left Wyoming too late in the summer, lost precious time hauling their wagons over the boulder-strewn canyons of a questionable route through the Wasatch Mountains of Utah, got bogged down along the Humboldt in Nevada, and arrived in the Sierra to find the passes blocked with snow. Forty-two of their eighty-nine perished of starvation by the shores of the lake that bears their name, a mile below the pass.

But the lake and the pass and the route over it were discovered by another group, the Stevens Party, whose harrowing but successful transit two years earlier is not nearly so well known. From Wyoming to the Humboldt sink, Elisha Stevens and his group of forty-eight men, women, and children followed the tracks of another wagon party led by the mountain man Joe Walker, unaware that his trek a year earlier had ended in disaster with the wagons abandoned and the people just barely alive when they staggered into California. Near today's Sparks, the Stevens Party quit Walker's track on the advice of a Paiute chief, Truckee, and headed directly west across the Forty Mile Desert, blazing the trail that the railroad and Interstate 80 follow today. They then followed a river, which they named the Truckee, into the Sierras until it forked at a lake. In late November, the snow was already two feet deep and the party was desperate.

Stevens split his people into three groups. A small, light traveling contingent of young, well-armed men and women trekked up one fork as a "break-out" party. Stevens led six wagons and the main body of his people, including the women and children, up the other fork, which apparently led to the head of the rocky pass. And three young men stayed at the lake with five wagons and the bulk of the possessions until a return party could take them out in the spring.

Both of the traveling groups got through, though not without hardship. The "break-out" group discovered Lake Tahoe and arrived first at Sutter's Fort. Stevens's wagons were snowed in on the western slopes and his group survived the winter in shelters built beside the Yuba River. The three young men remaining at the lake built cabins and settled in for the winter until the snow piled up so deep that all game disappeared and they had to slaughter their last cows. It was time to get out, so they made makeshift snowshoes and started up over the pass. The youngest, Moses Schallenberger, couldn't make it. Sick and exhausted, he returned to the cabins expecting to die, while the others eventually made it to Sutter's Fort.

Moses discovered some traps left behind at the cabins and set them out. His first catch was coyote, the flesh of which was revolting, but it kept him alive. Later he caught foxes, whose meat he thought delicious. He found books in the possessions he was entrusted to keep and lived the winter on fox and the poetry of Byron and letters of Lord Chesterfield. In late February he saw a figure approaching through the ten-foot drifts. It was Dennis Murphy, of the original party, who had spent the past month involved in a California revolution that took him as far south as Los Angeles. Upon returning to Sutter's Fort and hearing that Moses had been left behind he set out to see if the lad was still alive.

Murphy took the time to make good snowshoes and taught Moses how to use them. Together they made it over the pass. In the spring, the men of the party went back for the wagons and what possessions hadn't been looted by Indians. The Stevens Party all got through, with two extras in the form of infants born during the passage. It is almost entirely through Moses Schallenberger's diary that we know of these events, the Stevens Party not being blessed with so many writers as the later Donner Party. In 1955, historian George Stewart wrote, "These are the ones who discovered the pass and took the wagons over, who kept out of emergencies or had the wit and strength to overcome them, who did not make a good story by getting into trouble, but made history by keeping out of trouble."

The train ride through the pass is impressive, even in this winter of little snow. How those pioneers managed to lug their wagons over these granite ledges I will never understand. The thought reinforces a notion I have had before while struggling to get in a winter's supply of firewood in New Hampshire with the help of a chainsaw. Our pioneers must have had a physical capacity unimaginable today. There are two possible explanations. One is that modern life has sapped us of the ability to perform sustained feats of muscle and endurance. The other is that the pioneer experience called forth only certain men, creating a kind of natural selection and assembling an "all-star" cast of remarkable physical specimens whom it is fruitless for most of us to strive to emulate. Today there is no single endeavor or occasion, short of the day when Omaha becomes a cinder, which might make them emerge as an identifiable group.

On the west slope of the Sierras, the trees and vegetation tell me how far I am from home. Palms and cacti, orange trees and tall slender junipers and cypresses dominate. The soil is a dusty sand, and there are unfamiliar hardwoods, some of which have their leaves in this season and some of which have shed them as our New England trees do. The impression is one of seasonal disorientation. For one of my northeastern environmental experience, it could be spring, summer, or fall here. The one season that doesn't seem right is the one that we are actually in, the last traces of snow having disappeared abruptly in the Sierra foothills. "The country is so big, you cannot say it has the same October," wrote Thomas Wolfe. Ditto for February.

The human marks on the landscape are less alien. Approaching Sacramento, we ride by several large housing developments, which are intriguing in that they have no houses. The streets, traffic signs, sidewalks, electrical installations and meters, and even mailbox address markers are all in place awaiting the building of homes—a supreme example of California confidence.

There are touches of Spanish architecture here and there, but for the most part, man's imprint is all too familiar—the McDonald's arches, the green interstate signs, the malls and parking lots, and split-level housing. One of the distressing lessons taught by a trip by land across America is how free enterprise and popular democratic government have conspired to foster the same kind of standardization and uniformity in the works of man that one would expect from a centrally planned economy such as those in communist countries.

But the day and the moment are too glorious for distressing theoretical speculation. I search for a way to characterize the high I am feeling as we roll toward San Francisco Bay three thousand miles down the tracks from the Springfield station. It's the same as that I felt on my first Amtrak trip to Florida five years ago—a sense of being far from home that is backed up by a tactile feel of the landscape I have crossed to get here.

As the train skirts Suisun Bay, Terry North shares a farewell beer with me before we part company at Oakland. He points out the mothballed fleet of World War II ships, and I wonder whether air travel will ever render these trains a similar fate. Somehow I begin to feel a touch of that sublime confidence of the conductors I have talked to in Iowa. Today I believe there will always be a passenger railroad in America. It was no jackalope when Asa Whitney first proposed it, and it isn't one now, even in an age when most people would consider a contemporary cross-continent train ride more unlikely than a stock takeover of a sexual Disneyland in the Nevada desert.

Stevens, Donner, Whitney, Vanderbilt, Pullman, Forbes, Dodge, Ames, Lincoln, Casement, Moffat, Stanford—to call this an epic catalogue is no hyperbole. So many of their stories are tales of individual initiative and feats on the truly grand scale, yet they led "a cast of thousands." Their journey spanned massive dimensions of time and space. They were tested by nature, their fellow men, and the gods themselves. And at the end of their trials and toils, through triumphs and tragedy, they were successful. They truly affirmed the view of a world unlimited. My journey, in three days and nights of comfort and ease, across three thousand miles of the route where they drove their spikes binding the land into a nation is testimony to that victory.

But the route I have ridden so far was only a tenuous first link. Forging a single track to central California was a mighty, practical accomplishment, but its ultimate significance lay in its pointing the way toward an even greater vision—the network of lines like this connecting not just a few widely separated key points, but the entire continent, its great places and its small, its cities and its farms, its inland valleys and its seacoasts, its towns and its empty spaces, mountain and plain, east-west, north-south, near and far—so that boys and girls lying in their beds in places like Bloomington, Illinois, would hear the fast express howl through at midnight and dream of Oregon or New Orleans, Texas or New York City. My journey has just begun. Twenty-five thousand miles of passenger runs still ply those dream routes. My quest will not be finished until I have ridden them all.

Crossing the Bay Bridge on the shuttle bus from the Oakland station to San Francisco Transbay Terminal I already miss Terry's companionship. Casting about to fend off an attack of traveler's loneliness, I strike up a conversation with an attractive young woman with long blond hair who seems to know her way around the Bay Area. Shortly I feel myself succumbing instead to traveler's fantasy—free-spirited California girl takes easterner in hand and brings him to nirvana in her apartment on Nob Hill. I ride the fantasy, staying cool, pumping her for advice to help me survive for two days in San Francisco—nothing more. She is helpful and matter-of-fact, and just plain friendly—she would have been a fine train companion. As we get off the bus, I ask where her trip originated.

"Charlotte, North Carolina. Just rented a house there. I'm tired of San Francisco. I'm getting my stuff together so I can clear out for good."

"You flew into Oakland?"

"Nope. Took the train all the way, about four thousand miles. I was on the same train you came in on this afternoon."

"Why didn't you fly?"

"I wanted to see America."

Chapter Four

Roots and Driftwood

The Coast Starlight

THE *Pullman Hotel Express* arrived in San Francisco on June 12, 1870, two weeks out of Boston. Editor Steele described the pouring of a flask of Boston Harbor water into San Francisco Bay. In speeches, the Bostonians exulted that they were the prototypical Americans of a new age, having been the first to experience the immensity of the continent from the rails, touchstones to a nation's future. Meanwhile their California hosts, eager to realize the first tangible monetary benefits of the railroad, grumbled a bit about their guests' Yankee penuriousness until the *San Francisco Bulletin* editorialized about how "these same flinty New Englanders give larger sums . . . for educational and charitable purposes than any people on earth." During the return trip, Steele expanded on what the journey had taught everyone concerned: "Americans will know each other as never before. Hooray for the railroad!"

In keeping with Whitney's dream of the railroad's making America the center of the world, the commemoration of my arrival here is a ride on one last set of tracks, the cable cars, to the harbor and Pier 35, where the cruise ship *Canberra* is just in from a two-week crossing from Australia.

At the Powell Street turnaround, cable car operator Charlie Cortez rotates the car on its turntable.

"Don't call these trolley cars," he tells me in his thick Spanish accent. "They got no motors. Just the lever that reaches down into the slot in the street and clasps on to the cable when I pull on it like this." He pulls the huge lever and the car inches forward. "Travels nine and a half miles per hour. That's how fast the cable moves under the street. I tell you more about it at the other end of the line."

The cable car seems full to me, but more people manage to squeeze on at every stop. By Chinatown, well-dressed women hang from the platform step. As we begin the incredibly steep descent down Hyde Street, with the bay, the Golden Gate, and Telegraph Hill displayed in a spectacular panorama this sunny February morning, Charlie says, "Oh, oh," and lets the car roll free for a few terrifying seconds. A dozen riders, including myself, look toward him with panic on our faces. "Just checkin' to see how many new riders we got," he says, laughing. He narrates the sights. "There's the Transamerica Pyramid. They say it's some kind of a fallacy symbol, but I never could figure out what that means. Down there at the docks you can see the ferries. We got lotsa them here in San Francisco—ferries all over the place. What you smilin' at, young fella? You don't believe we got a lot of ferries in San Francisco?"

At the end of the line, Charlie tells me the story of the cable cars as he bustles around polishing the brass. "They put in the cables to do something about the horse manure. See, at one time the city used horses. But they wore out pretty fast pulling the cars over these hills, and the streets used to be filled with horse manure. If there was a flash rain before the honey-bucket men came along, it could get real ugly."

Once labeled Hallidie's Folly, for Arthur Hallidie, inventor of the system, the cars became fixtures in San Francisco after their inauguration in 1873. The system has been rebuilt twice in recent memory, once in the 1940s and again between 1979 and 1984 when it was declared a National Landmark. Each time innovations have been eschewed out of an almost devotional dedication to authenticity. "If cable cars needed windshield wipers, the good Lord would have made them that way."

By midmorning the February chill has burned off, even down by the docks of Fisherman's Wharf, where Charlie waves farewell from his cable car as he eases it back up the Hyde Street line. He told me earlier that I was like any other tourist to San Francisco. "They all got a homing instinct for Fisherman's Wharf. The first thing they do is get on the cable car and ride down there and hang around by the docks on the bay. Some, that's all they ever see of San Francisco."

The boat that I came down here to see looms up over the warehouse of Pier 35—the SS *Canberra*, out of Sydney, Australia, via Honolulu. Where the rails meet the docks, this is the junction that made America the center of the world. I bring no flask of Boston Harbor water, and the glitzy tourist strip on Jefferson Street might just as well be Fort Lauderdale.

Not far from the berth of the *Canberra*, the waterfront today reveals the other side of San Francisco. You see derelicts in any big city, but there is more human flotsam in San Francisco than I have seen anywhere else, and it isn't just the leftovers from the sixties, though they are well represented. There are elderly and young men, women with kids and men in terminal midlife crises, blacks, whites, Hispanics, but very few Chinese. There are alcoholics nipping on brown-bagged bottles, and drug addicts sitting on benches with the drool just pouring from their nostrils and lips into puddles on the sidewalk. There are bag ladies asleep under cardboard on the grandstand facing the bay and sixties hippies playing the songs of revolution and love on guitars with broken strings just outside the entrances to fashionable Pier 39 boutiques. Wild-eyed lunatics shout curses at strangers across the Embarcadero, and muscular, athletic young men in tattered sneakers panhandle along Jefferson Street. By the Aquatic Park, the "pigeon people" speak only to the feathered friends so numerous that they wear them like clothing, and shabby old black men sit on Municipal Pier, Otis Redding's "dock of the bay," wasting time.

The common wisdom holds that the mild climate is responsible for the preponderance of street people in West Coast cities, but I wonder if perhaps many of them are washed up here by the national westering tides. Like human driftwood, they gather here by the shore at the end of the continent, but it is the land they have crossed and the ocean that bars their further drift. That American instinct to move on toward the setting sun, ever westward, a better life always just over the next rise, through the next passage—perhaps here is where it ends for many.

Beyond the postcard panoramas, these are the sobering impressions I take away with me from San Francisco. I realize that I too am bitten by that drifter's urge—it is in our American blood. In a few months, I will run out of rails to ride, but I have a family and roots back in the granite hills of New Hampshire. Here arises a tension that is one paradigm of the American experience: that between the urge to settle down and the urge to move on—roots and driftwood. San Francisco, thriving with its own well-founded sense of community—its preservation of historic buildings and network of mass transit—but cluttered with the desperate rootless here at the end of the line on the last shore of the continent; San Francisco teases the American traveler with his own unresolved contradictions.

A day later, riding the shuttle over the Bay Bridge to Oakland, where I will board the *Coast Starlight* for Los Angeles, I recall the San Francisco girl moving back to Charlotte by way of the train so that she could see America. I wonder why she is quitting San Francisco; I wish I could talk to her some more. She said she would be riding the *Broadway Limited* to Philly, where she would catch the *Crescent* for Charlotte after four days of squaring away her affairs here. I check my itinerary and the Amtrak timetables and discover that I will be riding the *Broadway Limited* the same day on my return journey.

It was the dream of just that kind of predictable, reliable transportation that drove the clamor for railroad building in California. In the decade following the Gold Rush of '49, travel to and from California, as well as within it, was a nightmare.

Collis Huntington's journey was typical. He departed New York City aboard the steamer *Crescent City* on March 15. Eight seasick days later, the ship anchored a mile off the mouth of the Chagres River of Panama, where passengers and their freight were literally deposited on the beach. There was no harbor, no welcoming lights of a seaport city. Travelers continued from the beach up the Chagres River by native boat and then by mule over the continental divide to Panama City on the west coast. The land crossing took five arduous days through tropical rain and swarms of malaria-bearing mosquitoes.

At Panama City, mobs of restless gold-seekers camped in tents outside the crowded city waiting for one of the three Pacific Mail steamers bound for San Francisco. Those who could not find passage on one of the steamers took their chances on the irregular visitations of sailing vessels in transit to California by way of Cape Horn. The wait for passage had mortal consequences as malaria took its toll among those who were forced to encamp in Panama City the longest.

Huntington made his way on the Dutch bark *Alexander von Humboldt*, which sailed into doldrums and was becalmed for five weeks off the Central American coast. When the winds finally blew the ship into

Acapulco, the starved passengers and crew revolted when they saw how scanty were the provisions purchased by the owners for the remainder of the voyage. The owners were left ashore and the ship sailed for San Francisco under potentially mutinous conditions. A month later, five months out of New York, Huntington sailed into San Francisco Bay.

And this was the fast route. The longer voyage around Cape Horn could be even more unpredictable, and the overland crossing was worse still—only three years had elapsed since the Donner debacle.

But Huntington did not come to California to build railroads nor even to seek gold. He came to do what he had always done, with his brother Solon, back in Oneonta, New York—sell provisions. He quickly recognized that San Francisco, with its "flimsy shanties" and tough men "adrift, milling back and forth" in seemingly endless pursuit of gambling, whoring, and drinking, was already too far to the rear of the action to support his business. Several attempts at setting up shop in the mountains themselves where the miners worked proved too unsteady as the sites of the most intense activity continually shifted with new strikes. He settled in Sacramento, at the head of the Sacramento River, which provided a water route for his goods coming in from the port at San Francisco and from which trails fanned out toward all of the significant mining sites. The thought that this location was ideally suited as the natural jumping-off point for any railroad that might cross the Sierras never occurred to him, though it created spasms of concern among San Francisco interests who feared that a transcontinental railroad terminating in Sacramento might relegate the Golden Gate to secondary status. Thus amid the cacophony of lobbying for various routes to California, one powerful voice was raised opposed to the whole idea—that of San Francisco.

Still the thought of railroads must have loomed large to Huntington as it did to all Californians during these years. The entire population of this explosively growing province had endured a voyage like Huntington's, or worse. Every item of trade in the local economy, still tethered to the centers of production in the east, had to make that same journey as freight. Whitney's dream of a transcontinental railroad found its earliest root here amid folk who couldn't have cared less about making the United States the center of the world. They just wanted to end the awful separation that had been the sacrifice demanded by their visions of gold and empire.

One man, Theodore Dehone Judah, decided to do something about it. After cutting his engineering teeth building railroad bridges in Connecticut, he had been hired by Sacramento interests in 1854 to build a twenty-one-mile railroad to Folsom to expedite the movement of goods up to the placer deposits. The Sacramento Valley Railroad was the first in California, and it hatched a bug under Judah's skin. For the next seven years, he turned a series of engineering jobs into reconnaissance sorties for a rail route over the Sierra Nevada. During this time a new gold and silver rush mushroomed on the eastern slopes in Nevada. Judah traveled and spoke throughout California emphasizing this as the immediate prize. When Congress and the Lincoln administration finally authorized a transcontinental railroad in 1862, Judah already had the western segment of the line laid out and a constituency to support it. The Central Pacific, thanks to "Crazy Judah," actually had rails laid while the Union Pacific was still haggling over routes.

Among the California merchants whom Judah had approached for financial backing were Collis Huntington and his new partner, Mark Hopkins. For the paltry sum of $1,500, they bought in on the ground floor of the fledgling Central Pacific Railroad. They were joined by fellow Sacramento merchants Leland Stanford and Charles Crocker. Thus originated the partnership of the "big four" that would change the map of America as no one ever had before. That Judah himself did not come to make a fifth in that combination is due to a situation which echoes the story of the Union Pacific. Huntington, Hopkins, Stanford, and Crocker were initially less entranced by the dream of running a transcontinental railroad than they were by the immediate reality of reaping hefty profits from the construction of the first miles of the line. Thus a dispute over the standards of construction led to the break in which Judah first tried to buy out the big four; when he failed, they moved to buy his interests.

In a desperate maneuver to secure financial backing, Judah embarked for New York via the Panama route, possibly to seek a partnership with the Vanderbilts—which would have vanquished his small-town merchant adversaries in California. He never made it. He died of malaria contracted during the horrendous Panama crossing which he had worked for nearly ten years to render obsolete.

California got its railroads. The big four went on to build the Central Pacific Railroad over the Donner Pass route Judah had laid out and to consolidate it with half a dozen shorter routes, including one that reached northward toward Oregon and another that brought San Francisco into the fold. Crocker, as head of the enormously profitable construction company that built the road, brought in the Chinese labor that added a new face to the American melting pot, the same Chinese who, during the final race with the Union Pacific, set the record of ten miles of track laid in one day. But eventually, his fortune established, he wanted out. Stanford became governor of California and used his post to promote the building of his railroad in ways that would make even our sleaziest politicians today look like angels. Yet finally he too lost the fever and dwelt increasingly on his horses and his political avocation. Hopkins lost his health and died.

Only Huntington, destined to become the greatest rail baron of them all, inherited Judah's bug for building transcontinental railroads, eventually welding the only coast-to-coast empire ever assembled under one man's control. Though his biographies relate a tale of restless, incredibly serendipitous opportunism, the end result of his life's work suggests a relentless drive to connect his western empire with the east—to weld his new roots to his old.

Between Oakland and Salinas today, the run of the *Coast Starlight* over the original Southern Pacific route to L.A. looks just like New Jersey except for the occasional palm trees and Spanish architecture. Nothing but the backsides of decaying industries, truck farms, and junk—old refrigerators, rusted autos, ruptured couches, piles of tires, discarded fuel tanks, and trash, trash, trash.

Things aren't much better inside the train, where I face an eleven-hour ride to Los Angeles as a day-tripper in coach—I just couldn't justify the expense of a sleeper for a day run. There's a crying baby right behind me and someone with a stereo tape player turned up a little too loud somewhere else in the car. Traveling coach on Amtrak isn't necessarily unpleasant—except when the train is crowded. Today there is not an empty seat in the car.

Entering the Salinas Valley, we pass what looks like huge flooded fields. These are drying flats for the Morton Salt Company, whose white mountains of salt make me wonder what happens when it rains. Then there are vegetable farms with their dark, rich-looking soil, and not a stone in sight. This is hobo territory, where even today a subculture of transient workers hops freights to follow ephemeral work in the valleys of the West Coast. The mountains that rise on both sides of the valley are treeless, and again I am struck by the sense of seasonal disorientation that the California landscape holds for me.

Finally there are the meticulously tended orchards, frequently presided over by contrasting ramshackle dwellings surrounded by more junk. This is John Steinbeck country. Here his Okies ended their long drift westward only to discover new hardship. It is also the vegetable basket of America. It should look prosperous, but the images of squalor and struggle are all too evident as we roll through. We pass migrant-worker villages where the accommodations are rows of derelict school buses. Just west over the Coastal Range are the surfer beaches and golden sands. The proximity of these scenes to California paradise gives a meaning to Steinbeck's title *East of Eden* that I had never thought of before.

Crossing the Coastal Range after lunch, I discover a new dimension to rail travel—open air. One of the frustrations of modern passenger travel is the lack of an open observation balcony or windows that can be raised. I push my luck with the train crew and open the window on the lower-level door and hang out to take pictures. It is a warm spring California afternoon. Being able to smell the countryside and hear the outdoors sounds of the train is a whole new travel experience. I get a touch of the feeling that riders of freights talk about and realize that those folks have the same advantage over me, in terms of contact with America, as I have over air or interstate travelers. The experience is especially impressive on a Superliner, because one is so close to the passing ground at the lower-level door.

The train winds through the treeless Coastal Range, passes through a tunnel, and, after a stop at San Luis Obispo, where I cut my hand carving a souvenir piece of cactus, descends toward the Pacific.

From my open window perch, I can smell the ocean before I see it. Then there it is, the vast swell of the Pacific, down about a hundred feet from the cliff the train traverses. I never really saw the Pacific in San Francisco, just the bay, so this is another milestone. What an irony that it is commemorated by the PA announcement telling passengers to look east to see the Minuteman missile site and the gantry towers of Vandenberg Air Force Base and the West Coast Shuttle Launch Pad. Just a few miles beyond the base we pass the site of the only direct enemy attack on the continental United States since the War of 1812. In 1942, Japanese captain Kozo Nishino fired seventeen rounds from his submarine at the Elwood Oil Field. Damage was minimal, but the event contributed to the Nippon-phobia which resulted in the infamous resettlement camps for Japanese-Americans whose fathers crossed the Pacific to settle here, put down roots, and share in the American dream.

The train follows the barren cliffs for 130 miles with the Pacific surf to the right and vast, empty hilltops to the left. It passes through the man-made greenery of Santa Barbara, where I'm told there is no unemployment because the cost of living is too high even for people with just one job. There is a spectacular Pacific sunset out beyond the oil-drilling platforms and channel islands—golden, then pink, then flame-orange, and finally absolute purple. Dinner takes us inland, over another rocky pass and down through the San Fernando Valley. I see rivers of light pouring down the mountainsides in the darkness—the southern California freeways. We are approaching Los Angeles.

It's hard to imagine Huntington's once omnipotent transportation monopoly, so overshadowed as it is today by the automobile. Yet in 1869 it was vulnerable on a variety of fronts to competing railroad schemes. The Union Pacific proposed a parallel to it through the Feather River route over the Sierras, north of the CP's Donner Pass crossing. The UP envisioned its "short line" to Oregon that would then enter California from the north. And a series of proposals for railroads across the flat southwestern deserts presented a continuing threat on the southern flank. These latter were especially ominous because of the ease of building that route and the growing national sense that the southern states needed some economic boost after the ravages of the Civil War.

As merely the shorter western leg of the first Pacific railroad, dependent for survival upon the cooperation of the larger UP, the Central Pacific could never hope to compete with any railroad which operated a continuous line from the Mississippi to the coast. Thus the associates bought up everything leading into San Francisco, plus the major line under construction northward toward Oregon and, most important, a seemingly innocuous little line from San Jose down the coast to Gilroy, a line which held franchises and land-grant rights all the way to the southern California border, the Southern Pacific.

Initially then, the monopoly characterized as an octopus in political cartoons of the day and in the title of a Frank Norris novel was in reality a desperate struggle to defend the tenuous roots established at great cost in dollars and sweat by the Central Pacific Railroad. Huntington would argue against his detractors to his dying day that those roots were the underpinnings of the success of the booming California economy. He never understood why Californians came to hate their railroad so vehemently.

But at some point in the late 1870s, the drive to extend the Southern Pacific as a defensive shield for the Central Pacific changed to an unabashed quest for total monopoly of California transportation. The memory of the costly race against the UP to Promontory became an obsession to Collis Huntington, and he vowed that his railroads would never again face a competitive threat on their own territory. Growing profits from the Central Pacific financed Huntington's Southern Pacific empire, which eventually stretched from Oregon to the Gulf of Mexico, finally even gobbling up the Central Pacific itself. Vast landholdings acquired initially as state grants made the SP California's largest landlord, and conflicts with homesteaders occasionally resulted in bloodshed, as in the infamous Mussel Slough Massacre. Huntington could make or break struggling California communities by his ability to set rates and routes, unchallenged by competition. San Francisco, in particular, perceived the SP's stranglehold as stifling its destiny to be the greatest Pacific port. And San Diego had even greater grievances: the SP left it without any rail route whatsoever. By the end of the century, the Hearst newspapers would build an empire of their own largely out of the vitriol they poured out daily onto the head of Huntington and his railroad.

During these years, new railroad-building drifters with route proposals were welcomed by a California populace eager to break the iron economic grip of the CP/SP combination. First there was the Atlantic & Pacific through northern New Mexico and Arizona, then the UP's "Oregon Short Line," then Jay Cooke's Northern Pacific across the northern Rockies, and finally the Texas & Pacific, through the desert southwest, sponsored by no less a figure than the president of the Pennsylvania Railroad, Thomas Scott, and later by Jay Gould. Huntington succeeded in destroying or delaying them all by building or buying the California end of each proposed route. And when a second transcontinental was ultimately completed all the way to New Orleans, it was the Southern Pacific's. Only the Atchison, Topeka & Santa Fe, in conjunction with San Francisco interests that would finally have their day, eventually succeeded in cracking Huntington's California empire, but those are other stories.

Los Angeles' Union Passenger Terminal is one of the most beautiful in America. Built in the 1930s with a Spanish influence in its Art Deco design, it still invokes two golden ages, those of Hollywood and the preairline railroads. Through this gateway, Bogart and Dietrich, Gable and O'Hara, Tracy and Hepburn rode the Santa Fe's *Super Chief* to Chicago or Southern Pacific's *Sunset Limited* to New Orleans or the Union Pacific's *City of Los Angeles* to Vegas or Salt Lake.

The prevailing motif is one of archways except for the square mission-style tower and its clock. Inside, the architecture generates a cool darkness, altogether appropriate for a station that is a haven from the hot, dry southern California sun. Overhead, magnificent chandeliers hang from the dark hardwood beams of the vaulted ceiling.

The floor plan creates the appropriate impression of a terminal, rather than a hub station, as does Chicago's Union Station. The station has a front end, the entrance from Alameda Street, and a back end, the train platforms. In between there is a logical progression from waiting room and ticket stalls, to the concourse with its restaurant separated from the waiting floor by a shoulder-high partition, to the baggage-claim area, to the double doors leading into underground walkways to the various train platforms.

Angelenos complain about the upkeep of the place and in particular about the pigeons that have taken roost inside the high concourse room and wing freely about as if the place were some kind of aviary, but I rather like the musty sense of age and wonder if the place might lose some of its charm if it was scrubbed squeaky clean and antiseptic.

Out on the platform, there are three Amtrak trains sitting chugging between runs. One is the *Desert Wind*, just in from its overnight run from Salt Lake through Las Vegas. A day train to San Diego is taking on supplies for its lounge car, and another from San Diego is waiting for attention. The engineer with this last train gives me a friendly wave. I motion for him to come down to the platform, and he does. His name is Lester Hornsby, and he asks, "Ya wanna see the inside of the unit?" I'm up the ladder in a flash.

Inside the cab it's hot and noisy; we have to shout.

"Ya ever been in the head end before?"

"Not since I was a little kid. My grandfather was an engineer on the GM & O."

"He wouldn't recognize much here today." He notices me staring through a little hatchway into a small cubicle located down several steps in the very nose of the engine. There is a whiff of odor wafting from that direction. "Yep, that's the crapper. It discourages a guy from sitting there and reading when he ought to be up here keeping an eye on things. If shit happens, that's where it will happen first."

"The fireman or assistant would still be up here, wouldn't he?"

"Only on long overnight runs. We don't carry a fireman on short runs like this one to San Diego anymore. Union finally knuckled under."

Lester admits that the fireman is no longer really needed, thanks to modern automation and safety equipment. Even the legendary "dead man's pedal" has been replaced. It was too easy to abuse—you could lean a heavy wrench against it and leave the driver's seat. Today the seat is wired. A klaxonlike horn blasts if the engineer leaves it. There is also a randomly timed alarm that the engineer must respond to when it sounds or else the brakes automatically kick in.

The engineer's seat is on the right side of the cab. It is surrounded by gauges and controls. Just to the left hangs the communications phone, a key tool in modern railroading. "I don't scratch my ass without checking with somebody somewhere through that phone."

Hanging down almost in the line of sight out the windshield is a huge speedometer, about a foot square. It would be hard for an engineer to disregard it. "When you got power that'll take you faster than most of the track in the system can stand, speed limits get to be pretty important," Lester says.

"Most of my San Diego run is ninety miles per hour, which is pretty good. The alarm is set for ninety-three. If I hit that speed, the same safety mechanism that replaced the dead man's pedal kicks in. Same routine—the train will stop if I don't respond and slow down." There are some routes that have automatic cab signaling which works by radio signal. If the train passes a slow or stop order and the engineer doesn't respond, the emergency mechanism kicks in. That's what governs the high-speed corridor between Washington and New York, and parts of the Santa Fe route in southeastern Colorado and the Illinois Central in southern Illinois have it as well. "Can't run over ninety without it no matter how good the track is, national rule," Lester explains without any of the cynicism that interstate drivers evince in talking about the national fifty-five-mile-per-hour speed limit.

American diesels are properly called diesel-electrics; the diesel engine is linked to a huge generator that powers electric traction motors mounted directly on the wheels. This eliminates the necessity of some sort of mechanical transmission between the diesel and the drive wheels. Increasing the speed of the diesel causes the generator to pump out more voltage, thus increasing the speed of the electric motors. No gears ever need to be shifted; the flow of power from standstill to the top speed of ninety-seven miles per hour is smoother than in the most highly refined automatic transmission of any road car. All-electric lines are rare in the United States, outside of the busy northeast corridor. In America, the distances and the possibility of changes in routes are too great to justify the tremendous expense of installing electric catenaries. The country is just too big and too restless.

Amtrak's engines are mostly F-40s, the latest and most efficient diesel passenger engines ever built. Since this writing, Amtrak has introduced a new engine, the F-69. Just behind the bulkhead of the cab are racks of fuses, relays, and various function modules. Virtually all parts requiring frequent servicing or replacement are clustered in this location. Then there is the monster engine generator and the sixteen-cylinder, three-thousand-horsepower diesel that powers it. At the rear, the engine is connected to the smaller service generator, which cranks out the power for the heat, lights, and appliances in the passenger cars. Many pre-Amtrak railroads did not have this "head-end power" feature. Power came from battery banks and/or generators on individual cars, and heat was delivered by steam lines, a holdover from the days of steam engines. The old arrangement was notoriously inefficient and unreliable. Finally, there are the air pumps for the brakes and a handful of other applications, including power tools and power doors on some of the passenger cars.

Lester has to get back to work, but I want to hang around. "They're gonna break the train and take the cars out to the service yard. If you wanta stick around, just stay down and out of the way—and no pictures of me!"

Each platform bay has three tracks, one adjacent to the platform on either side and one in the middle with turnouts just before the track stub for the engine escape. When the yardmen have detached the air and power lines, the coupler is released and Lester eases the engine forward with the slightest movement of the throttle. He communicates with the yardmen by hand signal and radio telephone, every move confirmed in duplicate. "Those guys' lives are in my hands. More guys get hurt in simple little operations like this than in any other railroading situation." So much for my asking to handle the throttle.

We have moved toward the stub, past the turnout. The switch is thrown, and now Lester backs into the escape track and we pull away from the platform and out into the yard.

The controls appear pretty simple, consisting basically of four levers: the throttle, reverse, air brake, and dynamic brake. The dynamic brake makes use of the electric motors' braking power. We pass the switch engine that approaches on the adjacent track to pick up the cars we have left behind.

Lester doesn't have much to say now; he seems a little nervous about having brought me along as we roll through the yard at five miles per hour. Even though we are not carrying passengers, this is probably a violation of Amtrak rules. I don't want to ask.

We pass a triple lash-up of Southern Pacific engines rolling in the opposite direction. "I used to do that," Lester says.

I wonder why he made the jump. Conductors and trainmen have told me they switched to get in out of the cold, but as an engineer, Lester was already working inside.

"Well, not quite," he explains. "A freight engineer does everything. But for me it's the regular schedule. A freight engineer's train may be called for three in the afternoon, but he never knows. He may not pull out till midnight. Then there's seniority and job security."

I ask the archetypal question: "What makes people become railroad engineers?"

"A lot of 'em, it's in the family. Dad was an engineer or a conductor. Me, I was just restless. I hitchhiked from California to New Jersey when I was sixteen. On the way back, I was waiting for a ride in Kansas outside of Hutchinson, and a big ole Santa Fe hotshot came humming by. I knew I wanted that. I went to work for the railroad right outa high school. It's the perfect job for me. I got my family and a nice house in Anaheim. But I get to put two hundred miles between me and them every day I go to work."

We've come some distance from the station and have switched tracks and changed direction. I'm getting a little uneasy about how I'm going to find my way back through this complex yard.

"I'm going to stop just past the turnout up here. That's where you get off."

Lester points out the service road I can follow back to the station. "Just don't go wandering around in the yard. It's a dangerous place, and when you get hurt and sue Amtrak, I don't know you, never saw you."

Lester's tone changed as soon as he broke the rules for me. I apologize to him for it and climb down the ladder—backward, just as he has insisted that I do. As I leave I don't wave; he is looking around nervously and doesn't even acknowledge my presence on the ground beside his engine.

Back at the station, as I'm coming up the corridor normally used by rail employees only, I hear what I swear is a familiar voice. Bursting out of the women's room is George, the sleeping-car attendant of the *Lake Shore*, gold tooth, hearty laugh, and all.

"I thought you were going to quit this work," I holler to her.

"Who you talking to?" she says. Then she recognizes me. "Well, Ah'll be damned. You still riding, honey? Well, Ah tole you Ah was gettin' outa them eastern slumbercoaches. Now Ah'm doin' Superliners to Seattle. Ah jes needed a change o' scenery. You pretty far from home now. Ah bets you gettin' a little homesick."

I am, but I want to know how it was so easy for her to arrange a change of route.

"That ain't hard. There's always somebody lookin' for a change. How ya think I got myself tied up with that rattle-bucket back east to begin with? But ah always come back west."

"Is this really home?"

"What's home? My family's in Chicago, mostly. I guess this is home now. Ah got friends here," and she gestures to the three other women who are now impatiently waiting for her down the hall. "Good luck, honey. You ride to Seattle sometime, maybe I see ya again."

I will be riding to Seattle several months hence, but somehow I don't think George will be doing that route when I do. For now, the easy chatter and laughter she shares with her friends echoes all along the hall even after they have turned the corner and disappeared.

The *Sunset Limited,* which I will be riding to New Orleans, doesn't leave till 10:55 tonight. With the evening to kill I wander over to Pueblo Park, across Alameda Street from the train station. The park commemorates the site of the founding of Los Angeles, but its dominant theme is a celebration of the proximity of Mexico. Within the park, Olvera Street is lined with little shops and stalls that look as if they have been lifted right out of Chihuahua. It turns out they actually have.

Besides the predictable leather goods, ponchos, and hats, there are shops selling pots, woven goods, bark curios, toys, wood carvings, knives, Mexican clothes, and, of course, fragrant burritos, enchiladas, and tacos. The thoroughfare is so crowded that browsing becomes something of a contact sport and I instinctively button my wallet pocket. I associate places like this with tourists, but here everyone is Mexican. There are moments when I cannot see an Anglo face in the crowd.

Everyone looks, but few seem to be buying. The places doing the most business are the food stalls, especially selling snow cones. It's late in the afternoon, and I theorize that the tourists who provide the bulk of the trade are largely gone for the day and that this is when the indigenous Mexican population gathers to enjoy familiar sights and to be with their own kind, but not necessarily to buy.

Inside La Golandrina Restaurant and Bar I put my theory to the test. The barmaid is a strikingly attractive Mexican girl with tousled black hair, long painted nails, and a ready smile. She asks me my name and guesses that I am new to Los Angeles.

"How can you tell?"

"You got traveler's eyes, always looking around, checking everything out. Anyway, the people who come in here are pretty regular. I've never seen you before." My theory is in trouble already.

"I would think you get a lot of tourists here. The train station's just across the street."

"Oh, we get tourists, but they mostly just wander by. They don't usually come in, sit down at the bar, and order a beer. Our clientele is mostly Mexican."

Her name is Rhonda Blake, her father an American expatriate in Mexico and her mother Mexican. She has lived in Los Angeles for six years. She wishes she could get away to go back for the Mexican festival traditionally held the Tuesday before "Fat Tuesday" (Mardi Gras). I guess that there are enough Mexicans in Los Angeles to support a pretty good festival right here.

"Oh, there will be a festival here, but it's never as good as in Mexico. And it won't be on the right day. Here it's always a problem—nobody wants to have it on Tuesday because that's a workday. So it has to be on a weekend. That spoils it. In Mexico, if there's a festival, workdays don't matter."

But life here on Olvera Street is good for Rhonda Blake. "I'm surrounded by everything familiar, but it is America. I always wanted to live in America, even when I was a little girl. My daddy would tell me about it and I would just dream."

"So Olvera Street is pretty authentic?"

"Oh, completely. Every little shop—they're called *puestos*—has been brought here from someplace in Mexico. And they're all owned by Mexicans. Everybody that is Mexican in Los Angeles comes here. It's like a little Mexico."

The bartender, Gerardo Solis, joins the conversation. He teases Rhonda. "Her father's an Anglo, gringo, Yank, white-eyes. Talk to me. I'm a Mexican. You could take a picture of me but my face would break your camera."

No way. He is handsome, with his black eyes, black mustache, strong jaw, and shiny black hair. He says he has been working since early this afternoon, but his shirt is spotlessly white and his red kerchief still looks crisp.

He brings me a pile of freshly made taco chips and a bowl of salsa—supper. The salsa is not like what I have bought in jars back home. It is thin, translucent, and golden red, with only a few traces of peppers and spices floating around in it. "This is the real thing," says Gerardo.

It is delicious. What surprises me is that it is not garishly hot. It is almost like a slightly thickened, spiced vegetable soup broth with a musky flavor.

"In real Mexican salsa the peppers sting but don't bite. And you don't taste onion. Don't believe what they serve you in the Anglo fast-food places."

When I tell him about riding trains he says, "You ought to ride some trains in Mexico. We got three classes. I always ride second class," he says with dignity. "Third class is all pigs and chickens. You gotta watch your money and your woman when you ride third class. First class is for the rich people—you know, the politicians and their friends. And they don't have it on all the trains. But second class is nice. It's like the coach class on your Amtrak trains. Only the trains in Mexico are older and the seats seem a little softer."

The rail connection from San Diego is the lifeline of Mexicans in Los Angeles. Buses bring them from Tijuana to San Diego. From there Amtrak brings them to the L.A. station, just a block away from Olvera Street and its familiar images of home. "Everyone coming from Mexico passes through here," says Gerardo.

For Gerardo and Rhonda, life in America is a fresh adventure. Gerardo remembers the poverty of Mexico, but it's the one thing he doesn't want to talk about. "Why should I want to feel bad about my country? I am happy to be a Mexican in America. Someday maybe I could be as happy in Mexico. But not today."

Meanwhile, beside me at the bar, a short, balding Mexican dressed in a business suit has been listening to our conversation. His name is Alfonso Miranda.

"I run the bakery next door."

"So you're a baker?"

"No, I'm a businessman. I own the bakery. I hire the bakers. I come from Mexico five years ago and today I do good business. It's easy to make money in America once you learn the Anglo system—you convince someone who has money that your business can work, and they don't quite throw it at you, but almost. In Mexico there is no money to start businesses with."

"Isn't there a wealthy class in Mexico?"

"Sure, but nobody ever sees any of that money. There's no system for putting it to use. Here you just have to learn the secrets of the system."

"What are the secrets?"

"Like I told you, you have to get money to get money. The difference is that in Mexico it just can't be done. That's what I love about the Anglo system."

On Olvera Street I'm reminded that the American syndrome of restlessness and putting down new roots is part of something larger than easterners drifting west. It is the genesis of the "melting pot," that phenomenon that would never have happened if there weren't people in other places with an urge for going. When I leave La Golandrina for the station across the street, the group at the bar has grown to include half a dozen Mexican entrepreneurs enjoying the success of their American dreams.

Later as I'm waiting for my train in the restaurant of the station, I meet Allie LaRoche, a Canadian from Fredericton, New Brunswick, who is traveling to a new job in Phoenix with his young family. He is a construction worker, and with his flannel shirt, dungarees, and callused hands, he looks the part. His route has been the Canadian railway VIA to Vancouver, a bus, and the Amtrak *Coast Starlight* to L.A.; tonight he's waiting for the *Sunset Limited* to Phoenix.

"People think I'm crazy to ride all that distance on the train, but I just love cross-continent trips. I like the train because you just get on and go."

His wife is supervising his three preschool boys, who are roughhousing on the lawn in the cool evening darkness outside the window of the station restaurant. She calls him periodically to issue stern directives.

"Why Phoenix?" I ask.

"It's the work and the housing. When I found out what I could get there, compared to what's available at home, I just told my wife, 'Let's go.' There's nothing for a young family in Fredericton. So here we are."

"Nothing except changing seasons," I say, giving voice to a growing feeling of homesickness that has been building since I first saw the treeless hills of California. Fredericton is not that far from New Hampshire.

"Boy, you're sure right there. You know, I've been a long way from home a lot, but it's going to be hard getting used to this southwest climate. I don't think I'll miss five months of snow, but you can't even tell what season it is here."

My thoughts exactly. But I am boarding a train that will begin my journey back to familiar surroundings, back to a family waiting in a town that I have lived in for seventeen years and have no intention of leaving. Allie has uprooted his family from everything familiar for a place in the most alien corner of another country where the housing is plentiful and cheap. The only thing he can count on is that the people will speak English.

Most of them, anyway. "I don't know much about Mexicans, but they tell me I'm going to see a lot of them on construction crews in Arizona. Makes me nervous."

Allie is scared, though his construction-worker bravado won't let him admit it. He worries about unfamiliar surroundings, unfamiliar people, whether his children can make friends in a place that never heard of snow, whether his wife will resent him for dragging her across the continent to live in a desert.

The one recurring theme that heartens him is the image of the house

he will have in Phoenix, the house that is going to make all the difference in his family's life, the house that would make Phoenix or Vancouver, Ottawa or Tombouctou a place he can call home. It's an image of
fixity, rootedness, shelter, that made him take to the road. But the
house is only a starting point. Allie reminds me of the Pueblo Mexicans
and their faith that life across the border would be better. He and they
both present a new perspective on the old theme of "going west." There
are places where the same drive converts to "going north" or "going
south" or even "going east." It's just the urge for going.

When the call comes for the *Sunset Limited* sleeping-car passengers
to check in, we queue up next to another check-in line for people going
on a "Findlay Fun Tour." I had noticed luxury passenger cars with the
Findlay logo out in the yard this afternoon. A retired couple, Merle and
Charlotte Jameson, are taking the tour. Merle, with his three-piece
suit and dignified gray head, speaks with a deep quiet voice that is used
to giving commands. Charlotte, with her bluish rinse, wears a fur tiara
and diamonds at her throat. They are as excited as two kids.

"It's real old-time luxury rail travel. Two weeks through Mexico. They
hitch the Findlay cars on to Amtrak to ride as far as El Paso, then we
hook up to National Railways de México for the rest of the trip," he
explains.

She elaborates, "Naturally it's the real crystal and linen and fine
china, the rosewood-paneled drawing room, fresh-cut flowers, and real
gourmet dining. But it's also a style of service. They pamper you in
ways a person has no right to expect in this day and age. I'll have my
hair done, my nails manicured—a tailor will even cut and fit garments
from fabrics we buy at stops along the way."

For Merle it's simpler than that. "I'm interested because I'm seventy.
We just like to travel. I spent my life earning the means to do this kind
of thing. Now we spend our golden years enjoying it. We've been all
over the world looking for travel experiences that are a little out of the
ordinary." He spent a "lot of years doing the predictable things" people
do to get ahead. He started a business in Florida years ago, moved it to
New Jersey, then back to Florida. He didn't have to retire—he owned
the company and was chairman of the board—but he wanted out. He
wanted to do "something better" for these years.

"We heard about this opportunity while we were on a riverboat tour
up the Yangtze in China. Over dinner one night people were talking
about how the Yangtze trip was the best they had ever taken. But an
English couple kept insisting that these Findlay tours in America were
even better. So here we are."

When they get the call to board, they wave goodbye and their eyes twinkle like children's before Christmas.

I might have thought that the urge for going was connected somehow with having a modest position on the ladder of economic wealth, but the Jamesons testify otherwise. The urge to pick up and go isn't unique to any particular place, people, or time. George said it best: "Birds gotta fly, fish gotta swim, people gotta jes' keep on truckin'."

Chapter Five

———

Soap

THE *SUNSET LIMITED*

A L L right, crew. Get your act together—we got passengers coming. Attendants, hit the ground!" snaps the voice of service
chief Jay Fontaine over the PA of the *Sunset Limited*. I am already
settled into my compartment, since I tagged along with the Findlay
group, whose amenities include entraining ahead of the crush of regular Amtrak passengers. Boarding is quick and efficient, and at 10:55
P.M. sharp, Fontaine comes on again: "The *Sunset Limited*, bound for
Phoenix, Tucson, El Paso, San Antonio, Houston, New Orleans, and
intermediate points, is about to depart. This is the last call for visitors
to leave the train. Get your last kiss and get back out there on the
platform or you're going to pay for a train ride."

In the sleeping car, I hear the usual clatter of people settling in for a
long two-night run, but there is also the clink and slosh of ice in glasses
and a lot of good cheer. No need to visit the bar car tonight. Sam Root
rattles around in the compartment next door. He looks like the old
cowboy who never dies—tanned bald pate, leathery skin, rough hands,
well-worn boots, blue jeans, and western-style flannel shirt. He has
never taken the train before.

"What'll ya have, pardner?" he asks and produces one of those portable bars that traveling salesmen use. He pours two bourbons, one for me and one for Eddie Dunn, a tired-looking, phlegmatic older fellow from Rhode Island in the compartment directly across the corridor from mine. On the other side of my compartment an elderly couple from Boston are full of questions about how to operate the features of their bedroom. Eddie and I are the only people in the car who are veterans, so we spend the next half hour kibitzing as the attendant, Bill White, does his job of introducing people to their accommodations.

Sam has spent his whole life working Rocky Mountain cattle ranches. "Yep, I'm the real thing, I guess, a cowboy, ranchhand—retired, you understand. I'm enjoying my golden years. They call this train the *Sunset Limited*—well, here I am, just riding off into the sunset with a bunch of New Englanders." He guffaws heartily, drains his glass, and pours another.

Eddie doesn't share Sam's zest for life in retirement. His talk has a whining quality that contrasts jarringly with Sam's exuberance. In appearance my two companions couldn't be more opposite—Sam tall, wiry, and hyperactive, Eddie short, overweight, and very slow-moving.

"I just can't take the New England winter anymore," he complains. "My wife's gone and I don't have much family left, so I don't have anything to keep me from riding out the winter on the train—Vegas, Frisco, L.A., San Diego, New Orleans, anyplace the train goes where it's warm and there isn't any snow." Eddie will spend the summer on his yacht in Narragansett Bay. He says that's why he's never considered moving to the southwest, but later, when Sam is preoccupied, Eddie confides, "I'd have to be awful sick before I'd move out here even for my health. This country is god-awful dead. Nothing grows. Even the mountains don't look like mountains."

But Sam's laugh and the anticipation of a long, convivial ride to New Orleans brighten even Eddie's spirits as the train rolls through the sprawling lights of Pomona and San Bernardino and out into the southern California desert. The good cheer spreads down the corridor of the sleeping car; other travelers join in, standing in the doorways of our compartments, until sometime after midnight when we withdraw one by one to turn in. In bed, I listen to the clatter of the tracks, muffled and distant in the huge Superliner car rushing through the desert night, and drift off comforted by the thought that for the first time since I started, that sound is taking me toward home.

Morning's first image is not a cactus, but Phoenix office towers. Over breakfast, Sam tells me that growth in Phoenix is creating the conditions that people come here to escape. Smog and pollution, primarily from exhaust emissions, is especially acute, since the desert is a great place for the kind of atmospheric temperature inversion that is normally associated with warm valleys. Pollen from the vegetation that people transplant here to banish the desert is starting to affect allergy sufferers; in the dry climate, it doesn't take nearly as much pollen to be a problem as it does in more humid zones. But even that aspect of the climate is changing. Man-made bodies of water and irrigation sprinklers are increasing the humidity of the area.

But east of Phoenix, there is desert that is unscathed, nothing but saguaro cacti, mesquite, sand, and craggy mountains in the distance. To the north lie the Superstition Mountains, where German prospector Jacob Waltz discovered a rich silver vein, never again located after his death—the Lost Dutchman Mine. After Tucson there is the Davis Air Force Base boneyard of mothballed aircraft preserved by the dry climate, some dating back to World War II, but then the scene quickly returns to the tan-brown-red tones of undisturbed southwestern desert. During the Civil War, Benson was a stop for the Butterfield stagecoach, which made the journey from St. Louis to San Francisco in fifty-five days. The hardships its passengers must have faced are inconceivable from this comfortable air-conditioned vantage point.

Long before, it was here that the first explorers from across the Atlantic set foot in what is today United States territory. In 1539, the Moroccan Esteban mistook the mirages reflecting in the desert sun off straw pueblo rooftops for gold. Coronado's resulting search throughout this region for the "cities of gold" introduced the glamorous era of Spanish colonization. Today much of the desert sleeps as if these expeditions had never occurred. Only the rail route itself and the occasional encounter with the thin strip of Interstate 10 and its periodic rest stops with picnic-table shelters and camper hookups betray modern man's presence in this alien landscape.

It was the intention of the builders of the Union Pacific and the later Santa Fe to change the face of the earth along their routes. They created communities and imported their inhabitants from as far away as the Russian steppes to accomplish that goal. Here that was never the case. The Southern Pacific route between Los Angeles and New Orleans, the nation's second transcontinental railroad, was never meant to be anything but a bridge across a barren desert connecting a California empire with the east. It's the airplane that has made metropolises out of young Phoenix and Tucson, not the railroad.

From the standpoint of topography and climate, this is the route that would have been the easiest to build first, had not the southern secession forced the issue to the advantage of the Union Pacific. Most of the route is relatively flat, and the crossing of the continental divide is accomplished without tunnels at only 5,200 feet altitude. There is no winter snow with which to contend, and underground aquifers ironically make water less of a problem here than it was for the UP in central Wyoming. Long stretches of the route could be laid in straight lines on firm desert hardpack.

Yet the route was finally built by men who were not enthused over these advantages but terrified of them. After the Civil War, a great clamor rose up calling for national sponsorship of a southern transcontinental as a gesture of reconciliation to the south—almost a kind of "affirmative action," which would give the south a mercantile advantage and help it catch up with the rest of the nation as part of the reconstruction process.

To Collis Huntington and his partners in California, this was nothing less than their worst nightmare. It was hard enough maintaining their monopoly defending the vulnerable CP in the face of California popular sentiment; this southern route had a national constituency as well as practical expediency on its side.

Huntington marshaled his considerable powers of persuasion, including huge bribes, in an attempt to dissuade Congress from sponsoring the Texas & Pacific, a line proposed by Pennsylvania Railroad president Tom Scott to run from Memphis over the southwest route to San Diego. When Scott put former UP engineer Grenville Dodge to work laying track in eastern Texas in 1878, Huntington employed his standard tactic, pushing the tracks of the Southern Pacific toward the California border opposite Yuma, Arizona. If Scott persisted in building his road, he would have to accept the Southern Pacific's terms for entry into California or settle for a route ending in the middle of a desert.

But Scott was stubborn. There would be no deal to let the SP control the western end of his route. If need be, he would build a parallel route from the border to the southern California coast. War was declared.

Despite widespread sympathy for the southern states' cause, Huntington had some arguments of his own. He declared that Scott's real intent was to link the T&P with the Pennsy at St. Louis to establish a transcontinental monopoly which would not serve the south at all. He claimed to have proof that the proposal had gotten as far as it had only because of bribes to the Republican and Democratic national committees totaling $300,000. And, most significant, he played upon the now widespread distaste for federal land grants and loans to railroads. He boasted that if the nation must have a southern transcontinental, he could build it without federal assistance.

His partners were aghast at this last promise. They were just beginning to enjoy the fruits of their first empire and had no relish for starting a second, especially without the sustenance of the federal trough. Anyway the SP's charter only allowed it to build to the California border.

Huntington forged ahead. While continuing to negotiate with Scott, he ordered ten thousand tons of rails to be shipped up the Colorado River to Yuma. He finagled a franchise out of the Arizona legislature and began looking for a likely Texas line at the other end. Meanwhile the negotiations with Scott led to a compromise bill authorizing joint construction of a southern transcontinental by the T&P and SP. But Congress had had enough. The bill was resoundingly defeated and Scott vowed to build his line on his own.

Huntington was prepared for this. The Colorado River presented the only major obstacle to a southwest line, and the engineers of the SP had identified the site opposite Yuma as virtually the only bridgeable stretch of the river. With a franchise in hand from the friendly Arizona legislature, Huntington began building the Colorado bridge, despite the fact that his tracks were still miles away and would have to cross federal Indian lands to get to it. The T&P was effectively blocked at the river.

However, as long as the federal government refused permission to cross the Indian lands and was willing to call upon the garrison at Fort Yuma to enforce that refusal, Huntington was stymied, too. But two thousand miles away in Idaho, an upheaval involving another Indian reservation provided him with his opportunity to move. Troops were called from throughout the southwest to pursue Chief Joseph and his band of Nez Percé in their thousand-mile odyssey across the northern plains; the garrison at Fort Yuma was reduced to four men.

Using the pretense that high waters of the river threatened the unfinished bridge, Huntington persuaded the War Department to allow "temporary" tracks to be laid through the reservation to the bridge but not across it. Then at 2:00 A.M. on a Sunday morning, Major Dunn and his four-man garrison heard the sounds of rails being laid. Outnumbered and ignored, the major informed the armed tracklayers that they were technically under arrest and then retired to the fort. By morning the tracks reached Yuma.

Surprised and delighted, residents of Yuma awoke to find a work train and no less than the *San Francisco Express* itself, loaded with passengers and mail from the Golden Gate, steaming into their city. Arizona had its first rail service.

Washington was furious. By rights the government could have forced the SP to tear up the track, so blatant was the railroad's disregard for federal authority. The War Department ordered the drawbridge raised and rushed troops back to Yuma to ensure that no further trains crossed it.

That was fine with Huntington, as long as he had two engines and a passenger and mail train parked on the Arizona side. Time and the good citizens of Arizona were on his side. A flood of telegrams and letters poured forth from Arizona petitioning the government not to take away their railroad. Shortly an executive order was issued allowing permanent train service over the bridge into Yuma. "Seize and hold." When law, money, and diplomacy failed, Huntington secured his goals by other means.

At 2:45 in the afternoon, we cross the continental divide. It is almost imperceptible. We wind up a shallow ravine and cross a slight rise in the endless flat desert between clumps of ancient mountains, and we're over the hump. I wonder how the nation's development would have been different if the Southern Pacific's so-called Sunset Route had been the first transcontinental. Would New Orleans have occupied the role of Chicago as hub of the nation? Would Atlanta have taken the role of feeder-gatherer from Cincinnati? Would Memphis have replaced St. Louis as the gateway to the central west? Would California have placed its allegiance with the south instead of the north? Riding this smooth, fast route today reminds one of the significance of Lincoln's choice of the Union Pacific route for the first transcontinental thoroughfare.

Near El Paso, the PA points out the spot where the tracks pass within thirty feet of a marker which signifies the Mexican border. I have been hanging out the open window in the door to take pictures of the barrios just across the border where the battle against illegal aliens and drug smugglers is most intense, and I'm reminded that one of the arguments used by northerners against this route's being the first transcontinental was the security risk of a line running so close to a foreign border.

When I close the window and turn around I'm confronted by a dark-complexioned woman with jet-black hair wearing heavy gold jewelry and an almost oriental Indian gown. She doesn't smile and her face has a grim set to it that reminds me of women who have seen either too much sun or too much trouble. I wonder if the desert sun has gotten to my head, for in her hand she holds a stack of $20 bills, maybe two inches thick. She peels one off and stuffs it in my shirt pocket. "Get yourself some lunch," she says. I protest and try to return the bill. She shushes me and points impatiently toward the doorway of the special bedroom for people in wheelchairs that is always located on this lower level. Through the door I don't see anyone, but I do notice more elegant, extravagant, and foreign-looking garments hanging inside the bedroom door.

She asks me, "Have we left Mexico yet?" I construe her meaning as New Mexico, so I tell her yes, we are just entering Texas. She pats me on the back and gestures for me to run along like a good boy. Halfway up the stairs I stop and go back down. I ask her why she gave me the money. "I like to be nice to people," she says and absolutely will not take the $20 back. She appears to be on the verge of getting angry with me, so I leave. Later in the afternoon I make several trips to the lower level pretending to use the bathroom, but my strange benefactor is nowhere to be seen. The door to the special bedroom remains closed.

Shortly the aroma of dinner cooking in the diner car distracts my attention from the mystery lady. At lunch I was surprised to find real New Orleans–style chicken gumbo and Cajun red beans and rice that made me want to meet the chef. Before dinner, I get a chance to explore the galley on the lower level beneath the dining room, and I meet Romedell Lambert.

Romedell is a young black saucier from a New Orleans family of chefs. He wears a spotless white chef's uniform and a starched cap. His stainless galley is just as pristine, and he wants to pose for pictures with the steam tables, the broiler, the oven, the refrigerator, the cutting board, the dishwasher, everything including the kitchen sink. But he won't talk, except to advise me to order the barbecued ribs tonight and the Creole catfish tomorrow if I want to know about Romedell Lambert.

Dinner in the diner on this train is showtime. Randy Jacobs is one of those waiters who sings, tells jokes, teases, dances, and still has time and energy to flutter around doing his job with an attentiveness that generates big tips. "You like those silk flowers? We get 'em fresh from China every day." "You'll forgive the plastic platters, I hope—you see, we're moving and we haven't unpacked the Sheffield yet." " 'Course that catfish is fresh—Romedell's downstairs killin' 'em right now." He carries on a running flirtation with Barbara, the diner steward. Barbara is an attractive young black woman who wears her makeup like a model. Her long painted nails don't seem appropriate for a working woman, but they don't seem to get in her way. She manages her all-male crew with a variety of poses, gestures, smiles, and strokes which seem to say, "You do this for me and I will make you the man every boy wants to be."

The crew enjoys boasting of the celebrities who frequent the train. Sportscaster John Madden used to be a regular before he acquired his specially outfitted bus and he still rides the route from time to time. Kim Carnes's rock group has been a recent regular. Her entourage always reserves a double deluxe suite and provides as much color (and noise) as a glamour hound could want. But the *Sunset*'s longest-standing celebrity connection is Pearl Bailey, who has been riding this train since the days when she was accompanied by such as Humphrey Bogart and Bing Crosby.

It isn't just the Hollywood connection that is responsible for the *Sunset*'s special panache. The fact that New Orleans is at the other end is just as significant. Sometimes the baggage car carries more musical instruments than baggage, according to service chief Fontaine.

Romedell's ribs are spectacular. As we cross the Rio Grande into El Paso, the dining car is filled with the noise of people in high spirits, and the famous sunset for which this route has always been named begins to form. I've already seen three fine sunsets from trains in Iowa and Utah and by the Pacific, but this one is a spectacular in three acts. For prologue, there are the lengthening shadows of the rust-red crags across the desert floor which brighten to a burnished gold, ever more intense as the sun swells just above the horizon, where a sharp line of purple separates sky from earth. The color intensity builds to the climax of the second act as the sun is dying down and suddenly the sky and earth swap colors and brightness. Now the sky is bright gold, the desert is blue, and the sun takes on the red of the rocky crags, which now break up into puzzle pieces of stark brown and absolute black. In denouement, the black spreads to swallow the land entirely while the sky above the now sunless horizon passes through the spectrum from gold to orange to pink to deep crimson and finally to a violet that lingers like the mood of a tragedy. Someone claps, and the diner is filled with applause—for Romedell, for the sunset, for the pure joy of travel on this remarkable train. Randy takes the bow.

As I leave the diner to head back to my room, I spot the mystery woman, dining with an even grimmer man who wears dark glasses while he eats. She fixes me with her gaze as I walk past but never speaks, never smiles. Her companion wears a ring with a diamond a quarter of an inch across. He scowls and appears to stare straight ahead while he eats, though behind the glasses one can't tell for sure— he could be looking right at me. The train winds through a canyon where a century earlier another inscrutable man worked to conceal his true intentions.

With the Arizona connection, the SP was guaranteed at least a share in any southern transcontinental route, but Huntington had no intention of repeating the partnership arrangement that the CP had been forced to enter into with the UP. The Texas & Pacific was forging westward through Texas and Jay Gould was building his Missouri Pacific southwest from St. Louis. The SP began laying its stockpiled ten thousand tons of rails in a dash across the Arizona and New Mexico deserts. The critical point was a Texas canyon east of El Paso through which only one line could be built.

The SP had no charter to build in Texas, but Huntington found a railroad that did, the small Galveston, Harrisburg & San Antonio. Thus while the T&P, now dominated by Jay Gould himself, built westward confident of victory, Huntington bought into the little Texas line and merged his construction company with it. While SP tracklayers were still working in south-central New Mexico and the Galveston railhead was somewhere near San Antonio, construction crews of the new outfit laid rail from El Paso eastward through the canyons despite the lack of a continuous link at either end. There were advantages in not being dependent upon federal land grants and bonds and the rules under which they were granted.

By 1883 the SP had reached New Orleans, and Gould's T&P terminated at a connection with the SP at the lonely spot of Sierra Blanco. Gould was obliged to accept an agreement which reduced his road to the status of a feeder branch giving the SP connections through it to Memphis, St. Louis, and Chicago. The land grants formerly promised to the T&P now reverted to the SP, minus the western third of them, but that was a minor loss. Huntington built the route without federal assistance and ended up getting much of it anyway. Steamship connections from New Orleans to New York completed the sweep.

But Huntington still wasn't satisfied. By this time he had completed another project in the east, the Chesapeake & Ohio, as far as St. Louis.

By connecting several short Mississippi Valley railroads, he was able to build the Louisville, New Orleans & Texas Railway to New Orleans, so that in 1884, Huntington personally controlled a line stretching from Newport News to Oregon, the largest transportation empire in the world.

But building the empire was costly, and, ironically, the debt incurred led to the end of the SP's monopoly in California. And another railroad was making a bid to become a transcontinental during the 1870s—the Atchison, Topeka & Santa Fe out of Kansas. It had picked up the pieces of the failed Atlantic & Pacific and was headed across northern New Mexico and Arizona toward California even as the SP was pummeling Gould's T&P into submission. California interests, especially those of San Diego and San Francisco, cheered its approach. Huntington responded to the challenge with his usual strategy, building a line on his old California land grants across the Mojave Desert to Needles on the Colorado River opposite the point where the invader's old A&P charter terminated, but this time the SP faced a financial crisis that could be resolved only by the sale of assets. Eventually the Needles line was sold to the Santa Fe, and the SP's California monopoly was broken. The Santa Fe built into San Diego and northward to Oakland and even paralleled the SP into Los Angeles.

The details of that conquest constitute a story for another chapter, but the upshot by the turn of the century was similar to what was taking place in the east between the New York Central and the Pennsylvania. Competition brought rate wars, then more regular and efficient service, and finally the western version of eastern luxury: glamour. The Sunset Route strove with the Santa Fe's *Chief* route to become the romantic high road to glittering southern California. These were the first trains whose status was measured not only by Pullman-style physical opulence but by the style of the people who rode them. Huntington himself was among the first to grace the *Sunset Limited* with his prestige, always preferring it over the CP-UP Overland Limited route. His great nemesis William Randolph Hearst was another. As the entertainment industry grew in southern California during the early twentieth century, the SP and the Santa Fe would vie for the patronage of the great figures of the silver screen. Advertisements for the *Sunset Limited* portrayed graceful women and dashing men in romantic on-board scenes. Special features touted included the oil-burning locomotives, dust-free rock roadbed, and warm climate which allowed the dramatic experience of traveling with open windows throughout the trip. The train catered to the special needs of the beautiful people with such amenities as a library, barber, ladies' maids, buffet, hot baths, and manicure and valet service. Later advertisements featured various Hollywood figures ranging from Clark Gable to Ronald Reagan, photographed at their ease amid the silver and linen of the dining cars. The dynamic drive of Huntington's empire building spanned the continent and then, on the *Sunset Limited*, reached for the stars.

I've been looking forward to the evening scene in the bar car on this train, hoping to find some of the drama or glamour that is the train's legacy. As usual, the upper lounge is preempted for a movie in the early evening, but Jay isn't going to do a second showing tonight out of deference to the particularly social nature of the travelers aboard.

By 7:00 the downstairs lounge is already buzzing. I recognize Sam Root, bourbon in hand, sharing stories with the bartender, a plump young blonde who could be a college student taking a leave from studies. Otherwise, it's all new faces here. A young man with long blond hair and holes in his blue jeans scribbles notes on a pad at one of the booths. In between scribbles he drums with his knuckles on the table and hums emphatically. He is writing a song. At the far end of the lounge, in the seats near the rest rooms, two really ratty-looking young guys strike me as a couple of druggies headed for the dock on San Francisco Bay. They don't have beards but they need a shave. Each carries a woven wool purse or satchel. Their eyes are beady and their predominant color is just gray. Beside them sits a middle-aged couple who smile and watch the festivities without participating. Standing by the stairs, a handsome guy in his upper thirties with a mustache and a reddish face dominated by a striking Marine Corps jaw projects a macho image with his heavy brass belt buckle, his open shirt displaying a chain and shark-tooth pendant, and his metal-studded heavy leather watchband. The center of attention in the lounge is a tall, very young blond woman, dressed in fashionable black jeans and turtleneck, who speaks with a heavy German accent. Her companion, a tough-looking woman in tight blue jeans and a sweater, ten years older maybe, is traveling with her son, who listens to a Walkman and reads comics. They are both attractive, and the hippie rats and macho man appear to be competing for their attention. Others come and go throughout the evening, but these are the leads in the cast of the soap that unfolds on the *Sunset Limited* tonight.

The hippie rats and macho man fall all over themselves attempting to convince the girl with the German accent—her name is Karin—that she ought to like America. Macho man extols the natural sights of America, the trees and cliffs, gorges and mountain peaks, wide-open spaces and wildlife—sort of a hunter's-eye view of the nation. The hippie rats counter with the freedom to be whoever you want, the plurality of American society and its tolerance for diversity. Karin protests that she likes cities. Macho man says all cities are alike except for San Diego, which is his current address, and goes on about national parks and getting back to the earth. The hippie rats dig that too, but insist you don't need to go to a park to get back to the basics.

While this goes on, the other woman, the mother, introduces herself to me. Marilee Palmer is her name, and her son is Rob. She explains that Karin is nineteen, is Austrian, has been traveling in America for five months, and hates it here. Marilee is an "artist": she does commercial Santa Clauses in ink and water color for Christmas cards, coffee cups, knickknacks, and so on. She sells the rights to syndicates.

Macho man finally antagonizes Karin to the point where she storms up the stairs, but she soon returns and sits with me and Marilee. "I can't stand that guy. Talk to me so I don't have to talk to him." I ask why she dislikes America. Her eyes flash and she snaps, "Will you just listen, or are you going to beat me over the head with your Smokey Bear and Purple Mountains, Home on the Range business like him?" I promise, and she begins.

She passed her tests for university in Vienna a year ago and thought she'd take some time to visit her estranged mother, who lives in Virginia. She left Austria looking forward to the adventure of her life. Her friends were all envious; America beckoned.

But living with her mother didn't work out. "We never talked—she had to have the TV on all the time." She thought at first it was just her mother, not America in general, so she went up to stay with a cousin at Georgetown University in Washington. That's when she realized that "your country has a problem. Americans can't stand silence, so they never communicate." At Georgetown it was the stereo more often than the TV, but it was still the same thing. She found her American acquaintances at Georgetown either stiff or lewd. "Americans can't make jokes unless they're sexist or ethnic." She believes Americans have an unhealthy attitude toward sex and their bodies and is appalled by the hypocrisy of a people who use sex to advertise as we do and yet frown on going bare-chested at the beach. "They make it a dirty thing in their jokes and it becomes a dirty thing in real life. The guys are all saying, 'I want your sex, I want your sex,' and the girls walk around advertising, 'I got what you want, come and get it.'" She left Georgetown and has been traveling the country by train, bus, plane, and hitchhiking for several months. "It didn't get any better anywhere else—just TV, loud music, impersonal sex, boasts, and bullshit. And then some really bad things happened." But she's not telling any more.

The long-haired guy has joined us. Hair says he has played guitar with the band of bad-boy rocker Ozzy Osbourne. "A lot of great music has been written on trains," he explains. His family lives in New Orleans, and he is returning there for the first time in a year. "I split for L.A. 'cause I couldn't stand bein' poor. I never thought I'd end up playin' with anyone famous or nothin' like that. I just wanted to play in a band that made me enough money so I could stay outa bein' poor. I hate it, man. I'll do anything not to be poor again."

He played with various groups in L.A. and sold a song called "It's Getting Better." Then one day he heard that Ozzy Osbourne's band was auditioning for a new guitarist. "A guy called up, 'Hey, Ozzy's down here.' So I gave it a shot." For a year now he hasn't had to worry about poverty.

Marilee has gone upstairs and has returned with a collection of her Santa Clauses—"Father Christmas," she calls him. Her favorite is one of Santa soaking his feet and having a schnapps, entitled "The Morning After." The hippie rats feign interest, but there is a snicker in their comments. The title reminds me of my mistake the first night on the *California Zephyr* and prompts me to return to my room tired and disappointed.

About an hour later, there is a rap at my door. It's Marilee. "Can I sit with you for a while? I just had to get away from that guy." Then comes the rest of her story. She has two husbands, one in South Carolina, whom she simply walked out on with Rob several years ago. Since then she has married again in Oregon. "But he turned out to be a real bastard and I have to get on with my life." Now she is returning to the husband in South Carolina in hopes of a reconciliation. He hasn't invited her back; she just wrote to him telling him that she and Rob were coming.

The immediate problem is that last night there was a little hankypanky between her and macho man. "Now he thinks we're having an affair." She goes on to describe how he is a New Ager, a vegetarian, "a real gentle person," and a bit of an amateur psychologist. "He understands me better than I do. He knows how to push all my buttons. What am I going to do?"

I don't really want to play a role in this soap, so I steer her back to the bar car, where we find hair and Karin alone in the upper lounge, and they ask us to join them. I had hoped to get lost in a little larger company. The lounge is dark and quiet. There isn't enough moon to light the passing Texas landscape, so we sit and stare at the occasional lonesome lights that drift by in the blackness. Marilee says, "Well, tomorrow's the first day of the rest of my life. Let's see if I can do it better than I did yesterday and today."

"Nothing changes," says Karin, a more bitter tone in her voice after an evening of beer drinking.

"Yeah, you still wake up with yourself," says Marilee.

"Thozh are linezh from shongs," observes hair, who is slurring his words badly now.

"They're platitudes. I'm a great collector of platitudes. They help me make my life work," explains Marilee.

I remind her that platitudes are platitudes because they don't mean anything.

"Oh, that's not true. They mean everything. People couldn't live without them."

Macho man arrives, friendly, loose, civil. Marilee gives him a come-on hello and Karin sneers. He sits down and tells us all that Marilee is never going to make it back to her husband. Karin moves to the far end of the car and he continues, "You're searching for love and you think you'll find it where you found it before. But do you really think it's going to happen that way? Is it going to be anything like last night?"

He strokes the nape of her neck, and I'm embarrassed. It feels warm in the car and I want to leave, but Marilee urges me to stay. Now he goes to work on me. "You're here to protect her. I respect that. I'd probably do the same. But it's not necessary, right, Marilee? It's not really necessary, is it, Marilee?"

I've had enough. I tell macho man I will leave and go to bed if he will just back off for a few minutes, and, surprisingly, he does. While he's gone I tell Marilee, "I'm going to go to my room to go to sleep. While he's gone, you can go back to your coach seat with Rob. Tell the attendant you don't want anybody bothering you." She thanks me and I leave to go to bed.

Late at night, somewhere in west Texas, I am awakened by another knock on my door, this one quieter and more tentative. I roll over and try to ignore it, but when it doesn't come again, I'm wide awake. I pull the curtain and squint out into the dimly lit hall. There is no one out there, but something is sticking through the crack between the door and the jamb, a piece of paper or something, moving rhythmically with the curtains as the car rocks gently back and forth. I sit up and pull it loose: a $20 bill.

In the morning, as I stroll the consist, I find Marilee curled up asleep in macho man's arms in the very first pair of seats of the very first coach, the most private place on the train aside from the bedrooms. There is no sign of the mystery woman, and the door to the special bedroom downstairs remains closed still.

At breakfast I talk to hair, who is nursing a furious hangover. Karin got off at San Antonio to go to Dallas. From there she was taking a plane to Jamaica and never coming back to America. "No wonder she hates Americans. She's had a lot of bad experiences, man. Everybody she meets just tries to use her. What a waste, man. She was really beautiful. I mean, that girl was just plain glamorous."

By Houston, the colors and textures of the topography begin to approximate the familiar, the tan-brown-red color scheme of the southwest giving way to the chartreuse green of midwestern and eastern American spring. There are clouds in the sky, leafy deciduous trees, wildflowers and young crops. Sam, Eddie, and I ride in the lounge car discussing differences in the flora of various regions of the country.

Service chief Jay Fontaine joins us, and I ask about the mystery woman. He whistles and says, "So it's you this trip? Sure, I know about her, she's a legend on this train. Always tries to give away money to somebody. We were wondering. Usually she picks several, but so far this trip, we haven't heard that she approached anybody. You just might be the only one. You're marked."

The mystery woman has been a frequent rider on this train since her husband, a railroad man, passed away several years ago. The train crew seem to have an affectionate regard for her. Train legend has it that she was a movie star, that she has ninety-three grandchildren and great-grandchildren, and that her mother was Jewish and her father black. She is very rich, and the strange nameless, humorless man she travels with is even richer. But no one knows why she gives away money or how she comes to choose the recipients of her largess. Jay shrugs. "It's just part of the mystery and lore of the *Sunset Limited*."

The second afternoon the *Sunset Limited* winds through the swamps and bayous of Louisiana. I make a final visit to the lounge car, and it is empty except for the very unglamorous hippie rats. I turn to leave when one of them calls me by my name. "That was quite a soap opera last night, wasn't it?"

James and Richard Laffonde are twin brothers going home for winter break from college in California. With a strong southern accent and friendly goodwill that I haven't noticed before because I never really listened to him, James tells me that they live in a poor bayou shack like some of those the train is passing now. They attend USC on full scholarships and take the train because it's the cheapest way. "But we also like to just watch the people on the train. A lot of glamorous people ride this train. Where else could a couple of bums like us get to drink beer with the kind of chicks that were in here last night?"

I ask who they found most interesting.

"Oh, Karin," gushes Richard. "Never met any girls like her in our parish. But you know, for all her money and European clothes and fancy travels, I felt sorry for her. I never met anybody so all alone."

"Yeah, that plus she got raped," adds James. "She told us that some guys in L.A. took her up to their apartment. They said they wanted to take pictures of her for modeling. When she got up there they hurt her, really hurt her bad."

Now the Sunset Soap Opera is complete. At dinner, I keep my promise to Romedell, and indeed the catfish reveals his care, the spiced fried batter so thin it melts when I taste it, the flesh firm and flaky and still tanged with the river. Eddie Dunn and Sam Root are with me and play a little game timing the interval between the solitary egrets we pass in the swamp outside. There is one almost every half mile. Dusk gathers, the swamp woods voiding a sunset display like last night's.

Eddie is dreading the next leg of his travels, a bus ride to Jacksonville, Florida, but after that he will take the train to Fort Lauderdale and spend a few days looking at the pleasure boats on the Inland Waterway. Three years ago, a generous retired couple he met there took him to the Bahamas aboard their sixty-five-foot yacht. "Now that was a cruise," he reminisces. "They had caviar and attendants who brought you drinks all day long and pretty girls who came around and rubbed suntan lotion on you." After that Eddie adopted the practice of inviting sightseers in Newport aboard his boat each summer, hoping the gods of hospitality will reward him when he heads south.

Sam is looking forward to Mardi Gras in New Orleans. "It's the cowboy's Shangri-La, you know—always has been the only city where cowboys could come roaring in looking for excitement and bright lights and not feel out of place." Sam intends to "root and snort and raise a little hell and romance" and then return to the mountains with memories like a movie with himself in the starring role.

Later, as I get my things together back in my room, I play back my tapes, leaf through my notes, check the film in my camera, and realize that despite all my tools for capturing experience, ultimately the train ride slips through one's fingers. That's the way it is with travel, even when it is dramatic.

The western rail approach to New Orleans runs over the high, massive Huey Long Bridge. Until the bridge was built in the 1930s, all rail traffic to and from the west was carried on ferryboats across the Mississippi River. Crossing the bridge at 7:30 in the evening, riders of the *Sunset Limited* today are treated to a spectacular view of the lights of the river and the Crescent City, reminiscent almost of a nighttime airplane approach.

The train backs into the track stubs at the station past the huge futuristic shape of the Super Dome. On the platform, there isn't the usual rush to make connections that I've seen in New York, Chicago, and L.A. There are no more trains until tomorrow, so disembarking passengers tend to engage in more leisurely farewells. Some are making plans to get together somewhere in the French Quarter this evening, others just hang around and visit as if they were still riding in the lounge car of the train. As I shake hands with Sam and Eddie, Marilee and macho man walk by arm in arm with Rob trailing behind. In the window of the special bedroom, I spot the mystery woman. She is looking right at me, and for the first time, she smiles and waves.

I didn't find glamour on the *Sunset Limited*, but I certainly did find drama amid a setting at least as substantial as the sets of TV soaps. From the firm command of Jay Fontaine to the dining-room fun with Randy Jacobs, the attentiveness of Bill White, the culinary showmanship of Romedell Lambert, and the poise of Barbara with the long nails, this crew made their work either invisible or part of the show.

And the passengers—Eddie Dunn riding out the New England winter, Sam Root enjoying his golden years, Marilee trying to find her way back to her husband, hair in search of rock-and-roll affluence, macho man looking for love and satisfaction, Karin in flight from America, the mystery woman, and even the "hippie rats" who turned out to be so human after all—they all played parts in a piece of the romance I left New England in search of. This is what it must have been like when children mesmerized by the whistle of the midnight express made their first rail journey to a place that, till then, was only a name and a spot on the map, when the journey getting there was a drama itself, when traveling made the world bigger instead of smaller.

Chapter Six

Spirit of New Orleans

THE CITY OF NEW ORLEANS

I N 1971, Arlo Guthrie, the son of Woody, folklore great and author of
"This Land Is Your Land," recorded a song called "The City of New
Orleans." Overnight the hippie singer of antiwar songs of comic protest
(such as "Alice's Restaurant") earned his inheritance among the royalty
of the popular American folk establishment. The song did little for the
passenger railroads whose demise it mourned, but it helped span the
generation gap as little other music of the sixties generation had. Here
was a long-haired flower child who sang of images held dear by the older
generation. It was more than nostalgia; the song was a bridge between
past and present folklore that opened lines of communication between
more than one father and son. When I presented my own father with
the album for Christmas in 1972, it marked an easing of overt hostilities that had begun when I tried to explain the politics of "Alice's
Restaurant" to him during the Chicago convention in 1968.

I have come to New Orleans to ride to Chicago on the *City of New
Orleans*, Amtrak's version of the train commemorated in Arlo's song.
Even before Arlo, this train engendered more than its share of folklore,
epitomizing the nation's geographical, historical, and demographic

111

heartland. And with its southern terminus in New Orleans, this road represents a current of Americana counter to that of the empire-building routes I have traveled so far.

Though it still claims to be one of America's busiest ports (especially if one counts the river traffic), New Orleans's history as a transportation center is primarily one of decline since the advent of the railroad. In the heyday of the riverboats, before the bands of steel changed the transportation landscape of the country, New Orleans seemed destined to be the greatest center of transportation in the land, maybe in the world. Chicago was still a miserable, provincial hub for plank roads. New York, Philadelphia, and Baltimore were in fierce competition to divide the portion of the shipping pie left after Boston took its share, and even that Hub of the Universe began to lose its preeminence as the efforts of its competitors bore fruit in the Erie Canal and the New York Central, Pennsylvania, and Baltimore & Ohio railroads. None of these cities could rival New Orleans, and one glance at a map of the North American river system shows why.

Before the Civil War, the eastern trunk lines had already arrived at Chicago, but the prosperous shippers and plantation men of New Orleans saw little cause for concern. Though the railroads could move freight faster than the riverboats, the waterways still reached nearly a thousand miles beyond the rail lines. It was simply unthinkable that the rails could ever supplant waterways, especially for passenger travel. The trains' one advantage was speed, a small thing in the antebellum southern scheme of things. The indignities suffered by rail travelers guaranteed the continued preeminence of the grace and style of travel by riverboat and fast packet. But most reassuring was habit and custom. The waterways to New Orleans were already established as the method by which mid-America reached the sea. It would take a long, long time for the promotion of the upstart railroads to change that, and by that time, New Orleans would naturally become the hub for rail transportation as it had always been for water routes.

The Civil War blew that scenario to bits in two years. By 1862, with the Mississippi River route closed due to the war, the vast majority of the old river trade made the forced transition to the rail routes of the northern trunk lines. When the war was over, the bulk of that trade remained where it was.

When the second transcontinental route was built, New Orleans had plenty of competition. Atlanta and Richmond, with their convenient rail connections to the rival ports of Savannah, Charleston, and Norfolk, became the region's rail crossroads. Thus New Orleans played third string, behind Chicago and St. Louis, in the transcontinental rail network, and faced other upstart cities as a regional center.

Nonetheless, New Orleans still dominated two romantic chapters in the history of passenger railroads in America, one opulent and exotic and one homely and common as an empty whiskey bottle in a brown paper bag. The upscale chapter was largely due to the construction of a transcontinental water route two thousand miles away—the Panama Canal. Teddy Roosevelt's adventures with the big stick and the subsequent boom in tourism throughout the Gulf and Caribbean gave a new lease on life to the port of New Orleans in the early twentieth century. The railroads that terminated in New Orleans moved to capitalize on the advantage that New Orleans had always enjoyed as a port: the fact that passengers and freight coming down the river could be transferred at the river docks to oceangoing ships. The Illinois Central exploited this advantage by running its tracks right to a terminal on the waterfront where passengers off the super-luxury *Panama Limited* from Chicago could immediately board steamships bound for the exotic climes of Havana, Colón, or Caracas.

Passengers on the *Panama Limited* paid a premium to enjoy amenities rivaling those of the *20th Century Limited* with the added attraction of live entertainment by New Orleans and Caribbean musicians amid potted tropical flora in the club car, which earned the reputation of having the best bartenders in America. The Illinois Central conceded nothing to the eastern trunk lines in terms of efficiency either: the premium was refunded if the train was an hour late. Refunds were few, and the people of the rural Illinois, Tennessee, and Mississippi towns along the route regulated their days by the train's reliable and glamorous passage. For twelve years, the Sixth District Court in Vaiden, Mississippi, recessed every day at a precise hour so that its denizens could stand by the tracks to watch the glorious train pass.

But the connection between New Orleans and passenger railroading that is preserved in the modern American consciousness centers around a less exotic Illinois Central train for which passengers paid no premium, the *Spirit of New Orleans*. Poor relation of the super-luxury *Panama Limited*, the *Spirit of New Orleans* was the Illinois Central's daylight coach service to the Gulf. With no sleeping-car service (though it did offer a first-class-coach accommodation), it became the train of the ordinary man, as was the Illinois Central itself, the *Panama Limited* notwithstanding. Though it is now a night train, Amtrak's *City of New Orleans* today carries on that tradition.

During my stopover at New Orleans, Mardi Gras is just cranking up.

Amtrak's trains to New Orleans from Los Angeles, Chicago, and New York are always booked solid during Mardi Gras, and the *City of New Orleans*, in particular, is famous for its tradition of commencing nonstop Mardi Gras celebrations in its lounge car as soon as it pulls out of Union Station in Chicago for the overnight run south.

With an evening to kill before the train leaves in the morning, I ride around for a while with Cecil, an elderly black taxicab driver, before he drops me off at my hotel in the French Quarter. He grouses about the blocked-off streets necessitated by the parades. "Mardi Gras is jes' a big pain in da ass," he says. "Ah gotta work harder fo' less fares. Mostly I git two fares outa one drop from the train station. But not durin' Mardi Gras. And ah ketch half as many flights at the airport." But I notice that he hangs on every word of the AM radio announcer who is doing a sort of play-by-play call of the parade's progress. He needs to feel a part of the event that electrifies this city while making his work harder.

Later, on foot, I witness a near riot at Krazy Korner, where a crowd of rowdy youths, just back from the parades, take over the intersection for a while until horseback-riding cops clear them out with little mini-charges on their mounts. A hot dog vendor, whom I ask for an explanation of what is happening, just shrugs. "I don't know, man. You want a hot dog or what?"

But one of the cops talks to me after things have settled down and says, "Mardi Gras is just a pain in the ass for us. Most of the things you can do in a situation like this are wrong. So you don't even think, you just react the way you were trained in crowd control." I ask if there is a level of response beyond what I've seen tonight. He says, "Oh, yeah, but you don't want to see it."

Meanwhile the jazz pours forth from Preservation Hall and Pat O'Brien's. I buy a sixteen-ounce beer to go and cruise past the combat zone where crowds gawk through doorways at mirrors reflecting glimpses of strippers and hawkers shout, "Here come the girls," while female wrestlers challenge all comers.

In the morning Krazy Korner is tranquil; during the night the streets have been sprayed clean. By the time my train for Chicago leaves in the late afternoon, I have found my brand of pipe tobacco, eaten a marvelous Cajun lunch at the Gumbo Shop, strolled along the tracks by the waterfront with a gandy-dancer crew who still sing Leadbelly songs as they swing their hammers, listened to the steam calliope of the riverboat *Natchez*, talked with flower girls, street musicians, and hack drivers, who share the opinion that Mardi Gras is just a lot of work but wouldn't be anywhere else in the world this week, and watched a trainload of exuberant high school field-trippers from Illinois take over my hotel. Like Cajun gumbo itself, a visit to New Orleans is a colorful stew concocted from humble ingredients. So is the train that bears the city's name.

Though I am riding a train that bears the slightly revised name *City of New Orleans,* from south to north and at a time of revival of passenger rails under Amtrak, in the first hour out of New Orleans I can tell that Arlo knew his train well. In the bar car (read "club car") old men are indeed playing cards and drinking "with no one keeping score." There are eleven cars instead of fifteen, but once we're past the bayous, the dominant features of the landscape are the "freight yards full of old black men and the graveyards of the rusted automobiles."

At this time of year, the northbound run does have the feeling of carrying people who aren't going anywhere, since the action is in New Orleans at the end of the southbound run.

Item: A woman from Illinois is returning to the minor state government job she was shunted into after blowing the whistle on some corrupt state officials. She sought her vindication by running for election as county clerk but lost to "a high school dropout" who was part of the corrupt crowd. She rides the train and nurses the grudges she will settle when she wins election to state office next November.

Item: Another woman is an insomniac who travels the train because it puts her to sleep. "Most of your life you are so rushed, rushed, rushed. It's only on the train that you can slow down enough to remember how to sleep."

Item: In the dining car, two elderly gentlemen just stare and stare at train timetables during their entire dinner without a single word of conversation.

Item: A woman from Providence relates how she rides the train because of an intense fear of flying. Her company sent her to a young therapist who let slip that even frequent fliers have to repress a dread of flying. That did it. She takes the train and has settled for the lesser job that she has been permanently sidelined into.

Item: Another Illinois man who has lost a son rides the train and tries to write the book about fathers and sons that will conclude his mourning.

And then there is macho man—yes, the same guy who romanced Marilee on the *Sunset Limited.* When I encounter him alone in the men's room, he steps between me and the door as I am leaving and snarls, "How 'bout if you stay outa my way this time?" With no female audience, he has dropped all pretense of chivalrous cool and is spoiling for a fight. The timely entrance of a father and his two small sons defuses the tense moment. Sure enough, a little later I spot him again coiled up in the bar car with another vulnerable woman. As I walk past the booth where they are seated, he reaches out to shake my hand, now all charm and goodwill. His companion gushes, "You know everybody, don't you?"

Today the Illinois Central is derisively referred to as a "junkyard line" by railroad people throughout the country. Its management is said to be more concerned with selling real estate than preserving a national treasure and is selling even potentially profitable routes as fast as it can. Arlo was wrong about the fate of passenger railroading on this line: Amtrak will maintain it regardless of who owns it. But he was right about the institution, "the native son," which built the line. Today this railroad and the type of distinctively American public enterprise it historically represented are endangered species.

If the NYC in the east and the SP in the west are the epitome of Republican railroads, then the Illinois Central is Democratic. As early as 1837, Illinois was the first state to commit itself to a massive program of publicly financed canals and railroads. Though the state's population at the time was only a few thousand, the $10 million project won passage because of the lobbying efforts of officials who dreamed of feeding at the public trough. But the Panic of 1837 demolished the project before much rail-laying was accomplished, and the debt hobbled Illinois for a decade as settlers avoided its now astronomical taxes for the greener fields of Wisconsin and Iowa. Illinois became a developmental backwater and a symbol of investors' worst fears when the state finally repudiated the debt.

Yet out of these financial ashes arose one of the most successful public enterprises of the century. In 1851, the state chartered the Illinois Central and supported it with the nation's first railroad land grant of 2,500,000 acres. The company would finance itself through the sale of these lands and pay back to the state 7 percent of its gross income. The sale of the lands would provide the state with the economic development and population it so desperately needed. The route of the railroad, a north-south line running right down the middle of the state with a branch running northeast to Chicago, provided the inhabitants of the state's vast desolate spaces with a fast connection to the junction of the Ohio and Mississippi rivers.

The plan worked so well that within ten years, Illinois became the boom state of the nation while the railroad company turned steadily heavy profits. This was the model the builders of the Union Pacific and other western railroads attempted to duplicate, but no one else would ever make it work so well.

It wasn't easy, however. Attracting rail laborers and homestead settlers to the scene of the "Debacle of 1837" required the most ambitious program of promotion the nation had ever seen. Ads in New York and Boston newspapers for labor simply didn't produce any. Acting on the theory that the class of men wanted focused their attention elsewhere than on the newspapers, the IC management had huge gaudy posters printed and pasted thousands of them in bars, pool halls, and corner drugstores throughout New York. The pitch touted "A Rare Chance for Persons to go West," with wages of $1.25 a day and guaranteed employment for two or more years. Decent board was promised for $2 a week and special rates for passage west were offered through arrangements with east-west railroads.

Within months the IC had thousands of workers, mostly Irish, but increasingly German as well. Thus began the unique demography of Illinois which persists to this day.

Newspaper ads in scores of eastern cities were more successful in recruiting settlers to buy the lands along the route, but the program didn't stop there. Handbills were mailed to 100,000 selected farmers, and "Emigrant Guide" pamphlets were distributed at seed and feed stores. Placards were displayed on the sides of the horsecars of the New York transit lines, and agents toured the northeast to speak at town meetings and offer personal invitations to come west.

The hallmark of all of these pitches was artists' renderings of "typical" scenes of Illinois life: gingerbread farmhouses surrounded by leafy trees and well-maintained fencing beyond which grew corn tall as the house with an IC train steaming along the gently rolling horizon. No inhabitant of the flat, treeless Illinois prairie would have recognized the place, but thousands of New Englanders did. It was the homestead of their dreams—if the corn grew only half as high and the ground was only half as free of granite outcroppings as the illustrations suggested, this was the place for a generation of Yankees fed up with the harvest of frost-driven rocks that was the most prolific yield of their fields.

Thus began what New Englanders know as the "Great Emigration." Within one year, farm property values in parts of Vermont dropped 40 percent; entire communities pulled up stakes and headed for Illinois. From Boston to Burlington to Bangor, a great quiet settled over northern New England as now the most common postmarks passing through mailrooms named faraway places in Illinois.

The New Englanders brought their Congregational churches and Anglo-Saxon names to the prairie in a rare case where the Smiths and Wrights were newcomers to towns already populated by Kellys and O'Connells, Schmidts and Kimlers, who had arrived in the earlier wave of laborers for the railroad. When the IC's sporadic efforts at recruitment in Europe finally began to bear fruit in the immigration of Swedes during the Civil War, and with the "theft" of more Germans and some Norwegians from remote and rail-less neighboring Wisconsin and Minnesota, the demographic mix so characteristic of Illinois prairie communities was complete.

The state of Illinois established the railroad, which in turn established the state of Illinois. It proved that progressive government could indeed initiate successful railroads as well as could the self-interested tycoons who operated out of a place in New York called Wall Street.

In keeping with its role as a monument to democratic tradition, the *City of New Orleans* carries one of the rare dome cars in which third-class-coach passengers can ride in a glass "bubble" that protrudes above the roof of the rest of the train and enjoy the remarkable experience of being able to look out over the top of the entire train. Here I meet John Mills, senior inspector of train quality. He is on the train because he has been troubleshooting a problem in New Orleans. With a shock of silver hair like Phil Donahue's, John is the quintessential old-time railroader who is still a tree-shaking force. He gives me a membership form for the National Association of Railroad Passengers, a lobby that apparently wields power in Washington disproportionate to its number of members. John is a hardball Democrat who, along with Arkansas senator Dale Bumper, claims responsibility for the perpetuation of Amtrak's *Eagle* through Arkansas and my family's hometown of Bloomington, Illinois. "We let 'em know that it was a deal where if we didn't get funding for the route through Arkansas, they wouldn't get funding for routes they wanted somewhere else."

Mills is an expert on current passenger cars. He tells me that within the Heritage fleet of older cars, the vast majority were built by the Budd Company of Philadelphia, not Pullman. In modern times, Pullman, and other passenger car companies, sheathed their cars in stainless steel but did not build their frames of stainless. As a result they have rotted or rusted "in their guts. You can tell an old Pullman by rapping on the side and listening for the telltale fall of rusted steel—like Republican politics, gilded and glittering on the outside and rotten underneath." Only Budd, whose cars are trademarked by the fluting of the sheathing, built cars of stainless steel all the way through. The trade-off was in the finishing touches; Budd eschewed Pullman's brass, fabrics, and hardwoods. "Budd-built cars are like Democrats, a little homely and common on the surface, but solid at the core."

John says that there was some controversy when Amtrak selected the cars to be rebuilt in its Heritage fleet—"A lot of people complained about Amtrak letting beautiful cars go"—but the key criterion was structural integrity. Cars without a solid stainless steel center sill (the structural beam running lengthwise down the middle of the frame) weren't even considered. "Railroads can't stand to see cars crumble in wrecks. Cars have to be able to withstand crashes and look like a derailed model train, not a broken train." Mills is not optimistic about the vaunted Superliners. "They're all mobile-home construction. The Heritage cars will outlast them."

Mills will not sleep till his section of the train (breaking off at Centralia for the run to Kansas City) arrives at its destination. With the intensity of a man who believes that his vigilance might be the difference that saves a thing he loves, he will sit all night in the dome coach listening to the sound of the ragged tracks and looking for every opportunity to preach his cause to passengers.

A visit to the bar car introduces me to Mary Black, tender of the bar on this train for the past four years. Mary has worked on several Chicago-based trains but likes this one "because the people are more interesting. All kindsa weirdos ride to and from New Orleans. But I've learned to keep my distance." Her most interesting story is about a man who rode most of the route in the lounge car with two large stuffed animals at his side. Throughout the ride he carried on a monologue with them about the scenery, the politics of the day, and the other people in the car. Finally the teddy apparently "said" something unforgivable. "Let's not go into that. We've been over this. Don't bring it up again," said the man. But the teddy apparently persevered. At that point the man pulled out a pocket knife and violently ripped the teddy to pieces. Mary ran out of the car to get a conductor; when they returned, the man was all apologies and courtesy. He picked up every piece of stuffing and disappeared to his compartment for the remainder of the trip.

Mary says she has learned to be more circumspect in her relationships with passengers. Today she wouldn't pay enough attention to hear what led up to the teddy-bear stabbing. "You build a kinda wall, that you only take down when you want it down. I been burned a couple of times that I don't want to talk about. Some rough people ride this train."

The *City of New Orleans* makes no pretense of preserving a heritage of luxury. Tonight the most salient feature of this train is its speed. I time us doing ninety miles per hour over very rough track. As I am drifting off to sleep, the violent side-to-side jolting brings to mind the song about the most famous train wreck on this or any line, and I am comforted by Mills's revelations about the structural integrity of the car in which I am sleeping.

It was along these tracks that John Luther (Casey) Jones ran his steam engine at top speed on the rainy night of April 30, 1900, and spawned the greatest in the tradition of Illinois Central folk songs. He had just finished his own run and had volunteered to take over the run of another engineer who was sick. With his favorite fireman, Sim Webb, he pushed the *Cannonball* hard, making the night echo with his haunting trademark trill on the whistle.

As happens with myths, the lyrics of some of the well-known versions have key facts wrong. There is no such thing as a "six-eight wheeler": Casey's engine was a 2-6-2. The run began near midnight, not "about half past four." His widow protested for years, in an era before libel lawsuits, the line about Casey's wife fixing to get a new husband "on the Salt Lake Line." And the most immortal lines of several versions—"Number Four stared him right in the face," "Two locomotives were a-bound to bump," "Around this curve he saw a passenger train"—have got the critical moment all wrong. What Casey Jones saw as he rounded that curve at anywhere from fifty to ninety miles an hour—accounts disagree—was the last few boxcars and the unprotected caboose of a freight which was still pulling into a siding where it was to stand as Casey's express passed. The freight was headed in the opposite direction and was too long to fit on the siding, so it was executing what was known as a saw-by, a maneuver in which the front end of the freight would be on the siding as Casey's train passed the first switch, and then would move out over that switch onto the main line, thus getting its rear cars clear before Casey's short express could reach the switch at the other end. Casey's speed was too great for the freight to complete the maneuver before he reached the far switch.

Why was there no flagman from the freight warning Casey of the saw-by? At the inquiry the freight crew testified that they thought the man from another express running just ahead of Casey's was still there. Did Casey tell his fireman to jump? The fireman said so. Had Casey brazenly disregarded speed limits? The inquiry said so, but in those days, that was not uncommon. What is undisputed is that Casey did ride to his death blasting the whistle to warn crewmen in the caboose and working the reversing lever to the end, possibly lessening the carnage to the passenger cars in his charge.

The passage of Casey's tale from history to legend is a classic of the folklore process in relatively recent times. An illiterate black man named Wallace Saunders, who worked in the engine house at Canton, Mississippi, had tended Casey's locomotives for years and knew him well, often entertaining him and other engineers with simple home-spun ballads based on the stories that railroad men swap between runs. Within a few days of Casey's death, Saunders was singing the precursor of the well-known melody and the original lyrics as he crawled over the engines in his care. Another IC engineer and mutual friend of Saunders and Jones, John R. Gaffney, was impressed enough to offer a bottle of whiskey in a brown paper bag for the opportunity to write down the lyrics and melody of the song.

By 1902 the song appeared as the sheet music of vaudeville per-formers Bert and Frank Leighton, whose third brother, Bill, was an IC engineer who knew Gaffney. Already many of the details of the original had been tampered with. In 1903, the version by T. Lawrence Siebert and Eddie Newton was published and became the one best known to posterity. Not only were factual details of the original changed, but the authentic railroad usage of Saunders was now gone entirely, the bogus "six-eight wheeler" of their version replacing the authentic "high right-wheeler" (indicating a classy engine) of Saunders's original. But Siebert and Newton are credited with improving the meter and melody and adding the chorus that made the song creep into the nation's collective unconscious. Though lyrics to all versions are available today, that most often heard is the Siebert-Newton. It's just a better song.

The Illinois Central's debut as a breeding ground for folklore actually antedates Casey Jones and Wallace Saunders by some thirty years, and the central characters in the lore were not the dashing engineers or burly brakemen who worked for the railroad but those vagabond men who rode it for free, the hoboes. The decade following the Civil War was the first of the four great hobo eras (the others were the Depression and the periods following the world wars). Because of its mid-America north-south route, along which migrant workers could follow the sea-sons, and its frequent junctions with major east-west routes, the Illi-nois Central attracted more than its share of men who rode the rods and the blinds.

As early as the 1880s the cartoon hoboes Weary Willie and Happy Hooligan were portrayed as gawky fellows in tattered rags with stub-bly faces and booze-swollen noses who carried their few possessions wrapped in a red bandanna suspended from a stick over the shoulder. By the end of the century, however, observers noted the division of the railroad vagabonds into several classes which persist today: the hobo, who works and wanders; the tramp, who dreams and wanders; and the bum, who drinks and wanders. Sometimes the bum who doesn't even wander but merely hangs around railyards and drinks is called the home guard. The truly criminal wanderers, feared by all other rail vagabonds, were called yeggs. Partly because his freedom epitomized a repressed urge hidden within the breasts of many respectable Americans, the hobo in all of his manifestations quickly became a romanticized fixture of popular American culture.

The hobo is not only a folk character but a prolific creator of folk argot. It was the hoboes who initiated the American habit of adopting fanciful nicknames, and characters such as A No. 1, T-Bone Slim, Super-Tramp, Boxcar Bertha, Three-Day Whitey, Steam Train Maury, and Frypan Jack have carried on the tradition down to the present day. Many of the slang terms used by railroad men themselves probably originated with the hoboes, especially those with negative or ironic overtones suggesting the hobo's rather than the trainman's point of view. Thus an engineer is a hogger, a caboose a crummy. A slow, heavily loaded freight is a drag and an empty one is a rattler. Passenger trains are varnish, and a fast freight is a hot shot (or redball, a term which seems contradictory, since red signals slow or stop a train; but from the hobo's point of view, its speed says "halt" to a hobo fixing to catch out on it). Hoboes gave specific railroads monikers that have stuck down to the present. The Chicago, Burlington & Quincy is the Q, the Pennsylvania the Pennsy, the Missouri Pacific the Mop or Mo-Pac, the Great Northern the High Line. And in at least two cases, hobo nicknames eventually became corporate names in the Nickel Plate (New York, Chicago & St. Louis) and Frisco (St. Louis–San Francisco).

Contributing to the hobo's stature as a figure of folklore is the physical danger of the life he leads. It is the trainmen, fascinated by the deadly effects of the machines they handled on those who took their chances with them, who are the conduits of the myriad tales of hobo tragedy; by the end of my journey, I will have gathered a pretty fair collection of contemporary ones myself.

Here is a recent sample. Two hoboes were fighting over a bottle of Night Train Express (the preferred rotgut today) on the rear platform of a coal car on a train backing to spot a section of cars under a coal chute on the IC in Mississippi. One succeeded in throwing the other off the train but fell across the gap between his car and the next. He didn't fall onto the tracks, however, because his feet got tangled with the frame of one car and his upper body was wedged in the frame of the other. Looking down he might have seen his doom if he noticed that the coupling between the two cars was disengaged—the cut was to be made here. After the train stopped to allow the rear cars to separate and coast into position, the dragging-equipment indicator, a trackside device which photoelectrically checks the profile of the train's trucks and couplings, alerted the crew that something was amiss. What they found when they investigated was half a hobo.

Such stories are still a mainstay of trainmen's tale-telling, but perhaps because of their grisly nature, they never took root with the popular culture as did the stories of the ongoing conflict between hoboes and railroad detectives—"rail dicks" or "bulls." These have some of the same appeal as the familiar cartoon of the Road-runner and Wile E. Coyote: American freedom versus malevolent cunning.

The railroads hire detectives because of significant material losses attributed to hobo depredations. Regular law enforcement officers tend to advise hoboes to "leave town on the next train," precisely what the railroads don't want to happen, so their detectives are usually little more than hired thugs whose job is to beat up or otherwise intimidate hoboes into staying off the trains. A bull's work is successful when his section comes to be one of those known and avoided by hoboes. Word of mouth is his publicity, violence and intimidation his trademark.

Hoboes today identify various railroads as more or less hostile. The UP, IC, and most sections of the Santa Fe are considered hazardous. Much of the SP is considered safe if one knows certain hotspots. The Burlington Northern, the modern conglomerate built from the Burlington, Northern Pacific, and Great Northern, is considered almost friendly.

During the first quarter of the twentieth century, many hoboes found some degree of safety in membership in that American brand of pseudo-communism the Industrial Workers of the World, better known as the Wobblies. Possession of the Little Red Card signified one to be an honest migrant worker, as opposed to a tramp, bum, or yegg. Wobbly cards were therefore always in great demand, and many trainmen, some of whom were also Wobblies, would make allowances for a card-carrying hobo, though the flashing of the card could backfire. Some bulls of particularly virulent anti-communist strain would be provoked to even greater violence at the sight of the Red.

It was the Wobblies who provided the organization to institutionalize many aspects of the hobo contribution to American folk culture. They published the pamphlets popularizing the hobo's argot and promoting legendary hoboes as models of the free worker of the world, unfettered by property. Sometimes his life was portrayed as an ideal of life in a capital-less, classless society, other times he was portrayed as the ultimate noble but oppressed victim of capitalist inhumanities.

But the Wobblies' most significant specific contribution to American folklore is the *Little Red Song Book,* which collected, through twenty-eight editions, the political folk songs and parodies which celebrated the workingman's life and his imminent emancipation from the bonds of capitalism. Many of the most colorful of these songs featured the hobo and his life of worker's freedom. These were heady times for early unionists, and for the red wave they felt themselves to be part of as they sang their songs of protest in union halls and around jungle campfires along the routes of the rails. They justified some taking of liberties with already established legend.

Joe Hill, the Wobblies' poet laureate and martyr after his death at the hands of the state of Utah in 1916, wrote "Casey Jones, the Union Scab." The song ascribes Casey's fiery end and his subsequent placement in the steamiest corner of hell as retribution for running his engine during a union strike.

The Wobblies have passed, but the romanticizing of hobo life continues in the 1980s in the hobo conventions held throughout the west, modeled after the annual affair in Britt, Iowa. Today these are commercial and media events at which aficionados who are not practitioners of the life gather with their Winnebagos, Webers, and camcorders to rub shoulders with those who are. The climax of the gatherings is the election, by the nonhobo tourists, of a King of the Hoboes. The mainstay is the yarns of the hoboes, usually preceded by the standard invocation "You don't know much about railroads and hoboes, do you?" An answer of no guarantees the most colorful stories. The events and the publicity they have generated have sparked a mini-revival of freight hopping, much to the chagrin of railroad management, which has taken the trend seriously enough to inundate railroad magazines such as *Trains* and *Rails Illustrated* with letters urging their editors to warn the public of the dangers of the railroad right-of-way.

Ted Conover, an Amherst College student who became a hobo for fifty thousand miles for his dissertation, published as *Rolling Nowhere,* concludes that today's hobo is a sociopath with little resemblance to the happy-go-lucky character of romantic folklore or the noble figure of Wobbly propaganda. The crux of his argument is that there is little social fabric within the jungles and partnerships of the hoboes. Conover frequently witnessed men turning violently on partners they had traveled with for tens of thousands of miles. He found that beyond the predictable need to project a facade of cynical toughness was a chronic pathology of lying, especially to those of the "brotherhood" that one might need to rely on in times of trouble. His hoboes were not transcendentalists who lived for the moment, but rather fanatic "planners" continually concocting long-range schemes involving complicated train routes to various sites of work, larceny, or freeloading, routes which were never actually followed. Though they espoused a code of tribal ethics, his hoboes more often than not violated those rules at every turn, and their enclaves were more contests of naked aggression than models of communal living. Conover concludes that their world makes the term "jungle" more appropriate than anyone might have ever suspected.

Those characters who have succeeded in making themselves cult heroes, such as today's Frypan Jack, are regarded with some suspicion by the hard core who inhabit the remote jungles far from the Winnebagos and journalists of the conventions. Most hoboes today live well outside of our culture and its folklore—and do not appear to have another of their own. Many of these conclusions will be born out by encounters of my own on subsequent train trips. Though the life continues, the spirit has died.

In the night I am awakened from a dream of riding in an open boxcar by the pressure of the beer I have drunk during the evening and so confront one of the inconveniences of the first-class single roomettes on eastern Heritage cars—the toilet is under the fold-down bed. There are two choices: raise the bed, disrupting the bedding and fully wakening myself, or throw on my bathrobe and use the bathroom in the (fortunately) adjoining bar car. Ironically, I don't have this problem when my compartment is the second-class slumbercoach—the narrow bed leaves room for the toilet to be serviceable. Somewhere in the history of sleeping-car design, it was decided that persons traveling alone in first class would care more about having a wide bed than about being able to use the toilet during the night.

I opt to use the public bathroom in the next car, but as I step into the vestibule connecting the cars the world slips away. With a painful crash I am tossed on my behind in a swirl of cold white which crystallizes through my sleepy vision into snowdrifts. Tales of hoboes walking in their sleep and falling off trains flash through my half-dreaming mind.

But this is no dream. During the night we have run into an Illinois blizzard, and the snow has leaked into the vestibule. Fully awake now, I open the window of the Dutch door and am blasted by dense snow coming out of pitch darkness at eighty miles an hour. I shiver at the thought of the hoboes sleeping in open boxcars rushing along through wintery nights like this.

But after my business in the next car is concluded and I crawl back into my snug bed in the warm roomette with the snow blazing by the window, everything is just fine. I am reminded of snuggling down in the bed at my grandfather's house in Bloomington and hearing the far-off sound of the midnight express. The moment is not thirty years away, but only the flickering of the eyelids drifting between dreams.

One of those dreams conjures up another railroad folk song, "The Phantom Drag." Out of the turmoil and disappointment of a million rides to nowhere, hoboes fantasized about the "phantom drag," a freight which would carry them beyond the pains and indignities of this life into a better world. The train is always headed west, beyond the sunset, and the engineer is no other than Casey Jones himself. The train number is "Ninety-seven," from another hallowed song of a great train wreck in which the engineer died "with his hand on the throttle, a-scalded by the steam." It is a "redball" that has stopped, giving the hobo his shot "to stake his soul" on a fast route to the "distant westward shore." But the bitter winter night carries him instead into eternity. "No one knew, not even the crew, they were hauling a frozen 'bo. All in a heap his body lay, on the frost-covered boxcar floor; that's the first thing the car-toad saw when he opened up the door. When the inquest was through all the jurymen knew that he was only a frozen vag. No one will ever know the name of the 'bo who was riding the phantom drag."

Morning in Champaign, Illinois—I was born here and haven't seen the place since I was a baby. As we roll into town I peer out my window at a world that is white. It's creepy, like eternity, one night after leaving the flower stalls and greenery of steamy New Orleans. But farther north we stop at Kankakee, a town on the auto route from my first childhood home of Elkhart, Indiana, to Bloomington, Illinois. I believe a lifelong interest in geography grew out of following our progress on the map as we drove that route to Grampa's house. Even today, Kankakee conjures for me a personal folklore of going home: my grandfather coming in sooty and garrulous off the train, his cigar smoke, the St. Louis Cardinals on the huge Emerson console radio, hot ketchup on meatloaf, pouring lead soldiers in molds in my grandfather's basement, Sundays of church and long afternoon backyard family picnics, drawing railroad tracks with chalk on the sidewalk under the mulberry tree, carrying my father's gym bag after watching him turn double plays as shortstop of the hometown team.

There were other childhood auto trips to the midwest from Virginia, Colorado, and upstate New York. These rides home from my father's latest career rung began as experiences with the texture of American earth and the faces of its towns. We would stop to hunt rocks in the West Virginia Appalachians or gather walnuts in the southern Indiana hills or just cruise the small towns of southwestern New York looking for likely diners. In Bloomington the first discussion around the Emerson radio always centered on our reports about the route we took—traffic, detours, shortcuts, new pavement, bridges, and how to get around the cities that always seemed to swallow up routes that had previously been good. But the advent of the superhighway and the interstate system changed all that. Like nothing since the railroad itself, the interstate system has altered the face of the land, cluttering it with the garish flotsam and desolate wreckage of economic decisions made in air-conditioned offices by men and women who travel by jet.

Eventually we stopped going home to Bloomington. The time of my first continental travels still haunts and rings with a resonance for me that no other time since can. Is it a stage of young life that men at all times have remembered, or is it the tailing end of a platform of experience, uniquely American, uniquely my generation, that we left behind somewhere in the mid-twentieth century? I still have many miles to ride to find out.

As we approach Chicago my childhood reveries are interrupted by the characteristic rattle of frequent diamond crossings. These are places where east-west lines cross over the IC tracks at grade, the diamond being the parallelogram-shaped track structure installed at the point of crossing. The track sound invokes another legend of the IC.

During the construction of the IC in the 1850s, the rules and etiquette of grade crossings involving competing railroads had not yet been established. As the IC approached Chicago from the south, two competing Michigan roads rushed to become the city's first connection to the east. Since the IC had a contractual agreement with the Michigan Central to share a line into the city, Central's competition, the Michigan Southern, regarded the IC as its enemy, and the Southern built its east-west line into the city first. It believed it had blocked the IC–Michigan Central north-south route into the city, which had to cross its tracks.

The position of the Southern was that the IC would have to build an expensive bridge or could not cross at all. The issue was brought before the courts.

But while the courts were considering the case, late one night in April 1852, the guard stationed by the Southern at the crossing point found himself bodily hustled away from his post by a gang of sturdy fellows working for the IC. The night air was rent by the sound of rail cutters, and then the clanking sound of the installation of a diamond. The new day saw a spanking new diamond glinting bright in the morning sun, and by noon, an IC work train had rattled across it.

Still the issue was not settled. Both railroads stubbornly operated as if the crossing did not exist, setting their own schedules with no reference to or cooperation with the schedule of the competing railroad. The Southern refused to recognize the violation of its physical property; the IC refused to acquiesce in the blockade of its chartered route. As has happened so often when stubborn principle or ideology has made fools of otherwise rational men, crisis intervened to smarten everybody up. One day in 1853, an Illinois Central passenger train and a Michigan Southern freight arrived at the now-named Grand Crossing at the same instant. When the smoke and dust cleared, eighteen people were dead and forty were seriously maimed. There were angry mobs and inflammatory news headlines screaming "Murder at the Crossing!"

The two railroads met and agreed that all trains would make full stops at the crossing. After a few months of this wasteful foolishness, everybody knuckled under to reality and developed cooperative schedules so that trains of both roads could pass the crossing in safety and without stopping.

Two significant precedents were thus established. The lesser was that legally chartered railroads could not be blocked by others crossing their paths, but had the right to lay the diamond to make crossings at grade where necessary. The greater was that crisis and tragedy would be sure to succeed where men had failed to accommodate their principles to the demands of new realities they were so busily creating.

To the right of the train as we come into Chicago, a line of dark towers looms through the snowmist. These are "the projects," monuments to good public intentions gone bad. Closer to the tracks are more of those bypassed streets where the people have no ticket to ride even this train of modest pretensions. The cityscape reminds me again of the "crossing-crisis principle." Here an intractable reality exists, just as surely and solidly as the hurtling trains of competing railroads crossing a diamond whose existence we don't want to acknowledge. When the collision finally shakes us, the crisis will get our attention. The victims will be the innocents who are caught up in the turmoil of crisis and the not-so-innocent ideologies whose blinding effects make crisis inevitable. Fair-minded, compassionate men will mourn the sacrifice of the former, but not of the latter. Songwriters and taletellers will memorialize the upheaval with lore that will echo in a new generation of ideals and bitter memories.

Much of my route so far has focused on the triumph of the "great American enterprise." On the old Illinois Central route from New Orleans to Chicago, the "Spirit of New Orleans" invokes the disenfranchised, the countercultures, and the crises whose memory both enriches and humbles the American spirit. Here the pendulum of history has reached the end of its swing. It pauses, turns, and falls back, trailing a more ambiguous folklore behind.

Chapter Seven

_____

God, Country, and Freedom

THE *BROADWAY LIMITED*

O U T of the northwest roared the Alberta Clipper, not a train but a monster cyclonic winter storm system feeding on moisture from as far away as the northwestern Pacific, the Gulf of Mexico, and the Great Lakes. By midafternoon I have given up all hope of walking the streets of Chicago as I have those of San Francisco, Los Angeles, and New Orleans. Fifty-mile-per-hour winds and snowdrifts on Canal Street have frozen my enthusiasm. Union Station is warm and filling with people, not just the usual travelers and commuters but a whole body of bewildered folk who will take a train for the first time in their lives. The Chicago airports are all closed.

Crowds of travelers used to the routines of air terminals swarm at the Amtrak ticket windows for seats to Detroit, Indianapolis, Milwaukee, Minneapolis, St. Louis, Kansas City, Cincinnati, Pittsburgh, Cleveland, Washington, Philadelphia, and New York. Nothing has defined the American character more than the freedom to travel. The storm has demonstrated that it's not just the political right that is so taken for granted, but the technological ability to do so. This crowd is angry, and if the technology of travel fails here, there will be a riot.

By 4:00 it is apparent that the storm has created problems even for the railroad. All of the trains due in from the far west are delayed. The *Empire Builder* from Seattle, due at 3:08, isn't expected till around 5:00, the *Southwest Chief* from Los Angeles, due at 3:15, till after 6:00. And the *California Zephyr*, from San Francisco, is so late that no arrival time is even projected. Amtrak has been scouring its yards all afternoon for additional coaches to add to tonight's trains, but there simply aren't many to be had. As tempers fray around me, I treasure my ticket for warm, snug, reserved slumbercoach 7 in car 4001 on the *Broadway Limited*.

But I've been traveling alone long enough now that, all travelers' fantasies aside, I'm craving simple companionship amid this crowd of strangers—a familiar face who already recognizes my humanity. If my memory, sense of the calendar, and knowledge of train schedules are sound, I should encounter one when the *California Zephyr* finally arrives.

Sure enough, at 7:15, when the *Zephyr*'s arrival is announced, among the crush of passengers rushing to see if they have already missed their connections there bounces the blond ponytail, now under a fancy suede cowboy hat, of the young woman from San Francisco who is moving to Charlotte. "Hello, San Francisco–Charlotte!" I call out.

"Hello, San Francisco–New Englander! Where do we catch our train?" she returns. Humanity reaffirmed, we now exchange proper introductions, and she is full of talk. Her name is Winter Dewsnap, for her grandmother Winterble, and thus she captures Romedell Lambert's prize for best name of the trip. She has a terrible cold because the heat in her sleeper on the *Zephyr* didn't work last night. The cowboy hat and high tooled leather boots are mementoes of a closed chapter of her life in the west. She has no regrets.

I ask if the train satisfied her urge to see the country. "Yes, and what a country," she says. "Where else can you live one life for twenty-two years, try on another one three thousand miles away for five years, and then chuck it and on your way home see a dozen other lives you might give a try sometime?" She is excited to be free of San Francisco and headed for home, where people are plainer and where people had better be a guy waiting for her in a pickup truck at 3:00 A.M. tomorrow night when the train is due in Charlotte or she will just sit tight and ride all the way to New Orleans and maybe stay there for five years. But first she has to get from here to Philadelphia, where she will catch the *Crescent* headed south.

When we board the *Broadway Limited*, Winter Dewsnap and I

discover that we are next-door neighbors—traveling companions for the duration. Our slumbercoach compartments are so small that from our seats we can look out our compartment windows and then lean into the corridor to chat about what we see without ever getting up. As the train pulls out into the maze of yards that crisscross Chicago, the horizontal snowstorm blurs the rose pinks and electric blues of city lighting into an abstract impression of a city—it's impossible to really pick out specific features of the urban landscape.

After the yards, the *Broadway Limited* is very fast getting out of Chicago; no slow meander through suburban countryside here. The reason for this lies outside the window a hundred yards away in the roaring blizzard. The New York Central tracks parallel the Pennsylvania's tracks for some distance to the east of Chicago. In the days of the intense competition between the Central's *20th Century Limited* and Pennsy's *Broadway Limited*, the Pennsylvania deliberately laid its route so that a visible race could develop between its train and its vaunted competitor, whose PR people made such a big deal of their train's speed. In its obsession to guarantee that the *Broadway* would always be viewed as an equal alternative to the popular *20th Century Limited*, the management also set up the train's schedule so that it would depart Chicago at the same time as the Central train and decreed that it would never be outrun. The races that developed were legendary and dangerous enough that in 1926, the two railroads negotiated a truce on speed. But old habits die hard. Today's Amtrak descendant of the Pennsy train still roars out of Chicago at well over eighty miles per hour, even into the teeth of a blizzard that has brought all other forms of travel to a halt.

A truly friendly voice on the PA announces free snacks and half-price hot toddies in the bar car. Winter pops up at my door and suggests we check it out. This train ride is going to be all right.

The bar car is warm and full of friendly, cheerful people. A quick survey shows that aside from Winter and me, only two patrons are train regulars. The rest, a couple dozen, some of whom struggle to stand with drinks in their hands cocktail-party-style, are first-time riders. The train has already worked a congenial effect on their spirits.

By the service counter I spot service chief Gene DeAngelis. With his curly hair and contagious smile, Gene is one of the most genuinely warm people I have ever met on a train. Tonight he has a trainful of first-time passengers, and he regards them as an evangelical minister might regard a flock of potential converts. "These blizzards are a godsend. Anyone who likes working on the train and doesn't bust his butt to make the most of these runs is a fool." Gene is going all out. The free snacks and the half-price hot toddies are his initiative, not normal amenities for this run.

But Gene is also a worried man with a problem on his hands. The equipment Amtrak has given him for this run is in bad shape, particularly the dining car. He's afraid that breakdowns caused by the cold weather will cancel any goodwill he and his crew can create with good service. So he is off the train in the snowstorm at every stop, crawling under cars, rapping on pipes, and looking for trouble.

After he returns, snow-frosted, from one of his outings at a stop in northern Indiana and joins us at a table in the lounge car, I try out a theory I've heard about the austerity of the Reagan years being good for Amtrak, and he responds. "Well, yeah, it's good if you think it's good to stretch a rubber band as far as possible to see where it will break. But then you'll need a new rubber band. And if you had passengers riding the old rubber band when it broke, then who's going to ride your new one?"

Tonight the freezing temperatures are doing a job on his aging Heritage car's plumbing that could mean the loss of its water supply. "Now how am I going to feed people in any kind of style without water?" Temporary repairs haven't been possible because of the weather. "If you take these cars off of the head-end power that generates the heat, you've got forty minutes before pipes freeze and you really wreck the car." As it is, he doesn't think his pipes will make it through tonight's wind chill, and then the waiters will have to tell the diners that there simply is no water. The chef could still cook with water brought in buckets from other cars. Gene hopes his passengers like milk, wine, beer—anything but water.

As the noise of good cheer in the bar car escalates, Gene introduces me to Peter and Joan Smythe, a well-dressed middle-aged couple from Australia sitting in the next booth sipping toddies. They've vacationed in the United States since their business, insurance, put them on easy street. Shouting to be heard above the combined track rattle and human chatter, Peter says the States have a tremendous allure for newly wealthy Australians. Where else in the world can you go and travel a whole continent where everyone speaks your language? Joan says that people returning to Australia from the United States always talk of how they felt right at home in this country on the other side of the planet from theirs. They appreciate the homogeneity of America. "And yet you have more pluralism than in any country in the world. You speak the same language everywhere and buy the same brands and

shop in the same stores; but your southerners are so different from
your Yankees, your midwestern farmers are so different from your
California yuppies, and your minorities are big, vocal minorities. I
don't know how you all manage to get along as well as you do."

I remind her that we have fought a Civil War and that we still have
lots of people who haven't really bought into tolerance of diversity. "You
mean your flag-wavers and Bible-thumpers," interjects Peter. "But
nobody takes them seriously, right? Your country just has so many
people of good, pragmatic common sense. That's what makes America
the model to the world of modern pluralistic society."

Before we part to go to bed, the Smythes point out that there are
facets of American life that they do find very disturbing, especially the
level of crime and violence. They insist that Australia has lived down its
outlaw past and is today a much less violent and more law-abiding
society than the United States. The government even just recently
passed a law totally banning all handguns. Several well-publicized
cases of shooting sprees by a few crazies created a tidal wave of public
outrage overnight. Unaccustomed to the kind of violence that we take
for granted, Australians simply revolted and their gun-lobby types
were just blown away.

American history is replete with tales of the kind of lawlessness that
the Smythes decry, and some of the worst of those involved the railroad
as a catalyst. Even before the network of rails could have its revolutionary effects on the way a newly mobile public thought and acted, the
mere building of some of the early roads sparked conflagrations in such
places as Shin Hollow, New York.

The Erie Railroad, the first serious attempt to lay rails from New
York all the way to the midwestern hinterland, danced with disaster in
a variety of forms for decades. First there was the wrongheaded notion
of building the roadbed on wooden pilings, then the adoption of an
idiosyncratic six-foot gauge, the decision to terminate at a small town
on the Hudson River twenty miles upriver from New York City, and
finally the failure to act on an opportunity to buy the Harlem Railroad,
which later brought the New York Central into the city itself. On top of
all this loomed the ruinous financial schemings of Daniel Drew, Jay
Gould, Jim Fisk, and others which led to the legend of the "scarlet
woman of Wall Street." But at Shin Hollow, the railroad demonstrated
its power to provoke an archetypal mindless violence that still lurks,
like a bleeding ulcer, on the underbelly of the American character.

The Erie had imported thousands of Irish and German workers to do the job of laying rails without paying much heed to the demographics of the men they brought together. First there was the problem of religion, the Catholic Irish and the Lutheran Germans mutually antagonistic as oil and water. Then there was the problem of alcohol and sex. The railroad thought of the flourishing brothels and saloons on the hillsides at Shin Hollow as harmless diversion, a necessary outlet for rude men who toiled all day in sweat and pain. Finally there was the presence of almost tribal factions among the Irish, of which the railroad managers were blissfully ignorant. The men of Cork and those known as the Far-downers avoided conflict in their homeland by geographical separation. Here in America the railroad brought them together in a setting where they found that they not only drank in the same taverns and worked on the same jobs, but also shared the same women.

Thus one night in 1847, the aggressive, liquored Far-downers marched on the camp of the men of Cork with stones and rifles and drove them out. Two days later they resumed the attack. Many were wounded and one man died before the Far-downers prevailed upon the railroad agent to pay off the Corks and send them packing.

After an inconclusive raid on the German camp, the aggressors regrouped several days later to further scourge the Corks, who still lingered in the region harboring hopes of getting their jobs back. The Corks slept in slapdash lofts supported by posts loosely driven into the ground (perhaps in emulation of the engineering of the railroad itself). The Far-downers met on the mountain, primed themselves with whiskey, and then swarmed down to cut out the posts from under the sleeping Corks. They beat them all to bloody pulps.

Again the victorious Irish turned their attention to the alien Germans, but now the aroused Germans were ready, armed with shotguns and organized for battle. When the Irishmen swooped down in the early hours of the morning on the German camp, they encountered formal battle lines bristling with primed firearms. The Germans fired in volleys and decimated the disorganized ranks of the Irish. Those who could fled with the daylight, vowing revenge for the Shin Hollow Massacre.

But by then the company had called for militia, and the appearance of uniforms and a small symbolic cannon quelled the rioters. Other incidents occurred along the Erie line when uncongenial combinations of Irish factions met, but these flareups were written off as mere friction among lower orders of foreigners. The railroad managers never dreamed that these events foreshadowed much larger explosions among fully Americanized men brought on by the homogenizing impact of the new technology itself. In this case it had canceled the buffers of geography that separated enemies. Later it would bridge the distance that separated men incited to violence by a solidarity of rage.

In the morning, east of Pittsburgh, the snow outside is different, now heavy and wet. It doesn't blow in sheets past the windows, but continues to fall in great half-dollar-sized blobs. Just as I followed a continental thaw in my trip west, I now seem to be matching the eastward progress of one of those storms we New Englanders watch approaching for days on our TV weather forecasts. In the dining car the subject of talk over breakfast is primarily the storm and the fact that, for some reason, there is a water shortage this morning. The breakfast coffee is heavy and potent; later the lunch soup is thick and salty. Stepping off the train at the Johnstown station, I see Gene's backside sticking out from under the dining car.

"It blew at three A.M.," he explains as he wipes his hands on a rag. "Ice in three joints. We lost all our water. Now I'm afraid of the damage it did to some electrical stuff. I don't want to have to tell all those good people that not only will there be no water at lunch, there might be no lunch." Moving on to the positive, Gene reminds me to get pictures of Horseshoe Curve before Altoona. As long as a crowd doesn't gather, he has no problem with my opening the Dutch window in the vestibule to get a better shot.

The scenery at the Pennsylvania Railroad's Horseshoe Curve isn't really as impressive as some I've seen on the Denver & Rio Grande in the Rockies or the Southern Pacific along the California coast. What has made the sight so famous is that this is a horseshoe of a four-track main line—thus the name *Broadway*. During the heyday of the railroads, an observer could sit by this spot and watch a continual parade of trains up and down this grade on what was the busiest route of the world. The site is also significant in being the first great horseshoe curve in one of the earliest attempts to leap a mountain range.

Philadelphians had watched with chagrin for seventy years after the Revolution as the nation's political capital moved away and rooted itself in Washington and its intellectual capital coalesced around Boston. Burghers of the "city of brotherly love" had once entertained illusions of building a democratic Rome, before which all other American cities would pale in significance. By the time the nineteenth century was well underway, they had to adjust to a different vision, one of a string of great, competing east-coast metropolises, each with its own claim to leadership, heralding the pluralistic future of the new nation. Philadelphia at least still led in finance and commerce.

But in the mid-1840s the appearance of railroads foreshadowed a third vision, one totally unacceptable. With Baltimore & Ohio construction crews toiling through the Appalachians with their sights set on Pittsburgh and the Erie Railroad, despite setbacks and gross mismanagement, threatening to link the upstart city of New York with the upper midwest, Philadelphians saw themselves threatened by mercantile pincers in the neighboring seaports to the north and the south. There were even some who feared that the combination of the Erie Railroad, the Erie Canal, and the newly developing string of central upstate New York railroads might someday enable the rude port of New York to surpass all her neighbors and dominate as Philadelphia had once seemed destined to do.

In 1846, a group of Philadelphia men incorporated the Pennsylvania Railroad, its goal Pittsburgh. The state's "Main Line of Improvements," dating back to the early 1830s, consisted at the time of a series of canals and short railroads with inclined planes over the Appalachian ridges separating the level links in the system. Cars were hauled up these planes by ropes or chains connected to fixed steam engines at the top of each ridge. Cars moving up one side of these steep ridges were balanced by the weight of cars moving down the other. The journey from Philadelphia to Pittsburgh involved a number of inconvenient changes of conveyance and could take up to a week. The mandate of the new railroad was to weld this patchwork system into a continuous rail line that must, under legislative fiat, reach Pittsburgh ahead of the feared Baltimore & Ohio.

Under the brilliant management of John Edgar Thompson, the Pennsylvania Railroad did just that. With no competition yet for the stretch between Philadelphia and Harrisburg, Thompson wisely built first the most difficult section of the line, from Harrisburg to Pittsburgh. Near Altoona, Thompson and his engineers faced the greatest obstacle, the high central divide of the Alleghenies where the approaching valley on the east side simply isn't long enough to allow a decent grade to the top. Thompson hit on the expedient of beginning the climb up the side of the preceding ridge to a point where the ridges met at the head of the valley and then doubling back with a sharp curve to continue the second half of the climb up the eastern slope of the divide itself. It was railroading's first great horseshoe curve, and it worked because though it added miles to the length of the route, trains could travel fast enough over it to easily beat any known conveyance traveling more as the crow flies.

By the Civil War, Thompson had succeeded not only in building a continuous line from Philadelphia to Pittsburgh but in extending it through consolidation of existing lines and new construction all the way to Chicago. With the accumulation of branch lines to Cleveland, Cincinnati, and St. Louis in the west and extensions to New York Harbor in the north and Washington in the south, the Philadelphia railroad men eventually found themselves possessed of a potential empire stretching in a broad band all the way to the Mississippi.

Unlike the managers of the Erie, the early New York Central, or the later Union Pacific, the men of the Pennsy saw their interests from the start as lying in the best possible operation of the railroad itself. The railroad always paid dividends and yet was among the first to make such expensive innovations as steel rails, air brakes, and a block signal system. It came to be known as "the standard railroad" of the world.

But though it may have been first among peers, the Pennsy never truly established an empire like that of the Southern Pacific, nor could its characteristics set a true standard. The reason was competition. By late in the century, the Pennsy competed with the New York Central, the Baltimore & Ohio, the Erie, the Grand Trunk, and others in linking the growing midcontinent with a string of Atlantic Seaboard cities stretching from Hampton Roads, Virginia, to Portland, Maine. In this sense, unifying and homogenizing force that it was, the railroad also worked as a force for diversity, for pluralism. No single region, city, or combination of political, ideological, and business interests of the east could ever quite lay claim to the heartland as its province. There was just too much energy abroad, charging the land through the lines of the competing steel rails. Soon the charge of that network would explode in conflagrations seldom seen in this country before or since.

The train climbs the chasm that leads to Horseshoe Curve, and the moisture-laden wind chills me under my jacket as I hang out the window of the vestibule. It doesn't look promising for photos as an icy mist drifts across the gulf between the train and the tracks on the other side. Winter Dewsnap has followed me with her camera, and a woman who works in another car has come by and started a bit of a row about my having the window open. After some shouting, she leaves to get help to remove us, the clouds clear momentarily, and I get my shot of the engine passing in the opposite direction on the other canyon wall.

I have read in sources as late as 1975 that one of Pennsy's distinctive K-4S steam locomotives is displayed beside the tracks at the bend of the horseshoe, and thus I am surprised to see in its place an early GP-3 diesel, a type used in the 1950s by the Pennsy, the NYC, and many other lines. The K-4S was Pennsy's standard-bearing workhorse in getting hundreds of trains a day over this hump in a crusade that would never allow the "water-level route" of the NYC the monopoly of the New York–Chicago trade that it sought. Conrail, which now operates both lines, has apparently decided to maintain a symbolism that promotes a generic image of modern railroading rather than an idiosyncratic relic of the past.

Today the inside set of tracks around the curve has been torn up; the traffic simply no longer justifies four sets of valuable rails, which are needed on lines falling into disrepair elsewhere. But the crushed-rock bed, the ballast, is still there—an effort by Conrail to preserve either the skeleton of the *Broadway* or the option of someday relaying the track in better times.

Just as a Conrail engine pulling a rattler of empty automobile carriers appears on the adjacent track heading in the opposite direction, the car attendant who hassled us earlier returns with an assistant conductor to whom I haven't yet introduced myself. He diplomatically reminds me of the rule prohibiting opening of the Dutch doors while the woman clucks with her arms folded in vindicated disapproval, and my open-air view of the horseshoe is concluded.

Back in my slumbercoach, my car attendant, Beachey S. Thompson, is making up beds, and he apologizes for the incident at the window. He leans at my door to expound his theory about women and authority. "Some of 'em got identity problems that makes 'em sticklers for the rules, so they're always buttin' into other people's jobs and territories. What they don't understand is that people do their jobs different." He's got his way of running his car, and he respects her way of running hers. He wouldn't think of expecting her to do her job his way and wishes she would do the same. "But it doesn't work out that way. So ya just ignore 'em and sometimes turn the other cheek. It takes a lotta tolerance to work with a woman with a rule book in her head."

This same woman called him "an Amtrak dog" once, so he and her old man had to "box it out" to settle that one. That was before he learned tolerance. Today he wouldn't think of settling a problem he had with a woman by squaring off against her guy, "a man I should feel sympathy for 'cause he takes her crap regular."

For the sake of argument, I suggest that maybe being a stickler for the rules is just some people's idea of being conscientious, of doing a good job.

"Naw, that ain't it," he insists. "It's people that got holes in their souls. They don't really know who they are so they feel more secure if their work follows some set of rules that never changes, like a kind of Bible or something. And when they see somebody not doing it their way, they get threatened, like it's gonna really hurt them personal somehow."

He returns to his work, moving from compartment to compartment with hands fluttering between gestures of emphasis to his talk and strikingly efficient movements in the changing of the bedding in the bunks. Beachey likes his job—feels it's one pretty fair deal and finds it difficult to imagine times when railroad men had to strike and strike violently to achieve the status and working conditions they have now.

In the early days the same railroads that fostered the paradox of unity and pluralism in the land also spawned paroxysms of division and solidarity in the nation's first and most violent confrontations between labor and management. The year was 1877, and in Pennsylvania, it looked as though the centennial decade would be marked by yet another revolution.

The trouble began with the Panic of 1873. Like many industries, railroads cut pay to cope with dwindling revenue without cutting stock dividends, secure in the belief that with widespread unemployment, they could get away with it. Yet, as capitalists would learn to their chagrin in the next century, widespread unemployment generates masses of desperate men whose spasms of rage tend to infect the gainfully employed with the instinct to revolt. In Tompkins Square in Manhattan, a riot of twenty thousand unemployed men with their women and children set the tone for the mood of the employed for the next decade. As tales of blood in the New York streets spread along the rail routes of America, the workingmen of the railroads organized into brotherhoods increasingly dedicated to solidarity in defense of their livelihood rather than traditional fraternal social ritual.

In June of 1877, the Pennsylvania cut pay 10 percent. Labor lay quiet, so other railroads followed suit. Still nothing happened, so the Baltimore & Ohio made its move, a 10 percent cut of all wages over $1 an hour. B&O firemen and brakemen in Baltimore walked off the job and were quickly replaced with men from the ranks of the unemployed. Then all hell broke loose.

When firemen and brakemen walked off the job in Martinsburg, West Virginia, twelve hundred freight cars quickly accumulated and jammed the tracks. B&O officials prevailed upon Governor Matthews to call out the local militia, but with the corps manned largely by relatives of the strikers, the move succeeded only in adding armed, trained soldiers to the ranks of the rebellious.

Matthews called out the militia of distant Wheeling and, leading them himself, marched on Martinsburg. En route he encountered mobs of angry citizens who supported the stance of the strikers, and before arriving in Martinsburg he thought better of personally leading the charge and retired to his capitol to petition the President for help.

Soon all along the B&O line federal troops with bayonets confronted angry mobs with clubs and rocks. While the company offered promotion and "a fine medal" to employees who would remain on the job, the 6th Regiment of the National Guard was set upon by a mob of two thousand wielding two-by-fours and stones. When the terrified weekend soldiers fired into the masses, thirteen citizens were killed and a hundred more seriously wounded. Gatling guns, artillery, and regular infantry finally enforced the B&O timetable over the rebellious route, and the strike on this road was quickly broken, but it was just the drumroll for what was yet to come.

The Pennsylvania had initiated its pay cut some time earlier and in July rubbed salt in the wound by decreeing that henceforth freight trains would be doubled in length and pulled by two engines to cut down on manpower needed. Pennsy crews grumbled but stayed on the job until news of the B&O strike reached Pittsburgh. As word of the mayhem in Maryland spread throughout the Pittsburgh yards, men climbed down from their engines and cabooses and walked away, leaving them steaming on the tracks.

The company requested troops, and as usual the men of the local militia stood passive while the strikers stopped train after train coming into Pittsburgh from either direction. Federal troops and artillery were called out and confronted a crowd on Liberty Street. Rocks flew and two volleys were fired: twenty men fell dead, and the wounded included a woman and her three children.

Rumor spread throughout the city to walks of life far removed from railroading. Wives and children of strikers had been publicly executed, the troops had orders to exterminate all strikers, artillery was firing on workingmen's homes. With such wild stories flying, crowds from all parts of the city began to converge on the railroad yards. Troops at the roundhouse were surrounded by a crowd estimated at twelve thousand. Three soldiers were shot down as they ran, and the crowd swelled further as word went out that a contingent of the hated troops was bottled up inside the roundhouse.

While the mob raged and the terrified soldiers peeped out from the

building, a group of particularly fiendish workers loaded a gondola car
with coke soaked with flammable oil. The death car was set afire and
rolled into the roundhouse, which exploded in flames. Panicked, the
soldiers boiled out in all directions, firing randomly as they ran. The
crowd surged upon them. Miraculously, most of the soldiers managed
to escape alive, though badly mauled. But twenty strikers died at the
"Battle of the Roundhouse."

The smoke billowing up from the roundhouse incited men and women
throughout the city to anarchy. Shops were looted for guns and bread as
the spirit of revolution marched the streets and people knew by instinct
what to lay hands upon. Only in the churches, now filling with those
fleeing the horror on the streets, did men of peace call for reason in
prayers to God.

But now all Pittsburgh caught fire, literally and figuratively. The
blazes started in the long coal trains stacked up in the yards and spread
to the Union Depot and Hotel and the offices of the railroad. As night
came on, the city glowed bright with hundreds of conflagrations while
the crowds cheered the flames, harassed the beleaguered firemen, and
cursed the railroad that had made Pittsburgh one of America's most
prosperous cities.

By morning when General Winfield Scott Hancock arrived with an
army of three thousand regulars, Pittsburgh's rage was spent. Dazed
crowds passively watched as the federal troops occupied the city and
the firemen watered the steaming cinders.

But with Pittsburgh quiet, the rage of '77 sparked tinder in other
cities along the Pennsylvania line. Altoona, Johnstown, Bethlehem,
Easton, Reading—one by one they all blew up until over ten thousand
regular troops manned the rail lines throughout the state, and the
death toll mounted. Trains that moved that summer did so with a
Gatling-gun car at the head of every locomotive.

The flames of revolt jumped the firebreaks separating states and
railroads. In New York, strikers on the Erie halted traffic by greasing
or tearing up rails, as well as by pulling crews. In street fighting in
Buffalo, eighteen hundred soldiers of the Grand Army of the Republic
fired on mobs of strikers and killed eight. As it had in Pennsylvania, the
strike fever flashed out over the lines of the New York Central till there
was trouble in Rochester, Syracuse, and even Albany.

Westward the fever raged over the lines of the Lake Shore & Michigan Central all the way to Chicago, where sympathetic dockworkers
joined the striking railroad men. At the Chicago, Burlington & Quincy
roundhouse, midwestern railroadmen staged their own "Roundhouse

Battle," and at the Halstead Street viaduct, a clash between mounted soldiers and an enraged mob left a dozen dead in the street. Here the radical leftist Workingmen's Party took the lead in a general strike that paralyzed the city for several days.

Likewise in St. Louis, the struggle now painted itself in shades of red signifying something more than just the shedding of blood. The Wobblies organized a less violent and more orderly series of strikes whose real thrust was to propagandize a generation of revolutionaries for the coming Red Dawn.

Even as far away as San Francisco, striking railroad men spawned a general riot whose violence turned against the Chinese minority, the ultimate whipping boy in all California disputes.

By the end of the summer of '77, over a hundred people had lost their lives and many hundreds more had been maimed in this paroxysm of rage along the trunk lines of America. One by one the strikes were broken as three factors dominated: the guns of federal troops (but not local militias), the vast pool of unemployed standing ready to replace fired strikers, and the lack of coordination among the striking brotherhoods themselves. Later labor leaders like Eugene Debs and Samuel Gompers profited from the lessons learned in '77 to build powerful unions which eventually forced concessions out of management through collective bargaining.

But not until 1968, when a new technology flashed images of violence in American streets and Asian jungles into living rooms and campus dorms across the land, when the assassination of Martin Luther King, Jr., unleashed racial passions of far deeper cause than a mere 10 percent pay cut for rail employees, would such a massive spontaneous outpouring of rage be seen in America. And even then the death toll would mount to less than half that of the explosion nearly a century earlier.

The events of 1877 demonstrated for the first time the revolutionary power of a new machine. The anger of those strikers was no greater than that produced by hundreds of other labor, racial, or ideological conflicts in our history. What was unique about 1877 was that the conflict occurred along tracks and telegraph lines whose ability to speed communications was still a novel thing. Would Pittsburgh have detonated if the news from Martinsburg had arrived several days later by older, slower methods of communication? Would Chicago railroad men have sat down on the job if they hadn't known that others were already at that moment doing so throughout the trunk lines far to the east? Americans had not yet adjusted to the heady thrill of timely knowledge of popular movements far away. In time they would, but in

1877 the railroad demonstrated painfully the power of new technology to spawn the paradoxical twins of revolution: ideological solidarity and violent division. In the latter twentieth century, peoples of developing lands everywhere would see other new technologies further attenuate the time and space between angry men sharing common cause, and again there would be blood in the streets and smoke above the rooftops as a result.

Beachey's struggle with petty tyranny and the upheavals of 1877 pale before the personal tale of Shahriar, an Iranian medicinal chemist now living in Chicago, with whom I have lunch. Gene has been able to hold the diner together, so except for the lack of drinking water we are able to have a fine meal of heavy minestrone and spicy Italian sausage.

Shahriar takes the train from Chicago to Philadelphia to be with his family. Unfortunately his best opportunity as a chemist was not in Philadelphia, where inexpensive housing and presence of other relatives had drawn him and his family when they fled Iran. He first came to this country in 1976, before the Khomeini revolution. He returned to Iran in 1980 to complete his doctorate at the university and was able to bring his entire family out as soon as he earned his degree in 1984.

Shahriar has the dark complexion of the Middle East. His jet-black hair is sparse, his forty-year-old face is deeply lined, and he would be better company if there were showers on board this overnight train. But the tall forehead and sharp, quick eyes do more than suggest intelligence, they aggressively project it.

Shahriar says that the Iranian revolution was a tragic disappointment. Intellectuals, scientists, and other people like himself originally supported it mainly to stop the killings and torture of the Shah's regime. "Everyone of our class knew someone who had been tortured or killed. We could only imagine how it must have been for the underprivileged." But there was never any intent, in the educated segment of society, to "dewesternize" Iran, as has been argued in several western histories of the conflict. "Nobody wanted to change Iran. There was a great national pride in our status as the most highly developed of developing nations. We just wanted to get rid of the Shah."

Neither did anyone dream that the very tools of that developing status, the technology of television and instant communications, would be the undoing of the class that had wielded them. Iranians were unprepared for the visual immediacy of the electronic age they had entered so abruptly. The intellectuals lost control of their revolution before it even started. The fundamentalists, led by Khomeini broadcasting his messages from Paris, swelled with power as the machines of the "Great Satan" they were committed to destroy welded the individual angers of millions of the uncomprehending into a massive rage.

Educated Iranians like Shahriar had always tended to be loose Moslems who distrusted the mullahs and their fanatically fundamentalist followers. "We were like your liberal American Catholics—those who practice birth control, who wouldn't outlaw abortions but still raise their kids on the catechism and go to mass once a week." The revolution has driven Iranians like Shahriar away from Islam, away from religion entirely. Today he is an "evangelical atheist." Khomeini showed him that religion is "a tool for harnessing fear, superstition, ignorance, and passion as an engine of power." He believes it offers the holder of that power the potential, if not always the reality, of a totalitarianism more absolute than communism, fascism, or autocracy. "How can you place limits on men acting on behalf of God? You can't. They can take a person, your wife, your child, and they can do, in broad daylight, anything to that person that they want. Who is to lift a hand against an agent of God?"

The mullahs viewed educated people as the enemy long before Shahriar realized that they were right. During his four years of doctoral study, Shahriar watched as the mullahs and their street thugs harassed the freethinking intellectuals of his circle. Wives would return from market quaking with terror after being followed by crowds chanting "Whore" because they didn't wear the chador. Children were beaten up at schools and tagged "puppies of Great Satan." Professionals who walked to work became unwilling participants in a fiendish game of "twenty questions" as street people demanded fundamentalist answers to questions of Moslem doctrine and delivered savage kicks to the behinds of the well-dressed men who answered incorrectly.

At first there was protest that such tactics would drive away Iran's educated class. The protests were straw for the fire; the harassment became systematic and more shrill and violent. Khomeini had succeeded in cleaving Iranian society in two. The ignorant reveled in their new status as soldiers of Islam. With no restraints on their age-old desire to lash out at those whose education was a fearful mystery, they wanted blood and the assurance of the simple certainties of medieval religion. "The law of Islam is absolute. Change is the work of Satan. Death in the service of the mullahs guarantees a personal place in heaven. All who do not subscribe to the letter of the one law are enemies, to be smitten to the last man, woman, and child."

The educated fled Iran. No attempt was made to stop them; indeed, the agents of the mullahs were more inclined to assist them in their departure. When Shahriar took his family out in 1984, he felt like one of the last survivors abandoning a sinking ship. He says that today there simply are no educated people left in Iran.

That's why he sees no hope. He harbors no illusions about ever returning to his native country. He loves his country just the way "one loves a violently insane father or a brother who has been put to death for heinous crimes." Without Khomeini, there will be civil war in Iran, and there are no moderate democrats waiting in the wings to take advantage of such an opportunity—only Iranian communists of the Pol Pot stripe, more mullahs, and a few of the Shah's fascists. "With Khomeini gone, those three forces will cut each other up for ages."

I suggest that other violent revolutions have moderated into a newly civil society. "Yes, but that happens only when there are people who will tire of fanaticism and when voices of moderation, restraint, and common sense finally have a chance to reassert themselves. I tell you there are none of those voices left in Iran. There are only the ignorant and fanatical, whose zealotry feeds on itself and is permanently self-perpetuating. The religious state has made hell on earth in Iran."

And it isn't just Islam that has this potential. Shahriar shows a solid knowledge of Western cultural history as he reminds me of men of enlightenment such as Galileo, who, when shown the instruments of torture by the bishops, concluded that indeed he had erred in calculating that the earth was not the center of the universe. He says modern Americans shouldn't become too complacent. There is an abortion clinic in Chicago near the lab where he works, and he witnessed an antiabortion protest there a few months before this trip. "You should have heard the things that crowd was saying to those young girls who were visiting the clinic. I could see what they wanted to do to those poor girls. It was just like Iran in 1982!"

Shahriar won't turn on a television on Sunday morning ever since the day he watched Oral Roberts prayerfully promoting a book on demon possession. "This man was actually telling me, here in America in the twentieth century, that my wayward teenager is possessed by devils that must be scourged out of him. You Americans don't realize, you've got your own ayatollahs right there on Sunday-morning TV." Shahriar thinks that it is conceivable that some subtle new leap in the media technology, something which is truly novel and for which we are societally unprepared, might yet provoke the baring of the primal, communal rage that destroyed Iran. Televangelism has convinced him that those who will lead it are already in place and well financed.

By now Shahriar and I have overstayed our welcome in the dining car; two sittings having been served while he has talked in his low, intense, only slightly accented voice. We move to the lounge car, where we sit down with Winter Dewsnap and Shahriar orders a Perrier and continues his dissertation. "The mullahs did one thing for me. Under them I learned that I didn't need to drink alcohol. Yes, they've made me a sadder but healthier man."

But Shahriar is happy in America. He feels there is a greater level of education in Europe, but prefers America because there is greater opportunity and less bigotry. "Your country, at least most of it, still really believes in pluralism. Europeans give it a lot of abstract lip service, but let's face it—Germany is a place for Germans, England for English. Those are racially defined nations. As such they won't accept anything but praise from foreigners. When a European asks you what you think of his country, he is fishing for a compliment. When an American asks, he is not satisfied until you find a flaw. And then you become fast friends."

Shahriar is quite taken with Winter's cowboy hat. She explains to him her theory about country-and-western music. "It gives people an outlet for sentiment and emotion that wouldn't be acceptable otherwise," she says. Shahriar likes that. In Iran such feelings are vented in bigotry and violence. She is intrigued by his criticism of the influence of our media, explaining her belief that what one learns from television makes it possible to adapt to living in different parts of the country.

"See?" says Shahriar. "I criticized something about America and now she wants me to understand her. We will be friends."

At 30th Street Station in Philadelphia, it is time for goodbyes. Shahriar is detraining to meet his family and Winter is heading south to Charlotte, while I will reboard the *Broadway Limited* bound further east to New York and home. Out on the station platform, Shahriar shakes my hand with lingering sincerity. When he wishes me well, the conventional words resonate with a deeper meaning than the usual parting sentiments. I suspect he has bade some farewells where there was little chance that there would be much faring well. When he calls me "friend," the word acquires a new definition in my vocabulary: one who has listened well across a cultural divide. Winter and I thank each other for simple companionship. I've seen that it's not easy being an attractive young woman traveling alone. She gives me a parting pose for a camera shot in her cowboy hat. As I watch the two of them disappear down the platform, she full of country-and-western music and southern fried chicken, he of his horrific memories, I am struck at the improbability of their juxtaposition in my memories of this train ride. Only in America.

A mumble of quiet profanity catches my attention, and there is Gene leaning under his derelict dining car. In a cheerful mood I josh him, "What are you worried about? You're done with meals for this trip—the pipes have burst and you've lost the water. Now you can take it off at New York and get it fixed."

"No way," he says. "We gotta turn it around and have it ready to leave for Chicago at two forty-five tomorrow afternoon. Since tomorrow's Sunday, it won't be till we get back to Chicago that we can take it off and get anything done to it."

Trains on Sunday. If theocracy ruled in this country as it does in Iran, there wouldn't be any. By 1850, American churches of a wide variety of denominations recognized in the railroads a growing threat. People then were content to honor the Sabbath by avoiding work, trade, and commerce on the first day of the week; but travel, especially rail travel, was another matter. As the railroads made travel an increasingly passive proposition, folks saw no spiritual harm in passing their day of rest in transit from one place to another. The prospect of a restful return trip on the second weekend day from some place of pleasant diversion contributed greatly to the growing "weekend mobility" of Americans everywhere.

But someone had to work to run those trains, and thus the clergy argued that Sunday schedules placed the souls of railroad men in jeopardy, and passengers themselves were at least accessories in the crime against the Sabbath. Even more to the point was the fact that as more people traveled on Sunday fewer remained at home to attend church. As clergymen watched attendance decline, a new dogma quickly developed and spread throughout the land like another "Great Awakening"— railroads that operated on Sunday were an abomination and placed the very soul of the nation at risk.

The Long Island Rail Road was the first to feel the wrath of the men of God. Rural farmers, who tended not to go anywhere on Sunday anyway and who also had their own scores to settle with the railroad involving frightened livestock and fields set afire by cinders, were quick to respond to the ministers' call for action. They ripped up rails, derailed trains, and torched stations up and down the line.

Political action groups in Massachusetts, Connecticut, New York, and Pennsylvania agitated for legislation to prohibit Sunday trains. "Sabbath committees" circulated fliers and petitions, which often had powerful effects in specific communities. One was Altoona, Pennsylvania, where trains of the mighty Pennsylvania Railroad, arriving from western cities on a Saturday night, would stop and stand until Monday morning. Altoona was "one city where locomotives keep the Sabbath," boasted a local clergyman in his sermon.

A well-circulated letter to an editor expressed horror at the sight of women traveling on "public conveyances during the Sabbath" and suggested that all of the fairer sex who did so must be of that very lowest order and oldest profession of women.

Sometimes the opposition could be quite civil and flattering in its campaign. The New York Sabbath Committee congratulated the railroads on being a great "civilizing power," one which "can be hardly overestimated. The snort of the iron horse as he rushes through the forest, or over the prairie, or along a valley, wakes the indolent to effort, and breaks in upon the stupor of helpless isolation. . . ." Nonetheless, the pamphlet of the committee went on to argue that if the locomotive was put to uses which disrupted the repose of the Sabbath and introduced habits into the life-style of Christians which undermined their fundamental adherence to the more valuable edifice of the Decalogue, "then it would be better if it did not run at all."

In the 1870s, the attacks against Sunday trains found common cause with the growing "Granger movement" which pitted farmers against the monopolistic rate-setting practices of the railroads. After the strikes of 1877, one misinformed Massachusetts preacher argued that "labor would not be obliged to strike for shorter workdays, if they would guard the Sabbath and keep it holy as a day of rest."

The railroads responded to the challenge of the clergy in a variety of ways. Virtually all railroads offered free passes to men of the cloth, who might have need of the railroad to travel quickly to some site of lost souls to preach a sermon of salvation. The Boston & Maine printed in its timetable the caveat "Persons purchasing tickets for Sunday trains will be required to sign a pledge they will use the tickets for no other purpose than attending church." The New Haven Railroad answered its critics with the explanation that it sent out one mail train on Sundays with one passenger car attached for use "only by those persons who must go on account of sickness or death or other urgent matter." At least one railroad attempted to establish church services in its coaches until an effective boycott deprived it of preachers to deliver sermons.

And there were some lines that knuckled under. The St. Johnsbury & Lake Champlain ran no Sunday trains and thus came to be known as the St. Jesus & Long Coming. Its executives' insistence in the matter forced its practical-minded managers, charged with getting out Monday trains through the snows of Vermont, to the expedient of sneaking plow trains out of St. Johnsbury without whistles, lights, or bells in the dark hours of early Sunday morning.

But most railroads bulled ahead, setting schedules without the guidance of scripture. One might admire them for refusing to submit to intimidation but for the fact that these same railroads during these same years were also stonewalling on issues ranging from monopolistic rate-setting to refusal to install safety equipment to the systematic corruption of politicians. And yet, somehow the dynamics of good common sense eventually forced railroads to reform on the latter three issues. Of the four great vices of nineteenth-century railroads, only Sunday trains remain. Indeed, though Amtrak schedules today list timetables for Sunday trains that differ from those of the rest of the week, generally the alterations are designed to increase Sunday ridership of weekend travelers, and virtually all of these trains are at full throttle, cutting through the meat of their route, during the hours of religious worship.

Past Philadelphia, we are back in the high-speed northeast corridor where modern electric engines wing their way down the track at over 110 secular miles per hour all seven days of the week. This is where Amtrak really hums, even through the wet snow, sleet, and freezing rain of the storm that has followed me eastward.

After 7,500 miles on the rails, I have had my first transcontinental ground-level look at America. Of course, the landscape is bigger and more varied than it is in imagination, the plains impossibly vast and empty, the mountains tiered in range upon range till one gives up looking for the last ridge, the desert crossings as alien as Mars in psychedelic sunlight, the Pacific cliffs so far away that now they seem not quite real. But the backyards of America that line the rail corridors, the marks of human works, are smaller, more predictable, and more inscrutable than one might have thought. At least the rails'-eye view confirms that the land still holds its power to humble and inspire. With a few notable exceptions—the Manhattan skyline, the rail line climbing the face of the Rockies' Front Range, the Golden Gate, the parade of ships on the Mississippi under the Huey Long Bridge, Horseshoe Curve—the continent continues to make the works of man appear unworthy and tentative. It suggests the possibility of so much more, just as it has since the first voyagers from the old world gazed awestruck at the new one they had found.

Then there are the train travelers, so different from the tourists one meets in the eighties along the interstates or in airports. For the steel-riders travel is not a disposable product, defined and packaged by the travel agents for consumption during some specified time period. They don't carry cameras, their goal is not fleeting memories or impressions to make on their friends back home, and their journeys often have no destinations. Always risking the fate of those who end up on the dock in San Francisco, they embody the restless American energy that perhaps offers some guarantee against the ultimate horror of Shahriar's Iran.

There the tensions between past and present, between custom and technology, between conformity and pluralism provoked a rift dividing the nation into opposing camps separated by walls of education, religion, and economics. There the struggle became a war with a victor—the ancient homogenizing forces of uniformity and simplicity. The result, according to Shahriar, is a place where the light has flickered out, where the dark is total.

Approaching New York, I wonder if that could happen here. If the problem is to maintain a pluralistic society without walls, then I suspect that travel is the natural enemy of those barriers, like the frost in Robert Frost's poem. But today's travel industry, with its infinitely innovative techniques for insulating the traveler from the regions and peoples lying between him and his destination, has been all too successful in helping us to take our walls with us. It isn't enough to have the freedom to travel; it is a matter of how we travel.

I may not have found much of America in this first sally across the continent. If my father were still alive, I think we'd argue over how I have just spent the past month. I haven't learned enough yet to make him understand why the search is so important—but I have confirmed my suspicions about how to look for America. Its most fundamental truths lie in prospects revealing combinations of contradiction held together by a monumental energy, like the plasma in hydrogen fusion—prospects that lie most open to the traveling eye along the right-of-way of the railroad.

There is a place near Newark where the tracks run on higher ground through a horrendous dump and abandoned graffiti-scrawled factories with not a plate of glass unbroken. Rusted bedsprings, tires, discarded hot-water heaters, automobile seats with their stuffing protruding, and all manner of human detritus line the tracks so that one expects to see a family of corpses any minute. But ahead and to the left, gleaming jets are landing at Newark International Airport, and the shape of

Giants Stadium looms in the distance. To the right the burnoff flames top the cracking towers of a huge refinery and dark slums merge into more prosperous tall apartment buildings of Jersey City, while just over the eastern horizon rise the glorious towers of Manhattan.

Like this train, the east is the essence of contradiction. It is wasteful, dirty, and awesomely productive. It is inefficient, decrepit, and fast as lightning. It is mean, criminal, and a fixture of enlightened liberalism. It is polluted, decaying, and full of people who regard the outland as savage. It is secular, profane, and soaring in spires toward the heavens. It is the home of mass man living in stunning combinations of diversity. And to this returning steel-rider, Galileo notwithstanding, it is the very center of the universe.

PART TWO

Spring Heartland

*Remember, our sons and grandsons are
going to do things that would stagger us.*

—DANIEL BURNHAM

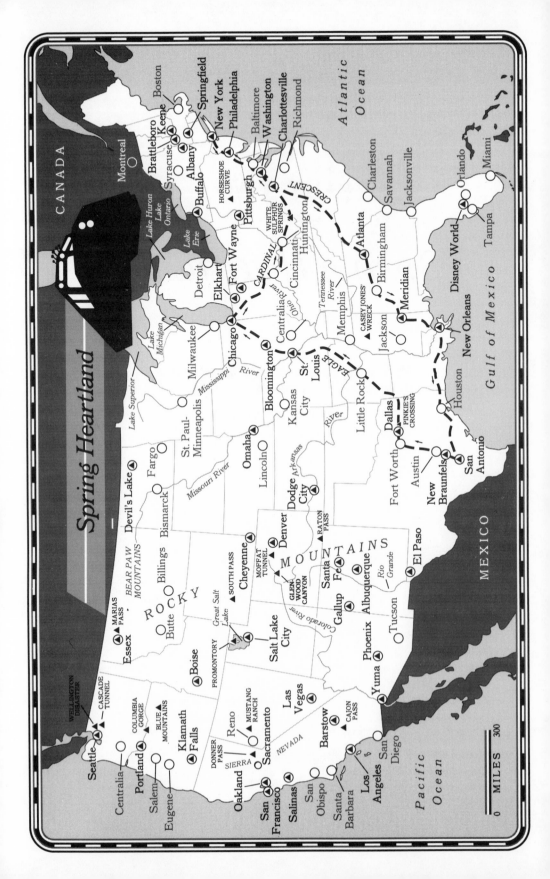

Spring Heartland

Chapter Eight

———

Old Habits Die Hard

THE *CRESCENT*

W͏E have no spring in New Hampshire. There is a long colorful fall, more than enough winter, and then, in the interval between winter and our short, precious summer, something we call "mud season."

Mud season is caused by the frost that is so deeply entrenched in the ground by the end of winter. It lingers in the soil, like an old habit that won't die. The result is mud just beneath the thin veneer of green, and a chilliness whose source is the atavistic earth itself. No one would ever confuse mud season with true spring. It's a wonderful time for Hampshiremen to travel into the heartland of America, anywhere south of the Mason-Dixon Line. I have a special excuse. In the south and midwest run the tracks of my grandfather's railroad.

A springtime ride on Amtrak's *Crescent* from New York to New Orleans via Washington, Charlotte, Atlanta, and Birmingham reveals a slowly changing seasonal spectrum that adds to the delight of escaping the unpleasant northern climate. The fields of the New Jersey truck farms have just been plowed, good brown earth lined with the first flecks of wild green along the margins. In the Philadelphia afternoon

155

the rowing crews are out on the river in heavy sweatshirts, but no one here would think of swimming yet. The cherry trees are in blossom in Washington, and in northern Virginia the springtime chartreuse laced with white dogwood is almost electric. By late afternoon in western-Virginia backyards, people are removing the covers from their pools and cleaning out winter's accumulated leavings. At evening stops along the Blue Ridge foothills, the calls of peepers are loud at the open vestibule doors. By the Georgia morning, vegetable gardens flourish in maturity, full-grown weeds are already asserting themselves, and the peach trees are past blossoming. All day long across Alabama and Mississippi the hot, red southern dust drives folks to the water in pools, under sprinklers, and down by the slow rivers to sit and fish. By evening in the Mississippi bayous, one has entered the tropics and the Spanish moss hangs like ragged drooping curtains of neglected plantation mansions. In New Orleans, a million flowers blaze as the air steams like jazz after the warm showers, and folks sip mint juleps and wipe their brows with white linen.

It wasn't always possible to ride the *Crescent* all the way from New York to New Orleans. Until late in the nineteenth century, the tracks of the south were laid in different gauges than the four feet, eight and a half inches standard in the north. Some were narrower at four and a half feet, but most were wider at five feet. The result was a physical barrier between the regions which hampered economic intercourse as effectively as did political differences. In some cases the reason was a conscious strategy of keeping the northern railcars off southern tracks, thus ensuring that the profits from freight and passenger traffic through the south would accrue to southern interests. In the case of some of the five-foot gauges, it was the farsighted notion that as rail equipment grew in power and size, the wider gauge would make more engineering sense. In other instances it was a more simple matter of cussed independence.

For a time, an attempt was made to develop through cars, called "compromise cars," with special wider wheel surfaces which could run on several gauges. These proved a great disaster in a number of sometimes grisly derailments. By 1900, southern railroads recognized that their odd gauges were just one more impediment to development and they relaid track to match the national gauge.

The irony is that, according to railroad legend, there was even less rationale for the standard gauge than for the various odd ones. The emperors of ancient Rome decreed a proper width for the wheels of their chariots—a measure that converts today to exactly four feet, eight and a half inches. When the first railroads were constructed in England eighteen hundred years later, the rails were arbitrarily laid over the ancient ruts of Roman highways. Initially lacking the technology to build their own engines, the early American railroads had to import their engines from England—engines whose wheels were set up for English track. Thus the Roman gauge came to America, where, with notable exceptions, it was declared the standard in 1886. By late in the century, American engines became the rule for the world, and despite England's later experiments with a wider gauge, America exported the Roman measure to other countries' developing rail systems. Today the gauge established by Emperor Augustus in ancient Rome is that used by most railroads in the world.

Though the relatively narrow standard gauge has hampered the development of railroads in modern times, the balancing of an engine nine feet wide on such narrow rails having long since pushed engineering to the limit, the changeover of rail infrastructure to a wider gauge is today considered an impossibility. Old habits die hard.

"This is definitely not the real *Crescent*," says an expensively dressed woman of patrician bearing in the lounge after dinner as the train pulls out of Alexandria into the Virginia countryside. "There were no crumbs on the tables of the real *Crescent*. There was white linen, crystal, china, and heavy silverware." She is sorry that the half-dozen people in the car today never got a chance to experience the real thing and has nothing but contempt for today's train, which she refers to as "the government's train to New Orleans."

"On the *Crescent*, one felt obliged to dress for travel. Anyone wearing what people wear on the train today would have felt at least out of place, and probably quite uncomfortable. Of course, on the train today, if one dresses as I do, one ruins perfectly good clothes."

But she continues to ride the train and to dress as she always has. She has tried air travel and is appalled by the barbaric conditions of passage without a private compartment, "and one certainly doesn't drive to Los Angeles." She is not impressed by the Superliners she has ridden between New Orleans and L.A. Though the cars are newer, the only real innovations on them are "that miserable stairway" between levels and the sound insulation that deprives one of the reassuring chatter of "Heinie Marouche."

Six blank faces in the lounge pause, wondering, who is Heinie Marouche?

"That's how you can tell a real old-timer like me. 'Clickety-clack' is an invention of silly songwriters. The real sound of the wheels on the tracks is Heinie Marouche. That's what everyone always called it. Listen." Everyone in the lounge car is silent and straining his ears, including the hefty black attendant behind the bar. Sure enough, one by one, we all begin to hear it, "Heinie Marouche, Heinie Marouche, Heinie Marouche," and occasionally when we cross the heavier clatter of a rattling switch a louder refrain of the same pattern, "Heinie Marouche, HEINIE MAROUCHE, Heinie Marouche." The woman says we will never hear the tracks the same way again.

Suddenly the lights go out and the woman groans, "And this is the other thing. So many breakdowns today."

The train slows to a halt in the middle of nowhere, Virginia. The eerie emergency lighting comes on to little effect as the sun sets over the Blue Ridge to the west.

When the train is stopped, conductor R. E. Haney and assistant conductor M. B. Woodburn enter the car and sit down with their radios crackling. The patrician woman leaves for her bedroom, shaking her head. We have apparently lost our head-end power, a short of some sort; the breakers keep blowing. Until the problem is diagnosed, we have been given a red board. "That means we're not going anywhere until they send out some experts on an engine from Washington. They'll snoop around and not find anything and then ride with us with the problem continuing all the way to Atlanta."

For an hour and a half, the train sits on one of the two main-line tracks of the Southern Railway just south of Alexandria. During that time, two long freights roll by and the evening social scene comes to life despite the lack of power. A TV crew from WYFF, Greenville, South Carolina, is on board doing a special for the tenth anniversary of Amtrak's takeover of the *Crescent*. After the "experts" arrive, the train twice starts up with power restored only to have it blow again. As the TV cameras roll, conductor Haney just clenches his teeth and says, "You just gotta have a relaxed attitude in this job." When the train starts up for the third try, someone begins the chant "I think I can, I think I can," and it spreads throughout the now-crowded bar car. The TV crew love it, and this time the train continues, two hours behind schedule.

The elegantly dressed woman returns, still disgusted. The TV crew, attracted by her strikingly formal clothing, pounce on her and buy her a drink. For the next hour she gives them their background on old-time railroad service. Her thesis is that there is no continuity between the past and the present. Some superficial details bear her out—the trains are not as pristine today and there is no white linen on the tables—but for one of my generation, this train and the history of its route and region encourage the opposite conclusion.

The men and women who deliver the service on passenger trains today still ride the entire length of the route, just as they did when they worked for Pullman; the train crew, the conductors, brakemen, and engineer work only their five-hundred-mile division. Thus though the conductor may be the head man in terms of authority, the train really belongs to the service crew, which includes a service chief (the boss), coach car attendants, the chef, the dining steward, the bartender, the waiters, and, of course, the sleeping-car attendants, formerly called porters.

Throughout the century before Amtrak, when service was provided mostly by the Pullman Company, the porters were exclusively black men recruited primarily from the Carolinas and Georgia. Early Pullman records were destroyed by the Chicago fire in 1871, but railroad tradition holds that the first porters were particularly well trained former household slaves who brought their considerable skills in maintaining southern graciousness onto the railroads in the years following the Civil War. Shortly it became customary for the Pullman Company to rely on the judgment of successful porters already in their employ to recommend new applicants for positions. Thus to a large extent, this tight community of black men chose and trained its own successors and was as responsible for the Pullman tradition as were the much-touted standards of Pullman management.

Well into the twentieth century, Pullman employment tended to be hereditary. Until the civil rights movement began to open new doors, the calling was second only to preaching as a stepping-stone to black affluence. Ambitious porters who didn't eventually go to college or into business themselves often lived to see their children do so. It wasn't so much a matter of earnings that made porters prosperous as it was the mobility of their station itself. Pullman porters saw the world, more of it even than most middle-class white men. They dealt on a day-to-day basis with moguls of business, and they practiced the rules of etiquette prevailing in the highest echelons of American society. They came to be keen judges of human nature and high practitioners of the art of "people management." In short, they developed a worldliness that was hard for a black man to come by in pre-civil-rights America. It is gospel among black service attendants today that many of their race who have risen to positions of power and affluence in the past few decades had fathers or grandfathers who worked for Pullman.

At the end of the run, the old-time Pullman porter set up his car for the next day and headed for the bunkhouse and the camaraderie of his fellows. Here commenced the oral tradition known in the trade as the Baker Heater League, for a type of obsolete heater once used on many Pullman cars. Tales ranging from heroism to simple embarrassment, from the tallest lies to profound truth, were the stuff of the Baker Heater League. If soldiers had their Sergeant York and engineers their Casey Jones, porters had the mythical Daddy Joe.

Daddy Joe was so big he could stand in the aisle and simultaneously make up the upper bunks on either side, one with each arm. He was so dark that passengers in upper bunks who called for him in the night wouldn't know that he was standing towering over them until he broke into a smile. But it was the power of his oration that was really his trademark. When a Mississippi flood inundated sleeping cars and passengers panicked, Daddy Joe delivered a speech so soothing that his charges stayed in the car until it reached higher ground. When his train was attacked by Indians on the plains, Daddy Joe climbed out on top of his car and thundered at them in their own language; tamed, they accepted the Pullman blankets he tossed to them before the train chugged off into the sunset. Confronted with a gang of desperate robbers in Oklahoma, Daddy Joe squared off with the leader in the sleeping-car aisle and, as his antagonist drew his gun, unleashed such a furious verbal blast that the offender misfired, dropped his gun, and was captured without a fuss.

But the most famous of Daddy Joe's lines was simple advice for his peers: "We don't get no tips till the end of the run." Whether Daddy Joe ever actually existed, the advice attributed to him was ingrained in the soul of every porter in the land.

The Baker Heater League also told stories documented by history. There was wealth for the porter who was left $2,500 in the will of Diamond Jim Brady. There was tragedy for Oscar Daniels, the only porter to have a sleeping car named after him, who died from the scalding he got when he closed the vestibule door against an exploding engine, thus saving the lives of all his passengers. There was only terror for porter Johnson who woke to find his two empty cars hurtling down a grade with no engine and no brakes. When he ran to the head end of the first car and saw no engine he mused, "This is queer railroading." When he ran to the rear and found the same thing, he reported, "Then I turned white." He was saved from "slapping an oncoming square in the mouth" by switchmen who shunted him onto an upgrade where he finally stopped. There was pure embarrassment for porter

Johnnie Jones, who took a load of shoes into an adjacent car to shine them, only to find when he had finished that the cars had been separated and sent on different routes.

But the greatest of the historically verifiable Baker Heater League stories is that of porter John Blair and the Skunk Lake fire. On the afternoon of September 1, 1894, the St. Paul & Duluth's train 4 was headed south from Duluth with a full load of passengers. Engineer Root could see smoke in the sky ahead of him, but there was no warning sounded at the stops he had made before Hinckley village. As he rolled south at fifty miles per hour, a stiff southerly breeze pushed a huge forest fire northward at nearly thirty miles per hour. Approaching Hinckley, Root saw blossoms of flame bursting in the woods surrounding the town, and by the time he stopped at the station, the town itself was ablaze. No one detrained. Instead, dozens of fleeing, panicked citizens of the town clambered aboard the train. Engineer Root threw the engine into full-throttle reverse and began backing up as fast as he could in hopes of getting clear of the fire's leading edge, which had now raced on in the direction from which the train had come. He never made it.

Never was there a train ride quite like this one,* with fires raging in the forests on both sides of the tracks till the ties themselves burst into flames and the cars seemed to be entering the portals of hell. Porter John Blair was attending the chair car that day and stayed cool even when the train itself began to burn. He ran through the cars with towels soaked at the drinking-water tank, wrapping passengers' heads and telling them to lie down on the floor. He wrestled with men who had lost their wits and doused the lamps that began to explode when the heat ignited their oil.

When the woodwork inside the cars began to burn furiously and women's hair flamed like torches, Blair went to work with a water fire extinguisher till there was not a drop left.

By now the train had pulled abreast of Skunk Lake, a mudhole that proved to be salvation for the riders of train 4 that day. Blair led the few other crew members who had not already been incapacitated by heat and smoke inhalation in assisting women and children off the train and into the cool slime of the lake. Only when the last passengers were out of the train did Blair himself, his clothes smoldering and his hair and eyebrows gone, stagger into the water.

The fire was one of the greatest forest fires of all time, killing over

* At least not till the summer of 1989, when a remarkably similar story occurred along the route of Canada's Bayline in northern Manitoba.

four hundred Minnesotans before it was brought under control. And yet, of the hundreds of terrifying experiences it generated, the story that is legendary is that of the train and the heroic porter who wore to his dying day the gold watch and badge emblazoned with a burning train which were his reward for his "gallant and faithful discharge of his duty."

But for all of its relative glamour and opportunity, the life of a Pullman porter was no sinecure. Pay was low (until the late 1930s about $20 a month), and a decent living could be made only through the careful cultivation of good tips. Porters bought their own uniforms, meals, and even the polish for shoeshines for the first ten years of their service. Older porters with seniority could bump a young porter off a good-tipping run on a whim, and the intimacy of a man's relationship to his white charges presented a minefield of potential dangers in which deference and discretion became the keys to survival.

The price of the opportunities provided by Pullman work was, of course, the fact of working in a subservient position as racially defined as slavery. Porters did not wear name tags and were addressed as "porter," "boy," or, worse, "George" ("Let George do it"). One George Dulany, a white man, instituted the Society for the Prevention of Calling Pullman Porters George and claimed to have cured more than ten thousand passengers of the habit that grated so on porters' self-respect. On Amtrak, attendants are no longer even called porters; they all wear name tags and introduce themselves by their first names as they greet boarding passengers. But old habits die hard. I have heard today's attendants, black, white, male, and female, addressed as "porter," "boy," even "George."

My sleeping-car attendant for the overnight run to Atlanta is Darryl Kent. Though my slumbercoach accommodation is not first class, Darryl scurries about the car offering better service than I have seen on some Superliner sleepers. Towels and washcloths are meticulously fluffed and folded, and the bunk is made up with a precise crispness that promises a fine night's sleep. Darryl makes conversation with all the passengers in the car and encourages them to think of things he can do for them. I ask him to tell me about his job.

For Darryl his Amtrak job is his ticket to ride out of today's vicious circle of unemployment among urban blacks. Guys he grew up with are still "back on the street going nowhere." He was lucky to be enrolled in a Job Corps program which trained him for keypunch, CRT, and office work. Though the training did not specifically relate to the work he now does for Amtrak, it taught him the language and the habits of successfully employed people. "There are rules to the game of being employable. The Job Corps taught me those rules—the right things to say to people, the ways to respond to situations, to be knowledgeable and intelligent."

He joined the Brotherhood of Railway and Airline Clerks and went to work as a bartender on a Florida train, the *Silver Meteor*. "Now that was a wild time, man. People traveling that train left me tips that weren't money, you know what I mean. Tips that are the beginning of bad habits. And I saw a lotta guys get sucked into that."

It's healthier for him here. "This train is not your fast track. A young guy like me doesn't need the temptations of that life. I like the slower pace of work here." He likes working the slumbercoach that is dropped off at Atlanta, though the greater opportunity for big tips on the first-class sleepers that go all the way to New Orleans is appealing. This route is reasonably short, and he gets a turnaround day in Atlanta for rest. "It used to be that dudes like myself would have, you know, like a gal in every port. You'd meet girls on the train but you couldn't do anything about it till your shift was done. There was an old saying, 'We don't get no chicks till the end of the run.'" But AIDS has changed the old habits. "Even at the end of the line, today they're all afraid and so am I."

Darryl is young enough that to him the Baker Heater League is itself a legend and Daddy Joe's advice has undergone a curious twist. But even in the 1980s, he continues the experience of the black Pullman porter who rode the rails to worldliness in the white man's society.

Though Atlanta still hosts major railroad yards of the Norfolk Southern and CSX conglomerates, the sprawling automobile-dependent city is not the rail town it once was. Founded in 1837 by Colonel Stephen Long as the terminus for the Western & Atlantic Railway, it was originally named simply Terminus, but in 1845, the city fathers invoked a legend worthy of the future they envisioned when they renamed the city Atlanta. Though residents of well-established and well-heeled Savannah and Charleston viewed the name as pretentious, particularly for a place whose claim to fame was the dirty railroad, Atlanta did come to be the capital of the "New South." For me, the city is a gateway to the history of southern railroads; Atlanta is the first city I have visited that traditionally has been a center of railroads not based in the north or west.

Though the first steam locomotives in the land ran on the Charleston & Hamburg in South Carolina way back in 1830, railroad building in the south lagged behind that in the rest of the nation for nearly a century. The men who played the key roles in welding together small start-up roads into great ones operated primarily out of the bastions of monetary power in the northeast, where opinions about the profitability of economic enterprises in the south and about the long-term effects of the south's "peculiar institution" were hardly sanguine. As late as 1893, J. P. Morgan, in explaining his initial refusal to take over the management of the lines that would become the powerful Southern Railroad, saw the problem in starkly racial terms: "Niggers are lazy, ignorant, and unprogressive; railroad traffic is created only by industrious, intelligent, and ambitious people."

The depredations of the Civil War certainly played their role, too. While northern railroads were thriving on the wartime traffic, southern lines were being torn up and plundered by both sides. The tale of the Louisville & Nashville, one of the south's earliest successful long-haul railroads, is instructive.

Before the war, the L&N ran a successful line linking Atlanta and the heartland of the south with the river trade on the Ohio. Like the states it traversed north of Georgia, the railroad attempted to remain neutral at the start of hostilities, but quickly the northern-leaning Louisvillers despaired at seeing so much of their local produce hauled off to the rebel south. They pulled up tracks and blew up bridges in ironic defiance of the Union guards attempting to preserve the integrity of the line, and set the tone of L&N operations for the next four years.

When the road's branch to Memphis was seized by a Confederate regiment, a major chunk of its rolling stock was put out of action, and the road became an issue in the strategy of the war. The Union belatedly issued an order forbidding the carrying of goods to the south, and the battle was on.

Confederate bands occupied the line as far south as Elisabethtown, Tennessee, until General Don Carlos Buell began his march through "neutral territory" to Nashville. As he advanced, he found that the dashing Confederate cavalry had shown a rare interest in the unromantic work of destroying track. The Confederates learned quickly that it wasn't enough to pull rails from ties and set the ties ablaze; L&N crews, working out of loyalty more to the railroad than to the cause of either side, quickly repaired such depredations. To really wreck a railroad, it was necessary to heat the rails red-hot and bend them into steel pretzels.

Nonetheless, the L&N repair crews accomplished the miraculous work of getting the line in shape so that trains ran over it again in April 1862. Union freight arrived in Louisville aboard cars with the standard gauge, four feet, eight and a half inches, and the cars had to be retooled for the five-foot gauge of the L&N. Before the union had a chance to make the same use of the L&N that it had of the B&O in eastern campaigns, General Braxton Bragg struck and occupied much of the line for the Confederacy.

Up and down the line the forces of Bragg and Buell skirmished throughout 1862. As the preponderance of the Union force began to make itself felt, the Confederates increasingly relied on the guerrilla tactics of General John Hunt Morgan's raiders. They dynamited tunnels, burned trestles, and tore up track in lightning strikes wherever Buell's forces were thin. Again and again the long-suffering crews of the railroad cleaned up after the rampaging soldiers and kept the line running. Cordwood needed to fuel the locomotives became increasingly scarce until the road hired five hundred freed Negroes and charged them with keeping the engines supplied.

Twice the Confederate guerrillas captured freights, set them ablaze, and headed them back down the track, unmanned and at full throttle, in the direction from which they had come. Both times serious collisions with oncoming passenger trains were averted only by the alertness and last-minute intervention of repair crews working near fortuitously placed siding turnouts.

Near the end of the year, Morgan's forces struck in one last desperate spasm. On Christmas Eve his poorly equipped army attacked Union cavalry at Glasgow, Kentucky, where Morgan vowed to "get them guns from the Yankees." He failed to capture many weapons, but did succeed in raiding the Yankees' supply of Christmas turkeys. Fortified with the roasted birds, his ragtag cavalry attacked a supply train on Christmas Day and again filled their stomachs though not their ammunition belts. Exuberant with feasting, Morgan's troops ravaged the L&N right-of-way one more time before retiring for the year. Again the tireless repair crews went to work, and immediately a series of devastating rains washed out much of the line they had just repaired. As the new year began, the long-suffering gandy dancers of the L&N must have felt that all the gods of war and nature were allied against them in their thankless task, but they made this neutral line angling into the heart of Dixie one of the greatest weapons in the Union arsenal.

There is a myth grown out of the war that Sherman's armies lived off the land in their march to Atlanta and the sea. Nothing could be further from the truth. The supply of Sherman's 100,000 men and 35,000 animals for his 196-day campaign was entrusted to the L&N, which ran 160 cars a day over its battered single-track line throughout the campaign. Both Sherman and his campaign historian, Robert S.

Henry, concluded that the L&N, with its connection through the Western Atlantic to Atlanta, was the key to the campaign which "resulted in the fall of Atlanta ... the final deciding act in the Confederate war."

While the battle-tested L&N survived the war and eventually even reached New Orleans, the only southern road with a history anything like that of the great trunk lines up north was beginning to take shape. After the war, a small haywire road, the Richmond & Danville, created a through route to Atlanta by buying up another little line, the North Carolina Railroad. In the 1870s the operation acquired additional lines into South Carolina and the Appalachians to the southwest. Throughout these years of depression in the south, it was the money of the mighty Pennsylvania interests that held these little projects together. When southern economic interests began to revive in the 1880s, the south began to build a major railroad of its own in the Richmond & West Point Terminal Railway, which picked up the pieces connected to the old Richmond & Danville and added the East Tennessee and the Georgia Pacific. By the 1890s the system, such as it was, had suffered the usual ills of overexpansion, unjustified payment of dividends, and bankruptcy. It had earned its place among the ranks of "real railroads."

It was at this point that J. P. Morgan made his infamous racial slur against southern railroading when Richmond interests approached him to take over the management of the southern lines. But Morgan relented, and his management built the great Southern Railroad over whose tracks I am traveling today. What Morgan brought to the south were the two hallmarks of successful trunk lines in the north: the building of first-rate track and facilities throughout the system and the aggressive seeking of acquisitions and alliances for connections to create a network of continental scope. By the second decade of the twentieth century, the Southern would link virtually all points of significance in the north with those in the south, with the exception of Florida, which remained in the realm of the Florida East Coast Railway and the Seaboard Air Line railroads.

But old habits die hard. Try as they might, the managers of the Southern could never quite succeed in making the service of the road conform to that of the northern trunk lines. Southern custom and habit could never adopt the "bustle" or "scurry" so characteristic of railroads in the north. Southern conductors proved themselves downright insubordinate on issues such as punctually pulling out of a station and leaving tardy ladies on the platform or interrupting the romantic farewells of parting lovers. Dining-car stewards insisted on a pace of service that required meal shifts of up to eight hours. But these idiosyncrasies became the virtues of southern railroading in the twentieth century. The Southern's *Crescent* connecting the northeast to New Orleans via Atlanta was one of the last two non-Amtrak railroads operating into the 1970s. My ride on the *Crescent* today confirms that it certainly wasn't the scenery which kept the route alive, as it did the Denver & Rio Grande route. It was a grace of service, a style of behavior, found only in the south, and despite equipment failures and the leveling management of Amtrak, traces of it survive on the run today.

Riding the *Crescent* in daylight from Atlanta to Meridien, Mississippi, I make a delightful discovery. The Heritage coaches on this train still have the old smoking lounges with three large comfy cushioned chairs, stainless-steel sinks, a large mirror, and a toilet in a separate compartment. Here I discover that I can smoke my pipe to my heart's content and strike up conversation with men who wander in for a smoke or a stretch. They offer a series of vignettes which initiate me into the habits of the deep south.

Phil Norlund, a Dallas ad man, sits down and clears up a mystery that has nagged me on previous trips on the *Crescent*. The dominant natural feature of much of this route today is not cotton or Spanish moss or even the plentiful southern pines. It is a vine that chokes virtually all other vegetation in the places where it is thickest. Phil tells me that it's kudzu, a ground cover imported from Africa twenty years ago. It was originally used for the margins of highways and for erosion control, but it spread so wildly that it came to be an ecological disaster, choking off all native forms of vegetation.

When it started engulfing trees, the paper and lumber companies called for action. A few years back the state stepped in and poisoned it all. " 'Course, five years from now," says Phil, "the cows will all die or the bass will stop bitin' or something else terrible will happen. This is what comes of messing with the natural order of things—like the killer bees."

He says that's what caused the oil bust in the western south— Louisiana and Texas. Just when the economy had begun to develop a natural balance of oil, cattle, cotton, foodstuffs, transportation, and manufacturing, along came OPEC and the oil crisis. The banks put all their money on oil, and today only federal support prevents total collapse of the industry. In Houston, foreclosures on mortgages are running at four thousand a month. People just walk into the bank, drop off their keys, and split.

When I mention my home in New England, he laughs. He knows guys who used to ride around with bumper stickers that read, "Drive 90—Freeze a Yankee." Today some of those guys have left Texas and moved to the northeast, where they abandon their Texas drawl and learn to like chowder and lobster. "You Yankees always get the last laugh, doncha?"

The talk turns to relations between the races. As in conversations with whites throughout the south, I am impressed by the earnestness with which Phil wishes to convince me that southern racism is a thing of the past. Here it is gospel that today northern hypocrisy is the greatest racial problem in America. But he concludes the discussion with a comparison of blacks to kudzu. "We brought in the slaves that didn't belong here and had to learn to live with the consequences—since of course you couldn't deal with that problem the same way they dealt with the kudzu." It's the first glimpse I have of a way of thinking about the racial issue that reminds me of mud season back home. There is great pride in the greening of superficial relations between the races, but there is a layer of slippery mud just below the surface that suggests an even more deeply imbedded frost of residual attitudes that won't thaw for generations.

Later a black man comes in. He's anxious to try to get a ride in the engine cab, but his desire is more than the usual. He is a motorman on a New York subway; he's riding the train to L.A. to escape the hectic life for a while.

Gary Lane grew up beside the tracks in Atlanta and then Southampton, Long Island. He says the trains in both places were so regular that people literally set their watches and regulated their lives by it. He recalls his mother's rule in Southampton—be in the house by the time the train whistle blows at 3:35 every afternoon.

He played chicken with the train as a kid. There was a cut in his neighborhood where the tracks emerged from a blind crossing into a station. He and his buddies used to ride their bikes into the crossing and see who could come closest to the train easing its way into the station. The apoplectic engineer would shake his fist at them and holler obscenities. Gary's greatest terror today is the thought of encountering kids playing that game.

But he doesn't see much fooling around with the electric subway trains, not even by the gangs who paint the cars with graffiti in the yards at night. "It's the third rail that does it—it really keeps assholes at a distance." Every time someone is killed by it, the tabloids pick up the story with gory pictures and headlines like "Man Touches Third

Rail—Looks Like Burnt Meatloaf." It happens just often enough to put a little respect into people.

But Gary prefers to talk about what he likes about his job. He believes the media put a bad rap on New York subways. "Sure, you need a little common sense—there are things you don't do in New York, but then there are things that I don't do in a small town here in Alabama." His favorite recollection is of a wedding performed on his train to Rockaway. People just riding the subway dropped their plans for the day and joined the wedding party. "By the time we got to Rockaway, that was the biggest wedding party ever. Now you just don't see things like that anywhere but New York, right?"

Gary doesn't remember having that kind of sense of humor when he lived in the south. "In Atlanta, all I remember is bein' careful. There was a mean white man who lived on our block, and if you met him walking down the sidewalk, you had to detour out into the road or he'd invent some reason to cuff you one." Gary doesn't like to think about his early childhood in Atlanta. For him, life began when his mother took him to Long Island. He views traveling into the south today as a kind of personal challenge. "I want to go to New Orleans and be the same fun-loving person I am back in New York."

A man who is so overweight that he has to sidle through the doorway to get into the smoking lounge joins me and chain-smokes four cigarettes before leaving. "It's all that good New Orleans cooking," he says as he eases himself into the chair beside me and Gary. "I took up smoking to cut down on my weight, so now I have two habits that are out of control."

Terry Lee Van den Grapt and I quickly discover that we were given the same names at birth. By family legend, I had always thought that the Lee in my name came from General Robert E. Lee. "No way," says Terry Lee. "You're a World War II baby, aren't you?" I was born in 1947. "It was from 'Terry Lee and the Pirates,' the comic strip. Lotsa World War II babies were named after that." Terry Lee was a rebel with a name that felt good on southern tongues. There were Terry Lee jokes and Terry Lee songs. "Lotsa people adopted Terry Lee as a nickname. You and I are lucky—we got the real thing." He wants to know how New Englanders like the name, and I tell him that I've never told anyone at home my middle name; I've never liked it. As I say this, I can feel the mud slipping beneath the green of our fresh friendship. "Why not?" he asks, but he doesn't really want to know, quickly shifting the conversation to the firm, safe ground of how far the train is behind schedule. I have violated the man's pride in his name.

* * *

In Meridian, Mississippi—located in the deepest part of the deep south—I detrain in search of roots. Though no one in my family ever lived here, my grandfather's route in Illinois was a part of the Gulf, Mobile & Ohio system formerly headquartered in Meridian, and somehow, aside from my name and the fact that my family lived in Richmond for a while, I always felt that there was something else southern in my heritage.

My lodgings are a disappointment, a chain motel on the outskirts of town at the junction of two interstates, but I am introduced to a piece of the soul of the region in the parking lot shortly after my arrival.

A shiny red pickup hauling a horse trailer pulls in late in the afternoon. The driver, a "cowboy" attending a rodeo nearby, has his wife, son, and two prize horses in tow. Meanwhile four young trainees from the nearby naval air base, two men and two women, are deep into a rowdy afternoon drunk. Led by a short stocky character built like a stump, they snitch cowboy's halters and sneak giggling back to their room.

When cowboy emerges from checking in to find his halters missing, the Navy trainees charge out of their room twirling the halters over their heads and hollering, "Yippee yi yo, git along little dogies!" as they gallop around the parking lot.

Cowboy challenges stump on his third circuit: "I don't appreciate you taking my halters."

"Well, why don't you try to take them back, motherfucker?" responds stump.

Without an instant's hesitation cowboy swings and lays stump out flat on the pavement. He turns on the other three, women included, and growls, "Next asshole." But there aren't any more now, and the Navy skulks off to lick its wounds.

Someone calls a cop, and his sympathetic advice to cowboy is to find someplace else to stay tonight if he values his horses.

After cowboy and his family have left, I encounter the Navy crew at the swimming pool. Stump is cooling off the bloody swollen welt on his face while his peers bad-mouth the cowboy in a streak of foul invective. An elderly lady who has been sitting by the pool gets up to leave, and stump is instantly out of the pool to encourage her to stay. He apologizes for his friends' language and his suspect appearance. He is all charm and tells her that she reminds him of his mother, only she is much prettier. She does stay and he sits down with her to talk about her grandchildren.

I encounter this fine line between charm and aggression again in the motel bar that evening. Somehow a conversation has developed with two young natives, John and Ike, about eating wild meat. Ike, a wiry, bushy-haired guy in loose jeans and a flannel shirt, is a wild-meat enthusiast and leads the conversation. John just nods approval of everything Ike says. "I eat all of it," says Ike. "Armadillo, coon, rattlesnake, deer, squirrel, even groundhog, though it don't smell too good when you clean it." Ike is amused to be talking to a New Englander about his favorite subject. "Never met a real Yankee before, just those city slickers from D.C. or Atlanta." He warmly shakes my hand, buys me a beer, and is full of charm.

He expresses admiration for northern fur-bearing animals. Apparently wild mammals in the south are generally much smaller than in the north; a 125-pound deer is considered a good kill in Mississippi. When I describe the coons I've killed raiding my garden he is impressed. "I'd like to barbecue a coon that big just once."

I return the flattery by complimenting the south on its huge bass and catfish. Ike's eyes sparkle with delight; apparently I am playing the game of regional comparisons just right. But I blow it.

It begins when I tell him I have just visited Atlanta. "Whatcha go there for? 'New south,' hell, that place is a shithole. And they think they're God's gift to the south."

I try to explain that I wasn't all that impressed with Atlanta either, though I have to admire a southern city that's made such progressive strides under a black mayor. Ike looks confused for just a moment and then his nostrils flare. I can see a shift into a wholly different emotional and physical stance—combat readiness. "Well, that's just great," he says, chugs his beer, and slams the glass down on the bar. Before I can figure out what to say next, he has paid his tab and, with John in tow, is out the door.

The pleasant young woman behind the bar can't help but comment, "I guess you pushed his button. He was ready to pop you one." I tell her about stump and the cowboy; and she says, "Well, that's our boys, some of 'em anyway. It's not really in their nature to fight, they just wanta be friendly. But their daddies teach 'em to go at it over the drop of a hat from the time they're little boys."

Her brother came home from school one day when he was seven years old and entered the house by the back door instead of the front as usual. Her daddy was home from work at the mill early and wanted to know why the youngster hadn't walked home down the street. When the boy explained that some older boys had teased him on the street the day before and that he was afraid to encounter them again, the old man called him a coward and no son of his. He refused to set eyes on the boy for a week.

One day weeks later, her daddy came home with a new .22 rifle under his arm. The family didn't have much money then, and she could tell her daddy had saved to buy it. He just said, "Son, this is for you. It's time to make you a man."

"It wasn't like Daddy wanted my brother to go out and shoot those guys who had hassled him in the street. But Daddy's son had failed his first test of manhood, I guess, and Daddy felt responsible. My brother was so glad just to have Daddy speak to him again, not to mention holding that shiny black rifle, that he took to it like a duck to water. Oh, it's the daddies that do it, all right. They got their own unfinished quarrels with the world, and the sons learn to carry on the fight."

In my room later with a copy of William Faulkner's *The Bear*, I try to immerse myself vicariously in the spirit of the region he wrote about. I've had no more success than most readers in deciphering the unintelligible mystery of the story's ending, but I know that there is a bear that has drawn blood, a boy and a gun, a noble dead black man, and an ashamed living white man who ends the story insanely busting up his gun with its own barrel.

William Faulkner's great-grandfather founded the railroad for which my grandfather worked. Colonel William Falkner wrote a novel, commanded Confederate troops in the war, and used his stirring oratory to inspire fellow Mississippians to support the building of a line that would eventually stretch from Mobile and New Orleans through Meridian to St. Louis and Chicago. It came to be known as the Rebel Route, and its history aptly seems a rebel yell of victorious defiance.

Initially built largely by prisoners driven by brutal bullwhip-and-rifle-toting guards, the lines that became the Gulf, Mobile & Ohio survived the carpetbagger years and became prosperous enough in the twentieth century to buy out the venerable Alton route running from Chicago to St. Louis. The Alton was no less than the route over which the first Pullman cars had run and over which the body of the slain President Lincoln had been carried to Springfield.

Thus the GM&O of the twentieth century, headquartered in Meridian, Mississippi, came to run the redoubtable trains named the *Abraham Lincoln* and the *Ann Rutledge*—the very trains my grandfather engineered. The management replaced the slogan "The Rebel Route" with "The Alton Route" in a show of conquest, not deference.

After all, it was in Alton, Illinois, that Elijah Lovejoy, a leading abolitionist before the war, was lynched.

Colonel Falkner met a bad end himself. In 1889, the conduct of business and politics in Mississippi was still very much a man-against-man proposition. Falkner had emerged victorious from a fierce electoral contest with one R. J. Thurmond for a seat in the Mississippi legislature. Just after the election, Thurmond met him in the street, a revolver in his jacket. Falkner raised a hand and opened his mouth, perhaps to utter some conciliatory oration, and Thurmond pulled the revolver and fired right into it, blowing Falkner's lower brain out the back of his head.

It's Sunday morning in Meridian, and the sun is already hot even though it's only April. Front Street, which runs by the station and along the rail yards, is deserted, as is 22nd Street, which intersects Front Street and crosses the yards on a bridge. I spot several freshly emptied Night Train Express bottles, the brand of cheap reconstituted wine preferred by rail-traveling hoboes, and one Richard's Wild Irish Rose, the brand of the home-guard winos who hang around the yards but don't actually catch out on freights.

Across the yards I can see a crew at work on track repair. A yard engine is making up a freight train down under the bridge. In the Amtrak station, a stucco-and-clay-tile abridgment of something that was obviously once much grander, Perry Fairchild catches up on paperwork. The northbound *Crescent* is due in a little after 11:00, and Perry is checking the manifest for any special instructions concerning the passengers who will board or disembark here.

"Hell, no, I'm not the stationmaster," he says by way of introduction. "I'm just a general all-around good ole boy flunkie." Despite his modesty, I can quickly see that Perry is a man of a newer south than Ike. To him there is nothing strange about encountering a Yankee traveling the *Crescent*.

He takes me out to the yard and points out the old GM&O headquarters, gifted to the city before the railroad sold out to Illinois Central. Illinois Central sold its GM&O real estate, and today Meridian is the crossroads for only three remaining railroads: the big Norfolk Southern, the regional Midsouth, and the local Meridian and Bigby, which still has its headquarters here.

He kicks a Night Train Express bottle and I ask about hoboes. "They're pretty rare today, but there were a lot of them just about five years ago. They'd come through here, especially in winter, and congregate around the burning dump at the far end of the yards. Then we got a real tough rail detective and we don't see 'em much anymore."

Perry declares that racial issues have become downright irrelevant in Meridian these days. He remembers stories about the bad times when he was just a little kid. "I guess they shot some of 'em and dumped 'em in a dam they were building up near Philadelphia, Mississippi. But that stuff's light-years away from my generation." He tells how just last week, as he was moving his family into a new home, his kids were outside making friends with the neighbor black kids. It turned out the black kids' mother had gone to school with Perry's wife and they all became fast friends over a few beers that very evening.

Perry honestly believes that segregation in this region was never as vicious as portrayed in myth. Though the blacks didn't have any of the better jobs, he remembers the dressing-down his mother got from white neighbors when she passed a black woman by on the highway. She was told that that kind of unkindness just didn't go in Meridian.

This is the heart of the region where the horrific events surrounding the death of Medgar Evers and documented in the film *Mississippi Burning* took place, but this time I hold my tongue and am rewarded with some good tips on the town.

At Perry's suggestion, I hike across the tracks toward the old GM&O headquarters, where the corporate name still shows in the flaking paint on the clapboards. Here my grandfather's time cards were sent and his paychecks signed. But inside, the old offices are cluttered with featureless forgotten litter, a few caches of tools used by the track crews, and cases of soft drinks.

Outside I spot a 2-8-0 Baldwin steam engine built in Philadelphia in 1928 and some old passenger cars, possibly awaiting refurbishing for excursion runs, and, across the yard, the unmistakable signs of a hobo jungle. It's a mini-jungle, just two hobos and their stuff, but it has the hallmarks I have heard and read about. Their bedrolls are hanging on the bushes drying in the sun after yesterday's drizzle. The hoboes themselves are moving about under a plastic tarp thrown over the branches, and I can see them take frequent slugs from a plastic milk jug filled with water.

A railroad supervisor who is checking up on the track-repair crew wants to know my purpose in being here in the yard on a Sunday morning. Satisfied with my presence, he gestures toward the hoboes and grumbles, "Those goddam sombitches. I call the cops and run 'em off all the time and they're always back. The other day, five or six of 'em just pushed over one of our old buildings here. I've found 'em sleeping right inside like they owned the place."

The hoboes have seen me talking to the supervisor, so when I cross the tracks to talk to them, they gather up their stuff fast and head on down the tracks. One of them, a young stocky fellow, hails me with the universal sign of contempt, an upraised middle finger.

I turn my attention instead to the track crew, who are repairing a bent switch where a derailment occurred yesterday. There are machines today that make this kind of work easy, but here, as on many southern railroads, they do it the old way. They use a rail jack, very similar to a large auto jack, to pry up the skewed rail from its spikes, and the jack is then used to bend the rail horizontally into its proper position. A gauger is laid on the rails to get the right width, and two burly blacks swing their hammers in perfect coordination to drive in the new spikes. The plastic hard hats they wear would offer scant protection if their coordination failed and a hammer blow caught one in the head.

Another crew replaces old ties with a similar routine. One man picks the earth at one end of each tie, a second digs out the loose stuff with a spade, and a third uses a rail jack to lift the rail. Meanwhile, a fourth with a tool like a big cat's paw pulls the old spikes, then uses a crowbar to pry the rail loose from the old tie. Two guys swing spades and sink the blades into the old tie, then pull it into the trench prepared by the pickers and diggers. The old tie is lifted out and a new one shoved in its place. Then the gauger is applied and the rail jack is used to adjust the rails. One man slides fishplates under the rail while another drops new spikes in place. The chore ends with the tandem hammer men pounding home the new spikes. It takes the crew about seven minutes to replace each tie. That means nine ties an hour, seventy-two ties—about a hundred feet of track—in an eight-hour work day. According to the Association of American Railroads, there are ten thousand miles of working track in need of tie replacement in the United States today.

Perry Fairchild has told me that the high point of my visit to Meridian will be Sunday-noon dinner at Weidmann's Restaurant, founded in 1870, listed on the National Historic Register, and run by the same family for four generations. It is located on 22nd Street just a block away from the tracks. On entering I am immediately overwhelmed by the setting. The dark woodwork, the wall clutter of black-and-white celebrity photos, and the real old wooden ceiling fans are the first keys to the past in this place. There are also deerhead trophies and stuffed swordfish on the walls. The floor is brick, and in the family dining area, at the far end away from the lunch counter, a huge fireplace presides. The ceiling is ornate tin. Seeburg jukebox speakers are mounted along a high wainscoting that bears rows of decorative dishes.

Sunday dinner at Weidmann's is plain food made fancy. It begins with a fruit-and-marshmallow salad that takes me back to my grandmother's kitchen in Bloomington. For the remaining courses, I choose cream of chicken soup, onion-smothered round steak, hash brown potato casserole, green beans wrapped in bacon and cloves, and homemade sesame bread. There are no throwaways in this meal, no packaged breads, no overcooked vegetables, no instant potatoes.

Young families and elderly couples begin drifting in after church around noon. Everyone knows everyone else. All are dressed in their Sunday best. The young mothers and their preteen daughters, decked out in ruffles and lace, give a fresh meaning to the term "southern belle." They display a perfect squeaky-clean beauty that I had thought existed only in fashion magazines and ads for facial soap. The fathers, on the other hand, could pass as Boston yuppies until they speak with an accent that clashes with their Brooks Brothers clothes. One of the older gentlemen, with his white suit, white hair, and perfectly manicured mustache and beard, makes Colonel Sanders look positively seedy. The children maintain impeccable manners throughout the meal and are rewarded by the opportunity to rummage through Weidmann's treasure chest for prizes when they leave.

Sonny MacWilliams, generally called Mack, is the current proprietor, having married into the family business. The last generation of Weidmanns produced only daughters, and the pattern will repeat itself with the fifth generation, since Mack himself has no sons. His eldest daughter has already married a man who will carry on the business.

Mack gets plenty of advice from patrons. There's a ninety-six-year-old lady who comes in every day to point out where Mack falls short of his predecessors; she has known all but the founding generation. Mack's mother-in-law, at eighty-seven, still takes a proprietary interest in the business, and then there's all the attention generated by the listing on the National Historic Register a few years back. "Yeah," says Mack, "there's a lot of pressure to carrying on a tradition. It wears me out sometimes."

Mack is a rail fan who isn't all that pleased about how change has affected Meridian. He recalls the days when the railroad was the major employer in Meridian. "They called it Meridian Shops then or just plain Shops. Everyone worked for the railroad—they'd come in and cash their paychecks here. You lived with the sounds of the railroad day and night. I hated to see it when the GM&O was sold out and they tore down half of the station." He shows me a collection of old framed photos of railroad action hanging on the wall facing the lunch-counter seats. In the center position of honor hangs a magnificent shot of the old Meridian station as it was in its heyday.

Mack was active in an effort to get Amtrak to run a train from Meridian to Dallas. The idea is not so farfetched as it might seem, as it would give the populous Dallas region a link, via the *Crescent*, with Atlanta and the northeast. The plan fell through because the U.S. Postal Service wouldn't deliver the mail contract that would have made the run financially feasible.

"Trucks running the interstates got the contract. That's what's changed Meridian, the interstates. Everything's being built on the outskirts now because of those interstates." It took a major public commitment to renovate the old downtown area, which was in a state of neglect, and now the big push is to sell Meridian as a site for conventions.

I am surprised that the bar in an adjoining room is open today. I had thought that Mississippi had blue laws. Mack explains that the state was totally dry until the 1960s, "but it didn't matter—everybody was into bootlegging." They'd bring up pickup-truck loads of booze from New Orleans. Mack had a friend who was pretty active in the trade. He'd lie low when the grand jury was in session, but the rest of the year it was wide open. He kept his supply hidden at the bottom of a lake. Mack recalls the adventure of going out there at night and helping him haul it up.

But there aren't any blue laws today. "People think of Mississippi as a conservative place that's kinda slow to change. But when change does come, we go all the way. Now they're making a big deal about illegal gambling on that casino boat, *European Star* they call it, out of Biloxi. But you watch. In a few years, Biloxi will be the next legal Las Vegas or Atlantic City."

Mack has personally seated every customer, and he knows most of them well enough to be able to make a casual comment to each about something that connects with their lives. Weidmann's is one of those precious institutions that bind a community to its past and integrate its present.

Later, as I doze in the sun on the station platform waiting for the train, my reverie is interrupted by a man who materializes from somewhere out in the yard and begins talking to me. He wears a T-shirt, denim jeans, and Nike sneakers. Occasionally I can see his eyes sparkle behind small wire-rimmed dark glasses. His skin is leathered and his bald head is deeply tanned. At first, I can barely understand what he is saying; his deep-south accent is heavy and slightly slurred. His idiom is peppered with halting phrases—"you know what I mean," "you know how it is," "in a manner of speaking," "like I mean this way see," "you unnerstan'." He has a habit of saying "in other words" when he hasn't said whatever he has to say in the first words yet. For a moment I think he's drunk, but he's not. He just has a story to tell.

Dan Stevens rides the *Crescent* back and forth between Meridian and New Orleans, "whenever I feel like it, you unnerstan'." It all started when he was twelve years old. He and a friend ran away, catching out on a freight to New Orleans. "In other words, we didn't mean nothin' by it, you see. Just a couple of kids lookin' for an adventure." Their daddies sicced the New Orleans police on them and had them arrested. The police told them what happens to runaway boys: they go straight to prison, chain gangs, the works. "Well, I wanna tell you, they scared the hell outa us. That's what put the fear in me right there." The boys begged to be let out, said how sorry they were and all that, but the police told them that the only way they would ever get out was if their daddies came for them and that was pretty unlikely, seeing as how ungrateful they had been. "You know what I mean, they said we chose this life when we ran away."

But their daddies did come, took the boys home, and whipped them good. "I never ran away again, but it didn't matter because I started drinking when I was fifteen and managed to fuck up my life pretty good anyway."

Dan was a desperate alcoholic for twenty-three years, the kind who kept a bottle under his pillow for comfort when he would wake up clammy during the night. He got to be Meridian's town drunk. His father owned a small mattress factory, and Dan learned the trade but could never handle the business because of his drinking. A wealthy town leader once wanted to hire him and asked a mutual friend, "Can that son of a bitch do anything?" The answer was, yes, he could make a mattress. The phrase caught on, and whenever people would cluck over his drinking, they would add, "Well, he can make a mattress."

Dan quit drinking when he was thirty-eight. "One night I got so desperate, I just said an honest prayer and the Lord done it. In other words, I had said dishonest prayers lots of times, like I mean see I'd ask the Lord to make me stop drinking whiskey and then I'd drink gin. But this time I was honest and He done it all for me." Dan doesn't have much faith in AA or psychiatry. "You know how it is, I been to a few of those sessions and all they do is see who can tell the biggest yarn about his drinkin'. No, the Lord'll do it if you ask Him honest—He's a pretty big guy, if you got a problem, why would you turn to anyone else?"

Dan suffered a severe stroke which temporarily paralyzed his right side shortly after he gave up alcohol. "My doctor says it was from the shock of going cold turkey, and maybe it was. But you know what I mean, I think it was a kick in the ass from the Lord, just to remind me."

Dan has a daughter somewhere, from a past marriage. Though he wishes he could bring her flowers, he won't talk much about her. Instead he tells of a friend who was a real street fighter. The man got shot in a barroom brawl—he laid a guy out with his fists and the guy got up, pulled a pistol, and shot him five times in the belly. He had a daughter and before he died he would bring the little girl to visit Dan when he was sober, knowing how much Dan loved kids. The rest of the town thought of Dan's friend as a rough, tough, bad man, and no one mourned his death. "But I knew better, see, he loved his kid and he cared for her real good—she probably hasn't stopped crying yet. He was a good father, despite his bad habits, you unnerstan'."

In the lounge car on the train to New Orleans, Dan drinks gallons of coffee and chain-smokes Camels, but he is free of booze and grateful for it. He has a disability pension from his stroke and something from his daddy's mattress business. He also picks up money from what he calls "serious gambling."

Real gamblers win steady, he says, almost all the time. The secret to successful gambling is to follow the gamblers' rules, every single one. If you fail to adhere to just one rule, you lose. The first rule is to settle for small gains, not get greedy. Never bet more than you're happy to lose. "In other words, you bet just the amount that you'd give away without blinkin'." If you do lose, never try to make it up. "Go fishing—the game will be there when you're ready again." You always have to start out fresh, never think you're in the red and you have to make something up. "When you're betting ball games, forget sentimentality—home team, shit like that. Save that for your mother, you unnerstan'. And if your mom's running against a racehorse, bet on the horse."

It's not easy talking to Dan Stevens, even after I get used to his idiom. He rarely answers my questions directly, instead pursuing a logic of conversation driven by his own compelling experience. And he frequently shifts topics without any corresponding change in his choice of words or details. Dan is saying for the umpteenth time, "Never risk more than you're willing to part with right on the spot. When you give away as much as I have in one lifetime, you learn that, you unnerstan'.

Don't bet what ya can't walk away from and do without right now. And if you don't wanta bet it, then for God's sake, see—hold on to it." As he says this he crushes my empty soda can with his fist; and it strikes me we're not talking about gambling anymore.

I rode a train to Meridian, Mississippi, thinking I knew what I was looking for. But the headquarters of my grandfather's GM&O railroad was defunct and the scenes of the town invoked only vapors of memory. I saw a parking-lot brawl, watched men work on the railroad the old slow way, and ate a good southern meal. I never expected that the most valuable experience of the town would be the gravelly voice that accompanied me on the train beyond Meridian all the way to New Orleans. If, as William Faulkner testifies in his novels, the history of Mississippi is a tale of irretrievable loss, then Dan Stevens is its true native son. I almost missed him. And six thousand miles later on a train in the deserts of Nevada, I found out that indeed I did miss something else in Meridian.

Dinner is served one last time on the *Crescent* as it approaches its 6:30 P.M. arrival in New Orleans. Few Amtrak trains serve a meal this close to a final destination—the crews are always in a hurry to clean up, close up, and knock off—but on the *Crescent*, they squeeze in one last supper. Why? "Because it's always been done that way," explains our chief of on-board services.

She is in a garrulous mood as the train crosses Lake Pontchartrain on the causeway. Two elderly couples have just made her day by complimenting her on the service during this train ride. She says, "Considering that we've had equipment trouble all the way from Washington, that's a real breakthrough."

The woman is a veteran of breakthroughs. Formerly an engineer on the Baltimore division of Conrail, she shattered two barriers by becoming the first black and first female engineer on the lines of the old hidebound Baltimore & Ohio. It was a little rough at first—the men would complain, "Why can't she sleep right in the bunkhouse with us if she's going to work with us?"—but it was a heady time and she loved it—she was queen of the rails. Then she fell in love, married, had kids, and quit. Now, with her children past diapers, she's returned to railroading as an Amtrak service chief. It means a cut in pay to what she got as an engineer, but at least she's in charge.

I ask if she has ever had encounters with sexists or racists who challenge her authority on the train. She laughs. "Oh yeah, not everybody's going to be bright—and sane." She's had to put a few hard cases off the train, but that's really rare. "You get people to accept your authority by making them comfortable and at ease in the situation. Like with my crew, I gotta keep them happy so they can keep the passengers happy. But if I got a problem with somebody, like if they're dogging it and making more work for the others, we straighten it out right quick."

I can see that our service chief loves the *Crescent's* grand entrance from the causeway over Lake Pontchartrain into New Orleans. The engineer has it cranked up faster than at any point I can recall since the northeast corridor, and we clatter past dozens of families having picnic supper by the tracks just so they can wave to the old train as it roars in off the water. It's showtime. The engineer salutes with the horn, and the dining passengers all wave. It's a great moment that makes her beam from ear to ear, and she swears there's no other job where you can feel so good at the end of a day. Tonight she will catch some jazz, have some laughs with friends, and get a good night's sleep before the run back to New York, where she'll have two days with her kids before the next shift.

My experience of the deep south this trip is like my reading of the ending of Faulkner's novel. There are profound and disturbing things going on here that make men of boys at tender ages and that I don't fully understand. But the rails'-eye view, as always, does offer some impressions. I rode to the south expecting to find certain parallels between it and my own New Hampshire. Both regions are bastions of conservativism grappling with critical issues of change. But in New Hampshire people consciously cling to the old habits while change occurs in subtle ways beyond their consciousness and control. The southerners I met are living the opposite experience. In response to their region's history, they actively participate in and articulate processes of change under the general rubric of "the new south." But frequently beyond their awareness abides a deep fixity which preserves the old ways, the old attitudes, the old mysteries in a kind of perma-frost of the past just beneath the greening veneer of surface change. I never met a southern white who would use the word "nigger" today as casually as I've heard it used at home in New Hampshire, but during the entire Sunday-noon dinner at the best restaurant in Meridian, Mississippi, there was not one black customer. I watched a number of track crews where blacks and whites worked side by side with never a whisper of "boy" or "boss," but it was always the blacks who swung the heavy hammers driving the spikes, the whites who placed the gauger and lined the rail. Blacks and whites alike would talk volubly about the progress and vision of their community leaders, black and white, but whenever I would ask specific questions about the past, I felt myself slipping in conversations, like an athlete trying to cut sharply on a greening playing field in mud season back home.

Unfortunately, issues of race and politics loom so large that one overlooks some precious things preserved in that southern cooler of tradition. The south has been the one place in my travels where the slower, dare I say more gracious, pace of life on the train followed me into the communities I visited. Here the experience of human warmth, intimacy, and easy friendships found on the train continued after I got off. For better or for worse, here, old habits die hard.

Chapter Nine

_____

Life and Death on the Love Train

THE *EAGLE*

SLEEP does not come easy in the last room of the last car on the westbound *Sunset Limited* from New Orleans to San Antonio. The trackbed is very rough, and without the steadying influence of a car behind it, the tall Superliner sleeper rocks back and forth violently. "Never go to bed early on a train; wait until you're good and tired," says the helpful Amtrak traveler's guide. But I have to detrain in San Antonio at 3:20 A.M. to catch the 6:00 A.M. *Eagle* to Bloomington and Chicago for the heart of the heartland trip.

I first see him standing under a dim light on the platform of some nowhere Texas station carrying his gym bag. I don't know why he brings it; there's almost nothing inside. His sneakers are worn and he looks so frail, so shrunken. I can hear him board the train and shuffle up the steps to the upper corridor. He comes to the glass door of my compartment: "Terry, Terry, is that you? Are we going home now?" He doesn't look at me, but hangs his head, ashamed to be so weak.

"Yes, Dad, we're going home. . . ."

The attendant's buzzer jolts me awake at 3:00 A.M. I've had the dream before a dozen times. Sometimes he wants to play catch or tennis or go sailing. Sometimes he just wants to watch a Sunday-afternoon football game. But he never asked to go home, not since he lay brain-damaged and dying at the Lahey Clinic. Something has changed.

I have seen stations where one would not care to detrain in the middle of the night and spend four hours. I picture the headline—"Rail Itinerant Found Murdered in Vacant Train Depot." But the smell of the car attendant's coffee pot and the cheery sound of railroad workers' voices on the platform are reassuring.

The San Antonio station's magnificent facade of red stone and tan stucco in Spanish Art Deco style suggests the community's pride in its heritage. The station's interior confirms it. The ceiling is festooned with woodwork filigree, recently cleaned and polished. One wall is dominated by a huge stained-glass window with a blood-red "Lone Star" surrounded by a mosaic of glass. The beams and trim of the overhead vault are dotted with hundreds of low-wattage bulbs, all lit. A wide hardwood staircase rises under the window and divides into two balconies that lead to offices upstairs.

After the bustle of the *Sunset*'s arrival and departure has subsided, a dozen passengers remain in the almost empty hall. Some try to sleep in various positions of agony on the traditional hard station benches. A huge old Texan dressed in a khaki suit and chewing on an unlit cigar paces while his well-coiffed wife tries to read. A young man wearing sneakers of different colors, one red and one yellow with a chartreuse lace and a black one, and a blue and a black sock, shorts, a Coors Silver Bullet T-shirt, and an Atlanta Braves baseball cap chain-smokes while lying on his back with his eyes closed. Two young black women on the bench next to me are getting acquainted. Apparently one is leaving a man who has not treated her well. He will awake in four hours and find her gone. But she's nervous about striking out on her own. She says she wants to find a "tolerable man" as soon as she can. The other, more experienced with this routine, asks, "Is this your first big move, honey?" It is, and the experienced girl relates how she's "made the big move" like this several times. "You picked the right train, ya know. We're gonna be riding on the Love Train."

I'm too tired to speculate or indulge in traveler's fantasies about what she means by the Love Train, and when the ticket agent rolls down the steel cage over his window, turns out his light, and disappears, the uneasiness about being alone in the middle of the night in a station far from home returns.

Around 4:00 A.M., three wild-looking men come in hefting a huge cardboard box. Two have scraggly beards and all three wear bandannas, one on his head, one around his neck, one on his sleeve. Head bandanna sits on the box and glares at the few passengers in the room, while neck and sleeve bandanna take up positions at each of the entrances, waiting, watching for someone. I picture headlines again— "Drug Gang Shootout in Station, Passengers Killed in Crossfire." Then the desperadoes shrug and disappear, leaving the box behind. The last thing I remember is staring at the bulbs in the vaulted ceiling and wondering how the maintenance people get up there to change them.

I'm awakened by the sound of the ticket agent's cage rolling up at around 6:00. Now more passengers have gathered. A rosy glow seeps through the windows and the blessed smell of coffee percolates through the hall.

The train is two hours late, but after an invigorating walk downtown to view the Alamo, this Texas morning begins to look and feel pretty good: not a cloud in the sky, flowers, bees, and birds everywhere. On the train at 8:00, crew chief Dave Minorek competently introduces the *Eagle* and announces its departure for Fort Worth, Dallas, Texarkana, Little Rock, St. Louis, Springfield, Bloomington, and Chicago. It's going to be a glorious day.

The route of Amtrak's *Eagle* today is an amalgam of several lines. Between San Antonio and Fort Worth, it runs on the Texas legs of both the UP and the Santa Fe and also over a stretch of the single-track Missouri-Kansas-Texas, better known as the Katy. From Fort Worth to St. Louis the route is the old Missouri Pacific (Mo-Pac), Jay Gould's UP-affiliated link to the Texas & Pacific project which was stopped short of achieving transcontinental status by Huntington's SP route from California to New Orleans. From St. Louis to Chicago the train continues over the rails of the old Chicago & Alton (later the GM&O), my grandfather's run—the heart of the "spring heartland" itinerary.

I don't believe anyone has ever kept a comparative tally of the number of deaths by violence along the various rail lines, but when someone finally does, the Katy will surely vie for top billing. Conceived in 1869 at about the same time as the Santa Fe, the Katy, backed by the likes of August Belmont, Pierpont Morgan, and John D. Rockefeller, was to take advantage of a government offer of land grants in Oklahoma Indian territory to build the first north-south link between the midwest and Texas. Again, a race developed—as it had whenever there was government largess at stake—this time between the Katy and the Kansas & Neosha Valley, since the land grants would go to the railroad that laid tracks into the territory first. Crews of the Katy attempted to settle the matter early by carting rails on wagons to the territory border without any pretense of having established a continuous line to that point. A gang of Neosha Valley thugs met them with shovels, axes, and clubs. The ugly, bloody battle that resulted brought the matter to the attention of President Grant, who issued an executive order calling for the laying of continuous tracks from each line's Kansas railhead before either could attempt to build into Indian territory.

Dispensing with the niceties of proper roadbed engineering, both roads went to work furiously laying rail directly on the prairie sod. Each succeeded in laying flimsy, rickety track into Indian territory at about the same time, but a terrible surveying error by the Neosha Valley people brought them into the Quapaw Indian reservation, where Congress's offer of land was not valid. Officials of the Katy cheered until they learned that the courts had determined that Congress had no right to offer Indian lands in any part of the territory. The deal was off.

But the Katy just kept right on building. The route reached Texas at Denison by 1872, and the towns along its route quickly earned a reputation surpassing even the hell-and-gunsmoke towns of the Santa Fe. Gambling, cattle rustling, prostitution, and armed robbery established themselves as the economic basis for such towns as Parsons, Muskogee, and Denison, even in advance of the railroad's arrival. In Muskogee, a cemetery containing the bodies of shootout victims was the first public improvement.

Riffraff plagued the line and the towns with random violence until Grant sent in the 10th Cavalry, not to battle Indians but to drive out "terminuses," who had earned their nickname from the encampments they set up at the ends of rail lines. Trainmen of the Katy went to work armed for battle as had the men of the UP during the Indian wars. Ironically, the Indians who inhabited this land usually watched passively as renegade white men wrought greater havoc on this intrusion into their domain than they could have hoped to do themselves.

Eventually the road stretched all the way south through Texas to the seaport at Galveston and north to St. Louis. But there was no Pullman influence bringing civilized ways to the route of the Katy, no Harvey girls (more on them later), no growing tradition of railroad gentility as along the Santa Fe. As late as 1923, the Katy was still the frequent prey of famous rail robbers, including the James and Younger gangs, the Daltons, and the Spencer gang. The latter two outfits met their maker at the hands of the lawmen of the Katy and are buried alongside the Katy tracks.

The management of the Katy always favored spectacle over civility, or as in one famous case, even over good sense. The Great Train Wreck was conceived by general passenger agent William George Crush, as a stunt to sell thousands of passenger tickets to spectators who would ride Katy excursions from points throughout Texas and the midwest to the site of the event. A town, named Crush, was constructed at the site to serve the huge crowd. Two trains had been specially spruced up for the event and had traveled the line publicizing the spectacle for weeks before the big day. At 4:00 P.M., September 15, 1896, they hurtled toward each other at sixty-five miles an hour in front of thirty thousand spectators. The engineers jumped and the crowd held its collective breath for the last seconds. A reporter for the *Morning News* wrote, "Words bend and break in attempting to describe it. It is a scene that will haunt many a man. . . . A crash, a sound of timbers torn and rent . . . then the boilers exploded and the air was filled with flying missiles from the size of a postage stamp to half a drive wheel falling on the just and the unjust, the rich and the poor, great and small."

It was a massacre. But after attending to the casualties, the crowd polished off the kegs of beer and lemonade provided by the promoters and boarded the excursion trains without a disparaging word concerning the event. It had paid to see the staging of a great disaster, Texas-style. It had gotten its money's worth.

It's hard to conceive the violent past of this route today as I hang out the open window in the lower vestibule door taking pictures of the wildflowered Texas countryside and soaking up the golden sunshine and clear air. This is one of the areas where Ladybird Johnson's famous campaign to reintroduce colorful wildflowers has been notably successful. The rolling green fields are spattered with them as we glide by at seventy miles an hour. Now there's corn, now cattle, here and there the glades of pecan trees, and always the flowers. A sign on a water tower identifies a nearby town and its Germanic heritage: "In Neues Braunfels . . . Ist Das Leben Schön!" (in New Braunfels, life is beautiful). This Texas spring morning, about an hour out of San Antonio, it certainly is.

An assistant conductor in the vestibule has a radio tuned to the trainmen's frequency. I've become accustomed to the laconic transmissions over these radios as part of the rhythms and sounds of train travel. "Just about twenty minutes behind schedule for San Marcos." Fuzz, blip. "Make up ten of it before Austin." Fuzz, blip. "Got a man by the tracks up here." Fuzz, blip.

Suddenly the brakes blast air and we make a full emergency stop with a grinding that sets the teeth on edge. Over the radio comes the frantic voice of the engineer: "Man under train—Jesus mother Christ—he just laid down in front of us!" The train comes to a complete halt in less than a quarter of a mile. Now the conductor's voice comes over the radio: "Let's go—meet me outside, chief."

Leaning out the window I can see the conductor and a man wearing gloves and gesticulating wildly walking the length of the train toward the rear. Over the radio, another voice, probably the fireman's, quakes, "He just walked out of the bushes up to the tracks. No time to blow, we just popped the brakes."

I rush up the steps and back to my sleeping car, which is at the rear of the train. From the window in the upper hall doorway I can look down the tracks behind us. About two hundred yards back, a shape lies on the ties. It does not extend over either rail.

Now comes a PA announcement from crew chief Minorek warning passengers that the train has struck a man and there will be a delay. Passengers nervously crowd around the window. It isn't morbidity, it is simple curiosity; like those who gather around the scene of a car accident or a house fire, they just have to see. Some have their quick look and want no more. A few others are drawn back again and again until the spell of death overcomes their inhibitions and they just stare and stare. The sleeping-car attendant, Melvin, has seen this before; it's not all that uncommon in Texas during hard economic times. He is the first to use the hushed word "suicide."

The conductor and engineer are making what railroad men know as the "long walk back." They have called the local police, the coroner, and an ambulance. There will be sworn statements taken before the train can continue on its way. The assistant conductor's radio crackles with orders to other trains on the route. The order board for this whole division is red. Nothing is moving anywhere on this single-track line.

Beyond the body a few cars and pickups accumulate at a grade crossing. Their CBs have broadcast it all. Finally three police cruisers, lights flashing, make their way through the crossing and down the dirt lane by the tracks to the site of the incident. An ambulance arrives, no lights flashing. By now there is a small crowd gathered around the body. Uniformed officers bend over it.

The PA announces that the train will be backing up to the "accident site." This sends most of the passengers in my car scurrying away from the window. Three of us hold our ground, and there it is. The man is dressed in blue jeans and an orange T-shirt. One foot is missing. And there's just no head where there should be one.

An hour and a half later, the train is on its way, but the incident has left its mark on the passengers, who pass through stages of nervous inhibition, to pensive gazing out of windows, and finally to ever more exuberant social intercourse. By evening there will be one hell of a party on this train. In discussions with the conductor, I try to reconstruct the scene by the tracks in the last half hour before the train arrived.

The man sat in his car down the lane from the grade crossing as the sun warmed the breezeless fields of wildflowers. It was a morning to make most folks glad to be alive. Only an overwhelming grief or desperate pain could cancel all of that.

He had chosen his spot well; the horn would blow before the crossing, giving him plenty of notice of the train's arrival. The engineer would be easing his attention just after passing the crossing, maybe lighting up a cigarette or making some small talk with the fireman.

The train was twenty minutes late at the crossing. The man would have been waiting here in God's own morning for at least that long, probably longer. Did he have his car radio on? Did he drink something? Was there doubt or irritation at the train's tardiness?

What is clear is the last minute, the time it took for the train to come over the rise with its horn blowing, clear the grade crossing, and meet the man on terms he dictated himself. He was out of his car as the train hit the crossing and into the bushes by the tracks. In the time that it took the train traveling at seventy miles per hour to roll from the crossing to the bushes, he calmly walked up beside the tracks. There was no hesitation as he timed it perfectly so as not to alert the engineer. With the train less than a hundred feet away, he just lay down between the tracks, with his body low so that the plow would not throw him off to the side, and put his head on the rail. The engineer instantly hit the brakes. At impact, the train was still running exactly sixty-five miles per hour.

The train comes to a full stop just outside of the San Marcos station, the next after the incident. I guess that the crew want to check the front end of the engine to be sure there are no traces of the tragedy to upset passengers in the station, but later the crew chief tells me that they had already taken care of that before starting up. There are schoolchildren waiting in the station to board the train for a field trip. This is an optional safety stop, a procedure that they usually forgo, but not today with a distraught engineer worried about forty children milling around the platform.

Later in the morning near Austin, the train makes another unscheduled stop as I am sitting in the lounge car, where a large gathering of passengers is rising to a level of sociability unusual for this early in the day. We are halted because a freight train ahead of us has struck a car at a grade crossing. Now the morbid jokes begin making the rounds. We are riding "the death train," "the pearly gates express." One man jests, "I guess we'll get there sometime, but it's too bad so many had to die to make it happen."

There are also serious stories. John Cowper, the young man with the red and yellow sneakers I saw in the San Antonio station, turns out to be a freight engineer on the Union Pacific, thus the red and yellow. His dad was an engineer on a UP passenger train when he struck a jeep carrying a group of young soldiers out on a date. He had to make the long walk back, and one of the soldiers, horribly mangled and whimpering, died in his arms. "My dad was a pretty good drinker, when he wasn't working, of course. But the day after that he went on a bender like I never saw before or since." He never recovered from the trauma of that accident, and John is convinced today that the accident caused his parents' subsequent divorce.

Someone else tells a story I've heard several times on Amtrak trains about the Metroliner in the northeast corridor. After an apparently unremarkable run, the engineer got off at Washington to discover a head wedged between the plow and the coupler of the lead engine. Rail traffic up and down the corridor route had to be halted until the rest of the body was located. When the torso was found, the case was adjudged to be a suicide.

Amtrak officials later confirm that suicide is not an uncommon problem. Some twenty-three deaths a year occur in the northeast corridor alone, over half of them suicides.

But today's suicide fascinates and befuddles the gathering in the glass lounge car. This was clearly no call for help or attention. Agreed. This man knew exactly what he was doing. Agreed. He must have either had some connection to the railroad or wanted to make it dramatic. Almost agreed, and then a controversy breaks out. The act of stepping in front of, not to mention lying down in front of, a speeding train defies understanding. Several who argue that suicide is an inherently cowardly act cannot conceive of the steel nerve it would take to do this. "He must have been on drugs." Others reject the notion of suicide as a cowardly act, arguing that this suicide proves their point. "What could take more courage than to choose the unknown of death over the familiar security of life?"

A theory germinates about active and passive suicides. Active suicides involve being the instrument of violence on the self, shooting, hanging, wrist-slashing, hara-kiri. Passive suicides are those in which one places oneself in the path of an agent of death: taking pills, leaping off a bridge, stepping in front of a train. Perhaps Hamlet would have chosen suicide if a train had been handy. The broaching of the literary fragments the group, some simply not familiar with the allusions, others flaunting their knowledge of them till the session breaks down into separate twosomes and threesomes heading off in different conversational directions.

All have agreed that the forces that surround the actual act of committing suicide are incomprehensible to the rest of us. Little do I realize that by the end of this ride, I will come to a closer understanding of those forces than I ever thought I would.

By midafternoon, the denizens of the lounge car have left suicide behind for the serious pursuit of levity. It's bingo time, and service chief Minorek is a high practitioner of the art of running the game. Every seat in the car is occupied by a player, and the bartender has been busy. Dave announces the rules and the fact that he will frequently change them in the course of the game, "So you'd better listen up." He has a card with the words "Dumb Dumb" printed on it to be worn by those who foul up on following the ever-changing rules. John Cowper asks how we will know when the rules have changed and is promptly awarded the Dumb Dumb card before the game even starts. There are little prizes for the winners—"very little prizes," says Dave, "since President Reagan won't buy us big prizes."

The participants include the usual contingent of elderly couples and divorced young and middle-aged women, some of whom are pairing up with single men; several overdressed couples to whom this entertainment is "cute"; some teenagers; two large families; and the huge Texan with the fat cigar from the San Antonio station. John is hamming it up and buying drinks for a streetwise young girl, who gives him plenty of encouragement. An elderly Mexican earns the Dumb Dumb card once before Dave realizes he doesn't understand English very well and favors him with whispered advice for the remainder of the game. At the other end of the car I notice a blond-haired young woman—the prettiest in the car—dressed in fashionable black. There is an empty seat beside her; she is friendly throughout the game, casting a particularly warm smile about her; but no one sits with her.

By the end of the game, Dave has made sure that everyone has been a winner at least once. He makes a cryptic joke about how those traveling alone on this train will be the real winners but gives no explanation why.

Fort Worth is a train crew division point, and as we pull out, the new conductor introduces himself over the PA. "This is Conductor Love here. I'll be with you to Texarkana, and I hope this will be the Love Train of your travels." In response to my query, Melvin says, "You never heard of the Love Train? Well, you're on it now. The man is a legend you don't want to miss."

As he comes through the train checking tickets, Conductor Love also shakes the hand of every passenger and makes a complimentary remark to each. He resembles no one so much as Santa Claus without the beard and mustache. He wears a gold pendant and a tie clasp in the shape of a crossing signal with little red lights that actually blink. His eyes twinkle and his laugh is a hearty Texan "ho, ho, ho." As he moves on to the next car he waves and promises, "When I get through with this chore, I'll see y'all again. We're gonna have ourselves a good ole Love Train party tonight." I notice that for the duration of his division, service chief Minorek, who is a pretty effective maestro in his own right, recedes into the background before the jolly presence of Conductor Love.

In the dining cars, strangers are frequently seated together, since seating space is limited, but I have noted that usually there is little attention paid to who is seated with whom. In the dining car of the Love Train, there is conscious matchmaking ordained by Conductor Love. "Nobody rides lonely on the Love Train." I am seated with the pretty woman in black who sat alone during the bingo game. Her name is Pamela Redding.

She is traveling from Yuma to St. Louis—has been on this train two days already. She has family in southern Illinois, but doesn't seem to like them very much; she complains about their provincial ways and archaic attitudes toward women. She prefers Yuma, where she says people live an urbane, cosmopolitan life without being in a big city. She flashes between anger at the family she is traveling to visit—"Illinois sucks"—and a warm friendliness toward everyone on the train, capped by a smile that declares goodwill, plain and simple. But I have to struggle not to stare at her bare arms, marked by dozens of long, thin scars that she does not try to hide.

During dinner, Conductor Love announces a special sight in downtown Dallas, Pinkie's Crossing. Pinkie is an old black woman who has lived in the same house near the tracks since 1905. She has come out to give a "big ole Texas wave" to the train every day for the past sixteen years. We are told to watch for members of her family who stand in for her when she can't get out of the house. Sure enough, as the train slowly rounds a bend and a crossing, there is a family of two youngish men, a young woman, and two children frantically waving at the train with their whole bodies. The engineer sounds a special toot which Pinkie can hear and recognize even when she hasn't left the house. As instructed by Conductor Love, every passenger on the left side of the train waves back to her family.

After dinner in the lounge car, Conductor Love has just finished directing his own riotous version of bingo and then trivia. He has introduced strangers, checked out who's married and unmarried, who's "naughty and nice." His matchmaking completed, now there is no one sitting alone in the lounge car, and the social scene he has orchestrated carries on with its own momentum. I sit down with him and Pamela in the lower lounge, where I'm allowed to smoke my pipe, and my personal audience begins.

Zeb Love has been with Amtrak for fourteen years, though he still is an employee of the Union Pacific (he will retire while I am writing this book). He has not made the crossover to full-time Amtrak work because this train only runs every other day and he likes to work steadily. When he is not the impresario of the Love Train, he runs freight trains, but his love is the *Eagle*. From a satchel he carries, he pulls out stickers reading "I'm riding the Love Train," photocopies of news clippings, hats, badges, even a change purse imprinted with his name and address.

He tells the story of Pinkie. Several years ago he noticed an old black lady waving at the crossing in Dallas. She always wore an old pink bathrobe. He started dropping off goodie bags for her—peanuts, cheese, pretzels, etc. He included his name and address. She wrote to him and told him all about herself. She'd been living in the same house for sixty-five years, and when she heard the train horn, "people better get out of the way because she's gonna get out to give the train that big old Texas wave." He finally called her and she asked, "When you-all gonna come and see me?" He told her to make him a pie and he would.

On the next trip, the Dallas ticket agent had a message for him that read, "Apple Pie Pinkie." He knew what it meant and told the fireman to stop at the crossing in Dallas, a serious violation of Amtrak rules. Pinkie was there with two big apple pies for him. On a subsequent trip he presented her with a brand-new pink nightgown. Thus began the ritual of Pinkie's Crossing. A reporter from the *Dallas Times Herald* was riding the train and noticed the passengers' response to Pinkie waving at the crossing. He did a front-page story about Pinkie's Crossing, and Zeb had his first celebrity coverage.

For Christmas, Zeb dresses as Santa Claus and distributes gifts, at his own expense, to children on the train and in the stations. One child, Jason, of Atlanta, Texas, became the focal point of another news item. The boy loved trains and asked for a teddy, a choo-choo, and snow for Christmas one year. Zeb, who had taken a fancy to the peppy little black boy who always came down to watch the train, brought him a teddy and a model steam engine; and indeed, the day he stopped to deliver the gifts, it snowed. Zeb has a picture to prove it.

Always looking for opportunities to promote train travel, Zeb has gone into elementary schools on his own to show pictures, hand out engineer hats, and punch imaginary tickets. "Those kids will be passengers on my train someday." When word spread that the *Gazette* was going to do a photo essay on Conductor Love as Santa Claus in the Dallas station one year, some two hundred people showed up for the event. Just this spring, he received a letter from a John Baker of Virginia. "Dear Conductor Love. Please stay healthy and don't go fishing or hunting the 19th of April. I'll be riding your train." Sure enough, on that date John Baker and his family rode from Fort Worth to Texarkana, just Conductor Love's stretch of the *Eagle*'s run.

By 1987 the Love Train caught the attention of Charles Kuralt for his "On the Road" segments, and Zeb achieved national celebrity. Kuralt found Conductor Love to be a natural TV showman. The segment begins with Love on the platform in Fort Worth, where a couple is deep in a lingering embrace. Love announces, "You got time to hug her just once more and then we're moving. 'Board!" A woman expresses her fear at her first train ride. "Oh, don't be scared, you're in tender loving hands now." He chatters as he collects tickets: "Oh, I mean to tell you, we got a purty one here. Pretty as you are, honey, you could ride on your nerve."

Kuralt introduces the segment, "The conductor is Zeb Love. He's the one who gives the love and makes this a trip to remember. These people who think they bought a ticket for a rail journey discover they've bought a ticket to a party."

All along the route, spectators gather at the stations to see the excitement. Kuralt acknowledges that more of them are out to see Love than himself. Together they wave from the vestibule in a tableau like that of the nominees at the end of a presidential nominating convention.

At the close of the piece, Kuralt asks Love why he does all this.

"Well, it kinda puts a spark in my heart that I can make somebody happy."

But the apotheosis of Zeb Love's career as master of the Love Train occurred July 4, 1987, when Becky Robertson and James Hughey were married in the lounge car of the train. Everything about the wedding was traditional except for its location. Hughey, a principal at David W. Carter High School at the time, was considered a conservative guy, except for his habit of turning cartwheels at pep rallies for each victory of his school's teams. The wedding party boarded at Dallas, in full dress. He wore pinstripes, she traditional white.

Becky's sister, Olivia, had fixed them up for their first date. Becky, apparently jaded by the dating scene, didn't want to go, but they went dancing and something was different from previous dates. They fell in love. When it got serious, Olivia, whose boyfriend was an Amtrak employee, suggested the train wedding. The reaction began as "What a crazy idea" but moved to "Why not, what fun!" The rest is history, as recorded by the *Dallas Times Herald*.

At boarding, Becky promised her mother, "Oh he's a good one, Mom." Vows were exchanged as the train pulled through Grand Prairie, Texas. Champagne was uncorked at Arlington, and the wedding party left the train with Conductor Love at Fort Worth for partying into the night. The train was ninety minutes late, but not a member of the party noticed. Said Becky at the end, "I can't believe the way I feel, just like being a kid, but better."

With a twinkle in his eye, Zeb says, "Now isn't that the way you wanta make everybody feel?"

Before arrival at the end of his division at Texarkana, I ask Zeb Kuralt's question: "Why?" He says, "You make yourself happy by making the world snappy. I just can't think of any other way to live. Here, look at this." He shows me one last set of pictures as if in summation. One shows the den of his house, where stuffed turkeys and whole stuffed deer are displayed in a recreation of a natural woodland setting. In another his backyard is extravagantly decorated with bunnies, eggs, and colorful baskets for Easter. Finally he shows me his pride and joy, his spectacular gardens of well-kept azaleas and dogwood. There is a lot of P. T. Barnum as well as Santa Claus in this man, but there is no profit in the showmanship, and he says he has never received even token acknowledgment of his contribution from his employers at Amtrak. He gets out of it exactly the same thing he gives to people whose lives he touches, love and joy.

Pamela has shared this audience with Conductor Love and has been the object of his flirtatious winks. He has surely noticed the scars on her arms but never flinched in acknowledgment. After he has left us to attend to some train business, she says he reminds her of *Miracle on 34th Street*. Already in his absence, one wonders if he was real. I can see that he has left a spell that compels her to tell her story.

Pamela was given up for adoption at the age of two, and spent her early childhood bouncing from one foster home to another. She was finally adopted by a New Mexico family, but it didn't work out. She never could conform to precepts like "Never date a Catholic" and "Stick to your own kind," and she rebelled against their entrenched attitudes. She also began to show signs of a manic-depressive emotional disorder.

As the ultimate rebellion against her staunchly Protestant adoptive family, she married a Catholic Mexican whose family spoke no English, but the marriage was a disaster. After her divorce, Pamela began writing letters in search of her natural parents.

She found them in a small rural town in southern Illinois, but her first few visits with them were a terrible letdown. In their boots and overalls, they ridiculed her stylish southwestern clothes. When she talked about her male friends, they suggested it was a bit whorish for a woman to have so many. Once she invited her sister to come to California for a visit, but the plan was scotched because "women don't go galloping around the country alone. They stay at home and look after their menfolk."

And yet, Pamela continues to visit them regularly. That's where she is going this train trip. "It gets pretty lonely living without a family. Even a bad one is better than being alone in the world."

I finally broach the subject of her scars. There is a long silence, and I fear for a moment that I've blown it as I did with Ike in Meridien. For the first time since I met her, the goodwill smile disappears. But gesturing to her rolled-up sleeves, she finally says, "Well, you can see that I don't try to hide it. How much do you know about bipolar disorders?"

The manic-depressive episodes that began in her teens increased in severity over the years; she's been in regular therapy and takes heavy doses of lithium medication. But she offers nothing more than the implication that the suicide attempt was just the result of inconsistent attention to her chronic illness. It isn't quite convincing.

It was hard to accept her condition, because she feared that it would isolate her from people. With her life history, rejection was the last thing she could tolerate. But it was a growing involvement with the mentally disturbed which helped her to come to grips with her own problem. Today she is active at home in a crisis center and has close friends who suffer from schizophrenia or other disorders. She is particularly drawn toward working with families to help them cope with the conditions of disturbed loved ones.

As the evening rolls on she talks animatedly, but not manically. She displays anger in discussing stories of intolerance and prejudice, humility about her experiments with drugs and the discovery that she was self-medicating with potentially disastrous results, and humor about stories that circulate among the community of psychiatric patients she knows. There is one about a town in New Mexico that has high concentrations of lithium salts in the water. "Everyone in that town is so cooled out. It's like a fountain of sanity."

I find it increasingly impossible to picture this calm, cheerful person as a suicidal manic-depressive, but when I thank her for her company and move to leave to go to sleep, she frowns. "The worst thing about a train ride is that you're always saying goodbye to people."

And then she returns abruptly to the topic of her suicide attempt. "It was last November. It wasn't like that man the train killed today—it wasn't a definite, determined wish to die. But it wasn't the old call for help or attention either. It was more like one last desperate cast of the dice—just a shot at a new game." Her numbers had been coming up bad for a long time, and when she thanks me for my company and heads back to her car, I remember that it was during her visit to her Illinois family last November that she had found out the reason why she had been put up for adoption. She hadn't been born out of wedlock, and there was no divorce or death. Her parents already had six children, and they didn't want the seventh.

In the morning, I'm on my grandfather's old route at last. From St. Louis to Chicago, the *Eagle* follows the route of the redoubtable Chicago & Alton. In a state containing the greatest track mileage of any in the country and dominated by giants like the Burlington, the Illinois Central, and the Wabash, the C&A's route from Chicago to St. Louis and Kansas City via Bloomington, Lincoln, and Springfield competed as one of Illinois's dominant granger railroads for almost a century. In the thirties, the road was bought by the B&O, which made it the westernmost leg in America's oldest railroad. In the forties, it was incorporated into the Gulf, Mobile & Ohio, the southern road based in Meridian, Mississippi, which ran the passenger trains *Ann Rutledge* and *Abraham Lincoln* along with the *Rebel*. In recent years the road was bought by its century-old nemesis the Illinois Central, which was more interested in selling railroad real estate than in running modern railroads. Today the route has been sold again to the Chicago, Missouri & Northwestern, a railroad entirely owned and managed by one wealthy private individual. Its future is very much in doubt.

Like Pamela Redding and so many others I have met on the trains, I am returning to the place of my family's past in a ritual which sooner or later is pursued by so many of us rootless, mobile Americans. We have a feeling that there is something in our past to be found, something terribly important—some lost grail of ourselves. In my case there is no tale of adoption and suicide, but there is a death—two deaths—and ghosts that have driven me eleven thousand miles to set something right.

My last visit to Bloomington was a train trip with my father and family in the summer after my junior year of high school, 1964, a few years after my grandfather died of lung cancer. We rode the declining *20th Century Limited* from my family's home, at that time in Fayetteville, New York, just outside of Syracuse. I always thought my father chose that mode of travel for some of the same reasons that I choose it now.

Just a few scattered impressions of that journey remain: the strangeness of the dim lights in the Cleveland station at 2:00 in the morning, the craning of necks in Elkhart in search of the same familiar features of memory that eluded me on my recent *Lake Shore Limited* trip, the aromas of hot food and the clink of silverware in the rumbling diner of the GM&O train we took from Chicago to Bloomington, the chronic heartache for the high school sweetheart back home whom I had not yet even been courageous enough to kiss, and the pride with which my father showed me his father's calling—a pride he had never revealed before.

My first image of Bloomington this trip is my last memory from that one. The Bloomington train station itself is not notable, but what travelers through here have always remembered is the highway bridge over the tracks at the station. It is built of two straight concrete sections that meet at a crowned angle in the middle, thus testing the ground clearance of cars running over it. It always reminded me of the flattened roof of a church.

Under it, before boarding the train that would take me back to Fayetteville that summer long ago, I opened some mail that had come for me in Bloomington. It was a letter from my girlfriend. It smelled of perfume. Inside there were few words, but the paper was covered with lipstick kisses. When I looked up from my cloud, expecting my father to

be impatiently urging me to board, he was standing in the train vestibule smiling down at me, beaming, with the peak of the church bridge
directly above his head, as full of life in my mind's eye today as Conductor Love. He was an impatient man; but that day, at that moment, he
would have waited for me forever.

Today the bridge has a huge crack running raggedly through the
joint at its peak. Hunks of concrete dangle from the bird's-nest-infested
underside, but a decent crowd of people mills about on the platform.
Among them is an aunt from my mother's side with whom I will stay
during my short visit to Bloomington.

Much of Bloomington is changed today beyond my recognition. Route
66 is gone, replaced by Interstate 55; commercial activity has moved
from the downtown to the sprawling malls that envelop and suck the life
out of the hearts of so many small American cities. But Miller Park still
has its surprisingly substantial zoo. No eastern city of comparable size
would support such an institution, but here it thrives, even in the mall
culture. There is just not that much competing diversion in the flat
Illinois prairie.

The rail yards and the west side neighborhoods that surround them
are still there. The neighborhoods, which were the epitome of respectable workingman's gentility during the heyday of the railroad, fell into
shabbiness at the railroad's decline. Today they have been restored
through the process of gentrification that is usually identified with big
cities. But the rail yards themselves have continued to slide. The
prospect from Division Street Bridge reveals tracks twisted like
snakes, empty, cavernous shops, and a handful of battered freight cars
that aren't going anywhere. The continual whistle of the switch engines
is gone, and the staccato slamming of the long trains taking up slack is
almost unimaginable in the breezy silence today.

In a sense, the story of Bloomington is the story of mid-America since
the industrial revolution. Before the railroad, the site was just a lonely
spot on the Illinois prairie. When the Chicago & Alton was built as the
shortest route between Lake Michigan and the confluence of the Missouri and Mississippi rivers, Bloomington was founded as the site of the
road's service shops at the exact midpoint of the run. There is no river or
lake or other geographical feature to key the siting of a city here.

The C&A shops dominated the growth of the vibrant little city for
more than half a century. Here Bloomington native George Pullman
and his partners turned out the first Pullman Palace Car. Later the
Delmonico, the first dining car, was built here, as was the first reclining
coach chair, and the C&A, whose route on a map when extended to

Kansas City resembled the shape of a reclining chair, came to be known as the "reclining chair route."

The Bloomington shops generated more than just modern rail equipment: they earned a reputation as a training ground for the most highly rated railroad mechanics in the business. "You're one of those smart son of a bitches from Bloomington" became a familiar greeting to Bloomington mechanics sent out to troubleshoot problems on other railroads throughout the midwest.

By the 1920s another illustrious Bloomington native began building a new business on a vision of a very different posterity. George Mecherle saw the automobile as the key to America's future and founded his State Farm Insurance Company in anticipation. The depression of the thirties hit Bloomington hard, as its economy was almost entirely based on one very vulnerable industry, the railroad, and by the fifties, State Farm had replaced the railroad as the dominant employer in Bloomington. Route 66, from Chicago to L.A. via Bloomington, was the apotheosis of the nation's future. As the railroad continued to decline, the nearby Caterpillar tractor factory and, in recent years, GM's new Saturn plant have completed the transition of this city from its rail roots to its auto-dominated present.

The introduction to the McClean County Historical Society's *History of the C&A Shops* recalls the seminal point in Bloomington's history:

In 1922, the future of Bloomington looks as impressive as the past. It is good that Bloomington's economy leans so heavily on such a thriving industry—our nation's railroads. That is in sharp contrast to the state of automobile travel. There is talk of building hard roads in Illinois, but you cannot drive in any direction from Bloomington after last night's downpour without getting your auto mired in axle-deep mud.

A farmer from over near Merna, George Mecherle, has been pulled out of several bottomless mudholes in recent weeks as he has motored around from farm to farm trying to sell his new State Farm car-owners' insurance policies.

Mecherle has an uphill battle. As I stand here watching two thousand good workers head into the C&A yards to start an October workday in 1922, it is easy to imagine that it will always be like this.

As an engineer, my grandfather, Ira (Frank) Pindell, came to be associated with the *Rutledge* and the *Lincoln* in a flamboyant manner that presaged Conductor Love. Frank came to Bloomington from southern Indiana with two of his five brothers near the end of the last century, when the effect of the railroad on Ohio River traffic had turned his home county into a depressed area while making Bloomington a place of opportunity for a generation of future railroad men. But the brothers' original plan had nothing to do with railroading. Isaac (Ike), the only educated man of the three, was the kind of man who drilled for water and found oil, which is exactly what he did when he moved on to Kansas. But he never got rich from it, because he spent all he made in failing efforts to duplicate the trick. Frank and brother Harvey tried wheat farming and didn't like it. Harvey returned to Louisville, where he became a conductor on an interurban line and worked his way up to superintendent of Louisville public transportation.

Frank, whose education ended in eighth grade, stayed in Bloomington and went to work as a cook for the track crews of the C&A. He got five and a half cents an hour for his labor in those days. He was promoted to train fireman before the sixteen-hour limit went into effect and complained about the occasional twenty-hour workdays. He married Bertha Schutt, a stern unforgiving woman in her youth, a religious fanatic in her old age.

Frank was smart and enthusiastic enough that he worked his way up to engineer, eventually on the very best trains, the *Ann Rutledge* and the *Abraham Lincoln.* In one of the few vignettes related by my father, he recalled Frank bringing home the huge diesel manuals night after night and struggling to comprehend the new technology. It took him half a dozen tries before he passed the exams that allowed him to continue through the forties as engineer on the diesel-powered trains.

They called him Speed throughout the C&A and later the GM&O because of his penchant for beating the timetable on his passenger runs and because he was "fast" at cards. He never had an accident, and he was proud of that, but, oh, how he loved to run fast. My Aunt Lorene relates the story of a trip she made to Chicago with a friend when she was in high school. She didn't know that Grampa was the engineer, but he saw her get on the train. All the way to Chicago, the train roared down the track at high speed, pitching, swaying, bucking, and getting to every stop ahead of schedule so that it then had to wait for the schedule to catch up with the train. When Lorene detrained in Union Station, there was Grampa waiting on the platform with his arms folded. "Howdja like that ride?" he challenged.

Grampa had a weakness for gambling, but Grandma set him straight once by taking Lorene and holing up for two weeks with a relative.

Afterward she told him that if he ever gambled again, she'd leave him and never come back. That cured him, at least as far as anyone ever knew, though he began to play punchboards, cardboard displays set up in grocery stores. You would punch out a little hole that had a number on the back, and if your number matched a daily number, often kept in a capsule in the cash register, you won money or a prize put up by the establishment. Grampa was a whizz at punchboards; it seemed as if he intuitively knew which holes had the right numbers, and he won all the time. Lorene and her husband ran a grocery store near the tracks and it was embarrassing to have to tell customers that Father had won the punchboard again.

In later years I can recall the Sunday-afternoon Pit games in Lorene's house over the store in which Grampa would cheat like crazy and look you in the eye and wait for you to decide whether or not to make a fuss about it. If you did, he'd take it back and do it again later. If you didn't, he'd still do it again later.

This same mischievous lust for fun was a part of his life on the railroad. Grampa was a traditionalist about clothes, and he stuck with the old solid blue dungarees long after most had adopted the now classic blue and white stripes. He finally took to the stripes, too, but when a new generation started wearing solid white caps and overalls, that was too much. He didn't approve, and if he got a chance as his engine rolled by young trainmen wearing the whites, he would open the injector valves, letting out a blast of steam and oil that would blacken the offenders. More than once, Lorene recalls young trainmen tracking oil into the store and announcing, "Well, your dad got us."

Grampa knew everybody, and said he'd met only three people in his entire life that he didn't like. One was a fireman who showed up for one run so drunk that Grampa had to do both his own job and the fireman's, as well as take care of a sick drunk who threatened to fall out of the cab at every lurch of the train. He didn't turn him in, but the next time the guy showed up drunk, Grampa did the two worst things to the man he could think of. The second-worst thing was to turn him in and get him fired; the worst was to declare that this was a man he did not like.

Grampa never had a wreck and never ran over anybody, but he worried about it all the time. In contrast to the mischievous side of his nature, he took things on the road very seriously. He saw a hobo killed in the yard once and couldn't take his train out for his next call. When a friend was fired for getting in an accident and the union maneuvered to get his job back, the controversy tore Grampa in two, because he knew undisclosed details about the circumstances and believed the man had been derelict in his duties.

When Grampa died, a crowd showed up for his funeral. Family members report that most of the faces were strangers to them. He was a "character" in an age when being an engineer on the fast passenger trains was a high calling; when a simple, uneducated man could achieve celebrity by running the crack passenger trains ahead of fast schedules. Grampa had retired before the railroad really began to die, but time left his kind behind, and his own son was probably his first contact with the man of a new age.

Five blocks from the rail yards, I find the corner of Empire and Madison streets. Here there is a small store that was once a butcher shop. Across the street is a house with tall peaked gables—they always reminded me of a church. In front of and behind the house, huge mulberry trees tower like ancient giants, their droppings staining the sidewalk where two generations of sons could be found during the long midwest afternoons making tracks with chalk and waiting for the engineer of the *Ann Rutledge* to come home. There is still stained glass in the entry windows, but the house has been resided with yellow vinyl. This was once a house of St. Louis Cardinals fans, but today, at the back step a sign like a real estate marker reads, "Cubs Clubhouse."

This was the house of my father, who spent his entire boyhood in this one place, and the rest of his life in rootless pursuit of his modern American dream with me in tow. There is one mulberry tree in front of the house in which the seventeen-year cicadas blared like sirens one summer long ago. My father took me out to the tree; he had watched it grow since he was a child. He explained to me what his father had taught him seventeen years earlier about how the cicadas live in the ground for all those years before breaking forth with wings and flying to the top of the tree to make their song and seek mates. He showed me their holes in the dirt by the roots and traced their paths up the crevassed bark of the tree.

Tonight after dark I return to my father's house with the intention of stealing the Cubs sign. There is yellow light glowing in the windows and I hear loud conversation inside. I can't do it. Instead I find myself drawn to the cicada tree out front.

I never before gave much thought to the circumstances that led my father to become a noted scientist in medicinal research, but here by his tree it's all clear now. His father's dream was the railroad, and Grampa never understood why he wanted to walk away from that simple life to chase a will-o'-the-wisp at the university, but my father had his own dream—he wanted to be somebody. They quarreled. Grampa would offer no support for his college education; didn't believe that the son of a simple railroad man could make it. After his marriage to my mother, they lived on peanut butter sandwiches and struggled to meet tuition payments in Champaign, where I was born. My father never rode a train again until that summer following Grampa's death. Each career move took him farther from Bloomington—Elkhart, Richmond, Denver, Syracuse—and the visits here became fewer. When my grandfather died, my father would wake up crying, "Dad!" night after night after night.

The cicadas tonight are silent, asleep in their hibernation in the ground under the roots of the mulberry tree. The crevasses in the huge tree's bark are now so deep I can sink my hands into them and pull. Slabs of bark come free. Furiously I tear and tear at it till I can taste the drops of salt from my eyes—so much to atone for, so little possibility of doing it. Among my travel things during my return trip to New Hampshire are carefully wrapped objects: a rail spike from the Bloomington yards, a curious iron gear from an old engine, and several six-inch-long chunks of mulberry bark—gifts for my children.

Chapter Ten

Desperadoes

THE CARDINAL

I N addition to the *Lake Shore Limited* of the New York Central route
and the *Broadway Limited* of the Pennsylvania route, Amtrak runs
a third line from Chicago to New York. The *Cardinal,* misnamed
descendant of the old *George Washington,* follows the route of the
Chesapeake & Ohio, today part of the CSX system, down through
Indianapolis and Cincinnati, along the Ohio River, through the gorges
of the West Virginia Appalachians, over the Virginia Blue Ridge, and
then on to Washington and the northeast corridor. If you take the train
from west to east, you pass through daylight scenery that rivals, in
drama if not in altitude, that of the routes of the far west. This train is
no speed merchant as are the other two Chicago–New York expresses.
Like the western trains, this is a slow land cruise.

Though the C&O qualifies as a true trunk line with its terminals at
Newport News on the Atlantic Seaboard and Chicago on Lake Michigan, its primary function has always been as a conduit for the bitumi-
nous coal of the West Virginia mines. Collis Huntington's grandiose
scheme for this road had been as the eastern leg of his "true transcontinental"—a line stretching from coast to coast and owned by one

man. But economic reality proved stronger than Huntington's ego; like its competitors in the region, the Norfolk & Western and the Virginian, the C&O has since followed the fortunes of the mining industry through good times and bad. Its route today is a tour not only of high scenery, but of hard times. During my trip, the display of natural and economic history outside ends up having to compete for my attention with the soap opera of sex, drugs, and rock and roll unfolding inside.

My first impression of some of the key characters in the show is not auspicious. As the train rattles through the Indiana night, a glamorous but very young beauty holds court in the bar car before a pair of seedy-looking guys around forty and a younger blond fellow who dresses and carries himself like a surfer. He wears a blue bandanna and loose pants with gaudy blue swirls. One of the older guys has graying shaggy hair and a mustache and reminds me of a tired Anthony Quinn. The other, perhaps a little younger, maintains a smirking, sardonic expression on his stubbly face. Over his muscular frame he wears a T-shirt which reveals some nasty scars, the kind one might get from knife fights. He calls the beauty queen Cream Cheese, and she takes the moniker as a compliment.

In the booth across the aisle sits a character who makes me just plain nervous. Tall and mustachioed—Fu Manchu–style—his eyelids droop with drink and malevolence. He looks like the kind of character who could twist a knife in your belly and laugh. He is hanging on every word of the conversation in the booth across the aisle and interjects slurred, crude remarks that would get him thrown out of most respectable bars. The big, burly black bartender sits one booth away, obviously keeping an eye on the situation.

The girl is a Miss Teen America contestant and is traveling to Phila-delphia to make a rock video for MTV. She flirts, "You guys have to take a train to Cedar Grove sometime and come see me." At first I imagine that I'm overhearing a slightly indecent interlude, considering her age, which is only fourteen, but then it is clear that she is practicing for the bit she will do in the video.

The guy in the blue bandanna says, "That's pretty good. I thought you were eighteen and was thinking of asking you out." She explains that part of her training is to be able to pass for much older—and to be able to handle herself around older men. Practicing or no, the effect is the same. I notice that the offensive mumblings from the dirty drunk coincide with flourishes of her feminine art. When she flashes her beauty-queen grin, he slurs, "Oh honey, grin, grin, grin again."

I order a beer and when Cream Cheese's chaperons appear at the door of the car to shoo her off to bed, I take her place in the booth with the seedy guys while the young fellow moves down to a booth beside a foxy blonde whose tough-looking burr-headed friend has just gone to the bathroom. The Anthony Quinn character is Will LaChance; the sardonic fellow is just Jim.

Will is a Vietnam vet, a promising dental student before the war, an underemployed architect after. Jim describes himself as a "migrant actor" who has done spots in soaps, ads, and community theater. Will is quiet and intense; Jim is boisterous and opinionated. Apologizing for being an actor during the age of "the actor President," he says, "It took two hundred years to build the country and eight to tear it down." On the President's popularity: "It's not popularity, it's drug abuse. America's been on Valium for eight years."

Jim is going to Washington looking for acting work. He has no appointments or contacts; he doesn't even have a reservation for a place to stay. "And I've got no money, so it looks like a dead-stick landing," he says, laughing. He's done this before and values the experience of hard living. Eating out of dumpsters, sleeping on park benches, and even panhandling the tourists help to build his acting repertoire.

He says the train is a great place for actors to study character and plot development. Will agrees. He rides the trains because he is a "people watcher."

Jim espouses his theory of "ironic countertruth": the idea that truth is not at all elusive in American society, it is usually the exact opposite of that which our myths propagate. To him, American mythology is not aggrandizement or distortion of history, but counterhistory—stories in which black becomes white, crooks become heroes, forward becomes reverse, "like looking in a mirror, where everything looks right except it's all exactly backward." First of all, he argues that "capitalist" America has really been traditionally a socialist society. For example, the builders of the American travel systems over the years have promoted themselves as the epitome of risk-taking capitalist enterprise. The truth, says Jim, is that they have replaced the masses as the recipient of the dividends generated by socialist enterprise. Government built and paid for the interstates that made empires of General Motors and the trucking industry. Government built the airports that fostered air travel, the Caribbean resorts, and the entire economy of Hawaii. In earlier times government built the canals and roads and provided the security for the pioneers. Even the railroads received grants of land, though they built the rails and stations themselves and paid taxes on the whole enterprise ever after. Ironically, says Jim, and scholars of rail history agree, the railroads are the closest thing to true capitalist enterprise that we have; and yet they are destined to survive only through direct government subsidy.

To Jim, the recent decline of American glory is simple. The key to the success of the country during her rise to greatness was always the commonsense reality underlying the preposterous myths: the closet socialism of the government, the unspoken tolerance of moral diversity, the collective sympathy for the downtrodden and the unsuccessful, the unacknowledged fabric of communal living stretching all the way back to the Puritan common ground. "Somewhere in the past forty years, the country began to take its myths seriously," abdicating the public role in the building of a great nation. The result, he says, is a society marked by what private enterprise, moral rigidity, the success ethic, and antisocial individualism do best: "ticky-tacky housing developments and condos for narrow-minded people who drive obnoxious cars on crowded freeways to eat at sleazy fast-food restaurants and shop at malls decorated with plastic plants." The irony is that they have embraced a communalism so much poorer than the traditional unspoken American socialism that they reject. And the great monumental buildings, the parks, the rail lines themselves are endangered species in a world where what survives is what produces short-term profit and passes the ideological litmus test. "Another ten years of this and America will just be a trash heap."

But tonight Jim is less interested in society's global ills than in what is happening around us in the bar car of the *Cardinal*. Taking a cue from Jim and his nicknaming of Cream Cheese, Will and I assign names to the other characters in the car. The young blond fellow told Will and Jim earlier that he rides the trains specifically to hustle women. He claims a success rate above 50 percent—thus he is Top Gun. The blonde is Goldie. The sleepy drunk in the booth across the aisle is Jesse James. He claims to be a successful outlaw, having pulled off several liquor-store heists with a toy pistol and collected DWIs in six different states in the past year without ever landing in jail. We, of course, are the Desperadoes.

Meanwhile Top Gun loiters around Goldie at the other end of the car and leans over to whisper in her ear every time her friend (whom we name Rambo) goes off to the bathroom, which is quite often. Finally Rambo returns to find Top Gun sitting in his place with his arm around Goldie. Rambo stares at Top Gun, hands on hips, and for a moment it looks as though there will be a fight. Then he picks up Top Gun's beer can, chugs it, crushes it in his fist, and leaves. He storms in and out of the car several more times until the bartender warns him off. Top Gun is half Rambo's size but has never shown any sign of fear, his smirking smile brazenly glued on his young golden-boy face.

The bartender has his hands full tonight. Jesse James has been speculating out loud about robbing a train, something he admits he hasn't tried yet. He guesses there's some "pretty good coin" in the conductor's cash box. When the conductor strolls through, the bartender makes his move. "One more offensive or threatening word out of you and you're off the train at the next stop. The state police will be waiting."

It's another tense moment as Jesse's watery eyes ooze with malevolence. But he breaks the tension by laughing, "Ain't anybody got any sense of humor around here?" He gets up and staggers out of the car.

Top Gun and Goldie have disappeared. Jim speculates that they have gone off to consummate their acquaintance. Just when I begin to feel sleepy and conclude that the action is over for the evening, Top Gun returns, cursing the conductor. "He walked in on us and kicked me out, can you believe that?" He says Goldie is really something, "hot and fast, man." But just as he was deeply engaged in making sure she felt his appreciation for her enthusiasm, the conductor opened the door, which he had forgotten to lock, and ordered him out. I'm not sure I believe him until the conductor comes by, points his finger at Top Gun, and threatens that if he finds him in the sleeping section again, he'll put him off the train.

There is nothing unusual about Top Gun's activities, train trysts being one of the favorite subjects of stories told by many of the Amtrak employees I have met, and I will witness several myself during my journeys. And there is no rule restricting who sleeps where once a bedroom is reserved and paid for. Somehow Top Gun has really pushed this conductor's button. Will speculates that maybe he has a thing of his own for Goldie. I wonder if the confrontations with Rambo and Jesse James have put the crew on edge.

At Indianapolis, a division point, a new train crew comes on; Top Gun and Goldie are reunited for the night without further interruption, and I go off to bed, this day's episode of *The Desperadoes* concluded. In the morning Jim says that the new conductor resolved the mystery. Will was right; the guy was enamored of Goldie himself—has a history of falling for attractive female passengers—and is today in deep trouble for his harassment of Top Gun.

The most scenic portion of the route of the *Cardinal* begins as we pull into Huntington, West Virginia, during breakfast. Named for Collis

Huntington, the founder and twice president of the C&O, the city was once the western terminus of the C&O. Today it is still a major division headquarters and site of the kind of car and engine shops that have deserted Meridian and Bloomington. The Collis P. Huntington Railroad Historical Society maintains a museum here and runs one of the longest steam train excursions in America today, a day-long round trip that covers 150 miles to White Sulphur Springs and back.

East of Huntington, we enter the Kanawha River Valley, where the deep blue water, the green hillsides, and the white, pink, and purple of the dogwood, red-bud trees, and mountain laurel mingle outside my window like oils on an impressionist artist's palette. I have heard people rave about the fall color in this part of the country. This spring-time version is just as wild, shifted toward a different end of the spectrum.

The river, a tributary of the Ohio, is navigable here, and this fact plus the presence of the railroad and the vast raw materials of the mining country have generated industries one might not expect to find in this spectacular natural and pastoral setting. Near Scary Hill is Nitro, site of World War I government munitions plants that manufactured the explosive for artillery shells. At Institute, I'm told the plants still manufacture methyl isocyanate, the pesticide involved in the Bhopal disaster in India. In South Charleston, Union Carbide, Olin, and the U.S. Navy manufacture chemicals, some of which are so secret that local employees don't know the name of the products they produce. DuPont, International Nickel, and Elkem Metals Alloy all have plants here, none of them the "clean hi-tech" industry favored by municipal planners in my part of the country. But in a region whose reliance on the vicissitudes of the coal market has retarded its full recovery from the Great Depression, there is an economic desperation that makes such squeamishness an unaffordable luxury.

I have lunch with Rambo, who is now sober and cleaned up. Except for the tattoos reading "Dust to Dust," he hardly resembles the rowdy character I saw last night. A former legal aide, now a nuclear power plant operator, he is soft-spoken, articulate, and surprisingly knowledgeable. He identifies wildflowers growing by the tracks by their Latin names and points out construction on a bridge for Interstate 64, explaining that it will be the last interstate completed in the United States because of the engineering problems encountered in these gorges.

He never mentions Top Gun but does confess that he rides the train to meet available women like Goldie. His is the first independent confirma-

tion of what I have observed throughout my travels: trains are dispro-
portionately populated by young, often divorced, attractive women.
"Maybe it's because it's cheaper than air and safer than buses. Maybe
they ride the train to escape bad memories. I just know the train
usually beats any singles bar I've ever been in. There're a few of 'em on
every ride, and there aren't a dozen other guys hustlin' 'em—usually."
In all of my train travels, I meet only two guys who acknowledge this
reason for taking the train. It's their bad luck that they both happen to
be riding the same one.

By the time we have had our coffee and paid our checks, Rambo
waxes even more confidential. "I made a real ass of myself last night.
But you watch. The guy gets off at Alexandria, Virginia. I'll have till
she gets off at Philadelphia to salvage something from this trip. Otherwise this train ride doesn't exist."

The afternoon ride through the New River Gorge reminds me of my
earlier ride through Glenwood Canyon in Colorado. The rocks and flora
are different, of course, and the works of man are more complex than
the building of an interstate (though that happens here, too, as Rambo
pointed out at lunch). Remnants of old coke ovens lining the tracks
merge into the machinery of Hawk's Nest Dam, generating power for
steel plants hidden in the adjoining canyons. An aerial tram carries
sightseers up to the Hawk's Nest overlook above the ruins of coal
tipples and company housing. The verticality in this old eastern canyon
really is awe-inspiring.

In Thurmond, contradictory images dominate as I watch affluent
white-water enthusiasts ride their expensive hobby in the froth of the
river while old women wave forlornly from tattered dwellings along the
rail route. Thurmond is a flag stop, but today no one flags, and one old
woman, her face tooled and tanned like old leather, leans out from the
Banker's Hotel and raises her hand almost in supplication as the train
thunders through. I swear there are tears in her eyes.

At Prince the rails run along Main Street, where some kind of
downtown festival is supposed to be happening. There are flags and
banners, platforms and street stalls. But this Saturday morning, the
street is nearly empty, and it is a grim hello I receive from the man
standing at a T-shirt stall beside the station stop.

Hinton is a mecca for rail enthusiasts: each fall this little town acts as
terminus for the New River steam excursions from Huntington. But on
this spring day the town has the same hangdog look I have seen all
through West Virginia. Just past Hinton we rumble through Great

Bend Tunnel, where John Henry, the legendary "steel-driving man," laid down his hammer and died.

Only at White Sulphur Springs do the works of man begin to do justice to the magnificent works of nature that preside over this route. Here the world-famous Greenbriar and other spa hotels grace the vale with their prosperous presence. The hot mineral waters still attract the rich and famous, the political and powerful, along with everyman and his family. The Greenbriar's guest book reads like annotations of the *Congressional Record*, and yet is filled with the John and Jane Does, the Stan and Mary Washinskis, the Mario and Theresa Mantrocellis.

As we climb through the Blue Ridge Mountains into Virginia during the late afternoon, the lounge car is filled with quiet scenery watchers. There's a middle-aged couple from Grand Rapids who wear old clothes to ride the train, "like camping." A businessman works for a mall developer and isn't too comfortable about the fact that so many malls are being built on sites where tracks have been torn up. A young man from Colombia is traveling the United States to learn English. A young female Peace Corps vet, who was stationed in Bangui of the Central African Republic, is riding the train to recapture a feel for her own country.

I'm sitting with Will and Jim amid this group about a half hour before Charlottesville when two tough-looking young black men come in and sit down, and I can feel an electric tension charge the car. They are both dressed in ratty sneakers, dungarees, and fatigue jackets but sport huge gold diamond rings on their fingers. They make no effort to converse with anyone. Instead one of them pulls out a fat roll of $50 bills and ostentatiously begins counting them. He must have several thousand dollars in his hands. The other keeps his hands in his pockets. One by one the other people in the car get up and quietly leave till all that are left are myself, Will, Jim, and the bartender. We nervously replay bits and snatches of conversations we have had earlier and eye each other in a kind of game of chicken—who will be the first to bail out. The newcomers ride in silence to Charlottesville and get off the train.

Jim breaks the ice. "Real desperadoes. Running candy."

The bartender confirms, "Jamaican cocaine dealers. They're not usually so obvious about it. You know, we don't even carry any weapons on these trains." Drug running by train happens, but no one knows to what extent. I've witnessed the aggressive customs checks on the *Montrealer* coming into New England from Canada, but there is no such scrutiny of what people carry on trains traveling within the United States. Amtrak officials are concerned enough that they have recently inaugurated efforts with law enforcement agencies to make busts on the trains to discourage an explosion of the problem.

Jim opines that today's drug scene is becoming a replay of prohibition. "Outlaw the user and you create big business for the underworld. One of these days people will smarten up and realize that the worst thing about our current drug problem isn't the fact that people get addicted, it's the fact that innocent people get intimidated, brutalized, or killed by guys like those desperadoes. Big bucks bring big violence when it's outside legal business. Legalize drugs under government regulation and control and you put those thugs out of business."

Will agrees. "They just flashed those bills knowing nobody would dare to do a damn thing—like they were just omnipotent. I'll bet if any of us had said a word to them, he'd be a dead man now."

Amtrak officials point out that trains are remarkably crime-free. Except for some petty theft on trains standing in big-city stations (mainly New York), the incidence of crime on trains today is well below that of society as a whole. I've seen that passengers regularly leave their things unprotected in open rooms and on luggage racks. The advantage of close community helps. Passengers do tend to take an interest in what's going on around them, so there are always plenty of witnesses; the train's radio communication to stations down the line makes escape pretty tough. And there hasn't been a railroad holdup in the United States in years.

It wasn't always that way. In its heyday, the railroad was the conduit of riches, publicity, and status, just as the airlines are now. Whether the prize be money or political publicity, the glamorous transportation systems have always been a target of the criminal mind.

The first rail holdup occurred in southern Indiana near the route of the *Cardinal* on the Ohio & Mississippi Railway in 1866. A terrible war had just concluded and society had not yet assimilated all of the men trained for violence by its recent history. It was a simple inside job. Two masked men, wielding pistols, and initially posing as passengers, entered the unlocked express car from the adjoining coach and demanded the keys to the safe. After removing $13,000 in cash they pulled the brake cord, and as the train slowed, dumped a second safe out the door into the darkness and followed themselves.

They were captured, and while their trials were postponed, the so-called Reno gang became a scapegoat for a burgeoning phenomenon which made all too much sense. A year later the same train was held up in the same way by two different men who were caught red-handed in the act by a new breed—the rail detectives of Pinkerton's. It made no difference that these were different men; the deed was ascribed to the same conspiracy.

Throughout the next year, other robberies in Iowa, Illinois, and Indiana were attributed to the Reno gang. When the first train murder was performed on an unfortunate mail-car messenger, who was beaten and thrown from the fast-moving train in southern Indiana, the law proved itself able to capture the villains, but not to protect them. A mob of enraged vigilantes seized the men and hanged them without ceremony from a tree by the tracks where the messenger had died.

Late in 1868, three brothers accused of train robbery awaited trial in a jail in New Albany, Indiana. Vigilantes attacked, overwhelming the poor jailer in a tough fight, and, dispensing with symbolism, hanged the alleged miscreants from the rafters of their own cells. Here the legend of the Reno gang died—the men were the last three surviving Reno brothers.

Scottish immigrant Allan Pinkerton founded his detective agency in Chicago in 1850 with foresight that the Reno brothers eventually brought to bloom. At the time there was no national law enforcement agency that could cross state lines. Bandits thrived on the jurisdictional limits of local sheriffs, and Pinkerton saw an opportunity in this quaint custom. As a private operation, he could cross state lines, search without establishing cause, and raise general mayhem among wrongdoers—as long as he got the right men.

The Reno gang and a later series of holdups in Kentucky and Tennessee provided the Pinkertons with an opportunity to establish a reputation that grew with the expansion of the rails. When a train was held up in Kentucky and the perpetrators fled to Tennessee, Robert and William Pinkerton, sons of Allan, trailed the culprits across state lines to Gilman, a primitive backwoods town on the banks of the Mississippi, known for its distrust of strangers and harboring of violent men. The Pinkertons simply marched up to the largest cabin in the place, after dark, and, without knocking, burst through the door and walked in. Seven startled faces, including those of two women, disappeared as the light was snuffed out and shooting began. The Pinkertons captured two men but two more escaped. Within a week, they nailed the two remaining members of the gang in Illinois.

In 1977, William C. Linn, a Pinkerton vice-president whose service dated back to the nineteenth century, was interviewed by a *National Geographic* writer and recalled a visceral hatred for the memory of the Reno gang, yet acknowledged that they made the Pinkerton success story possible. Bill Linn's most virulent anger focused on Jesse James and the myth which is the best illustration yet of Jim's theory of "ironic countertruth."

"The James gang was just about as nasty, bloodthirsty, and messy a bunch of thieves and cutthroats as you could ever put together. . . . The idea that Jesse James was a kind of Robin Hood . . . is crazy. James had as much in common with the merry men of Sherwood Forest as he had with Tyrone Power, who played the role of Jesse in one of the films."

Rail historian Stewart Holbrook, noted for his folksy tolerance of many who strayed from the Protestant ethic, deplored the folklore that made Jesse out as a Civil War hardship case who was " 'kind to his mother and little children'—that is, all little children except those who happened to be on the trains that he and his goons wrecked in order to rob." He went on to lament the hero worship of a man who "showed an indifference to human life that should put him . . . beyond the pale of consideration" as a human being.

What James certainly does deserve credit for is the innovation of wrecking trains in order to rob them. His first rail job (after many successful bank robberies) struck a Chicago, Rock Island & Pacific train in 1873. James's men had pulled up the spikes from a rail on a sharp curve near Adair, Iowa, but left the rail lying loose in place. As the train roared around the bend, the gang yanked on a rope attached to the rail to pull it out of place; the engineer thus had no chance to decrease speed before derailing. The engineer was killed when the engine overturned, and the gang swarmed out of the bushes to ransack the train, loading valuables into their trademark grain sacks. Thus began the pattern which somehow escapes the legends: nearly every robbery involved the death by violence of innocent crew or passengers.

The Pinkertons were called in as the gang continued to prey on trains from the Dakotas to Tennessee. Two Pinkertons were killed along with one of the Younger brothers in a gun battle, and the game of cops and robbers became a blood feud. Perhaps this was where the Pinkertons made the fatal public relations error which led to the Jameses, rather than themselves, becoming the heroes of the myth. Following the modus operandi established at Gilman, they traced the Jameses to their home in Missouri and chucked a huge bomb into an open window. Jesse and Frank were not home at the time, but an innocent friend, Archie Samuel, was killed and the James boys' mother had her arm and shoulder blown off. Henceforth the press never relented in portraying the Pinkertons as the thugs of the railroad and the Jameses as American Robin Hoods.

To make matters worse, the Pinkertons and the combined efforts of state and national law enforcement officials failed to make a single arrest in the James-Younger robberies for three years. The Granger movement and the labor unrest that led to the strikes of 1877 surely played a role—the gang could always find folks willing to give them shelter and cover.

Ironically the James-Younger gang was put down not by Pinkertons or federal marshals, but by a student and some other respectable citizens of Northfield, Minnesota. When the gang held up the bank in that sleepy Minnesota college town in 1876, medical intern Henry Wheeler was roused from his nap on the porch of the Dampier Hotel. He scrounged an old carbine from inside the hotel and began blasting away. Somehow the street was suddenly filled with other citizens doing the same. Half of the gang were killed or captured, though Jesse and Frank escaped in a panicked, cowardly desertion of their compatriots.

The gang was finished, though Jesse and Frank would rob a few more trains, in one case shooting the engineer and fireman to death in cold blood after the robbery was completed. Jesse was finally shot in the back by gang member Robert Ford, and Frank reformed to perform with Cole Younger in the Frank James Wild West Show in the early 1900s.

Why did Jesse James become a national hero? Bill Linn suggests that it was his penchant for public relations, especially in the aftermath of the Pinkertons' bombing disaster. "He actually gave out a news release before he left the scene of one robbery. He even suggested the headline: 'Most Daring Train Robbery on Record.'" The paper used it and established a precedent echoed by the presidential election of 1988. Desperado Jim, riding on the *Cardinal* with me in April of that year, correctly predicted that the election would go to the candidate whose handlers most successfully dictated headlines to the national media.

Ironically, the romanticized legend of Jesse and Frank James might possibly be deserved by another pair of less well-known train robbers: Christopher Evans and John Sontag of California. The elusive story of their predations on the greatest predator of them all, the Southern Pacific, deserves a special chapter in the story of making tracks, of which more in its place.

Bill Linn did have kind words for another train robber mythologized by film: Robert Parker, better known as Butch Cassidy. Cassidy never killed anyone in his U.S. robberies, though things got out of hand when he and the Sundance Kid took their business to South America in 1902. Cassidy was known for little kindnesses, such as leaving his horse for a small boy who befriended and protected him during one caper. Cassidy's gang helped the Pinkertons recover from their public relations debacle with their own legend: of a dangerous outfit driven out of the country by the efficient, relentless pursuit of the Pinkertons. The popular movie of 1969 aptly portrays that pursuit and the myth of inevitability that made the Pinkertons so feared in the criminal world at the turn of the century. Linn met a survivor of the original Hole in the Wall Gang (sometimes known as the Wild Bunch), Cowboy Joe Marsters, who "suggested to me that the government should turn over law enforcement in the whole country to the Pinkertons, who would clean up the place in two weeks."

By the Alexandria station, the denizens of the bar car have returned. No one mentions the coke dealers now, except Jim, who espouses his theory that invisible, institutionalized, societal crime spawns conspicuous, charismatic, individual crime. The rail robberies of the later nineteenth century were a response to the greater robbery of the "robber barons" and their "economic rape of the nation." The Mafia booze business during prohibition was a response to a constitutional amendment whose effect was to limit Dionysian cheer to an upper class who could imbibe behind walls of privilege. Terrorists do to unwitting travelers what oppressive governments and outdated political arrangements do to their people all the time. Pervasive white-collar crime is a response to Vietnam and Watergate, where the news media took off the emperor's clothes and showed the world that cheating was the way that government played the game, "so why in God's name should private enterprise be holier?" And the drug abuse today is a response to the "Crime of the Century," as defined by the English rock group Supertramp, which took its name from a fabled American hobo. The crime is the depersonalizing of modern life and the labeling of those who refuse to participate in the purging of libidinous selves as insane.

As we approach the capital, the haunt of those who have power to refute or validate Jim's theories, various characters on the train prepare for their departures. People exchange addresses, telephone numbers, and promises to keep in touch. Top Gun and Goldie have been nuzzling and snuggling and Rambo has been lurking.

Top Gun makes a big deal of his farewell to Goldie, but when he hits the platform in Alexandria, he is immediately embraced by a miniskirted redhead who is waiting. Jim and Will choke on their laughter as Goldie spits, "Bastard, bastard, bastard!"

A sizable contingent, including Jim, departs during the engine change in Washington. His parting shot: "What this town needs is a good actor. Look out, D.C., here comes the Desperado." Will seems genuinely touched at the loss of his friend. Now it is just he and I.

We sit in the bar car as the train accelerates toward Baltimore beyond the speed limits of the trunk route we have followed so far—80, 90, 100, 110 miles per hour. The heady feeling always stimulates conversation along this route, and Will, who so far has remained so taciturn, begins to talk. He has just come from a reunion of some of his Vietnam buddies in Bakersfield, California, and he's going to another in Philadelphia before returning home to Detroit. The main activity at these gatherings is the showing of Vietnam movies. He's seen them all: *Apocalypse Now, The Deer Hunter, Platoon,* and dozens of cult flicks like *Winds of Sand* and *Streamers*. He says the films always provoke talk about the things the films miss, such as the terror of hits at night, the leeches, the tropical heat alternating with the monsoons' numbing cold that got so bad that guys would huddle together for the shared body warmth.

Will was in college studying to be a dentist at the University of Michigan when he was drafted in 1967. He was ready to go, never gave a thought to seeking a deferment or evading the call. Still idealistic, he wanted to prove that a thinking man could be a good soldier.

Newcomers to Vietnam were called cherry boys, but they didn't stay naive for long. When a green officer straight out of college ROTC joined Will's unit a month after he arrived, Will was the veteran telling the guy not to wear his bars on his helmet. The guy didn't listen, and the next day he was shot right through the bars.

Will was a Ranger assigned to long-distance reconnaissance patrols out of Leikei. LRPs, pronounced lurps, they were called, and since they spent long periods out in the bush, they became "a little squirrelly" and were feared by the outfits that operated out of fixed bases in more secure areas.

One of the first lessons of war for the cherry boys was not to form close friendships. "You'd lose a piece of yourself every time a friend got it. I made up my mind to save friendship for after I got back home." Another lesson was the anonymity of killing: "When you had to kill, you had to kill." Will recalls entering a village where a boy ran out into the street and dropped a package. As the soldiers approached, it exploded, wounding six men with shrapnel. Will eventually learned to fire at anything that looked threatening.

Will believes the war was lost during Tet. "I don't care what they say about Tet being a terrible defeat for the enemy, after that nobody cared anymore, nobody wanted rank—that's when an Army's done—it all fell apart. By the end of '68, things just didn't add up anymore." It became acceptable, even laudable, to be motivated primarily by fear. "Just cover your own ass, keep the mind together, survive." More and more the talk was about horror stories. Will says the story in *Apocalypse Now* of the NVA's cutting off the arms of Vietnamese children inoculated by the Americans was a familiar tale making the rounds in late 1968. Another held that Cong women passing for Saigon prostitutes would insert tubes containing razor blades into their vaginas and that a man would bleed to death through the penis in four minutes. "I have no idea whether that story was true, but it didn't matter. Everyone believed it."

When his tour was finished at the end of 1968, Will celebrated his survival by "getting shitty drunk for the flight back." That turned out to be a mistake, because it left him in no condition to cope with the shock of home. The planes landed in San Francisco at weird hours of the night. Will remembers walking around the city in his dress greens totally disoriented, "as lost as I'd been as a LRP in Nam. We had a phrase over there—when the shit would begin to hit the fan, you'd say, 'Here we go, here we go.' Here I was home—with the streetlights, TVs in store windows, taxi drivers almost running me over, and signs saying, 'No GIs allowed.' I remember thinking, 'Here we go, here we go.' I'd been dreaming about home every day for a year, and when I got back, I was still an LRP in Nam."

Will hung out at Berkeley for a while, then enrolled at San Jose State and studied architecture. Eventually he married, did Lamaze classes, had kids, got divorced, and returned to his original home in Detroit. I ask him what it was like when life finally settled down for him, when things finally started to make sense again. He says, "When did that happen? You saw those two guys with the money today."

Life for Will is still on the edge. Marriage and family are impossible in his world—but he's not hustling one-night stands like Top Gun either. What he is doing is a metaphorical replay of his war experience of huddling up with companions for security against the cold. More than anyone I have met on the trains, Will is intense about striking up friendships and sharing experiences of the harsh world. He keeps a little notebook with hundreds of names, addresses, and phone numbers of people all over the country with whom he has found companionship. As the end of the run has neared, he has grown increasingly sentimental, maudlin even. But there is one last laugh as we detrain and spot Rambo snuggled up with Goldie telling her how he once saw a man commit suicide by lying down in front of a train.

Off the train in Philadelphia, Will sticks close to me until my brother-in-law arrives to take me to his home for a reunion with my wife and kids. When I shake Will's hand in farewell, it trembles and there are tears in his eyes—just because we rode a train together and shared some American scenery and low comedy. Will is the human embodiment of West Virginia and of Jim's skewed view of American history. To me, he is the victim of the "Crime of the Century."

I thought that a springtime rail journey through the heartland of America might invoke the simple, pure images of a Norman Rockwell coffee-table book, but it didn't. For every portrait of innocence and fecundity, I found a contrary tableau of disillusionment and blight. From Meridian to Bloomington to West Virginia, the common motif was a pattern of loss that textures our history, collectively and personally, like the characteristic strokes of an idiosyncratic artist's brush.

Back home, in front of my TV where programming and advertising conspire to make greed a virtue, violence a way of keeping the peace, and sex an ornament of success, I muse on Jim's theory of "ironic countertruth." We have so often made virtues of our worst vices—the myth of bold Americans setting forth to pursue fine ideals obscuring a corresponding story of betrayal and abandonment. I wonder what touchstones of unalloyed truth I can pass on to my children besides a rail spike and a few pieces of mulberry bark.

The end of this journey leaves me unsettled, dissatisfied, impatient for the next and last. Like pioneers fleeing the old world, I feel driven by a yearning for a fresh start—farther west.

PART THREE

Summer West

*Most men who have really lived
have had their great adventure.*

—JAMES JEROME HILL

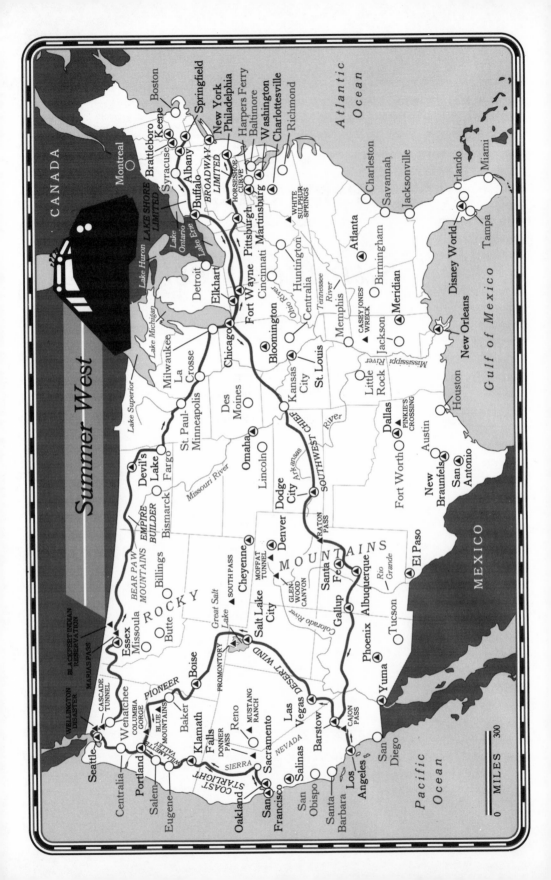

Chapter Eleven

––––––

Taming the Trail

THE *SOUTHWEST CHIEF*

B Y mid-June in New Hampshire, mud season is past, the black flies are gone, and the heat of the south begins to drive vacationers toward the cool forests, lakes, rocky shores, and mountains of New England. It is the beginning of a long period of tourism that continues through the fall foliage and into ski season. Many of us Hampshiremen ritually prepare for this onslaught by departing for a few weeks in June.

And so begins the last and longest of my rail journeys. This time my object is the northwest, by way of Los Angeles and the Mojave Desert. I have already gone transcontinental by the usual east-west route; now I want to travel the west as westerners might, following north-south routes connecting cactus deserts to sagebrush deserts, connecting barren faultline mountains to rainforest mountains. Westering dreams opened these lands and sustained the American faith for over a century. I want to find what remains of them by tracing the old trails to the farthest corners of the continent.

My route to the West Coast from Chicago runs over the old Santa Fe line, today's *Southwest Chief* on Amtrak. I saved this westbound route for the last trip because of the legend of its role in bringing civilization to the American west.

The Santa Fe Railway system, which is today one of the most profitable in America, was the high-minded, impractical pipe dream of Colonel Cyrus Holliday, who had a romantic notion of linking the imagined riches of Santa Fe, the capital of the old Spanish southwest, to the Missouri River with a rail route over the old Santa Fe Trail. The railway's peculiar institutions and unique role in passenger rail history were the result of the efforts of an Englishman, Fred Harvey, who brought a missionary's zeal to the task of making life along that route civil. The story begins in an era predating the founding of the first New England settlements.

In the thirteenth century, before the European Renaissance that would lead to the European settlement of the New World, there was already a trading center at the place that would later be called Santa Fe. Here in a high valley was shelter from blizzards, plentiful water in an arid land, clay and wood for building, defenses against enemies, and a junction of trading paths already worn deeply into the red-brown rock and soil. The pueblo was located equidistant from sources of gold, turquoise, fur, silver, copper, shells, and salt. Here in the 1500s the Indian traders met white men moving rapidly up from the south on four legs. These new men brought feathers and trinkets and tools and guns and violence—but most important, they brought their four legs. At first the natives thought they were dealing with supernatural beings who could part from their legs until they understood that the four legs belonged to animals, beasts of burden that would change their lives forever.

The natives now had the wherewithal to vastly extend their trading activity, and the pueblo became a repository of exotic goods collected from gatherings far and wide. To the white men from the south, such richness had to portend gold, and for three hundred years the Spaniards searched the American southwest for the gold that wasn't found until 1848 at Sutter's Fort in California. De Vaca, Cortez, and Coronado terrorized the natives in their search for the elusive source of the wealth whose real underpinning increasingly came to be the horses that the Spanish introduced. In 1599, after a year of fearful strife, Don Juan de Onate established his capital in the high valley and named it San Francisco de Santa Fe. The native trade melded with the Spanish flow up from Vera Cruz and the string of galleons from across the Atlantic. By the late 1700s when the first English-speaking wanderers arrived from the new American colonies over a desperate dusty trail from the rivers of the east, they couldn't believe their eyes.

The Santa Fe trail was never the result of careful scouting and planning as were some of the other pioneer trails of the west; it evolved from Indian legend, explorer's tradition, and not a little wanderer's blarney. But it did get travelers from the Missouri to Santa Fe, often with enough water along the way for sustaining reasonably robust human life. From Santa Fe another old Spanish route wound up over the Colorado, through the Wasatch Mountains of Utah, across the desert, and over another then unnamed range to the Pueblo of Our Lady, Queen of Angels. It was all there, a southwest passage by land from the Missouri to the eventual site of Los Angeles, when Lewis and Clark made their journey to the northwest, but it belonged to Spain and then Mexico. Yankee perception of good trading opportunities would change that.

In 1821, Captain W. H. Becknell led the first wagon train across the prairie and desert to Santa Fe from the Missouri River. He brought not settlers but traders, who exchanged $3,000 worth of American goods for $15,000 worth of Santa Fe silver and gold. A few years later the second train did even better, returning with $190,000 of silver and gold on an outlay of $30,000. The Mexicans were furious at the new trading competition and so levied a stiff tax on each wagon from the east. The Yankee traders responded by concentrating their loads in half of their wagons just outside Santa Fe and hiding the empty ones to be picked up and reloaded surreptitiously on the return trip. Then the tax was added on to the price of their inbound cargoes; the Mexicans ended up paying their own tax and then some.

In 1846, General Stephen Kearny captured Santa Fe, and two years later the capital was turned over to the United States government along with nearly a quarter of a continent in the Mexican cession. Texas came into the Union, and gold, real gold, was discovered in California. Santa Fe dwindled to a small trading outpost and wayside rest along the southwest trail to California. By 1850 the Oregon and California trails were thought to be faster and safer, and then the clippers around the cape proved an even greater competition. Manifest Destiny seemed to have bypassed the city that was once the jewel of the southwest. It lingered only as a memory in the dreams of romantic men, in the real life of a desert-bitten crew of hard-drinking, hard-gambling and hard-fighting ruffians, and, of course, as home for the natives who had been there forever and seen waves of white men come and go.

So when, in the mid-1850s, Colonel Cyrus Holliday began dreaming of investing the fortune he had made on the Pittsburgh & Lake Erie Railroad in building a line from the Missouri to Santa Fe, it is no surprise that people scoffed. The great national project of the Union Pacific was just beginning to gain sympathetic ears. But events began to focus attention on Kansas, and Holliday made sure that his dream was planted firmly in the midst of this opening historical arena. Kansas was to become a state, and its status with regard to slavery was not yet decided when Colonel Holliday himself laid out its future capital, Topeka, by literally drawing lines in the dust. When Kansas was declared a free state and the bloodshed began, Colonel Holliday was solidly ensconced in Topeka arguing that a railroad at least linking Topeka to the Missouri River would help bind the state to the Union. He got his charter in 1859 and in 1863 designated Atchison as its starting point on the river. No one knew that eventually the expected great Missouri River city would rise farther south at Kansas City. Thus the name of the legendary railroad—the Atchison, Topeka & Santa Fe.

But the Civil War and droughts—"a railroad into that desert?"—would hold up construction until 1868. By this time the Union Pacific was nearing completion and the Kansas Pacific was already begun and dominating rail traffic in north-central Kansas. Plans were in the works for a Northern Pacific at the 50th parallel, and the Southern Pacific was stirring in southern California. No one but Holliday saw the ATSF as a contender in the transcontinental race, and even he spoke only of the old Spanish capital in the mountains of New Mexico as the object. How could he hope to compete?

Since well before the war, the vast cattle herds of Texas had been growing. As the first rails of the UP and then the KP snaked across the plains, the ranchers turned their eyes away from the rivers and southern ports to the north and the prairie grasses that might provide forage for long drives all the way from Texas to a rail junction in Nebraska, Colorado, or Kansas, where the live beef could be loaded into railcars for cheap shipment to Chicago. In 1867 the drives began, and Colonel Holliday watched first the UP at Omaha, and then the more southerly KP at Abilene profit from the traffic. The Santa Fe route was more southerly still, making for shorter cattle drives and greater profits for those positioned to take them. In time the drives would all lead to a dozen hell-and-gunsmoke ATSF towns, including Newton, Wichita, Emporia, La Junta, and of course Dodge City, but before the ATSF could civilize the wild west it had to invent it along the now nearly abandoned ruts of the old trail. Its successful strategy for competing with the other railroads in the early 1870s did just that.

Waiting for the *Southwest Chief* in Chicago's Union Station 120 years later, I contemplate the route that I am about to take and that evolved from Colonel Holliday's dream. It begins here in Chicago and runs through Kansas City, Topeka, the string of old cattle towns, Las Vegas, Albuquerque, and Flagstaff and finally to L.A. It misses Atchison and Santa Fe entirely, but continues up the California valleys to San Francisco. It certainly is the fastest rail route to the coast, the only line to maintain eastern standards of speed over the vastness of the west. This route takes a civilized thirty-nine hours, versus the nearly fifty hours of others to the coast. You can see the remnants of the old Santa Fe Trail for much of the route.

The beginning of my journey is as uncivil as any yet. Apparently, in his zeal to be helpful, a ticket agent has sold me an economy bedroom that is reserved for the sleeping-car attendant in the working-conditions language of his union contract. All other upstairs economy bedrooms are taken, and so I am diverted to a lower-level one. These rooms are fine if you don't like to descend the stairs to the bathrooms or to meet any other people on the train, but I always request an upstairs room so I can have as much contact with travelers passing through the corridor as possible. For the first time I throw the kind of fit I have cringed to watch other unreasonable passengers perform many times before. There are sharp words on the platform, and an uneasy truce while the service chief makes a call. When he returns he takes my bags and commands me to follow him. He leads me upstairs and to the left. Oh God, I think. A coach seat—the economy bedrooms are all to the right. But he stops in the bedroom-car corridor and extends his hand toward the door of one of the deluxe rooms. "How's this, compliments of the *Southwest Chief?*"

Wonderful. A deluxe double, all to myself, all the way to L.A. The room measures seven and a half by six and a half feet. Just inside the doorway there is a closet, vanity, and sink with hot and cold running water, a three-way mirror, 120-volt electrical outlets, and little cupboards and shelves underneath for towels, washcloths, tissues, cups, and ice. Along the entire opposite wall runs a couch, long enough to really stretch out on, even when it's not made into the double bed it becomes at night. Above the couch an upper bunk is folded into the wall. Facing the couch at the other end of the large curtained picture window stands a reclining swivel armchair. In a separate compartment in the corner behind the vanity there is a toilet and hot shower, and a table can be folded out from the wall between the chair and the couch. There are the usual Superliner air conditioning, airline-style reading lights, and music and announcement sound channels. But the best thing about a Superliner deluxe room, aside from the shower, is the curtained glass door opening onto the corridor and its window. Thus with the curtain open, the passenger has a view out both sides of the train, even with his door closed.

The sleeping-car attendant whom I was threatening to displace stops by, beaming, and asks, "What time is the party?" I tell him it starts right after dinner. So while the train highballs through Joliet and Streator, Illinois, I enjoy the ease of a hot shower; I want to take advantage of this stroke of luck before it disappears. There is actually enough room in this compartment to make dressing for dinner a pleasurable activity, and I make the most of it. Out comes the jacket, tie, and slacks for the only time in the entire trip. There will be fresh salmon for dinner. Civilized, really civilized.

During dinner I barely notice the signs of severe drought as we pass through the stricken Illinois farm belt. The convivial atmosphere in the diner is too good. My table brings together four solo travelers: myself, Fred Diehl, Randy Wesson, and Lana Meagher.

Randy, a large fiftyish man who shouldn't be spending much time in the diner, is traveling to Dodge City to see his sister-in-law. We have been talking about the outlaw past of the Santa Fe route, and Fred asks jokingly, "Is your sister-in-law an outlaw?"

"Well, apparently yes," laughs Randy. "I'm going to Dodge to bail her out of jail." He is responding to a desperate letter he received a week ago, something about bad checks and credit-card fraud. He took the train from his home in Chicago because he gets motion sickness from the small airplanes that fly into little towns like Dodge. I wonder why people don't get motion sickness on trains, and Fred explains that it's vertical motion that does it. Despite all of the rocking and swaying of railcars, they don't heave up and down because the grade is so steady.

Fred asks if Randy is an athlete, though the question seems a bit inappropriate considering Randy's girth and gait. But Randy answers that, yes, he is a former pro ice hockey player who has lost the battle for fitness since he quit the game. How does Fred know?

"Athletes are always the ones to get seasick," explains Fred, a professional sailboat skipper who has dealt with many a seasick athlete. It puzzled him until he read a Navy study that confirmed what he had always observed. It's because of the athlete's finely tuned sense of balance, his inner ear. Gymnasts, baseball players, ballerinas, skiers, and, yes, ice hockey players are especially susceptible.

Fred Diehl, of Newport, Rhode Island, is a skipper of an excursion sailboat, a sixty-two-foot sloop named *The Winds of Love*. For a total of about $10,000 a week, he will take six passengers just about anywhere there's water and the wind blows. He only needs one crew member, since the boat is highly automated and motorized, sheets and cleats and manual coffee grinders having long since been replaced by electrical controls. Navigation is by satellite.

Fred is on vacation from all of that. This stocky, blond-bearded, thirtyish sea dog wants to see the continent by land for the first time. He is riding to Flagstaff to make a bus connection that will take him to the Grand Canyon. Later he will take another train to Las Vegas for the gaming tables and the women. Fred is unmarried and unabashedly on the make. When I tell him about the preponderance of single women I've observed on the trains, he winks with delight. He'd like nothing better than to find a harem on this trip and then, with that out of his system, maybe a girlfriend or even a wife. "I've been married to that boat too long."

Lana is amused by Fred's barefaced announcement of his intentions but is not available. About forty, she is an attractive elementary school teacher and mother of three whose absent husband weighs 275 pounds "and is not fat." She wears a fistful of heavy hand-crafted silver and turquoise rings. "From Santa Fe," she says. "You can buy them from Indian craftsmen during the long stop at Albuquerque. I've been collecting them for years." She has traveled this train back and forth to visit her family in Michigan ever since she moved to the West Coast eighteen years ago, a year before Amtrak was instituted.

Lana can narrate the ups and downs of diner service on this train. In the last year before Amtrak took over, even the once-proud Santa Fe passenger department was actively trying to discourage passengers so that they could drop passenger service. Except on weekend runs, when a reasonable facsimile of old-time diner service actually still prevailed, cold sandwiches were the rule. In the first years of Amtrak, four-course meals were served on real china with stainless dinnerware and linen tablecloths. "It was spectacular, but a little depressing because you knew they couldn't keep it up. There was a feeling that the high level of service confirmed the rumor that Amtrak was merely intended to preside over a glorious demise of passenger railroads." Then came the budget cuts, and by 1980, all food was microwaved and served on plastic with plastic dinnerware. "It wasn't even as good as airline fare, and the cutback in service personnel meant that you were treated poorly in the bargain." Since 1984, however, Lana has observed a fitful improvement to the relatively good standards of today. Occasionally the microwave regime would appear for a while, but then the chefs would come back. She says that the service we are enjoying tonight is as good as any since the early days of Amtrak.

Tonight's dinner has been good. The waiters have been efficient and pleasant, but there are still those damnable plastic platters and the oppressive blue plastic tablecloth. I'm sure Fred Harvey would not approve.

Englishman Fred Harvey came to America in 1850 seeking his fortune at the age of fifteen. Following his arrival in New Orleans, he worked in various fine restaurants and by twenty had opened his own in St. Louis, where he married and began a career as a restaurateur. But the Civil War wrecked his business, and he wound up working for river packet boats and then on the Burlington Railroad as a freight agent.

Until the "dining-car wars" of the late 1880s, passengers traveling west of Chicago were subject to gastronomic horrors that challenge description. There were no dining cars beyond the Mississippi, because of an agreement between western railroads to avoid competition in this money-losing service. Trains stopped for mealtimes at wayside eateries which often were little more than lean-tos of buffalo hides. Passengers would sometimes carve themselves hunks from week-old buffalo carcasses hanging on hooks and roast them over open fires. The better eating houses were notorious at best. Passengers would bolt what food they could during a five-minute stop and then the remains of their dinners would be salvaged for service to the next train. The fare was usually unidentifiable slabs of meat, beans, hard bread, and something called "railroad pie," a horrendous concoction of stewed leftovers in dough that might pass for either breakfast, dessert, or a dinner main course. The places were filthy and fly-ridden, the service careless and crude.

Fred Harvey thought he could do better and proposed a cooperative venture for providing good food service along the route of the Burlington. Management turned him down. No one enduring the miseries of the prairie crossing cared about food, and no one ever came back to the same place a second time. Fine restaurants are dependent on repeat customers, Harvey was told. Maybe in fifty years when the country was more settled.

In 1880, Harvey approached the Santa Fe, which gave him an old depot building in Topeka in which to try his ideas. Within a month, the first Harvey House was a roaring success, not only with train crews and passengers, but with local residents, who spread word throughout eastern Kansas that here was a place that actually offered clean napkins and tablecloths, polished silver, and good food. A second Harvey House and hotel at Florence convinced Santa Fe management that Fred was on to something, and thus began an association that would last until the 1950s.

The string of Harvey Houses that began to stretch along the old Santa Fe Trail like oases of civility in a barbarous desert ironically constituted America's first fast-food chain. Like today's McDonald's they catered to the long-distance traveler who could afford only a short stop for meals. Their menus were standardized and based on wholesale foodstuffs carried as freight over the same routes traveled by their customers. Their pitch to the consumer was cleanliness, predictable food and prices, and the cheerful smiles of the young women who provided service.

But there the resemblance to today's emporiums of indigestion ends. Harvey Houses created at least the illusion of slow, unhurried service. Trainmen would pass through the cars with menus taking orders at a point on the route one station ahead of the Harvey House stop, then all orders would be telegraphed ahead to the Harvey House so that when the train pulled in, the first course would be waiting on the tables and the main courses already sizzling in the kitchen. Choices of drinks would be indicated at each diner's seat with the "cup code." A cup sitting on the saucer right side up indicated coffee, upside down meant hot tea, upside down and tilted beside the saucer meant iced tea, and so on. When diners sat down at their appointed places, drinks waitresses would appear and miraculously pour the requested drink, as long as no one messed with his cup.

The price for dinners from the regular menu was fixed at fifty cents. Menus, though standardized, were issued in four-day rotating sequences so that even travelers on long journeys wouldn't see the same menu until the fifth day. Recognizing the value of Harvey's chain to Santa Fe passenger business, the railroad carried the foodstuffs at drastically reduced rates, which made it possible for the houses to afford the very best. In turning down a proposal to introduce cold-storage eggs into the menu, Harvey made his legendary declaration against processed food. "The intrusion of such a gastronomic atrocity between a host and his guest is an unpardonable breach of the laws of hospitality."

To Fred Harvey, civility was not a matter of custom but of immutable law. It was Harvey orthodoxy that in fine restaurants food was meant to be served by attractive young women of good cheer and unblemished character. Thus the Harvey girls became as much a part of legend as Fred himself. He recruited them throughout the East Coast and the more settled big cities of the midwest with simple ads calling for "young women of good character, attractive and intelligent, 18 to 30, no experience necessary." Their contract stipulated behavior as stringent as that required in a convent, and they had to promise not to marry for at least a year. Stern matrons supervised them in dormitories which they never left without their uniform of plain black dress, stockings, and shoes, Elsie collar and black bow, and the ubiquitous white ribbon tied in the hair. When they finally did marry, it was usually to the railroad men, ranchers, and prosperous businessmen who provided the foundation for the small but growing "respectable" class of Kansas, Colorado, and New Mexico. Thus they contributed more to the taming of the west than the gentility of the Harvey Houses; they provided much of the stock upon which the civilized society of the west was built.

A second law of civility which Fred Harvey personally enforced was the requirement of coats for dinner. The rule was simple: no coat, no service. Every Harvey House had on hand a supply of alpaca jackets for those who arrived coatless. Tales are legion of gun-toting cowpokes who would demand, with great gales of profanity, to be served coatless. They were ignored. In 1882, some cowhands and their foremen rode their horses into the dining room of the Harvey House in Las Vegas, New Mexico. Mr. Harvey happened to be present, and raising a hand of command, he informed the rowdies that "ladies dine here." When the shamed cowhands left, Harvey set them up with a free lunch in another room—after providing them all with jackets.

When an Oklahoma Harvey House refused service to the unjacketed chairman of the State Corporation Commission, who claimed that coats were against Sooner customs, Harvey's right to insist on coats was litigated all the way to the state supreme court. The decision in Harvey's favor pointed out that without such a right, restaurateurs and innkeepers might next be serving people without shirts or even in breechcloths. The opinion suggested that the highest court could do no less than encourage Harvey's laws of civility in the barbarous climate of the times.

But there was one place where an exception to the law was made—
the Harvey House at Santa Fe, where the centuries-old traditions of
caballeros combined with the more recent informal spirit of the artists
and writers who settled there to make the rule inappropriate. Santa Fe
had its own customs which predated Fred Harvey.

Though uniform in standards and rules, Harvey Houses made no
attempt to present a uniform physical appearance as so many of our
modern chains do. The combination of old Spanish and native Indian
design in architect Mary E. J. Colter's creation of the "Santa Fe style"
allowed for radical variation in design from establishment to establishment. And it was Harvey himself who initiated the much-imitated
practice of setting up fine restaurants inside old railroad cars. In 1884,
at Holbrook, Arizona, the Harvey House consisted of five rickety old
boxcars with the paint peeling off them, but inside was the usual
immaculate setting with Irish linen, English silver, crystal and imported crockery, and, of course, the Harvey girls and the Harvey food.
Holbrook became a frequent stop for traveling gourmands who would
tell their friends about the dreary boxcars at Holbrook and the diners'
delight inside.

By 1888, even the profit-hungry Union Pacific had begun to attempt
to imitate the Harvey formula, though with indifferent success. Now
there were enough railroads competing for the passenger trade that
many lines put on dining cars and the "dining-car wars" were on in
earnest. Harvey ran dining cars on the Santa Fe with the same standards and rules as in his houses, even though that meant operating at a
loss, which the railroad, recognizing the value of good public relations,
gladly absorbed. Here began a Santa Fe tradition of being the only
transcontinental line that could match the style and substance of the
great trains of the east. A traveler riding on the *Kansas Express* in
1888 was so impressed that he kept his menu for posterity and left it
with his estate:

Blue Points on Shell
English Peas au Gratin
Filets of Whitefish, Madeira Sauce
Potatoes Français
Young Capon, Hollandaise Sauce
Roast Sirloin of Beef au Jus   Pork with Applesauce
Turkey Stuffed   Cranberry Sauce
Mashed Potatoes   Boiled Sweet Potatoes   Elgin Sugar Corn
Marrowfat Peas   Asparagus, Cream Sauce
Salmi of Duck   Queen Olives
Baked Veal Pie English Style
Charlotte of Peaches, Cognac Sauce
Prairie Chicken, Currant Jelly
Sugar Cured Ham   Pickled Lamb's Tongue
Lobster Salad au Mayonnaise
Beets
Celery   French Slaw
Apple Pie   Cold Custard à la Chantilly   Mince Pie
Assorted Cakes   Bananas   New York Ice Cream
Oranges   Catawba Wine Jelly   Grapes
Edam and Roquefort Cheese
Bent's Water Crackers   French Coffee
Wednesday, Nov. 14, 1888   Meals 75 cents

Harvey expanded the news butcher service to include fine books, perfumes, drugs, and novelties at stations along the route. Skeptics scoffed that no one would stop in stations to buy anything beyond newspapers, cheap books, and candy, but the station merchant arcades of the twenties and the underground malls of today are testimony to the astuteness of Harvey's vision.

When news butchers began hawking their wares on the trains of many railroads, a new dimension of tawdriness appeared. The fraudulent "Paris Package" was sold in lewd, conspiratorial whispers as a collection of "snappy" pictures not to be viewed until the passenger left the train. Inside, the package consisted of a series of postcards depicting a young woman partially undressing for bed, alone, but with provocative captions such as "Looking for trouble." Another production called "Only a Boy" delivered on the conspiratorial promise with truly obscene depictions of a young boy's initiation into manhood through casual encounters with women of the world on a train.

But not on the Santa Fe. Harvey's on-board news butchers offered the *Chicago Tribune*, Chaucer and Shakespeare, Dickens and Hawthorne, and, of course, the King James Bible.

When Harvey began building luxury hotels at scenic out-of-the-way spots along the route such as the Grand Canyon, the Sangre de Cristo, and the Mojave Desert, the skeptics were there again to argue that people wouldn't pay luxury prices to ride a train across godforsaken nowhere to stay in a five-star hotel at the end of the earth. Establishments such as the Montezuma Hotel at the Sangre de Cristo hot springs and the El Tovar and Bright Angel lodges at the Grand Canyon's rim proved otherwise. It was precisely the presence of true first-class luxury in the wilderness that explained their appeal.

Fred Harvey showed us that civility and elegance were profitable commodities in America, even in her wildest places, and in the process of the demonstration, his enterprises made those places less crude. Since then the roughest rudiments of the Harvey formula have been taught in hotel management schools for a century and imitated by hotel chains for decades. But I wonder how well the spirit of the lesson is learned or remembered.

Today near the Santa Fe tracks in Barstow, California, the familiar McDonald's arches gleam far across the Mojave Desert in the red-dusk dinner hour. Weary travelers off Interstate 15 thrill with delight when they pull in and see the place set up in three immaculate, gleaming silver passenger railroad cars. But inside are the familiar jostling lines at the service counter, the orders barked into echoing microphones, the never-changing menu, the harsh orange-violet glare of fluorescent lights, and the piles of paper and plastic wrappings that accumulate on the plastic tray as the food is wolfed down. They have attempted to mimic Harvey's archetypal Holbrook stunt here; they have got it exactly backward.

On today's train much of Kansas is traversed during the night. After a late evening of libations with my dinner companions and a handful of others who drift in and out of my deluxe room, I find it a real struggle to rally myself by 7:00 A.M. to view our passage through Dodge City. As I pop the childproof cap of my aspirin bottle, I console myself with the thought that I am arriving in a spirit and condition appropriate for a morning in this most famous of once-lawless western towns.

But I am not prepared for the tidy little burg that is Dodge City today. From the train you can see Boot Hill and Hangman's Tree on the left and a restoration of Front Street on the right, but there is too much green—grass, trees, and ferns in the windows of prosperous, gentrified boutiques. The Front Street restoration reminds me more of Disney World than of *Gunsmoke* and *High Noon*. In this town which invented by statute the phrase "Wrong side of the tracks" as a means of separating its notorious establishments from the haunts of the growing class of respectable burghers in the 1880s, there is a disconcerting neatness and order to the scene on both sides of the rails. Blame it on the railroad and Fred Harvey and his girls.

Over breakfast I meet a bearded young man named Don Welles, who boarded the train at Dodge. Don is a traveling tree and hedge trimmer, and considers himself a "mobile capitalist" rather than a migrant worker. He rides trains around the country looking for places with lots of trees that need trimming. It helps if the community appears to have the trappings of money, because he likes to charge whatever the market will bear. He guessed wrong about Dodge. As I was, he was impressed by the prosperous greenness of the place and so made an unscheduled stop two days ago. "Money and trees. It looked like a sure thing. But they've got three well-established, highly competitive tree-trimming services in this town already. Dodge City—who would've thought it!" Now he's on the train to try again at Phoenix, where he hopes there are more wealthy retired shade lovers than any local tree services can handle.

As the train climbs the high plains into the southwest corner of Colorado, the landscape begins to evoke images of the wild past of this area. The clumps of trees disappear shortly after Dodge, replaced by the sagebrush that will dominate my window views for the next two thousand miles. Don is depressed and curls up in the lounge car in a kind of hibernation that lasts all day as the train crosses the treeless southwest. By Las Animas there is more than enough dust with barren flat-topped hills on a horizon of billowing storm clouds. Here the Rio de las Animas Perdidas (River of Lost Souls) was named for a wagon train of settlers who just disappeared from their camp one night, assumed victims of an Indian raid.

At La Junta the famous hundred-mile view of Pikes Peak does not materialize because of the clouds, and I wonder what happened during cloudy spells to wagon trains depending on that landmark as the sign for when to turn southward toward Raton Pass. Here we pick up the third engine to help us over the Raton climb, America's steepest passenger rail incline, 175 feet per mile, a 3.3 percent grade. In the lounge-observation car people comment about how they can feel for the first time the actual sloping of the train on this incline. There are nervous musings from passengers innocent of the design of railroad brakes about what happens if a coupling breaks loose (the brakes engage automatically). Outside passes the old Wooten Ranch and a number of stretches of the original Santa Fe Trail, now marked off and preserved for posterity. A tunnel runs under the pass itself at 7,588 feet and leads to an equally steep descent down the other side of the easternmost protrusion of the Sangre de Cristo Mountains, past the ruins of the Clifton House, a layover stop dating back to the heyday of the old trail.

A look at a map creates the impression that the Santa Fe Trail, and subsequent rail line, was laid out so that it went out of its way to cross the rugged Raton Pass, but the route through the mountains was actually established to avoid the haunts of particularly hostile Indians in eastern New Mexico and the Oklahoma panhandle. A trail known as the Cimarron Cut-off connected Las Vegas with Kansas by the more direct route, but this was a risky alternative. When the railroad came, tradition weighed heavily on the planners and surveyors who never gave the cut-off a second thought. Besides, by routing through, and in a military sense thus occupying, southeastern Colorado, the Santa Fe preempted the Denver & Rio Grande's attempts to reach the river of its name by way of Raton Pass. At the same time the route guaranteed that the DRG would not be able to block the ATSF from reaching the terminal city of its name.

Between Raton and Las Vegas, the old wagon trains were guided by a landmark known as the Wagon Mound. It was supposed to look like a prairie schooner and its team, but I am damned if I can distinguish it from several other mound-shaped mountains on the opposite side of the trail. First clouds around Pikes Peak and now this. If it had been up to me to navigate civilization into this country, there'd be another Las Animas Perdidas marking a dead end far off the beaten track.

Las Vegas sprawls across a high-altitude meadow of surprising greenness. The old Harvey House, La Castenada, still stands in the town where vigilantes, inspired by the virtue of the Harvey girls, made war against the likes of Billy the Kid and other unsavory characters who, for a time, made Las Vegas their headquarters.

From Las Vegas the route climbs its second major pass, Glorietta, scene of a Civil War battle that kept New Mexico out of the Confederacy, and then descends steeply through Apache Canyon, a passage so narrow that passengers once collected rock samples through their open windows. After the verdant meadows to the east and the dense pine forests of the mountain crossing, the western slope presents the landscape one associates with New Mexico—sagebrush, dry red-brown soil, and still redder outcroppings of vertical rock. Finally the train pulls into Lamy, as close as it ever gets to Santa Fe. The city that inspired Colonel Holliday's dream lies north through a rugged canyon.

Before the luxury diners steaming to the coast, before the artist colonies at Santa Fe, before Fred Harvey and his girls, before the cattle drives and the roaring cattle towns of Kansas, there was just Colonel Holliday with his dream and a handful of New Englanders who were seeking their fortunes by following Horace Greeley's advice. In 1869, the year of the completion of the UP, the first tracks of the ATSF staggered into southwestern Kansas from Topeka. The modus operandi originally was to lay track into an area and wait for a settlement to grow up around it. Thus the surveyors initially dealt only with considerations of engineering expedience and the traditions of the trail. But quickly settlement leapfrogged out in front of the railhead in anticipation of its arrival. Now the surveyors dealt with a third consideration: the Santa Fe actually had places to go to. Thus the route across flat Kansas turns and winds more than geography would seem to dictate. Critics would later argue that the wandering route of the ATSF was proof of railroad rapaciousness in seeking federal land grants and loans based on track mileage.

Life along the line in the early 1870s was crude. Besides the barbaric wayside eating stops, there were Indian raids, buffalo stampedes, and bandits. The trains ran by the smoke-and-headlight rule before the telegraph lines were run, and thus cloudy days could result in awkward "prairie meets" of trains running in opposite directions over a stretch of single-track line. Before the invention of decent spark arrestors, passengers had to choose between stifling in airless coaches with closed windows or fighting the cinders that blew in through open windows. Conductors did what they could by fishing cinders out of afflicted eyes with horsehair loops or placing a flaxseed under the eyelid so that tears would offer relief. In later years the trick of rolling chewing gum to a point to pick off the cinder offered the best treatment.

And the railroad was not always welcome. The Indians knew trouble when they saw it and developed a superstition about crossing the tracks. They would gather at bridges over creeks, and trouble would often ensue. The cattlemen, upon whose goodwill the road would heavily depend, complained of prairie fires started by the sparks from the stacks and stampedes caused by the chuffing sound of the engines. Thus it became Santa Fe policy to shut off the steam when a drive came into view and drift past it. Rowdy passengers had to be asked to refrain from shooting at the cattle from the windows.

Dodge City was founded before the arrival of the railroad as Buffalo City, but the U.S. Postal Service, deluged with Buffalo Cities, later changed the name to reflect its proximity to Fort Dodge, a few miles away. It was the buffalo hunting, at its most destructive peak, that built Dodge. One Dodge citizen, Tom Nickson, claimed to have killed 140 in a single day. "Brick" Bond, with half a dozen skinners working for him, accounted for 200,000 in four years. By the late 1880s three million buffalo had been slaughtered around Dodge. One of Dodge's earliest enterprises gives the lie, however, to the legend that the millions of buffalo carcasses left on the prairie rotted as waste. Organized concerns crisscrossed the prairie gathering bones and hides to be made into fertilizer, which became a major source of traffic for the ATSF. "Bone money" helped many an early family of settlers get through their first lean years. But the railroad arrived at Dodge in 1873, and within a decade the buffalo, and the fertilizer trade, was gone.

Then came the Texans with their cattle drives and Mexicans with their gambling tables. Saloonkeepers and prostitutes provided the closest thing to a sense of community and Dodge became the hellhole of legend. Money from the cattle drives kept the enterprises pumped up, and the railroad, so dependent on order, struggled through the place of anarchy keeping a firm but low profile. Trains passing through Dodge at night would always put out all lights and run in the dark to avoid the bullets of drunken cowhands who thought shooting at passing trains to be great sport. Conductors carried Winchesters to assist them in disabusing Dodge residents of the notion that they were somehow exempt from the requirements of tickets. Prostitutes were politely asked to refrain from conducting their business on the train itself, again with the quiet persuasion of the Winchesters if necessary.

The shootouts popularized in western novels, movies, and TV shows were real and frequent, though the familiar bit of the good guy disarming the bad guy by shooting his pistol out of his hand is surely fanciful; neither the pistols nor their owners' skills were anything like that good. Most shootouts occurred at distances of less than ten feet. A premium was obviously placed on speed of the draw, and at that distance, the damage done by one .45 caliber slug made further shooting unnecessary unless the winner was striving for effect. Often there were two winners—or losers.

From the arrival of the railroad, law made fitful but firm progress in Dodge. One of the first laws to be effectively enforced, usually by gun-toting citizens themselves, was the ban against concealed weapons. Those found carrying a concealed weapon in a saloon often found themselves on the receiving end of their peers' exposed weapons post-haste. No summons needed to be served.

The commander of nearby Fort Dodge attempted to bring order to the town but more often found himself pleading with the governor for more help to protect his soldiers from the whites they were protecting from the Indians. It was Mayor Webster's establishment of the tracks as the dividing line between respectable Dodge on the north and the red-light district, now confined to the south, that initiated the critical showdown between the forces of law and anarchy. The tracks became no-man's-land in a battleground over the issue until the emergence of the regime of two brothers who had contracted with the Santa Fe to grade the route through Dodge. Ed and Bat Masterson became Dodge's first effective peace officers, Ed as marshal, Bat as sheriff. When Ed was shot by the Walker gang in 1877, Bat's blazing vengeance upon the leaders became the basis of legend. As recounted earlier, the ATSF would call upon Masterson's talents again during its clash with the DRG over the Royal Gorge. With his emergence, Dodge was on its way to respectability, and the railroad had a man it could turn to when more civil means of persuasion failed.

But even with law established, life in Dodge was still wild. Dodge never had a fire department till late in the century, the residents relying instead on the expedient of keeping barrels of rainwater on the roofs with the expectation that when a fire burned through, the barrels would tip and douse it. Homesteading settlers were not welcomed for decades. A dentist in Great Bend, hoping to persuade a group of farmers to settle there instead of at Dodge, wired a message to some Dodge cattlemen ahead of the immigrants' train announcing their imminent arrival and urging the ranchers to "show every courtesy." The immigrants were greeted at the train with a show of lusty gunfire and decided indeed that Great Bend was the place to be.

The railroad actively recruited homesteading settlers from Europe. In time other railroads in Oklahoma and Texas would do to the ATSF cattle towns what the ATSF did to Abilene and others up north. The cattlemen protested the invasion of Germans and Russian Mennonites who fenced and tilled the prairie, but the railroad men knew who held the key to their long-term future.

Meanwhile a great race was shaping up for the southeastern corner of Colorado. The area was critical to three railroads hoping to make good on their names. The DRG wanted to push southward to the Rio Grande. The Kansas Pacific wanted to go west to California. The ATSF wanted to reach Santa Fe. It has already been related how the ATSF lost the violent battle with the DRG for the Royal Gorge into the Rockies but won the more polite struggle for the Raton Pass into New Mexico by befriending Dick Wooten and his toll road over the mountain.

While the ATSF never shrank from a fight with competing railroads, its history is generally much freer of conflict with the Indians than was that of the Union Pacific and other transcontinental lines. One of the reasons is a classic of enlightened enterprise. The ATSF hired Indians to help build the railroad. The Navajo and Pueblo in particular seemed eager to wield shovels for grade work, and early ATSF foremen chalked it up to childlike simplicity. Some thought that after centuries of enslavement under the Spanish, the descendants of the ancient peoples of the southwest welcomed a task that paid them money. Though attacks with flame arrows spooked many a Santa Fe passenger, there is no question that the Indians of New Mexico and Arizona put far more energy into building the railroad than they did into attempting to wreck it.

Today the *Southwest Chief* makes a twenty-minute service stop at Albuquerque, where Tiwa Indian women sell jewelry at concession tables set up right on the platform by the train. Lana has spotted a seller she has bought from before and is quickly dickering over a striking bracelet. At one time the railroad presided over these concessions, guaranteeing a standard level of quality and price. Today, according to Lana, they offer the flawed pieces at the same moderate prices as the good ones. "*Caveat emptor,*" she says. "You won't get your money's worth here, you'll get more—or less. On the whole, if you're careful, you get quality handmade stuff for about half what it would cost in an L.A. jewelry store."

An "Indian guide" boards the train at Albuquerque to offer a historical perspective for the ride across the reservations to Gallup. In his talk, Gary Holtsoi, a full-blooded Navajo whose name means "warrior of the meadow people," talks about the land—always the land—and his people primarily in terms of the lasting marks they have laid upon it. He points out the pueblos, which almost seem to be a phenomenon of the natural volcanic activity that shaped the region; the lava beds infested with rattlesnakes drawn by their epoch-old heat; Church Rock, where a lovelorn Indian maiden leaped to her death; Red Rock Park, which according to legend got its color from a wounded stag and today serves as a meeting place for the Inter-Tribal Indian Ceremonial; the cliff dwellings of Gallup; and the concessions of the Indian craftsmen who still make marvelous things out of the earth and its minerals here.

Later, off-duty over a beer in my room, he tells me about himself. He is a handsome thirty-seven and wants to see his people share in the melting-pot process as fully as have the various European and Asian ethnic groups. He feels that, unfortunately, good intentions springing from white guilt have combined with white racism to deny Indians their fair shot at the American dream by creating for them a special status outside the pot. Though he makes part of his living as an Indian artist, tribal dancer, and master of an Indian marching band, he wants to see his kids achieve the same kind of status and integration that a second- or third-generation Italian or Irish family might aspire to.

He comes from a family with a tradition of "progressive attitudes" toward the changes wrought by white men, and, of course, the Navajo always were friendlier than their mortal enemies, the Apache. His great-grandfather worked for the U.S. Army as a scout helping to track down and capture Geronimo; he was an interpreter at Fort Wingate for most of his life, retired at seventy-nine, and lived to be 118. Gary's father was training to be a medicine man but was converted to Christianity by missionaries, who began working in the reservation in the early twentieth century. Not allowed to speak Navajo as a child, Gary became fluent in English and German and studied Latin. He has since learned his native language as an adult, but he is grateful to the Christian reform group from Michigan who provided the education that gives him the fluency and social mobility that his forefathers never achieved. He has roots and a heritage he is proud of "out in the reservation," but that's not where the future lies. It lies in the good colleges to which he will send his kids.

Gary contends that history has not generated the same bitterness toward the railroads among the southwest tribes as it has in the nations in the central and northern plains. The buffalo never figured so prominently in the way of life here, so the railroad's role in their demise casts less of a shadow over its history, and, furthermore, the railroad in some ways struck a harmonious chord with the traditions and heritage of, at least, the Navajo and Pueblo. Both nations prided themselves as builders, as movers and shapers of the land itself. Long before the coming of the railroads, these nations and their ancestors were builders of stone and earth dwellings, of roadways and irrigation ditches. Thus the white man's railroad, though perceived as a threat right from the start, was a work that inspired some awe and reverence too. The Santa Fe foreman who reported that the Indians were delighted to be allowed to play with shovels and get paid as well was correct in his assessment of their enthusiasm for the work, though he underestimated the reason behind it. Eventually the name of David Gallup, the Santa Fe labor recruiter who offered what the Indians considered good pay to do noble work, became part of the Indian lexicon. "Going to Gallup" meant that a man was going to earn some cash and share in the pride of building the white man's great iron road.

As we enter Gallup, New Mexico, named after David and today considered the Indian capital of the world, Gary points out the St. Valerie Catholic and Indian Center. Across the door hangs a sign reading, ". . . for I was hungry and you fed me." I can see a wave of sadness pass over his face as he speaks of the southwest Indians' continuing need for missionary work, but he refuses to blame it on the railroad or white men. "It's just backwardness. And that can be changed." He shakes my hand as he leaves with the firm grip of a man determined to do just that.

This second evening on the *Southwest Chief* is a time of farewells, as it seems that few of the acquaintances I have made are going all the way to L.A. Fred Diehl is off at Flagstaff to see the Grand Canyon and then the casinos of Las Vegas, and so is Don Welles, who will take a bus to Phoenix. He is animated now. "All those wealthy retirees need a lot of shade out here. Trees and money—I can smell it." Lana Meagher is going all the way to L.A. but has gotten hooked on the movie playing in the lounge car, so I'm on my own.

As I take my evening stroll the length of the train, I ponder the varying social milieus I have seen on different trains. There have been trains like the *California Zephyr*, the *Eagle*, and the Florida trains that roared with a neighborhood-barroom conviviality. There was the nightclub scene of the *Sunset Limited* and the shady social intercourse of the *Cardinal*. On the *Crescent* and the *City of New Orleans* a variety of folks rubbed shoulders, but the ambience was more like a blues den than a jazz hall. The daytripper's half of the *Coast Starlight* was like visiting a mall, and the fast eastern trains, the *Lakeshore* and *Broadway*, conjured up the set and audience from "Saturday Night Live." Tonight on the *Southwest Chief*, the darkened coaches are quiet. Children sprawl asleep over nearly a third of the seats; mothers and fathers read or converse in soft whispers in tight circles of light from the reading lamps. The lounge car is silent but for the sound track of the movie, which has mesmerized a subdued gathering of older children, a few retirees, and several couples who munch popcorn just as at the drive-in as the Arizona desert rolls by in the darkness outside. There has been more Coca-Cola sold at the bar tonight than beer, and only a small handful of smokers occupy the downstairs lounge over quiet games of hearts or rummy.

It has been an easy trip for service chief Michael Salyers—no cowpokes with six-guns, no cattle stampedes or Indian raids, no cannon-toting buffalo hunters or monte dealers, no drunks. The Santa Fe Trail is tamed. Salyers laughs and says, "Toughest problem I had on the whole trip was a guy who got on at Union Station and refused to let me move him to a downstairs room." Now that I think of it, Salyers's handling of that situation is right out of Fred Harvey's book.

Chapter Twelve

———

They Call the Wind Maria

THE *DESERT WIND*

L o s Angeles is cold. Even the hot enchiladas at the sidewalk table of
La Golandrina on Olvera Street can't warm me as I shiver through
brunch in the shorts and short-sleeved shirt that I thought would be
appropriate for my June layover in L.A. before catching the *Desert
Wind* out to Barstow and up to Salt Lake. A breeze reaching well inland
from the cool ocean ruffles the pages of my *USA Today*, which reports
temperatures of ninety-five and above in Boston and New England.

Across the busy lane there is a stall where Mexican jewelry is sold.
There is Lana Meagher examining pieces of silver and turquoise. Just
as I call out to her, I spot another familiar face talking with the
waitress by the gate. It is Gerardo Solis, the handsome Mexican bartender I met here back in February. It's the beginning of several days of
wind, cognitive dissonance, and fortuitousness; by Salt Lake, I will be
immune to weirdness and surprises.

Lana says she always checks out the stalls here on Olvera Street
during the layover waiting for her connection to Anaheim. Gerardo is
just arriving for work. With their company for coffee, the chill in the
morning air evaporates.

As we watch a long line of Hispanics forming outside of a government office at the end of the street, Gerardo explains that these people are Mexicans who are eligible for citizenship under an amnesty program for illegal aliens. They are waiting to get passports so that they can visit their homeland and legally return. The passport office is woefully understaffed, and many of these people will wait all day and fail to reach the head of the line by the time the office closes. They will stoically return tomorrow to try again. In February, I was intrigued by the aspirations of these new Americans; today I see the rest of the story—the yearning to reestablish contact with what they have left behind.

Just as a good breakfast provides a firm foundation for a day of work, so does good company for a day of solo travel as a stranger in new country. After farewells to my friends I cross Alameda Street and board the *Desert Wind* ready for anything.

Ten minutes out of the L.A. station, the train stops because the head-end power has failed. The conductor jokes about how smooth the ride is—"as if we weren't moving at all"—but after an hour, the unventilated smoke in the lounge car gives me a frightful headache. The battery-powered PA system is too loud as the conductor's gravelly voice explains our troubles and urgently calls for a man named Howard Swett to report to him.

As usual when there is some kind of delay in the train's schedule, the beer and cocktails (on this train it's margaritas) flow freely in the bar car and a lively scene develops.

A large, loud, ruddy man wearing a red bandanna dominates the gathering with his wife, who also wears a red bandanna. He is Jim O'Connor, pen name Bryan Quinn, contributor with Tom Safford to *Countdown to Zero* and *GI Guinea Pigs*. He introduces himself with a card that reads, "Jim O'Connor—Versatile—Optimistic—News Contortionist—Editorial Reply Nuisance—Orientated in Three Spheres! —Writer."

Jim is a vet disabled by radiation exposure in the Los Alamos testing of the fifties. He has leukemia, which was supposed to kill him years ago. "But I'm a cockroach. You know about cockroaches, don't ya? They've exposed them to enough radiation to wipe out the population of New York and they keep on crawlin'. When the day of reckoning comes, that's who's gonna inherit the earth."

Jim has fought a personal war with the Pentagon on behalf of GIs exposed to radiation during tests. Aside from the two books, he's done a TV documentary for PBS and written "hundreds of letters that rattled cages all over Washington." He claims to have had experiences similar to those of Karen Silkwood. They tried to convince him he was unbalanced and sent him to a series of psychiatrists to confirm it. One, a New Ager, diagnosed his problem as "being oriented in three spheres, simultaneously living in the past, the present, and the future." The New Age shrink told him he was just a man ahead of his time.

A year ago, he and the Pentagon made peace. "They decided it was easier to wait for the leukemia to kill me than to do it themselves." For his part, Jim promised to stop making life difficult for them. Now he says he is mellowed and just enjoying the humor of a crazy world.

Sitting in the next booth is a dusty, tanned, barefoot girl in her twenties, with boyishly short, cropped blond hair. She concurs. Her travels have convinced her that people are either insane or uproariously funny. She prefers the latter view.

Rachel is Australian, has just graduated from university, and is on extended holiday to see some of the world. She began by visiting her boyfriend, who has a diplomatic job in Zimbabwe, and continued on to Kenya, England, Canada, Mexico, and the States. She chain-smokes cigarettes because she is low on money at this point in her travels. She claims to be able to fast for several days if she has cigarettes, and then when she can pick up a few bucks, "doing whatever it takes to earn something," she can drop the cigarettes without any problem. She carries a duffel bag and a sleeping bag, has slept on dormitory floors, on and under park benches, on beaches and mountain tops, in the backs of pickup trucks and station wagons, and, of course, in the coach seats of trains and airplanes all over the world.

She supports her thesis with a tale from her experience in Africa. One Sunday at church in Kenya the "colonials," with whom she identifies, came dressed in coats and ties and dresses and gloves and stood in their traditional places at the rear. The natives came in their kangas and were jostled by American Peace Corps people in kangas rattier than the natives' who pushed to the front of the church in an ostentatious display of their "nativeness." A particularly outspoken native tribal leader later confided to Rachel, "Can you help us with those American Peace Corps people? We know they mean well, but why do they have to be so white about it?"

"Well, there it is. People are crazy all over the world," says Jim. "Once you understand that, you got the key to everything."

"You're damn right," says a tipsy elderly gentleman at the next table. "Especially out there in the desert where I live. It's the wind that does it. It never stops, just howls and howls till that howling gets inside your head. I'm crazy, that's why they're looking for me." He chortles conspiratorially and shares his secret—he is Howard Swett and he's not going to answer the conductor's urgent call nor tell us why.

The lively buzz of the bar car halts for a moment as the train jolts and the power comes on to the accompaniment of lusty cheers. Jim says he was having such a good time he forgot we weren't going anywhere. He proposes a toast to the mechanics, Mr. Swett, Australia, and the train: "Into the desert, where we can all get colorful."

Another man wearing sunglasses and a baseball cap, sitting at the table behind us, leans over and says with gravity and dignity, "Ah know exactly what Mr. Swett here means—there's songs about that, yuh know." Skip Reilly is a brakeman who has worked on a number of railroads, mostly those which run through the empty spaces of the west, but he is also the "Music City Drifter," first-prize winner in the Jimmy Rodgers Memorial Country and Western Jamboree of 1974 and 1975 at Meridian, Mississippi. I tell him I spent a few days in Meridian on my last trip and ask if he ever ate at Weidmann's. "Sure, that's the MacWilliamses' place. It was Elsie MacWilliams who got me into Jimmy Rodgers and C&W."

But first there was the railroad and loneliness. Skip began working for the Burlington on the Sterling-to-Denver division back in the sixties. Later he worked the Santa Fe from Albuquerque to Barstow. "The big empty country, the stars at night, and the wind that never stops blowing made a feeling that yuh jes' had to sing to keep from going crazy." But the music of the times, the pop and folk and rock of the sixties, was all about places with lots of people. "Ah jes' knew there had to be a music that had my feeling, the feeling of a brakeman alone in the crummy of a coal drag across the desert."

A friend he met on the line played a Jimmy Rodgers record for him, and it changed everything. About that time he switched to work for the Southern Railroad, which ran through Meridian. There he met Elsie MacWilliams, who was related to Jimmy Rodgers by marriage, and Skip began his career as a C&W singer.

Now I know what it was that I missed in Meridian. I was so intent upon the past the Meridianites didn't want to share that I was deaf to the one they kept trying to tell me about. I thought I knew who Jimmy Rodgers was. After all, hadn't I collected records like "Oh, Oh, I'm Falling in Love Again" and "Honeycomb" when I was a teenager? Skip explains that it's not the same Jimmy Rodgers. Jimmy Rodgers, the grandfather of C&W, was a railroad brakeman who died in 1933 at the age of thirty-three. His home was Meridian, one of the few places I have visited where I thought I knew what I was looking for.

Skip got his big break when he cut an album in Nashville titled *Dust Devils Play on the Santa Fe,* but it couldn't last because he hated the promotional work, and in C&W, promotional work is everything. But he's still in good voice, as he demonstrates to me later in the diner, singing the song he wrote as the title track for his album.

Today he and his wife ride the train to see the country and to hear people tell the kinds of stories that C&W songs are made of, stories of hurt and loss and yearning and sentiment. I ask if he can explain how music of such raw feeling appeals to so many hard, tough men, and women for that matter, as C&W seems to do. "Well, that's just it, see. It's an outlet, that's why it's so healthy." He tells a story about the time he broke his grandfather's railroad watch. He was climbing up on an engine unit to check a fan and had the watch dangling from a cord lanyard. The cord broke and the watch fell and smashed. "Ah wanted to cry, Ah wanted to hit someone, Ah wanted to tear muh face off. But Ah couldn't do any of those things. So Ah started making a song about it."

Skip wants to hear one of the stories I've collected, so I tell him about Pamela with the scars on the *Eagle.* When I finish he solemnly shakes his head and intones, "Isn't that sumpthin'. But see, there it is. Yuh got the makins of a helluva C&W song there—'Nobody Wanted the Seventh Child.'"

During dinner, the train climbs over Cajon Pass. Here the old western Spanish extension of the Santa Fe Trail crossed the last obstacle to the coast, and here the ATSF line from the east finally linked up with its lines from San Diego and Los Angeles to establish the fourth transcontinental route (the third was the Northern Pacific, completed just a few months earlier).

It was always a cruel joke of geography that the road which crawled across two thousand miles of New Mexico, Utah, Arizona, and California desert should face this last forbidding climb over the San Bernardino Mountains less than a hundred miles from the coast and the City of Angels that was its destination. Here a ragged race scratched out a living primarily from the cactus, which played a role in their existence similar to that of the buffalo in the lives of the Plains Indians, and here too, rugged desperate white men picked at the youngest rock in America, still actively volcanic just five hundred years before Columbus, for gold, silver, and copper. Some found treasure, others broiled their brains under the merciless sun. On the western slope near what is today the city of San Bernardino, Mormon pioneers from Utah failed to duplicate the miracle of Salt Lake in attempting to extend their fantastic state of Deseret. They trudged back over the pass to their tabernacle, chastened at finally encountering the limits of Christian human endeavor.

But the railroad got through by 1885, thanks to the toil of the Chinese laborers who cut the line with hand tools and survived by emulating the habits of the native Indians. Once the Santa Fe line was through, finally providing competition for the monopolistic Southern Pacific, the second California boom was on, and it has never stopped. Much of the traffic that built it has rolled over this pass.

Thanks to the initiative of the SP-hating San Francisco, the Santa Fe did not stop in southern California. Upon its arrival, the Santa Fe found the San Francisco & San Joaquin Railroad, the so-called People's Road, already laid out and waiting for a junction with the Santa Fe. Thus the Santa Fe invaded SP territory as far as the Golden Gate, establishing itself as the other great California railroad. And with its eastern extension from Kansas City to Chicago, where it connected with the Pennsylvania, it became the first coast-to-coast route involving only one connection between different railroads.

Cajon Pass is actually the intersection of the San Andreas Fault with the junction of the San Gabriel and San Bernardino mountains. It is absolutely treeless and characterized by looming black-and-brown peaks that look more like monstrous hunks of disturbed rock (which is exactly what they are) than conventional mountains. Occasionally they are shrouded in a heavy mist, an extension of L.A.'s famous smog, as they are today as the *Desert Wind* grinds and winds its way up the steep climb.

The first transcontinental *Chicago Limited* climbed through this mist on the morning of October 31, 1895. An hour out of L.A. it was reported lost, without a trace, as absolutely as a ship at sea. It simply didn't arrive at Victorville on the eastern slope, and there was no telegraph message about a breakdown or wreck from anywhere along the line.

In the late afternoon, the fireman from the train was spotted limping down the track into San Bernardino. He told his story. As the train had climbed through the heavy mist into El Cajon, he and the engineer saw a shape in the murk ahead of them. Fearing a head-on collision with an oncoming train, they both jumped, without shutting off the steam or setting the brakes. The train crashed through a wagon stuck on the tracks at a crossing and chugged on up the climb for several miles until the slope dragged it to a stop. The engineer had broken his leg and couldn't get to the train, so the fireman, with only a sprained ankle, had hoofed it back to San Bernardino to get help. A rescue hack was sent out to find the stalled trainload of passengers and brakemen spooked and bewildered by their empty engine cab. A new crew was brought in and the train continued on to arrive at Chicago only three hours late.

On the east side of El Cajon, we roll down through the wildest desert country I have seen yet. We follow the bed of the Mojave River through barren eroded canyons out into the Mojave itself. Here the water flows at a depth of twenty feet, and what water does show on the surface is usually a treacherous film over true quicksand. The dust kicked up by the train gets into the wind, which carries it for miles the same direction the train is headed, so that the train moves across the desert with its own dust cloud for company. There are no signs of the haunts of men. I have never been a fan of C&W, but somehow these vistas suggest a backdrop where the emotional excesses of that music seem appropriate.

Before we part company, Skip bestows on me a C&W nickname, "Rail Eagle." "Because of my story about the *Eagle* train?" I query.

"No," he says. And then in hushed conspiratorial tones, "Yuh know about the secret of the eagle? Well, it's the only creature that will leave its roots for freedom."

I have been offended by T-shirts all over the west bearing the image of an eagle superimposed over a huge ten-wheeler rig or a Harley motorcycle with a caption like "Born to Be Free" or "Live Free or Die" (cribbed from the license plates of my own New Hampshire) or "Land of the Free." Now, setting aside the belligerent jingoism the image conveys, I see a whole new dimension to the symbol and the myth. That is the story of my journey, of my father's, of the building of the rails themselves, of the history of America.

Barstow, California, runs along the edge of the underground Mojave River on the southern rim of a valley in the heart of the Mojave Desert. Named for Santa Fe president William Barstow Strong, it was originally founded by the railroad as a division headquarters and junction of the three main western legs of the ATSF, the main line coming in from the east, the Cajon Pass leg down to L.A. and San Diego, and the San Joaquin Valley line up to Oakland and San Francisco. Today it also serves as a connection with the Union Pacific route which runs down from Salt Lake City and shares the Cajon Pass with the Santa Fe for its connection to L.A. As a vital junction for two of America's most profitable railroads, Barstow is one of those rare places where the rails are still king, where the traffic off the interstate is still secondary in the local economy. Here the local McDonald's is set up inside rail passenger cars and the huge yards and shops of the Santa Fe dominate the town the same way the monumental buildings of government dominate Washington.

That's why I am getting off the train and why I am struck by the graffiti-marred wreck that is the station, the old Casa del Desierto, one of the few original Harvey Houses still standing. In Meridien, Mississippi, the old station, though truncated, was well maintained and presided over by a full-time stationmaster, even though it sat by a dying freight line and served only one daily train each direction. Here beside the nexus of two of the most profitable freight networks in the country and serving two daily trains in each direction, the *Southwest Chief* and the *Desert Wind*, with bus connections to a third up in the San Joaquin, there is no stationmaster, no taxi service, no phone, just a rattrap with a hand-painted sign over a filthy cul-de-sac in the ruins labeling it "Waiting Room." Inside, a scruffy transient Indian is sprawled asleep across the only bench amid the dust and broken glass.

The train pulls out and I am left alone with the wind, the Indian, the graffiti, and a leathery older couple who watch the train's departure leaning against their RV and sipping Coors beer. They laugh when I ask about a taxi but offer to drop me off at my motel. I wonder if this counts as a hitch, which I am sworn not to do, and decide that it doesn't, since it is their idea and not mine and since their presence at the station makes them somehow rail-oriented.

Inside the RV (Max says it stands for retirement vehicle) of Max and Bea MacLain, the air conditioning and the cool deep wall-to-wall carpet work the track-wrack out of my legs quickly. Max sits on the love seat with his feet up on the leather footstool, offers me an icy Coors from the refrigerator, and flips on a Dodgers baseball game on the TV. Up front, Bea drives.

They just came from their home in Bakersfield on a whim, thought they'd sit out by the tracks, quaff some beer, and watch some freights roll through, but it's too windy, so they're going back after they drop me off. Max asks Bea to read the odometer, and she reports, with some pride, that it now stands at 25,658 miles. "Not bad for six months," says Max. The RV is their vacation home, boat, airplane, campsite, and backyard patio all rolled into one. "By the end of the year, there won't be too many corners of the west we haven't seen from this seat." I ask if they've ever taken it all the way to the east. "Only once, and we didn't like driving across the plains. See, we like to drive and stop, drive and stop. Out here you can do that, because the mountains and desert are really just as much ours as anybody else's. But in the farm belts, you always know you've stopped in the fields of somebody's spread. The feeling of ownership spoils it. And in the east, hell, you're always in somebody's backyard."

I suggest I might have a little trouble spending all my time in a landscape where you never see any green or rain. "Rain. You ain't seen rain till you've seen it here. Right here in Barstow there's a real downpour, maybe twice, three times a year. And then this air is just solid water. It comes down so heavy that it brings tons of mud off the hills and they have to plow it from the streets the same way they do snow up in the mountains."

Over my second Coors we cruise slowly down Barstow's Main Street. The entire town is really one long gaudy strip paralleling the rail yards, just like Cheyenne. Bea points out the El Rancho Hotel, built entirely out of railroad ties, and Lee and Leon's Coffee Shop, where I have to stop tomorrow if I want some good Mex while I'm here. Barstow is particularly well endowed with inexpensive motels and fast-food joints, which serve its second major enterprise, the travelers off Interstate 15. At the eastern end of town we find the Best Western Desert Villa, where I am staying, but rather than pull to the right into its parking lot, Bea turns left into a breakdown lane and says, "Well, let's show him how good his travel agent was to him. Bring your camera."

We get out of the RV and Bea leads us down the embankment beside the road and through a hole in a desert-flower-bedecked chainlink fence, and there is the double-tracked high iron of the joint ATSF-UP road to the east and north just a few feet in front of us. Beyond the tracks are fields of green alfalfa under jetting sprinkler systems, and across the valley the purple line of the horizon above the Mojave Mountains. Here the term "high iron" has real meaning, as the ballast is built up a good five or six feet; the track is nearly at eye level from where we stand.

After ten minutes Max points to the eastern vanishing point of the rails, where a light gleams brighter than the little headlights on the nearby highway. "Here she comes." The light grows as I fiddle with my camera, and suddenly it is upon us, much more quickly than I anticipated, five Santa Fe GP-40s and a mile of piggybacks furiously drifting in with a rumbling whisper at passenger-train speed, at least sixty miles per hour. It takes my breath away. Then it's gone into the sunset and I notice that there is no caboose, just a little box with a winking red light attached to the coupler of the last car as the ringing in the rails subsides. "That's the rear-end device that has replaced cabooses on some of the western freight lines," explains Max.

Bea claps her hands together. "Oh, good luck, check this," and she points in the direction of the dwindling red light. Another white light gleams and grows beside it. "That was the downgrade inbound direction—here comes an outbound going upgrade." This time there is a warning. The air begins to shudder with the low growl of straining diesel engines. The rails whistle and hum as the growl becomes a roar that gets in the teeth, and the five engines of the outbound Union Pacific freight slash past with five rips of intimidating violence. Even my veteran train-watching companions giggle at this and stand a little more closely together. Max spots a hobo curled up behind a hunk of cardboard under the axle of one of the piggyback trucks and points. The man points back and flashes past. Then the volume of the world throttles down to the whisper of the irrigation sprinklers, the traffic on the highway, and the desert wind rattling the plastic trash amid the scrub along the right of way. Max and Bea see me to my room for one more cold Coors, and then they are on their way. Before bedtime I'm back out under the desert moon to catch three more fast freights, two inbound and one outbound, and later the ground rumble of a fourth carries me off to never-never land. I think back to the lesson of Meridian and revise it: "Sometimes you find exactly what you are looking for."

The Mexican lunch at Lee and Leon's diner the next day confirms the MacLains' advice. The platter of tacos and enchiladas is a county fair of southwestern tastes. The decor of the place is plain, with only one extravagant adornment: in a little grotto presided over by a trinity of three milk-glass lamps hangs a large painting of John Wayne. His disembodied bust looms in the heavens over a desert landscape of two buttes and a team of four pulling a ragged covered wagon. He wears a red bandanna and ten-gallon hat complete with a maroon felt band and tassels.

Travelers come off the interstate like caravan drivers seeking an oasis. An elderly couple from San Bernardino heading toward Salt Lake notice my fascination with the John Wayne painting and explain that it was a fixture in many of the cabooses that have now been taken off the freights. The woman says that she can speak with some authority about railroads because her grandfather was a railroad man who came out from Chicago on the Santa Fe. He was attacked by Indians with flame arrows and ate in the old pre-Harvey hash houses. She asks if I ever heard a song from the Lerner and Lowe musical, *Paint Your*

Wagon, and reissued by the Kingston Trio back in the sixties titled "They Call the Wind Maria." She says her grandfather worked on the railroad with the man who wrote its C&W forebear.

As it happens, I can recall the song: "Way out here they have a name for rain and wind and fire; the rain is Tess, the fire's Joe, and they call the wind Maria." She has set loose in my head a piece of music that will haunt me in lonely moments for a thousand miles. I thank them for the gift and leave to walk down the main drag, across the bridge over the yards, and to the old deserted station to spend the afternoon before the arrival of today's *Desert Wind*, which will take me to Salt Lake.

On the bridge I spot a hobo eating a cold can of Campbell's soup. He has the shakes, his tanned skin has a permanent patina of grime, and his long sun-bleached hair is tangled with weeds and burrs. His sneakers have tattered soles, and his blue workshirt is caked with dried sweat and God knows what else. But most engaging are his eyes, pale blue and staring at the vanishing point of the rails far out on the desert with a mad, wild glaze. I speak to him, but he does not respond, and the song of the desert wind is there in an instant: "Maria blows the stars around and sets the clouds a-flying; Maria makes the mountains sound like folks was out there dyin'."

There is no one at the station when I arrive. Today I notice that while the building itself is in a sad state of neglect, the grounds around it consist of manicured lawns, willow trees, and bricked sidewalks. Here is manifest the town's indecision about its vintage railroad station. I've been told that there has been talk of tearing it down, of rehabilitating it, of making it a National Landmark. Though nothing seems to get done, someone has cared for the setting. I spend the long afternoon hiking around the yards, photographing the freights that roll through, lolling in the sun, and napping in the shade of the willows on the grass that seems such a treat in this desert place. My only company is a scrawny little kitten that has strayed from a brood of wild cats inside the wreck. He attaches himself to me and won't go away. He has a badly infected eye, so I shove him away when he cuddles up to me, but when I drift off, I wake to find him purring on my chest. A wave of the most profound loneliness washes over me with a gust of the wind, and I think of a family with two children, about the age of my own, embarking from the motel this morning. The song is there again: "Before I knew Maria's name, and heard her wail and whinin', I had a gal and she had me and the sun was always shinin'."

I drift off again, and somewhere beyond Barstow I hear a voice speaking my name: "Terry, Terry—Terry, is that you?" Half awake, I prepare myself for another dreamland meeting with my father, but the feel of the dream isn't quite right and I can't see him. "Terry? Is that you?" Opening my eyes with a start, I see a jovial bearded man standing on the brick walk with a large duffel bag over his shoulder. It is Fred Diehl. I'm on my feet in an instant with the kitten hanging by its claws from my shirt.

If we had compared itineraries a little more closely we would have figured out that we would meet again. He took the *Southwest Chief* to Barstow after his trip to the Grand Canyon, spent last night in a motel just down the road from mine, and now is awaiting the *Desert Wind* to ride to Las Vegas.

After exchanging stories of intervening adventures, we explore the ruins of the Casa del Desierta, which frankly I was afraid to do before out of a fear of encountering unfriendly vagrants or the authors of the hostile graffiti scrawled across the walls. Indeed the large rooms contain evidence of encampments of some sort. There are ashes from cooking fires, Night Train Express bottles, human excrement, and more of the unintelligible graffiti that I have learned is not confined to the slums of northeastern cities. The stray cats stay out of sight, but we can hear them. Only the scrawny white kitten tags along in the open.

From the top floor we see an Amtrak bus pull onto the platform and disgorge a dozen passengers. Amtrak today uses buses over a variety of short connecting routes around the country where for one reason or another it cannot maintain a rail service. The buses are usually a poor substitute, but in California, coordinated bus-rail routes have been a fixture since the Santa Fe established the first one in 1938. The idea was to maximize speed by using buses for the portion of the route which involved slow circuitous climbs over mountain ranges, California's freeways offering faster passage in those regions. Then passengers would change conveyances for the flat runs through the valleys, where fast trains could make better time. Amtrak has carried on this Santa Fe innovation on many of its runs throughout California today. The coordinated bus-rail route connecting L.A. to San Francisco today by way of the San Joaquin Valley maintains an overall average speed of fifty-five miles per hour including stops and transfer for a total of about eight and a half hours, about the same one could do driving the freeway at the national speed limit without any stops for rest or meals. The all-rail *Coast Starlight* run on Southern Pacific tracks from L.A. to San Francisco averages an agonizing forty-two miles per hour for a total of eleven hours.

Among the passengers off the bus waiting for the train, Fred spots two attractive women and speculates, "If they're going to Las Vegas, there's the beginning of my harem."

Aboard the *Desert Wind,* Fred and I have dinner with a man who has followed Fred's route since the Grand Canyon. He has made a nuisance of himself by buttonholing passengers and tyrannizing them with his lectures on railroad history and his odd opinions about politics.

Maxwell Greene is a rail buff. I have met a number of people who describe themselves this way, but Max is different, a true original. When I sit down he is counting the $20 bills he has safety-pinned to a kind of money belt that he wears like a cummerbund under his sweatshirt. He speaks in a gruff raspy voice in which there is very little difference between a grunt of disapproval and a guffaw of delight. "Yeah, they think I'm a little crazy, but that's because I know too much—I've always known too much. That's the story of my life."

Max never worked for the railroad, and nobody in his family did either. It was his mother's Lionel trains that got him interested. She'd set up complicated layouts on the dining-room and living-room floors of their Long Island home and run two, sometimes three trains over them. All the kids in the family and neighbors too would get down on the floor with Mother and run the trains. He did this till he was eighteen and then tried to get a job with the Pennsylvania Railroad, but they took one look at his medical record, muscular dystrophy and astigmatism, and said, "We don't need you." So he took his 150+ IQ and went to work for Allied Chemical's engineering department. "But there hasn't been a day in my life that I haven't thought about trains running to faraway places."

During dinner, the train runs through the boundary of the Mojave and Death Valley, below sea level. "The loneliest stretch of track in America," says Max, confirming Skip Reilly's observation yesterday. The Union Pacific didn't build this line until 1905, even though its Utah Southern extension to the copper mines southwest of Salt Lake constituted more than a third of this route as far back as the 1880s. The combined opposition of the Southern Pacific and the Santa Fe to the entrance of a third colossus into the southern-California rail sweepstakes was that effective.

But nature had a hand in it too. Early explorers who survived this desert brought back one unanimous report: Don't go that way. One of the earliest such was the Spanish missionary Escalante seeking a new route to the California coast in 1776. On encountering the Mojave, he took a vote of the members of his expedition; they decided to give it up and trudge over an equally unknown route back to Santa Fe. The

American explorer Jedediah Smith came this way in 1827 and, despite making it to the coast, concluded that this was not the way to California. Mormons from Salt Lake tried this desert in the 1850s and gave it up for their friendlier one back in Utah.

Beyond the Mojave River, this is true desert; there is no tappable water table lurking beneath the sandy surface. Huge flat valleys where even the sagebrush grows sparse are bordered by sand dunes, red wind-eroded lava flows, and young, absolutely lifeless mountains. The scene is even more desolate when rare signs of the hand of man do appear—a dirt road that runs straight to the horizon or an abandoned shack with a broken corral fence. Most disheartening is the windblown refuse that is snagged in the sagebrush for a hundred miles beyond human settlement. It is mostly hunks of Styrofoam eroded to shapelessness by the passage across the abrasive desert, and plastic bags, the lightweight crinkly kind that even a strong man must struggle to tear.

"Look at that socialist plastic stuff," says Max, "and tell me who is crazy." Max has his own version of the history of passenger railroading in the twentieth century. The peak was embodied in the *20th Century Limited* of the early thirties—in such details as the six-wheel trucks that provided a smooth ride even over rough track, the Pullman standard of dimensions and accoutrements, and the heavy construction of the cars. But the young people of the twenties who grew up during World War I introduced what Max calls a socialist approach to railroading. They wanted to make it faster and cheaper. "That's the socialist way, you know, to make things faster and cheaper, from restaurants to schooling to railroads." So around 1934 the socialist influence determined the shape of passenger railroading with cars that were lighter, narrower, and lower and mounted on four-wheel trucks. This was the beginning of the decline of the passenger railroads. "The American people have always rejected the socialists' trick of trying to make less seem like more."

In railcars the old Pullman standard was that the ceiling be twice the height of a short man, ten feet. The socialists changed it to eight feet. In architecture, the old standard was to create enough space overhead so that the inside of institutional buildings like travel terminals felt like the outdoors. It was the socialists, according to Max, who thought that to be a waste of space and put in the suspended ceilings of soundboard at eight feet. The socialists invented fast-food restaurants, thinking that feeding the most people the cheapest food in the least time was the way to handle "mass man's appetite." Unisex toilets, no-smoking regimes, monorails, and Turboliners are more examples of the socialist influence today. "And then the women, all of the women are socialists today. Two kids with a working mother, that's the socialist way."

I suggest that maybe it's just the process of change that he tags with the term "socialist." "No way," he says. "I was one of the first to suggest ultraviolet to cleanse the environment of trains in the air-conditioning system. I want to see everybody's water fluoridated. Amtrak's special rooms for the handicapped are a more civilized gesture than anything Mr. Pullman ever came up with. And these trains, though they have the four-wheel trucks, have pulled back from the socialist standard—nine-foot ceilings, middle-weight cars, and real chefs in the dining cars. No, it's the uniform mass production of experience that I mean by the socialist way."

But the socialists themselves couldn't have ruined the passenger railroads. The *coup de grâce* was delivered by an American trait as endemic as our love of freedom. Americans have always loved the wide-open spaces. "Think about it—people might have come here from Europe as much for space as for religious freedom or economic opportunity. So there's a genetic predisposition for claustrophobia in our heritage." After World War II, a whole generation came home accustomed to the outdoor military life. "They all had claustrophobia, so they couldn't ride the train, it's as simple as that." The same is true of American farmers. "Oh, nobody ever says, 'I got claustrophobia.' Instead they say, 'I love the wide-open spaces' or 'Why do people have to live so close together?' We have developed a phraseology that covers up our great national secret. That's what made the automobile king." Through the windshield there is an illusion of space. The popularity of the bubble observation cars on the railroad confirms it—it's the only place on the train where space opens in all directions. It's also the key to the settling of the west and why travelers universally observe an ease, an openness, a friendliness in western folk. "Fewer of them are suffering the tension of chronic claustrophobia.

"What we really need," Max argues, "is a six- or even ten-foot track gauge. Unfortunately that's opposed by the Mafia, who, through the Teamsters, have vested interests in seeing the railroads die. But economics are on the side of the Mafia. The four-foot-eight-inch gauge of the old Romans is with us to stay."

Socialists, claustrophobia, Mafia. I suspect there's a lot of jackalope in Max's monologue, but there are also golden spikes. He may have the terminology wrong, but there is a trend in the land counter to the generous spirit of the railroad. To me it is embodied in the malls, condos, and fast-food restaurants, but I always thought of it as a product of amoral, anesthetic capitalism. Max's cosmology posits an unholy alliance between the worst of both worlds, public and private. And the diagnosis of claustrophobia is just as probable as the myth of "rugged individualism" in explaining the appeal of the open west and then of the automobile. The suggestion that the Mafia has had its hand in the shaping of the nation's transportation policy is not so farfetched when one considers the character and impact of the Teamsters, prime beneficiaries of the government's total subsidy of the interstates. Max's experience is of life in an eastern megalopolis. He is as much a stranger here in the Mojave as I am, but he offers insights as fresh and dissonant as the desert wind itself.

Later, after a few hours with my notes, I meet Fred in the bar car, where he is ensconced with the two pretty women from the Bakersfield bus. The blonde is Belinda and the brunette with Fred's arm round her is Lorraine. They are returning to their husbands and families in Utah, and Fred invites them both to join us in my compartment for a farewell party before he detrains in Vegas.

I have been visited on occasion during these journeys with traveler's fantasies, a product of loneliness and the illusion of freedom and opportunity. I'm sure that railroad men and traveling salesmen know the phenomenon well. By the time we cross the Providence Mountains toward the million lights of Las Vegas spread across the flat semidesert of Nevada, the atmosphere in my compartment is charged.

Fred has talked Lorraine into getting off with him at Vegas and suggests that we make it a foursome. The full moon casts a tangled web of shadows across the sage on the desert outside the window. I can see stuff blowing in the wind, and then the last verse of the song of the desert wind comes to me: "But then one day I left my gal, I left her far behind me. And now I'm lost, so down and lost, not even God can find me."

At Vegas, I get off to say goodbye to Fred. The station is just a tarmac platform on casino property surrounded by high fencing topped by razor wire. Despite the train chief's announcement that the stop is short, some passengers scurry inside for a couple of pops at the slot machines. The scene plays in silver-gray halftones—the raspy sound of the waiting diesel engines, the wind-whipped platform, the faces of the three pausing to know my intentions. I try to think of a few appropriate lines from Bogart, or even Woody Allen, but all that comes out is a confused mumble about a song in my head and a quest that still lies ahead. The conductor makes his last call, and I turn and board the *Desert Wind* alone.

In the morning on the Salt Lake City platform I can see Max waving to me from a dining car that has his six-wheel trucks, one of the old Santa Fe Hi-liner cars that inspired and are used interchangeably with the new Superliners. After the crazy, sleepless night across the desert, the very pavement seems to heave beneath my feet. And even here, in the largest city of the central west, the dry wind blows steady, west to east, now like a friend at the end of a late-night binge saying, "Go home, man. It's time to go home."

Chapter Thirteen

Quest for the West

THE *PIONEER*

IF among the ideals of mankind there is an "American dream," then within that ideal there is a "western dream." It predates the "cowboy dream" by more than half a century, and it is not to be confused with the "California dream," an emphasis on wealth, ease, and innovative society. Its true domain ranges between the haunts of those lifestyles, between the continental divides of the Rockies and the Sierras, from the southern limits of the Mojave to Canada. Its crossroads is Salt Lake; its highway is the old Oregon Trail; its history begins with a flat-tailed rodent whose engineering works made him easy to stalk and whose skin could be profitably made into stylish and practical hats.

Traders of three countries eyed the beaver of the region as the key to economic empire in the years following Lewis and Clark's journey across its northern reaches. Spanish trappers and missionaries worked northward from Santa Fe while British agents of the Hudson's Bay Company moved east from Fort Vancouver on the Columbia River and U.S. Americans came west from St. Louis. These early "mountain men" quickly discovered that for the most part, the native Indians were valuable teachers and allies in the struggle to survive in the wilderness, and they adopted their ways, followed their paths, and sometimes even married their women.

The exception to this harmony was the Blackfeet of the far north, whose belligerence, well known to other Indian tribes, effectively closed the trail blazed by Lewis and Clark. The first Americans to cross the continental divide from the east after Lewis and Clark were a party led by John Jacob Astor in 1811, still more than half a century before the arrival of railroads. Warned of fiendish Blackfeet tortures, they climbed unpromising passes south of Montana and struggled down the lower Snake River to the Columbia in a harrowing white-water ride that no westering party would ever duplicate. They founded Astoria near the mouth of the Columbia and faced disaster after their supply ship blew up. So in 1812 they sent a party of six led by Robert Stuart back across the continent to get help. Stuart avoided the rapids of the lower Snake by slogging from the Columbia through the Blue Mountains to the broad plain of the upper Snake, which provided a natural highway eastward until blocked by the wall of the Wind River Mountains. Here all previous eastbound expeditions had halted and circled back toward Oregon, but Stuart doggedly worked southward until he found a broad, flat saddle over the divide. From there he followed the east-flowing Sweetwater to the North Platte and the Missouri. Without realizing it, his desperate party had blazed the Oregon Trail from west to east.

For a decade, Stuart's route lay lost to memory amid the myth of the Great American Desert and the belief that the Rockies were for all practical purposes impassable. Then in 1822, General William Ashley recruited "100 enterprising young men" for an extended trapping operation on the upper reaches of the Missouri. The roster of his expedition reads like a Who's Who in the history of American mountain men: Jedediah Smith, William Sublette, Thomas Fitzpatrick, Jim Bridger, Jim Clyman, Black Harris, Kit Carson, Joe Walker, Joe Meek. They encamped and traded for pelts with the Indians in the first trappers' rendezvous on the Sweetwater River and established a tradition that mountain enthusiasts still preserve today.

Two notable discoveries grew out of this enterprise. Jedediah Smith, his head badly mauled by a grizzly and clumsily sewn up by Jim Clyman, led one group westward seeking a pass over the continental divide in 1824. Frustrated again and again, he rendezvoused with a Crow chief and by mimicking the mountains with little piles of sand confirmed that a broad gap through the mountains was out there somewhere. Wandering lost up a barren slope to a flat saddle, he broke the ice of a stream to find the water flowing westward. He was on the west side of Stuart's lost pass, the South Pass, key to the future Oregon Trail.

Later that year, Jim Bridger set out from the main group to cross the pass and arrived at the Bear River, whose circuitous meanderings through the northeastern quadrant of today's Utah had puzzled Oregon trappers for a decade. To settle a wager as to where the river flowed, he followed it to its mouth at a huge unknown body of water. Kneeling at the shoreline to drink, he spat out the salty water and said, "Hell, we're on the shores of the Pacific!"

Legends of a great salt lake went back as far as the Aztecs, who supposedly emigrated to Mexico from such a place, and to the French baron Lahontan, who in 1688 reported Indian tales of such a lake. Though Spanish trappers or missionaries likely discovered it before Bridger, none ever laid claim to it.

Even after its discovery, the lake lay shrouded in myths perpetuated by fantasizing mapmakers of the day. One vision saw it as an arm of the Pacific. A more persistent rendering posited an imaginary Buenaventura River running west from the lake through an unknown gap in the Sierras and into the Pacific. Despite the obvious implications of its saltiness and its circumnavigation by Jim Clyman, who found no outlet, in 1826, the myth of a river to the Pacific died hard.

Smith, Bridger, Clyman, Sublette, and others knew better—west and south of Salt Lake was nothing but the vast deserts of the Great Basin. The real significance of the Salt Lake was the fertile valley along its east shore where water flowed in fur-rich streams down from the Wasatch Mountains. For several decades this was the kingdom of the mountain men and their rendezvous until the fur trade began to peter out in the 1830s.

Meanwhile, Joe Walker crossed the desert west of Salt Lake and followed a river earlier discovered by Peter Ogden in northern Nevada to a place where it disappeared in a brackish sink into the sand. From here he struck out over the Sierras and arrived in California in 1833, establishing the Humboldt River route as the California branch of the Oregon Trail.

Now the stage was set. The first wagon trains headed out over the Oregon Trail in the early 1840s, the Stevens Party successfully traveled the California trail in '44, and the Donners foundered in '46. Brigham Young eyed the now nearly abandoned fastness of the Salt Lake Valley in preparation for his persecuted Mormons' final migration in '47. The railroads that would eventually follow these routes were still only a gleam in Asa Whitney's eye, but their potential to open up the magnificent harbors of landlocked Puget Sound played a role in the tough stance of the U.S. government leading to the partition agreement with Britain, which made the Oregon territory south of the 49th parallel U.S. soil in '46.

The mountain men made the passage on to new careers as guides for the wagons, but their contribution to America transcended trailblazing; they left a memory in the national consciousness of a life-style that chose the tyranny of nature over that of men. They created with their Indian partners a community shaped by isolation and the necessities of living in harmony with lands that could not be conquered by plow or ax. The men and women of the wagon trains viewed this domain as merely an obstacle between them and a very different kind of dream focused on the fertile valleys of the Pacific Coast. The Mormons sought their idiosyncratic haven out of a desire to escape one society and build another of their own. By the end of my ride on the *Pioneer* over the route of the old Oregon Trail, I will discover that both of these latter dreams still conflict today with the surviving western dream of the mountain men. The other dreams eventually consumed the frontier; the western dream keeps it forever alive.

Today Salt Lake City offers no clue to the valley's past as the seat of the mountain men—it is dominated by the prosperous devices of the Mormons and the railroad, two institutions antithetical to the mountain man's ethic. The most imposing edifices in the city are the Latter-Day Saints office building, the temple and temple square, the capitol, and the Union Pacific station. The Mormons and the railroad built this city, and though westerners today have strikingly divergent feelings about both, everyone agrees that Salt Lake is fortunate to be America's only truly planned city. Brigham Young and later the railroad men of the UP and DRG laid out a city from whole cloth with wide streets, deep setbacks, and huge blocks.

The streets are not only the widest in the United States, they are probably the cleanest. The populace are all tanned with that western color, fit and youthful, and the dry climate makes everyone look better—dry hair, fresh complexions. Everyone looks as if he had just dressed in fresh clothes. A popular T-shirt reads "No sweat"—that's exactly it, no one sweats. Even the elderly Mormons, in their straw hats, exude a youthful crispness that goes a long way toward making converts.

Four blocks from Temple Square, the UP station is a monument to space, light, and history. Its vast airy concourse is highlighted by two great murals on the opposing north and south walls. One depicts the founding of Salt Lake by Brigham Young and his Mormon pioneers, the other records the driving of the golden spike that connected Salt Lake to the nation by rail. But this magnificent station is no longer used for passenger service, though it is maintained as meticulously as the smaller UP station at Cheyenne; passengers pass through the DRG station just down the street. It is smaller but has its own dignity. The city historical association is setting up a museum in the concourse, and local hotels provide free taxi service to and from the Amtrak station at the south end and a special accommodation and rate for passengers like me coming in on a morning train and going out on a late-evening connection.

The most striking image throughout Salt Lake City is water: playing in fountains, pools, and gardens; served with a flourish in big pitchers with ice and lemon wedges in the restaurants; and intimated by the immaculately scrubbed sidewalks and streets. Water was the determining factor in the final rail routes, since the old steam engines couldn't run without it. And yet for all of these purposes the water of the Great Salt Lake itself is worthless. It's the water that comes down from the Wasatch Mountains looming above the skyline to the north, east, and south that slakes the insatiable thirst of men living well in the midst of such arid expanses. It was also this water that was the final key to the lasting triumph of the Mormons over the hostility of the land and the "gentile" society they came here to escape.

According to Mormon tradition, Vermonter Joseph Smith found the golden tablets and the magic lenses which enabled him to translate its ancient inscriptions in Palmyra, New York, in 1823. The Book of Mormon recounts God's dealings with the ancient inhabitants of North America, the now extinct white Nephites and the dark Lamanites, forebears of the native Americans. The theme of America as the site of God's contemporary chosen people and of latter-day prophets and continuing revelation quickly found apt converts among New Englanders steeped in the tradition of the Great Awakening. Prophecies of a latter-day exodus to a new promised land stirred the souls of men who had no inkling of how quickly these things would actually come to pass.

The Mormons were marked for persecution from the start. They were chased out of Ohio over a matter of the church's issuing of its own paper money; they fled Missouri when rowdy frontiersmen revolted against their doctrine, their practice of converting Indians, and their

Yankee origins; they were driven out of Illinois in 1843 when Smith had his revelation favoring polygamy. This was the last straw for an intolerant populace, and Smith suffered martyrdom when he was murdered in jail after voluntarily submitting to arrest.

Brigham Young stepped in quickly to assume the mantle of leadership. With a scholar's zeal he researched the journals of the western mountain men in the early 1840s and tallied up the advantages of the Salt Lake Valley. The Oregon Trail passed well to the north, avoiding the Wasatch Mountains lying east of the lake and the great desert to the west. The extent of the fertile valley was such as could be occupied by the Mormons themselves without fear of unfriendly neighbors settling on adjacent lands. The territory was still officially Mexican and so beyond the reach of U.S. courts. Finally, there was the water. The land would not support life without irrigation from the streams flowing down the west slope of the Wasatch, but by controlling the streams, the church could control everything. The site was pure genius, worthy of divine inspiration. Legend has it that Young spontaneously declared, "This is the place," as his wagons descended the Wasatch canyons into the valley, but history reveals that he knew it was the place long before he set out from Omaha.

In '46 and '47 the Mormon migrations began, paralleling the Oregon Trail on the north bank of the North Platte, crossing South Pass, and then turning southwest at Fort Bridger through the canyons of the Wasatch. For a decade the saints resided in their desert fastness safe from the fulminations of the nation.

Though the territory finally became U.S. soil, Brigham Young was its first governor. Though gentiles began to immigrate into the valley primarily for the mining, Mormon control of local industry, water, and land preserved their theocracy.

It was finally the railroad that brought about the end of an era, and yet, despite anti-Mormon propaganda to the contrary, the Saints welcomed the Pacific Road with open arms. Brigham Young saw the inevitability of the railroad and weighed its advantages and disadvantages just as he had done earlier in selecting the site of the promised land. As a source of corruption from the outside it was a problem, but as a source of wealth and power for the kingdom of the Saints located at the crossroads of the west it was a greater boon. Before 1860, Young's agents were agitating to ensure that the railroad passed through Salt Lake City and along the south shore of the lake. When the UP engineers demurred, Mormon surveyors explored the feasibility of a filled route directly across the shallow lake, presaging the Lucien Cutoff, which was built in 1906 and over which today's *California Zephyr* originally ran. But in 1868 the railroad engineers chose the northerly route over Promontory, and Salt Lake was left off the main line.

Still the Mormons contracted to build the stretches over the Wasatch to preempt the corruption of the hell-on-wheels construction towns strung across Wyoming; then they built their own connection, the Utah Central, from Ogden down to Salt Lake. They also initiated the Utah Southern, which would eventually become the Union Pacific's *Desert Wind* line to L.A., and the Utah Northern, which would become a part of the UP's line to Oregon.

Anti-Mormon forces imagined that the railroad would destroy Mormonism by opening it to invasion by the mainstream of American society, but it worked out just the other way around. Though the era of isolation was ended, Mormon money and organizational power spread outward over the rails of the crossroads to dominate a significant extent of the land and politics of the west. Mormons are still reviled by many gentiles in the west, not for their apostasy but for their wealth and power over the land and, consequently, the western dream.

Today the rail crossroads of the west is the DRG station in Salt Lake City. Here Amtrak attempts to carry on the Mormon tradition of planned orderliness in one of the world's most unusual extant passenger train junctions. Every evening the *California Zephyr* arrives from Chicago at 11:00 and the train splits in three: one segment bound for San Francisco over the old Central Pacific, now Southern Pacific route; one bound for Portland and Seattle over the old UP Oregon Short Line; and one bound for L.A. over the UP *Desert Wind* line. Every morning, between 6:00 and 8:00, the three eastbound runs from those routes converge and are merged into the big *California Zephyr* to Chicago. But the eastbound combination doesn't work very well, with delays on one of the feeding lines, the longest in the world, causing the *California Zephyr* to be notoriously late in arriving at Chicago. It seems to be the only thing in Mormon Salt Lake City that does not function with clockwork efficiency.

At the Rio Grande Café in the DRG station, I enjoy not only good Mexican food, but the lively celebrations of recent graduates from Brigham Young University. In Salt Lake, "Meet me at the station" is an invitation to party. Because of laws banning liquor sales without food, you have to have dinner before the place heats up. After 8:00, Mormon strictures notwithstanding, there are some tables where graduates play boisterous drinking games over foaming pitchers of draft beer, others where the intercourse is more cerebral. I position myself on the outdoor veranda beside the old DRG steam engine overlooking the tracks.

Out on the tracks the engines and additional cars that will make the two branch runs to L.A. and Portland throb, awaiting the arrival of the full train from the east, and passengers bound for the three corners of the far west begin to congregate. Their gear identifies them as mostly followers of the western dream: lots of cowboy hats, plenty of backpacks, fishing rods, lightweight mountain camping equipment, skis, and even a saddle and bridle. There are none of the briefcases that are standard on eastern trains, and my portable computer is the only one in sight.

The train arrives with a flourish almost on time at 11:00 P.M. The *California Zephyr* section going on to San Francisco is loaded first and unhitched from the other sections, and it pulls out. Then begins a great deal of switching and coupling; Amtrak trainmen in yellow plastic hard hats scurry around attaching cables and hoses and murmuring unintelligible communications into their hand-held radios. It's all very bewildering to two little old ladies who pace tentatively around the platform clutching their tickets and wondering aloud which car they are supposed to board and whether the train might leave without them.

"Come on, let's help them out," chortles a pleasant voice behind me, that of Lori Olsen, a charming young woman in her mid-twenties, a little overdressed for the train in a striking peach outfit. She talks to the two women, who reveal how distraught they are by literally quaking in their shoes while I examine their tickets. One has already lost one ticket and had to pay for another. They have lost sight of their luggage and are beginning the big rail trip to Seattle, which they have looked forward to for nine months, in mortal terror. Neither has traveled any distance from Salt Lake since their husbands passed away years ago, but they got tired of just looking at the distant mountains from the retirement home's porch. They've been westerners all of their lives. They wanted to ride the train out into the land one last time.

They're taking the *Pioneer* to Seattle, the train that follows the westernmost leg of the Oregon Trail, the same train I am taking to Portland and Lori is taking to Boise. Lori gets them settled into coach seats, and I check on their luggage. When the train is underway and the two women have showered us with thanks, Lori says, "Come on, Good Samaritan, let's go have a drink."

Lori is a student in a nursing program at Boise State College. She took three years off to run a computer consultant service in L.A., and now that she has had a taste of ascendancy in the professional world she is not sure she can tolerate the subservient role of a female nurse lorded over by male doctors. She is thinking about continuing on in medicine to get her own M.D.

In the meantime she is a self-described "western girl." Brought up in Idaho, she has traveled enough to appreciate her birthright. Life in California-dream L.A. was "the pits" except for the money and sense of self-actualization, "but you can get addicted to that yuppie stuff, so I got out in time." She has been visiting a sister in cowboy Texas, "an empty place full of Texans" that made her yearn for Idaho. She flew to Salt Lake so that she could make the final approach to her home in the real west by land, by train, under a big starry sky. She can't wait to put on pants and boots and go camping, riding, fishing, hunting—"That's what you do in the west, it's why you live here."

But her west is threatened by yuppies and Mormons and Ozzy Osbourne. I never met anyone this young—Lori can't be more than twenty-six or twenty-seven—with so many strong well-articulated opinions. "It comes from really knowing what you love," she says, "and from knowing well the things that endanger it."

It isn't just the "backcountry rednecks" who have invaded the canyons and dunes and mountains with internal-combustion monstrosities such as trail bikes, ATVs (all-terrain vehicles), and dune buggies. It's the yuppies who can afford such toys, who live elsewhere, usually on the West Coast, and who have "no more respect for a perfectly formed windblown desert dune than they do for each other in their fratricidal career combat. They come to small-town western Main Street from California and bring their money and priorities and just lay waste, waste, waste all around them." In time they may mellow out, and some even become good westerners, but by then damage is done and another wave of them has moved in. "Their learning curve is too long—we can't assimilate them fast enough."

Then there's Ozzy Osbourne and heavy metal music. It isn't just the words that are sexist or racist, "the very sound is fascist," built around a profound violence that lifts up the followers in waves of passion directed at anything outside of the order. The essence of the west is "the silence of the wind," but today young westerners carry Ozzy Osbourne into the wilderness and over the edge. Yuppies and heavy metal—they're the inevitable products of urban life, of people living too close together and too far out of sight of the mountains and the deserts. They don't belong here.

Mormons are another story. Echoing my Iranian acquaintance,

Shahriar, Lori believes the Church of Latter-Day Saints is a paradigm of organized religion in general, "a machine for generating money and power." Like many westerners, she resents their power and influence over the lands of the western dream. She is not sure she believes in God and Jesus, but if Jesus is real and returns to earth, "the first thing he will do is smite places like Salt Lake and the Vatican for how they have enslaved souls in his name."

Lori grants that part of her animosity toward the Mormons is simply the usual envy of people living on the plain toward the wealthy folk who live on the hill and own everything. But she insists that when you know what you live for, it's easier to see the hypocrisy in false philosophy. I gently suggest that maybe that's exactly how the Mormons and other proselytizing Christians feel. This makes her laugh, a genuine self-deprecating laugh. "You got me. But I wish that when they found those tablets up on their mountain they had just stayed there and let the rest of us find our own."

The bartender tells us we're going to have to find the answers to life somewhere else on the train because it's after midnight and he is closing down. Back in the darkened coach, people are trying to go to sleep while an eerie display develops outside the windows. The train is climbing through a very narrow canyon, whose walls and outcroppings appear to be just feet from the window. The glow from lighted compartments of the train casts weird moving veils across the variegated texture, color, and curvature of the strata in the rocks. High up the canopy of stars provides the only steady images in the moving tableau, which is like nothing so much as one of the high-tech rides of Disney World. "Now this is perfect," Lori says as she rummages through her bag and produces the Walkman that is standard equipment for all young women riding the experiential road. I fumble with the light-weight earphones, but the music is young and lovely, something about loneliness, emptiness, and an undefined quest in a place of beauty "under the Milky Way tonight." I agree, it is perfect. Who are the musicians?

"You're not going to believe this," Lori chuckles. "They're called The Church."

In the morning, I'm the only rider in the coach car who is awake to see the sunrise across the Snake River plain and the rose lamps it lights in the peaks of the distant Bitterroot Range. Occasionally I spot the dust cloud of a pickup heading across the plain toward a rancher's workday, or maybe for a westerner's celebration of the land. Little fishing parties pass by my window, sometimes just a man and his son with their rods, thermos, and lunch basket, sometimes larger groups with coolers, stoves, tents, and collapsible canvas chairs. Occasionally a fur-jacketed hunter with rifle stalks I don't know what across wet flats and tangled brush. "It's why you live here."

When Lori disembarks at the white stucco missionlike station at Boise, I am more tempted to get off the train than I was at Las Vegas. On the platform she asks, "What are you going to call this chapter when you go back way east?" I don't know—"Oregon Trail," maybe, or "Westering Dream." She suggests "Quest for the West."

I return the westerner's handshake and verbal commitment she has told me is standard in places beyond the reach of lawyers: "Done."

The novelist Joseph Conrad wrote about places in Africa during the nineteenth century that, being unexplored, still showed as white spots on the maps. There are no literal white spots on the maps of America today, but many an American child has gazed at certain remote regions of a U.S. map and been fascinated by the blank in his imagination as he tries to visualize the place. For some it may be northern Maine, or South Dakota, or maybe central Nevada. For me it has always been northeastern Oregon, the region between Boise and the Columbia River. The route of the *Pioneer* and the Oregon Trail plunges straight through that white spot in my map.

It is not the virgin forested wilderness I imagined, but a kingdom where all of the images of the western dream flourish. After Boise the route continues to follow the Snake River through a region that is, surprisingly, desert. The great western desert, between the mountain chains, runs all the way north to the Canadian border. There are even sand dunes here and fences erected by the railroad to prevent them from drifting across the tracks. The river is wide and slow and incongruously blue amid the otherwise tan, arid landscape. Fishermen sit in little groups along its banks with their gear and pickups. There's not a cloud in sight in the big purple sky framed by distant mountains on all four horizons. At the open downstairs vestibule window the air blows dry, clean, and cool—around seventy degrees. Just a typical morning in western dreamland.

Two retired veteran riders of western trains, Ted Hall and Ray Sylvester, join me, drawn by the whiff of outdoor air that I've let into the hermetic air-conditioned environment of the train. They are returning to their homes in Portland from a canoeing and fishing trip in Colorado. "You'd best appreciate these last breaths of dry air," advises Ted. I comment that though I'm enchanted by the dry western expanses, I'm a little homesick for wetness and greenery.

Ray smirks at Ted with a conspirator's expression. "Suppose he'll see any wet green today?"

"Gee, I don't know," says Ted. "Maybe if the fog ain't too thick." He explains that in the Blue Mountains we will begin to see clouds, which will thicken as we roll into the upper Columbia Valley. By the Columbia gorge through the Cascades there will be nothing but the dark green murk of the northwest rain forest.

Past Baker, Oregon, we enter the heart of the Blue Mountains. Now in the valley there is green, farm green, grazing green. To the northeast rise the snow-capped peaks of the Wallowa Mountains, and abruptly to the west tower the even higher peaks of the Blue Mountains, which are not blue at all today, but—green. Over their tops waft the first traces of clouds, with shimmering silver veils draped from them. "What's that?" I ask Ray.

"Verga," he says. "Rain that evaporates before it reaches the ground."

During lunch we ride through the winding high valleys of the Blue Mountains, where tall timber, including even some deciduous trees, sways in an animating breeze. Here is the closest thing to the dense forested wilderness of my imagined white spot that I will see in this ride. The diner is particularly lively today, with the talk ranging from the quarantined chickenpox case in bedroom A to the football rivalry between the Denver Broncos and the Seattle Seahawks, the proper caliber for clean-kill antelope hunting, hot spots for catching cutthroat trout, trail blowups on horseback, and effusive descriptions of perfect mornings in high mountain camps. But the dominant topic is the rain toward which the train is hurtling. Just when I have caught the fever of the western dream, it seems that the train is going to carry me into another milieu. I wish I could get off.

"This is country where people do just that, you know—get off the train of civilization," says Ray.

"Like ole D. B. Cooper, though in his case it was a plane," adds Ted.

"Well, he didn't really bail out here in the Blue Mountains. That was an error of the early news reports. It was in the Cascades, but the country was the same kind. Newsmen got the name wrong, too—he called himself Dan Cooper, but the D. B. stuck to the legend."

It was Thanksgiving Eve in 1971 when a well-dressed middle-aged man using the alias Dan Cooper boarded Northwest Airlines flight 305 with his briefcase. He paid for a drink with a $20 bill and then dumped it all over himself as he fumbled a note into the stewardess's hands demanding two parachutes and $200,000 in $20 bills. He cracked his briefcase just enough to reveal cylinders and wires that looked like a bomb.

In Seattle the passengers were released and Cooper's demands were met. Airborne again, the pilot followed Cooper's precise directions to fly him to Mexico at the slow speed of two hundred miles per hour at ten thousand feet. Somewhere over the Cascades of southern Washington, he parachuted out of the plane.

In 1980, an eight-year-old boy, camping with his family by the Columbia, dug a wad of $20 bills out of the sand at the river's edge. Their serial numbers checked out; the boy had found $6,000 of Cooper's cache. Otherwise no trace of Cooper has ever been found.

In published accounts, Portland FBI agent Ralph Himmelsbach speaks for those who believe Cooper never survived his escapade and that his remains have been biodegraded at the bottom of the river or consumed by wild animals in the mountains. Parachuting in the dark over wild mountains is a feat even skilled paratroopers wouldn't care to perform. "Even if he'd just sprained his leg it'd be a death sentence in that kind of environment. I think he got as far as a creek, died, and the spring floods took part of his pack downstream and eventually into the Columbia."

But a lively legend refuses to accept Himmelsbach's scenario. Cloud cover prevented search operations for two days after the hijacking—plenty of time for Cooper to make himself scarce. People around Ariel, Washington, form the core of those who happily believe Cooper is alive and spending his money somewhere, even though none of the marked bills have ever turned up in circulation. Says one, "It was too carefully planned for him to flub up at the last minute." The night of the jump, another local resident grabbed his rifle and rushed outside in response to a loud thumping on his roof. Another recalls seeing a small plane circling a rarely used airstrip by a cemetery that night. Others, suggesting they may have witnessed a rehearsal, recall that the previous night, at another lonely airstrip nearby, a strange plane took off with the aid of the headlights from a parked car, and returned forty-five minutes later, and then both the plane and the car departed. Searchers combing the area later found a woman's severed hand and another body—possible victims of a desperate hijacker?

The Cooper cult quickly spawned T-shirts, bumper stickers, at least one book, several hoaxes, a song, and the annual D. B. Cooper Day at the Ariel Store and Tavern. Ray has attended it.

"Biggest beer bash I ever saw," he says. The little town was overrun with all kinds of people, even a few real modern-day mountain men.

There was a D. B. Cooper look-alike contest (based on the FBI's composite sketch), hours of scenario exchanging, and several spontaneous search groups formed with the intent of finding new evidence before the effects of the beer wore off. "People want to believe that he made it—that he beat the system, and did it without hurting anybody. One of the favorite themes is that he was really a mountain man himself, disguised in a business suit he never wore before or after."

"Speaking of mountain men, that's another story that gets folks around here all in a lather still," says Ted. "Don and Dan Nichols."

"Now you're talking real bad guys, but you're right, some people make heroes out of them too."

With a book and a TV movie about the Nicholses already extant, the story of their abduction of Olympic athlete Kari Swenson is even more familiar than Cooper's. But in those retellings aimed at a nationwide audience, the focus is on the traumatized golden girl from Bozeman, Montana. Ray says that out here, it's Don Nichols who fascinates people.

Don Nichols grew up in the region of Ennis, Montana, son of a big-hearted, alcoholic father who took him on frequent trips into the mountains in times of sobriety. After his father died drunk in a car accident, he increasingly turned to the mountains, where a man could be free of what he called "the rotten system." His own marriage didn't work out, but his love for his son rivaled his love for the mountains. As the boy got older, the two of them spent whole summers in the mountains, establishing a series of camps, caches, gardens, and hideouts. Here, he taught his son, they would be safe from the poisons that rich men made people eat in the valleys.

Eventually the Nicholses moved into the mountains full-time and broke the tether to civilization. At his trial, Don testified that he developed the habit of striking his son only on the forehead so that he would break his hand before he would do the boy real harm. Danny testified that he worshiped his father's will and saw his omniscience in everything.

Danny's coming of age must have been the precipitating crisis. When they abducted Kari Swenson as she jogged through her daily workout, Don told her, "See, we need a woman for Danny. That's the only way he'll stay up here with me." Whatever they had in mind, it all fell apart quickly. A search party stumbled upon their camp the next morning, and Danny shot Kari, wounding her, as she shouted a warning. Don took cool aim with his rifle at the face of rescuer Al Goldstein and fired.

The Nicholses fled, Kari was rescued, and the manhunt for a murderer began. To many westerners this is the best part of the story. For five months the mountain men eluded capture until they were ultimately tracked down by Sheriff Johnny France, a character out of western lore in his own right. France really did track down his quarry riding a snowmobile and finally appealed to the father's love of his son, who after Kari's recovery was guilty only of abduction and assault, not murder.

Kari Swenson, despite the obsession of many westerners with the Nicholses and the media's interest in her as a member of the U.S. Olympic team, is herself a mountain girl in the mold of my friend Lori Olsen. She had been running in the mountains around her hometown for years, and her sport was the biathlon, which combines grueling cross-country skiing with rifle marksmanship. She is probably the only person in the saga who could handle a rifle as well as Don Nichols himself.

Ray says that every westerner today is intrigued by these two stories. They have become myths of an urge that lies at the fringe of the dream and have become central in one of the two ongoing debates that cook whenever westerners gather. There are still men today to whom the vastness of the west means the opportunity for escape from society's restraints. Marijuana plantations, survivalist camps, militant fundamentalist cults, and white supremacist commandos make the terrain as "hairy" today as it is imagined to have been in the days of the "wild west." Guys who would never take part in any of those things argue passionately that the west is the place where people like that can make their stand. It's a question of a guarantee of freedom that transcends words written on paper. Others argue that the true legacy of the mountain men is the communality of the rendezvous. Distance between men makes them good neighbors who accept unwritten laws of civility without coercion. In this view, Cooper and the Nicholses are deviants, casualties of the western dream gone awry.

The other westerners' debate, Ray says, is that between environmentalists and "pro-use" groups concerning the future of the land. The pro-use side argues that the land itself is a precious opportunity for economic and recreational enterprise, an opportunity that must be exploited to keep the larger American dream alive. Western environmentalists counter that the management of the west as a commodity has already led to the near-extinction of the buffalo, the beaver, and a human race. Both arguments ultimately involve the western struggle with its dichotomies, its contradictions, its uncertainty about just how much community and regulation is needed by men living in the vast stretches of land that separates them and with a history that has always viewed the land as an infinite resource.

In the early 1840s, the fur trade had died. The panic of 1837, high taxes in midwestern states resulting from canal building (and in the case of Illinois, early failed attempts at railroad building), malaria in the Mississippi Valley, and the American urge to push west that had been going on since Jamestowners moved up to the Piedmont and later into Kentucky—all of these factors produced the explosion of westward emigration over the Oregon Trail in the 1840s and the beginnings of the modern west within which the mountain man's west struggles to survive.

The first parties with wagons set out in 1841; at Independence one of them discovered to its consternation that no one in the group knew the route. These early wagon trains failed; those who got through did so by abandoning the wagons. By '43 the first wagons made it to Oregon, and with the exception of the Mormons, the bulk of the pioneer movement was to Oregon until the California Gold Rush of '49.

The wagons, which were small, lightweight vessels better suited to the arduous western mountain crossings than the legendary lumbering Conestogas of the earlier migrations across the eastern mountains, covered fifteen to twenty miles on good days over a trail two thousand miles long. Trails meant for wagons did not follow the contours of the land, as would the later grade-conscious railroads, because the wagons would capsize. They had to go straight up and over the elevations, often raised or lowered with snubbing lines around trees or rocks. After the first few waves of emigrants, navigation by landmark became unnecessary as the ruts of the wagon wheels and rows of markers for shallow graves made the route as clear as that of an interstate.

Historians have scoured the journals of emigrants for evidence of Hollywood's famous Indian attacks on ringed wagon trains, but there is none. More frequently one finds references to friendly, if awkward, encounters with hungry Indians eager to barter for food and white man's hardware. It actually was the railroads and the miners of the '60s which provoked the Indians to a level of warfare that would have surely prohibited all westward migration if it had occurred as early as the '40s. But Hollywood didn't invent the fear of Indians; the emigrants themselves did, traveling with more armament than they needed because of the rare, but horrible, stories of massacres.

By the '50s the journey was not so lonely as myth would have it. Fort Laramie recorded the passage of 36,116 oxen and 7,548 mules in the year 1850, and emigrant journals record many a meeting between traveling parties. One John Lewis described such a gathering at South Pass in 1852: "There were about 100 wagons there and we got the girls together and had a fiddle . . . and sutch another party was never got up all the way to Oregon. . . . O that I could all ways be on the plains . . . love is hotter her than any whare . . . they love with all their mits and some times a little harder."

But there was hardship and horror. One group found a man dying of cholera and diarrhea who had been left behind by an earlier outfit. He had chosen not to touch the sack of provisions they had left him.

A woman announced to her husband that she would go no farther and sat down by the trail. He left her there and continued on with the wagons and the children. When he sent one son back to retrieve her, only the woman returned, raving that she had bashed the son's head in with a rock. When the man rode back to find the body, she set fire to the wagons and burned them all before he returned.

A man who had promised to take his son to Oregon kept the promise by carrying the boy in a zinc coffin filled with alcohol. Malaria had taken the boy's life before he had left the Mississippi Valley.

Despite the hardships, the journals of those who reached the soon-crowded Oregon or California valleys often betray an itch for the marvels and wide-open space remembered from the journey out. One look at a topographical map shows that the arable valleys of the West Coast constitute a surprisingly small area compared to the vast agricultural reaches of the midwest or even the east. Those who moved west primarily for elbow room soon began looking back over their shoulders toward territory staked out by nobody but the enclave of Mormons around Salt Lake.

By Pendleton, the rugged Blue Mountains have given way to fertile ranch land. Here the Pendleton Roundup is the world's oldest and biggest rodeo, and here too the wool of the local sheep is made into Pendleton clothing. In the lounge car Kurt Ferguson, a big, burly man with a crew cut, points to the rodeo stands and says, "I used to do that." Kurt is returning to his home in Portland from a trip by rail way east that made him a different man for the second time in his life. "First I was a kind of a happy mountain man, then I was an unhappy Vietnam vet. Now I don't know what to call myself. Hopefully just an American who belongs and who can sleep better at night."

Before Vietnam, Kurt was an aficionado of the rendezvous still carried on by latter-day mountain men whose saints bear names like

Smith, Bridger, Sublette, and Clyman. Today's rendezvous are regional get-togethers of American Indians and "mountain men" publicized in magazines like *Muzzleloader* and *Buckskin*. Participants try to recreate the past by sleeping in tepees, cooking on flint-and-steel fires, wearing the old clothes, and eating deer meat (don't call it venison), buffalo, bear, turtle, groundhog, raccoon—and even tree rats (squirrels).

There's money in it, too. Many pay for the travel to each powwow with the deerhide jackets and antler buttons they make. And then there are the capotes, mountain-man coats made from Indian wool blankets. "A real capote is a sign of brotherhood with the Indians," says Kurt. "A full-blooded Indian has to make the blanket. A white man has to then cut it and sew it into a capote." He says that yuppies have picked up on the capotes and pay big bucks for them.

But then Kurt went to Vietnam in 1966, 1st Cavalry, 7th Infantry. Going in, he thought his mountain-man experience would serve him well, but it didn't work out that way. In fifty firefights, he spent most of his term in the Pleiku, Highway 19, An Khe region in close combat with the regular NVA 304th Regiment. "We got to know them well. You could tell when it was them instead of VC. Their hits were just so much more effective. There would be people dropping all around." The Vietcong, according to Kurt, are terribly overrated in the war lore. Once he was guarding a village after an air strike and he heard talk from underground. He lifted up a bamboo platform and found half a dozen of them happy to be taken prisoner. "Those guys were just like us, drafted into hell. Getting captured was their only way out. I could feel toward them like the old mountain men must have felt toward hungry, hostile Indians, men who you could respect because they were up against the same tough shit you were. But the NVA were different, trained professional cadres. Not men but killing machines. If they had had our weapons, the kill ratios would have been reversed."

I tell him about Will LaChance's catalogue of images the Vietnam movies missed, and Kurt adds a few of his own. He recalls the "wait a minute" bushes that would snag on your clothes as you were packing through the bush. "You didn't want to be separated from the column and you didn't want to hold everybody up. Just one of the million ways that a Nam march and bivouac was a far cry from backpacking in the Blue Mountains here." And there was guard duty when it was so dark and rainy that it didn't matter whether you had your eyes open or closed.

Kurt recalls returning from a series of desperate firefights and being ordered to go to the rear for R&R. It didn't work. "You couldn't relax around the friendlies after having Vietnamese women and kids shooting at you. And you couldn't relate to the GIs permanently stationed in the rear with their cute little booze tents and air-conditioned mobile homes. And finally you just couldn't get yourself presentable." So in the end Kurt and a number of the guys in his unit opted to stay in the field like mountain men who find less and less call to come down to the haunts of civilized men. "We became animals."

When he returned home, a lady spat on him in Seattle, and the excursions out into the mountains became a hollow reflection of the images that had sustained him in Vietnam. They were no longer pilgrimages toward something loved but escape from something loathed—his fellow Americans. "I guess I became one of those 'traumatized vets' you read about."

Kurt never gave a thought to visiting the Vietnam Memorial. It offended him that it was designed by an Oriental, and he had spent most of the past twenty years trying to forget his tour: "Who needed a memorial to make you remember?" But his wife urged him to visit the traveling memorial when it came through Portland. He found a dozen names on it that he knew, and that changed everything. Suddenly the Vietnam Memorial seemed like something that was his, just as the mountains used to be before Vietnam. He became obsessed with visiting the permanent memorial in D.C., but he couldn't fly there. Somehow flying and hitting D.C. cold seemed like a sure way to replay the bitter homecoming to Seattle. No, he would travel alone across the country by train, seeing the land and the people he fought for close up and stealing the time to do just what he had avoided for twenty years—remember.

"But still I wasn't prepared for the genius of that monument. It's the way the visitors looking for names become part of the memorial that does it. You never understand till you become part of it yourself. Buddy finds buddy, brother finds brother, father and mother find son, wife finds husband, and kid finds father."

The first day in D.C., Kurt spent eight hours looking for names he knew. There were scores of them, many that he last saw alive and didn't know had later been killed.

The second day he watched the visitors and their gestures of grief and caring. He began talking to them and making acquaintances and sharing his pain in a way he had not done since the early days of his hitch. That night he couldn't sleep and went down to the monument at 4:00 A.M. and found maybe a hundred people there with flashlights and candles—people like him drawn into a community of memory reaching back across twenty empty years.

The third day, he and a group of newly made friends focused on the mementoes left behind by visitors. Several hours with park officials convinced him that the planned addition to house these things—these relics of love and loss—would do more than a dozen patriotic statues to show him and the world that the men of Vietnam were loved, that they were not cast off by their country, that survivors like himself belonged.

Kurt called his employer in Portland and stayed in D.C. two days longer than he had intended. The train ride back has been a joyous blur of making new friends. He has a little black book packed with the addresses of Americans he hopes to stay in touch with. "Here I had been hating people for twenty years because I thought what you were supposed to do was forget." Now Kurt can't wait to go back into the mountains with some of his newfound friends to rendezvous in an environment where isolation and the challenge of survival make men better neighbors because of the spaces between them. Vietnam has taught him what happens when human community breaks down. He wants to get back to the frontier, where it still works. "Hell, I might even go back to the rodeo."

At last the route of the *Pioneer* meets the Columbia River, wide and slow and reflecting a big sky between a desert plain on the south and barren hills on the north. On the far shore I can just make out the Burlington Northern rail line, over which runs the Portland branch of the *Empire Builder* bound for Montana, Minneapolis, and Chicago. It's the first place since Barstow where human commerce is anywhere near dense enough to support parallel rail routes.

The Columbia has played at least as important a role in the economic development of the northwest as the Hudson, Delaware, or Ohio has played in other regions of the nation, but for the beginning of the run down into Portland, you'd never know it. The land this river cuts through is resistant to the terrain-altering works of man.

Soon, however, the sight of the river, dams, and barges and clouds building in the western sky suggests a transition is at hand. The *Pioneer* is leaving the domain of the western dream and entering one that thrives on the coast. The western dream could never prevail too near a coastline because its essence is land and space.

In the western dream, the land—all of it—belongs to everyone and no one, and every man has a right to unlimited personal freedom and elbow room in the quest for discovery amid its harsh grandeur. Men don't live closely enough together to place much value on any kind of social contact nor to develop habits of unfriendliness. This makes them paragons of antisocial goodwill.

It is the vastness and harshness of the land that makes communal individualism possible and makes communion with it so rewarding. In places like Denver and Phoenix, where development has overcome the land's natural resistance to population, the dream has become a crowded parody of itself, a mongrel of the more generic American dream with a life-style that could just as well be located in Coral Gables or San Jose. But along the route of the *Pioneer* the dream is alive and well despite its controversies and schisms. Riding on the *Pioneer* I have drawn a colored line across my blank mental map of the northwest, but for hundreds of miles on either side of that route, the white space is still there, a frontier where men and women can still tromp back into the wilderness and find their own tablets. "It's why you live here."

When railroads arrived in the region of the Oregon Trail, they closed one era and heralded a new one featuring a four-way contest reminiscent of the imperial struggle in the days of the fur trade. Grenville Dodge saw the potential for a UP connection from Utah all the way to the Oregon coast as early as 1868, when he sent J. O. Hudnutt to survey a route roughly paralleling the Oregon Trail. Collis Huntington later gobbled up every California line headed north in his trademark strategy of aggressive defense of his SP empire. By the early seventies, the second transcontinental sanctioned by the U.S. government, the Northern Pacific, was working its way toward Oregon from Duluth. And finally there was Jim Hill's renegade Great Northern, last of the five great transcontinentals, laying tracks west along the Canadian border in Dakota territory.

Ben Holladay was the prophet for rails, sails, and anything else that moved in the early days of Oregon. He patched together a transportation company in which the role of the railroads was primarily to get people and goods by the portages of the northwest's rivers. The real stars were the elegant riverboats which, for a time, enjoyed a heyday like that earlier on the Mississippi.

But Holladay's little empire collapsed and was taken over by Henry Villard, a man of manic energy and huge German financial backing, who reorganized Holladay's enterprises into the Oregon Railroad & Navigation Company. Under this regime, railroads were dominant and spelled doom for the steamboats. First he built south to connect with Huntington's California SP in 1879; then he built east along the Columbia and through the Blue Mountains to a point on the Snake River (ironically named Huntington) where the presence of a connection enabled the UP to finally build the Oregon route it had wanted for so long. The Oregon Short Line (over which today's *Pioneer* travels) was completed by 1884 and the UP had its second outlet to the coast, though again it involved a connection with a symbiont like the Central Pacific.

But Villard didn't stop there. In one of the most spectacular financial maneuvers ever, he accumulated enough capital through a "blind pool" (an arrangement whereby investors would buy in without knowing the object of the investment) to buy control of the unfinished Northern Pacific. Now Oregon had three great lines connecting it to the rest of the nation, all of them linked to the local Oregon Railroad & Navigation Company, now renamed Oregon & Transcontinental.

Eventually Villard's empire collapsed of its own weight. Huntington got the northern California link into Oregon, the UP got the Short Line all the way to Portland, and the Northern Pacific again faced its series of bankruptcies independently.

But these years illustrated the railroad's role in a new west—the west as commodity. Land speculators coined catchy slogans to promote the latest boom town sprouting along the fertile lines of the new railroads. Kalima on the Columbia was touted as the place "where rail meets sail." Investors were exhorted to "keep your eye on Pasco." The railroads and their attendant speculators could make or break towns. Yakima wanted too much money for the right-of-way the NP needed to pass through it, so the railroad built a route that was four miles north of town. Recognizing their blunder, the captains of Yakima began to move their town, piece by piece. First a key hotel was jacked up and hauled the four miles to the new townsite, then a furniture store followed, and finally the whole town. The new site was called North Yakima for a while, but eventually became simply Yakima. The old site was renamed Union Gap and languished into obscurity.

And one of railroading's greatest feats was accomplished here in the Cascades as a result of one railroad's desire to be master of the northwest territories. The Northern Pacific already had a connection to Portland through its contracts with Oregon & Transcontinental over the smooth line along the Columbia River, but it began eyeing a direct crossing of the Cascades toward Puget Sound.

Between 1873 and 1884, engineers of the NP scouted three passes—all difficult—through the range known to the pioneers as "the Last Mountains" for a route to the Puget Sound area. Different Puget Sound towns agitated for the pass that would bring the rails and economic stardom to them, and by the time the route had reached Yakima, Stampede Pass was selected. The route would necessitate a two-mile tunnel, and because of financing arrangements it had to be completed within twenty-eight months. The worst obstacle was that there would be no tracks to the tunnel site for some time. Everything needed had to be hauled overland through rugged mountain territory. Eleven bids were received, and ten of them were extremely high due to the terrain and the time limit. Nelson Bennett's was half as much as the others. People thought he was crazy.

On the day he got the contract, Bennett and his brother Sydney began clearing a road to the tunnel site. On February 1, 1886, they began to build the plank road through dense conifer forests and canyons and across rushing streams to the site eighty-two miles away and 2,300 feet higher than Yakima. They hauled whole sawmills, steam engines, drills, compressors, ventilators, waterwheels, and miles of pipe and track by the same methods used by the earlier pioneers to move their little wagons, averaging a mile a day while advance parties at the site began hand drilling in preparation. At the east portal the snow was six to eight feet deep, and the site of the tunnel entrance was found to lie behind a frozen waterfall 150 feet high and ten feet thick.

To spur the work Bennett offered a bonus to those who completed more than the necessary thirteen and a half feet per day. Though landslides, explosions, floods, blizzards, strikes, and cave-ins set the work back, the tunnel crept on and beat the deadline by seven days.

The feat exceeds even Crocker's laying of ten miles of track a day and has not been duplicated since. And all because the NP wished to avoid reliance on the Oregon Navigation route through the Columbia gorge to Portland and to be the first transcontinental with its own through line all the way from the Great Lakes to the Pacific coast.

The competition for railroad empires in the land of the mountain men mimicked the imperial rivalries that had gone on here decades earlier and that would soon be reenacted on the other rim of the Pacific. The seizing and holding of territory (by building rail branches), the subverting of smaller powers (little railroads), the carving out of spheres of influence (by domination of regional traffic), the ever-shifting pattern of alliances (pooling and rate-setting), the abrogated paper agreements (such as the prohibition of dining cars before the dining-car wars), and the establishment of puppet government (by owning influential politicians)—these hallmarks of imperial struggle characterize the railroads' impact on the land of the mountain men's western dream. There were big winners: the UP and Jim Hill's late entrant Great

Northern in particular; and losers, including Huntington's SP, which encountered in Oregon a strategy similar to that it had used to defend its empire in California; and the Northern Pacific, which staggered through a series of receiverships because its managers, never fully apprehending the colonial nature of railroading in the Gilded Age, failed to build the crucial branch line feeders in the naive belief that a transcontinental could survive merely as a transcontinental. But the greatest casualty was surely the frontier itself as the last white space in America's map was crisscrossed by the steel lines. It's one place where I can't quite cheer the triumph of the rails.

Along the waterway of the northwest the *Pioneer* rolls this afternoon over the line of the old Oregon Railroad & Navigation Company. As the river narrows and the land begins to evince the green touch of rainfall, the works of man become more apparent. The John Day Dam, the Dalles Dam, the Cascade Locks, and the Bonneville Dam have tamed the waters and turned their energy into light, heat, and money. But overhead the indomitable black rocks of the Cascade gorge rise ever higher in seeming defiance of these furious human machinations on the river. By the narrows of the gorge, the air drips thick with mist and rain. A steady west wind howls and froths the water, and I can see the five-foot swells out on the river that make this the world's mecca for windsurfers.

But in less than a half hour the train crosses a steel bridge over the Willamette River in downtown Portland. The river is jammed with ships and pleasure boats for the Rose Festival, which starts tomorrow. Above the railroad station rises a tower carrying a huge blue neon sign, "Go by Train." A very modest skyline is backed by cloud-shrouded green hills which cradle the city like—well, like no place so much as the New England seaports of Bath, Maine, New Bedford, Massachusetts, and New London, Connecticut.

The eastern pioneers were coming home here. Their hearts must have joyed to find these wet fertile green valleys beyond the vastness of the plains, the hostile chasms and canyons of the mountains, and the dust of the desert. Here in the Willamette Valley there was land for the taking which didn't require that men remold their environmental gestalt. It was an easy place to live, and it was a clean slate, where they could start over again and get it right this time in reasonably familiar surroundings. They named this place Portland, after Portland, Maine.

Chapter Fourteen

———

California Dreamin'

THE *COAST STARLIGHT* SOUTH

T HE settlers came over the mountains on the Oregon, California, and Santa Fe trails, around the Horn in tall ships, and, finally, across the deserts on the steel of the transcontinental railroads. The fulfillment of Manifest Destiny, the opening of a second American coastline, and the discovery of fertile soil in the valleys and gold in the ranges offered restless Americans a second chance to get it right, to begin again the new world that many believed had been despoiled on the East Coast. Here in the rain-frothed waters of Puget Sound and on the sunny shores of southern California, tradition and old-world customs, Yankee reticence and southern bigotry, urban squalor and vested interests were not going to hem in the dreams of men and women who thought they could do better. This was, and still is, the California dream.

As far back as 1844, mountain man Jim Clyman noted not only the dream's driving essence, but the shadows that lurked at its edges. Traveling with a party to Oregon, Clyman tired of the slow pace of the wagons and went ahead on horseback to the Willamette Valley. He was charmed by the sparseness of the settlement there but disturbed by the continuing restlessness of the settlers. "I never saw a more discontented community. . . . The long, tiresome trip from the states has taught them what they are capable of performing and enduring. They talk of removing to the Islands, California, Chile, and other parts of South America with as much composure as you in Wisconsin talk of removing to Indiana or Michigan."

Feeling the itch himself, he scouted his way down to California. His impressions have a remarkably contemporary ring. He commented on the mild climate, the earthquakes, and the general nakedness of the people. The food was so dominated by several kinds of red pepper that "Callifornia cookery is enough to strangle a foreigner." He didn't like the inhabitants very much—"The Callifornians [*sic*] are a proud, lazy, indolent people who do nothing but ride after herds from place to place without object."

Clyman met up with Lansford Hastings and set out east over the Sierras and Hastings's new cutoff across the Nevada desert and the Wasatch Mountains of Utah. When he arrived at Fort Laramie on June 27, 1846, he was the right man in the right place at the right time—only some people didn't listen.

On that fateful day Fort Laramie was a crucible of western history. Missouri governor Lilburn Boggs, who had just driven the Mormons from his state, was headed west with one party and the Donner brothers and James Reed were there with their party. Advance scouts for Brigham Young's Mormons lurked listening for clues to a route to their promised land.

Clyman counseled that the apparent California shortcut of the Hastings Cutoff through the Salt Lake area was a route to be avoided. Boggs heeded this advice and gave up on California, eventually settling in the Willamette Valley of Oregon after an uneventful passage. The Mormon agents, too, added Clyman's report to Young's growing list of reasons why the Salt Lake area was the place where Mormons would not be disturbed. Only the Donners followed the Hastings Cutoff to disaster and history.

Clyman had now seen it all and continued back east, commenting on the trailside grave marker of a seventy-year-old woman in Kansas. "This stone shows us that all ages and all sects are found to undertake this long tedious and even dangerous journey for some unknown object never to be realized even by those the most fortunate and why: because the human mind can never be satisfied never at rest always on the stretch for something new—some strange novelty." But in Oregon and California, the quest for novelty had run out of land.

* * *

Portland's Union Station today is crowded and disorganized. The south-bound and northbound editions of the *Coast Starlight* arrive at approx-imately the same time, and people don't seem to know which line to jostle each other in. I attempt to sort them out by noting who is attired for rainy Seattle and who is dressed for sunny California but am frustrated by a motley variety of garb that makes such distinctions impossible. When the trains arrive, the crowd surges through the doors in one mass and is divided by a platform chief who frantically directs people to the proper train. Inside, the coaches are so crowded that some passengers stand in the aisles as the train pulls out. I protest that I haven't seen anything like this since New York, but am assured by an assistant conductor that this horrendous state of affairs rectifies itself after a few stops in the Willamette Valley, whose inhabitants use the train as a local commuter.

I will get to know the *Coast Starlight* well; I have already traveled as a daytripper from San Francisco to L.A. on a previous trip. In keeping with my plan to travel north-south in the west this trip, I will ride overnight in coach south to Sacramento, where I will visit the Califor-nia State Railroad Museum. Then I will catch the westbound *Califor-nia Zephyr* for the short run in to San Francisco for dinner in Chinatown before finally catching the northbound *Coast Starlight* with a bedroom accommodation all the way to Seattle.

The *Coast Starlight* is a long train, the longest in the west. With two mail cars, a baggage car, seven coaches, a diner, an observation lounge, and three sleeping cars—all Superliners—it cuts an impressive figure as it winds along the Willamette River south out of Portland. Originat-ing in Seattle, it is a relatively slow train even by western standards, taking thirty-three hours to make the fourteen-hundred-mile run to Los Angeles (the *Silver Star* runs the same distance from New York to Miami in twenty-six hours). Because of its pace and the spectacularly varied scenery along the route, including Puget Sound, the Cascades, San Francisco Bay, the Salinas Valley, the Coastal Range, and the cliffs of the Pacific Ocean, it should be the ultimate cruise train filled with laid-back California-dreamin' passengers riding to see the country.

But it isn't. As the only long-distance north-south run on the West Coast, it's called upon to perform an intercity role (and in some places even a commuter role) like that of the fast trains of the northeast corridor. Thus it's always crowded with people in a hurry to be some-place sooner than this train will get them there.

Why don't they fly or drive the freeways? Conductor Arthur Geary explains that it's partly economic. North-south flights on the West Coast are notoriously expensive because of their relatively short distances and the lack of passenger turnover. The price of a coach rail ticket is such a bargain that people tolerate—just barely—the slow service. Furthermore, a growing number of people here are turned off to freeway driving, Art says. "At least on the train you don't get shot at."

An unscientific survey of the passengers in my coach car confirms Art's observations. A widow returning to Oakland from visiting her daughter in Seattle is saving money and avoiding driving by herself. Her daughter is writing a book on Chief Joseph of the Nez Percé Indians, and she has a draft of it to read. An obstetrician returning to Klamath Falls from a conference in Portland will get home five and a half hours later than he would have by plane but still in time for a decent night's sleep. He saved $100 and finds the train a good place to wade through the literature he picked up at the convention. A couple traveling on business to L.A. from Portland take the train as a cost-saving measure. A young Mexican girl is riding the longest distance, all the way to her family's home in San Diego from Seattle, where she has been visiting her older sister. She has never flown; her family is "too poor." A man with unmistakable American Indian features who has quit his job as a stevedore in Portland is returning to his estranged wife in Sacramento, where they hope to build a new life refinishing Victorian-era homes. He hopes she doesn't think him a big spender for riding the train instead of taking the bus.

No sign of a regional dream here, and for a while the terrain along the Willamette River has that same generic overcrowded commercial look that you can see anywhere in America. It's hard to picture pioneers hacking forests and carving out homesteads along this busy river.

But suddenly the characteristics of the settled valley begin to change, and soon I am looking at waterfalls, rapids, and steeply rising forested slopes as the train begins the climb into the Cascades. Again I am struck by just how small the Willamette Valley is, as I was when I looked it up on a map. It must have filled up awfully quickly.

It wasn't furs that first stirred the white men's interest in California nor even gold, climate, or land. It was religion, or the lack of it, among the tribes of Indians. In the late 1700s, Spanish empire building was always heralded by missions establishing Roman Catholicism and then the broader benefits of Spanish civilization. The missions of the coastal valleys of California constituted an organized system for bringing civilization to Indians, who, under a rather harsh mandatory regime of labor and instruction, were to be raised, in theory, to a level of self-sufficient civilization. Then through a process of secularization, the mission lands were to be broken up and distributed to the Indians, who were supposed to carry on as loyal and responsible subjects of the Spanish Empire.

But the system didn't work very well. The California Indians were nowhere near as culturally advanced as those the Spanish dealt with earlier in Central America, and were inherently disinclined to the sedentary life of cattle raising and rigid discipline. Thus the Spanish regimes came to be characterized by what often looked like slovenly care and brutality. When secularization was implemented, the Indians usually lost their lands quickly to white land sharks and, accustomed to no other kind of relationship with whites, settled into a pattern of labor for the rancheros which differed little from true slavery.

Such was the state when U.S. Americans began filtering into California in the 1820s, initially to exploit the hide and tallow trade attendant on the well-established Spanish cattle herds. It was the reports of these early sojourners of a miraculous climate, superior even to that of Oregon, that led to the boom of migration and settlement in the 1840s. Inhabitants of malaria-plagued Mississippi swarmed to a place which claimed never to have seen malaria except in one traveler from Missouri who was such a rarity that native Californians came from miles around just to view the novelty of a man sweating and shaking with chills.

One might argue that the settlers who made it to the West Coast were, by a process of natural selection, a special breed. They had endured the longest and most arduous trek and had established themselves in the lands of a foreign power far from the haunts of their fellow Americans. Thus the climate and the life of relative ease it portended seemed only a natural reward for their uniqueness. If they adopted habits of the native Californians and Indians which were at odds with the ethic of Anglo-Saxons back east, who was to challenge them? If the discovery of gold and easy wealth conflicted with the Puritan norms of work and moral staunchness born in the cold climates of northern Europe and New England, then they would adopt new norms more suited to a place where the sun always shone and constant struggle with the environment was a distant memory.

In the dining car this evening, I meet a modern California native who tells a tale that at first sets off loud alarms from my jackalope sensors, but by Sacramento I am convinced she has shared a genuine story of the California dream gone bad.

I had first noticed Sarah Webb in the Portland station because she wore a heavy leather-and-wool coat in warm weather and lugged a huge stuffed rucksack bag that she needed help to carry. But what caught my eye most were her eyes, tired and sad and faraway, with a downward slant to the lids.

She silently picks at her dinner while the third diner at our table, Bill Tillis, Jr., explains that he is the first of four generations of men in his family who hasn't worked for the railroad. He wishes he did but does the next best thing by riding the train whenever he can. His father, a fireman, was killed in a head-on collision in 1944 when a switchman missed his call and sent a highballing freight into another that was supposed to be waiting on a siding. "I've never forgiven the son of a bitch. It's one thing when your father dies of natural causes, but when you know a man caused it, it's hard to accept."

"I know," says Sarah, who until now has listened to our conversation in silence. "My father was murdered."

It's an awkward moment; I can tell Bill doesn't believe her, and he steers the conversation back to train talk while we pay our checks. Sarah has left the diner without finishing dessert, and I set out to find her. Twice I hike through all twelve cars of the consist with no success, but on the third try I find her in the trailing coach car with two small children in tow. She has shed her heavy coat now, and I can see that she is pregnant.

The two children belong to a mother sitting across the aisle from Sarah's seat, and Sarah is ready to divest herself of them. I suggest she come down to the lounge car and tell me her story. The mother rolls her eyes in disapproval—she's losing her baby-sitter to what must look to her like an unsavory dalliance.

Veterans of the early sixties, Sarah's parents are prototypes of two divergent directions so many children of that era have taken, especially in California. Her father saw a living in the desire for altered consciousness pioneered in Haight-Ashbury, and by the time Sarah was seven or eight, he was making big money as one of northern California's major dealers of amphetamines and hallucinogens. Eventually his trade was exclusively cocaine. It was a secret she learned to keep at a very young age. Her mother split and settled with her small garden of home-grown marijuana plants in the remote Washington Cascades. Yuppie vs. hippie.

Sarah and her older brother stayed with Dad. After all, he had money, a big house, fast cars, and a fifty-five-foot schooner that they sailed to Pacific islands where they hobnobbed with millionaires and famous rock musicians. But by junior high school, Dad's generosity had gotten Sarah strung out free-basing cocaine. "I blew off high school. Never had any friends my own age. I was like a vegetable—fertilize me with coke free-base and water me with booze. Finally I would end every day taking downers and throwing up before I could sleep."

After high school Sarah went to work managing a motel, convincing the owner that she was twenty-six. "Since I hadn't hung around with anyone much younger than that since I was fourteen, it was easy getting the job." But the drug habit stopped her dead in her tracks. One day she realized she had just spent a whole week doing nothing but hustling coke, making free-base, and getting high. She weighed less than ninety pounds.

"That was the end. I just stopped, called my mother, told her to meet me in Portland, and got on the train." She spent three weeks at her mother's house drying out. She gained weight, realized that her father had poisoned her youth, and has been clean ever since. Today she can spot someone high "a mile away" and can't stand to be even that close.

She had been working as a computer operator in San Francisco when word came of her father's death in Mexico. "We all went down, my brother, my mother, and me. They called it a car accident. But we had to identify him. His teeth were all blown away and the back of his head was gone. His partner looked the same way. There were no bruises or other broken bones. Everyone knew it was a shotgun blast to the head." The authorities were threatening, saying that it was big trouble to question a coroner's report. The three returned home without challenging them. "After all, he was a bastard. We didn't owe him anything."

But there was a scandal anyway, and when DEA agents tried to get Sarah and her mother to testify they holed up in a cabin in the Washington Cascades till it all blew over. It was there that Sarah got mountain fever, like so many of the folks I met on the *Pioneer*, and she might have lived happily ever after if she hadn't returned to her job in San Francisco and then gotten married.

It has been difficult talking to Sarah in the crowded, noisy lounge car. Loud, rude patrons have intruded several times on our conversation—one man spilled beer on her head—and finally Sarah says, "I can't take this shit. I'm outa here."

Fortuitously, Art Geary stops by and tells us that there is an empty coach at the front of the train normally reserved for passengers who board during the night. He suggests that we join him up there and that it would be easier to move Sarah's stuff by detraining at Klamath Falls and walking up the platform to the front of the train than to fight the crowded aisles inside the cars.

At Klamath, I help Sarah lug her heavy bag out onto the platform and begin the hike toward the front of the train. The night air is warm and fragrant with the smell of unseen flowers somewhere out in the darkness. The red lights of the semaphores down the line and the moonlight on silver peaks demand the attention of my camera. I stop to try a time-lapse shot and to light my pipe. Sarah smokes a cigarette. It's quiet; the platform is unusually empty.

Halfway through the time-lapse shot, two short blasts of the horn announce that the train is about to roll. Somehow we have misjudged the length of the stop and not heard the call of " 'Board!" from the conductors. Now all the attendants are back on board, and we scurry to the nearest open door just as the train starts to move.

Almost "duffiled"—writer Paul Theroux's term for being left at a station, coined when a man named Duffil was left behind by the *Orient Express* in Italy when he got off to get a bite to eat.

After struggling with Sarah's bags through the forward half of the train, we finally reach the empty car, where Art is waiting. He apologizes for leading us astray with bad advice.

Settled in, with a car to ourselves, Sarah resumes her story. Her husband was a man who "demanded everything and gave only money and security in return." They had a daughter, then divorced, but when they separated, the judge stipulated joint custody of the child with legal rights vested in the father, because of his income-earning potential and her past record of drug abuse. For the past two years Sarah has had to travel from her home in Washington to San Francisco every two weeks for her time with her daughter.

That's where she is headed now, but it's for the last time. The child she is carrying was fathered by a man she had been with for the past year and whom she thought she would marry, but he reneged. She is going to San Francisco for one last court challenge to the custody arrangement of her six-year-old daughter; if it fails, she is ready to throw in the towel and accept the reconciliation her ex-husband claims he wants.

Sarah is not bitter. She says she has always been strong, but she's tired. She wants rest, a haven. Living and raising children with a man she can't love doesn't seem so bad if he could keep his promise not to abuse her. "A far cry from 'California Dreamin',' isn't it? When I was a kid, my father and brother used to play that song all the time. They'd use it to convince themselves that this exhausting life they were leading was something that people everywhere else envied. What a lot of bullshit."

In the morning at 6:00 A.M. as I gather my stuff to detrain in Sacramento, Sarah's eyes are still tired and sad, even closed in sleep. Last night she told me there will be no smiles, no hugs, no cheer when she meets her husband in San Francisco—just a faded morning memory of a midnight dream of lost youth.

Captain John Sutter established himself in the Sacramento Valley in 1840 with a dream of operating a kind of baronial estate worked by tenants and laborers brought from his native Switzerland. The Swiss connection didn't bear much fruit, but over the next decade Sutter's agents, stationed at Fort Hall in Idaho, had considerable success diverting Oregon-bound settlers to the larger and sunnier valleys of California.

Lansford Hastings had gone to Oregon in 1842, been dissatisfied, and headed south to California, where he too began to dream. Sutter's feudal empire impressed him; here was the potential of vast land speculation as had existed in the Ohio Valley. Hastings returned east with Clyman and published his *Guide to Immigrants*.

Mormon Sam Brannon encountered Hastings in New York and was swayed by his talk of California. Brannon, leading Mormons who wanted to go by ship around the Horn to California, landed in 1846 at the place soon to be called San Francisco. They had no idea where Brigham Young would turn up and so settled in the area of Sacramento. Brannon set out east to meet Young, only God knew where, but when he did (in Wyoming), Young was not interested in Brannon's wild talk about California. Brannon returned to San Francisco in disgrace and assembled a mini-empire around Sacramento. He still fully expected the Mormons to gather there eventually, and he was determined to be prepared. He hooked up with Sutter and they agreed to build a sawmill on the American River.

On January 24, 1848, sawmill boss James Marshall spotted a shining yellow rock in the sawmill channel. Sutter and Marshall swore their workers to secrecy, but Brannon rode out and filled a small bottle with gold dust, which he took back to San Francisco, whispering "Gold!" Soon 230 ounces were put on display in the War Office in Washington, and the rush of '49 was on.

Brigham Young laid a curse on Brannon for not sending his tithes to Salt Lake—". . . your hopes and pleasures will be blasted in an hour you think not of—and no arm can save"—and though Brannon did eventually lose all his fortune and die destitute because of incautious speculations, he and the men who would soon come to build railroads in California saw that gold had radically changed the future of the west. The yeoman-farmer ethic favored by Brigham Young and the earlier pioneers could not compete with the fast track offered by mining.

Placer gold mining was initially a shortcut to wealth—no fields needed plowing, no trees needed felling, no tunnels needed digging, no institution needed organizing. Even the climate helped, as the summer droughts exposed gold deposited in streambeds during the spring high waters. Again California functioned as an agent of natural selection, drawing from all corners of the country those most desperate, most loosely rooted, most hungry for quick wealth. Behind them followed more sober entrepreneurs who saw in their driving ambition a more substantial and permanent opening to fortune and power. Collis Huntington, Mark Hopkins, and others like them came to California in the 1850s, not the least interested in gold, but farsighted enough to build the railroad that would link this new California wealth to the rest of the nation.

But fast wealth brought fast corruption. Few of the newcomers brought their families or any kind of commitment to the new land; men planned to make their stake and then clear out for the east. Those who did have such a commitment, like Sutter, were often victimized by the overwhelming surge of unscrupulous characters. Sutter died penniless, his stores raided, his herds butchered, his crops despoiled, his lands trashed by squatters.

San Francisco quickly became a "jungle town" bullied by racist thugs posing as patriots such as Sam Roberts's Regulators, who terrorized the Hispanic community and eventually clubbed a woman to death for defending her child against rape. Inland forty-niners showed little of the diplomacy of the earlier pioneers or mountain men in dealing with Indians. Whole bands were brutally butchered when they got in the way, in sharp contrast to the policies followed during these same years by Brigham Young, who sent the chief of the Utes "tobacco for you to smoke in the mountains when you get lonely" in response to his raids on Mormon settlements.

Ever seeking shortcuts, the forty-niners were continually blundering into disasters worse than that of the Donner Party. During the first winter of the rush, Army troops were sent to bring in the scores of parties who simply were not going to make it over the mountains without help. The Donner disaster stands out because it was such a rarity; tragedy among the forty-niners would have been commonplace without interventions by Mormons, Army troops, and occasionally even Indians.

Gold and shortcuts. I picture Sarah Webb's father as an ill-starred forty-niner, arriving at his claim by a shortcut, made wealthy by its yield, and blown away in a barroom confrontation by a rival miner.

Just a few blocks from today's Sacramento station, you can cross a street and step into the world of Sam Brannon, John Sutter, and Collis Huntington. Old Sacramento is a completely rebuilt and restored replica of the old city around 1875, right down to the plank walks, hitching posts, and honky-tonk values of the merchants' signs. You can even find 54 K Street, where Huntington and Mark Hopkins began their march to empire. The buildings are all occupied by flourishing shops and boutiques, and if you didn't know what the place is supposed to be, you might mistake it for a modern mall with a very clever theme. Only the open sky gives it away.

By the old rail station, where generations of refugees from the east became Californians, today a half-dozen men in blue overalls, red kerchiefs, and bowler hats fuss over a steam engine which sweats and steams and smokes in preparation for hauling the museum's excursion train seven miles down the Sacramento River track. Al Shelley is the only one of the group who is a professional railroad man; the others come from a variety of walks of life: a dentist, a postman, a telephone operator, a pharmacist, a couple of businessmen. Their volunteer work on the old trains of the museum is their version of golf, fishing or gardening.

"Five years ago the UP gifted this engine to the museum," says Al. "We all gathered like boys around the neighbor's HO train set, except this one is life-sized." The train departs every hour, ten times a day. Aside from the half-dozen guys who service and run the engine, there are conductors and brakemen, ticket salesmen and service chiefs, gandy dancers and switchmen. Today there are more people working on the little railroad than there are passengers for it. "Fellows just come along and want to get involved—fulfilling some kind of boyhood dream, I guess. We try to find a spot for anyone who is sincere enough to come back again and again."

As the only paid employee of the museum, railroad restoration and maintenance specialist Joe Passentino is the head man here. "But I don't have to tell anyone what to do—everyone knows his job."

At the moment two men are lubricating bearings with a grease gun. Someone else is patching a leak in the tender's water tank while Al climbs around with a cloth and polishes the unpainted surfaces of the connecting rods, the bell, the whistle, and the bald head of a third fellow who meticulously tightens bolts. There is a lot of cheer and horseplay in their work, but their hands are sure and the engine gleams with their care. "What can I do?" I ask.

Joe gestures for me to join Al in the cab. I clamber up, and Al hands me the coal shovel, shows me the pedal that opens the firebox door, and says, "Fireman." Then he shows me the glass on which a piece of tape marks the correct boiler pressure and the fire rake used to spread the coals in the firebox. The coal flows by gravity feed and the vibration of the train from a hole at the base of the front of the tender. I discover that if I plant my feet just right, one on the lip of the tender and one beside the firebox door pedal on the floor of the engine cab, I can swing shovel loads of coal in one stepless motion from tender to fire.

Al opens the throttle and yanks the reversing lever to start us off the turntable and onto the spur where the old coaches used for the excursion rides wait. Al points at me and shouts over the breathing of the engine, "I hope you weren't planning on wearing that to church." My white shirt is already gray, a casualty of the coal dust and the soot-laden moisture that drifts into the cab from the stack.

We couple on to the coaches and pull into the old station, where a small crowd of excursion riders clutch their tickets and point dozens of cameras at us. "I've been in more movies than Clark Gable," says Al.

The interiors of the old coaches give the lie to the romantic notion that coach travel on these cars was more posh than in Amtrak's coaches today: no carpet on the floor, no air conditioning, no reclining seats, little kneeroom, plain painted metal walls and ceilings, and only three central light fixtures on the high ceilings. The treat is that the windows open and you can hear the whuff, whuff, whuff of the steam engine.

The little train ride itself is depressing. The tracks parallel the verge of a freeway along which autos and trucks whiz by at three times the train's speed. Only when I'm in the engine cab shoveling coal do the sounds of the train drown out the noise of the cursed highway. But as with any toy train operation, the real fun is the coupling and switching back at the station sidings and the engine house turntable.

Al asks me about my work and I tell him of my journey. He is impressed. "You sure you're really from back east? Quitting a job to pursue a dream like that—that's very California. I never met an easterner before who operated that way."

Al urges me to tour the main museum housing scores of historical railroading exhibits and twenty-one vintage engines from different eras. The museum has benefited from the SP's generosity and its continuing need, even in contemporary times, to placate a public with a long memory.

I have already related how Collis Huntington and the others known as the "big four" built the monopoly of the Southern Pacific from their humble beginnings as hardware merchants on K Street in Sacramento. The hatred so long felt by Californians toward the SP ran deeper than did animosities toward regional railroads elsewhere in the country. Aside from San Francisco's special reasons for antipathy, described earlier, perhaps Californians saw the monopoly as an excrescence of the eastern corruption they fled west to escape. Perhaps because the railroad represented the best bypass yet, the shortcut-loving Californians couldn't bear to see such a good one co-opted by a regime whose clearly stated purpose was to run it "for the utmost possible profit." Or perhaps it was simply frustration at feeling economically cribbed and confined by a corporation that stood wherever one turned throughout the state.

The immediate grievance which led to the infamous Mussel Slough Massacre and the adventures of history's most interesting alleged rail robbers was land. As the SP built southward from San Francisco, it acquired land grants from the state along the routes, announcing that when titles had been validated it would sell them to farmers at $2.50 an acre. However, much of the land was already settled by pioneer squatters, many of whom were belatedly engaged in acquiring their own titles to land they had cleared long before the railroad came through. Most probably would have paid the minimal $2.50 just to get their own clear title, but when the railroad's grants were settled, the SP announced land sales at prices of $10 to $30 per acre. The San Joaquin Valley settlers, many of whom were in danger of being put off lands they had cleared twenty years earlier, organized to fight first in the courts and if need be by other means.

In April of 1880, hundreds of settlers around Mussel Slough gathered at Hanford for what was meant to be a peaceful barbecue and organizational meeting. The SP chose that very day to send a U.S. marshal into the area with a shadowy Mr. Crow, thought by many to be an agent of the SP, to begin dispossessing farmers of their land and homes. They were met at the Brewer farm by a number of armed settlers who had gathered for the barbecue, and Mr. Crow began shooting. When it was over, five farmers and two law officers were dead. Seventeen farmers were later tried and sent to prison for the murder of the two lawmen, and the dead farmers went unavenged—for a while.

Enter Chris Evans, a grain clerk working for the Bank of California, who had walked to California over the line of the first Pacific Railroad. His job provided him with ample opportunity to hear farmers' stories of grievances against the high-handed practices of the SP, and furthermore, members of his wife's family were dispossessed of their farms in connection with the Mussel Slough Massacre. His best friend was one John Sontag, a former brakeman on the SP who harbored deep grievances over an injury and subsequent poor treatment of it at the company hospital that left him maimed for life.

The night of February 22, 1889, two men began robbing the SP trains at places near the various grain warehouses where Evans worked. The masked men—one tall, one short and stocky, just like Evans and Sontag—would climb aboard the cab as the train pulled out of a station, brandish pistols, and order the engineer to stop the train just outside of town. After grounding the engine crew, they would demand that the messenger in the express car throw out the safe. If he refused, the robbers' next move was to set off a charge of dynamite under the car. Sometimes this was enough to get the safe out of the car, sometimes not. If not, and the messenger was still alive, the next step was to threaten the lives of the grounded engineer and fireman. While the mystery robbers showed no signs of the gratuitous bloodthirstiness of the James gang, they didn't hesitate to start shooting when things didn't go smoothly.

For four years the SP was robbed regularly by the methodical bandits, and Evans continued at his job in the grain warehouses throughout this time. At least twice, the desperate lawmen and agents of the SP charged the wrong men, once a fireman on the robbed train who had actually struggled heroically against the bandits and once the members of the infamous Dalton gang. At one point more than fifty men resided in various jails as suspects in the robberies. The general public, remembering Mussel Slough, cheered every new report of holdups on the SP. The besieged lawmen were in an ugly mood.

Such was the state of affairs when John Sontag's brother, George, began leading the chorus of voices condemning the SP in a most incendiary manner. As he had been a passenger during one of the holdups, George was taken in for questioning and produced some contradictory testimony concerning the actions of his brother. Immediately two detectives went to Evans's house, which they believed they had seen Sontag entering by the back door. Walking in unannounced, they encountered Evans's daughter and demanded to see Sontag. When she answered that he was not there, they became abusive, and she ran out of the house to fetch her father, who was in the barn. When Evans entered the house, the shooting began, Sontag now present and taking part. The officers were driven off, and Evans and Sontag loaded up a wagon and headed for the mountains. Before they got away, another gunfight erupted and another officer was killed.

Brother George meanwhile was convicted of the last robbery, on slim evidence, and was severely wounded when he and some fellow prisoners mysteriously obtained guns and began firing at their captors.

Evans and Sontag thrived for a year and a half in the mountains among sympathetic miners and loggers. The manhunt for them involved so many deputies that eleven of them were shot by their fellow lawmen in the confusion of the chase. Several times Evans and Sontag managed to shoot their way back for a visit with the family at Evans's house, and once they had to battle their way out of encirclement by a posse.

Their end finally came at Stone Corral, where a large posse surprised them and pinned them down behind a couple of haystacks. The posse's fire was withering, yet the fugitives wouldn't die. Sontag's right arm was shattered by bullets, and he incurred several sucking wounds to his side and chest, and flesh wounds all over. In the morning he tried twice to kill himself, once grazing his forehead, once putting a hole in his face without hitting any mortal spot. He lived to tell his story to Evans's daughter before finally dying in jail, where the doctor said he had never seen a man carrying so much lead.

Evans fared a little better. His left arm was shredded, one eye was blown away by buckshot, and another volley caught his right shoulder, but somehow he managed to crawl away before the posse rushed the haystack in the morning and stumble six miles through wilderness to a cabin in the woods, where he collapsed in bed, a bloody rag. He sent a message that he would surrender if the reward money was given to his wife. The sheriff agreed, and Evans was brought in, recovered, and went to jail. But not for long.

With his left arm amputated, he could still wield a gun well enough with his right that when some SP haters smuggled a pistol to him he escaped. He thrived for some time on the lam with the aid of sympathetic settlers, and the lawmen gave up the notion of taking him by force. But his one weakness was his love for family, and a counterfeit message calling for his presence at the bedside of a sick daughter finally brought him to a place where he was captured by a posse "big enough to storm a fort."

One shouldn't expect a great California outlaw to recede quietly from the historical stage during his life imprisonment, and Evans didn't disappoint. In keeping with the California penchant for innovation and defiance of convention, the Evans and Sontag story became a popular theatrical melodrama, with Evans's wife and daughter playing themselves in the show. Evans himself wrote a book in prison, entitled *Eurasia*, which described a utopian government and presaged many of the political innovations of modern California, particularly in the areas of women's equality, education, and prison reform. And while he admitted the killings of several lawmen during his flight, he denied, even after he was paroled by Governor Johnson in 1911, that he ever robbed a train. There is only the slimmest of circumstantial evidence that he ever did, except for the fact that the SP robberies ended when he was incarcerated.

In the California State Railroad Museum there is a marvelous collection of railroad engines, cars, track equipment, and memorabilia, but little to remind the public of that dark phase of railroad history in California. Though there is a remarkable exhibit consisting of a genuine Canadian Pacific Pullman car, the *St. Hyacinthe*, which one can walk through and experience motion, sound, and passing nighttime lights, this is as close as most visitors will ever get to experiencing the real thing.

And that highlights a distressing note in today's visit. I walk through the *St. Hyacinthe* with a family who are unaware that you can still travel and sleep this way. I stand next to a couple looking at a display of a diner who bemoan the passing of dining on the railroad. A father explains to his son that the steam engine gets its power from the ignition of steam in the cylinders, just as in a gasoline engine. Again and again I hear people talking about how the museum displays a mode of travel that is a dead thing, a thing of the past.

I flee for today's Amtrak station. If I ran the museum, its most important program would be a shuttle van (or better yet a routing of the steam excursion train!) that would take viewers three blocks to witness the arrival of the *California Zephyr* and *Coast Starlight*.

Never has Amtrak looked so good. The westbound *California Zephyr* pulls into the Sacramento station two and a half hours late, but it is real, packed with passengers from Salt Lake, Denver, Chicago, Cleveland, Pittsburgh, New York. During my short ride into Oakland, I hear stories of their crossing of the continent: tornadoes in Iowa, mountain goats in Colorado, a midnight Golden Spike champagne party as the train crossed the Lucien Cutoff of Salt Lake, the "Canadian commando" who romanced all the women and handed out $50 bills, Irish, the red-haired lumberjack who got so drunk they put him off the train at 3:00 in the morning, and Sam and Sue, who rode the train to effect a reconciliation in their marriage and succeeded so well that neighbors in the rooms adjoining theirs got no sleep last night.

San Francisco Bay looks just as good as it did on my first trip, and crossing the Bay Bridge I experience that same thrill of exhilaration I felt back in February. But on the ground the streets of the city are windy and actually colder this June day, and again the lost human refuse that accumulates here on the western shore refocuses my attention. A current story in the paper about a son of a wealthy New England family who died on the street has provoked a frenzy of concern about the plight of homeless people—church groups, politicians, and social workers are all scratching their heads pondering how society might better care for the homeless who are the image of the eighties in urban America everywhere. I am provoked to ask a different question: Why, how, do they come to the end of the line in the first place? Somewhere the nation, not just California, has taken a shortcut, a Hastings Cutoff to the American dream of free and easy prosperity. The homeless are the ones who pay the price by being left behind on the trek.

Since my train from Sacramento was late, there is no time to enjoy a Chinatown dinner, so I settle for a burger and beer at the station bar at Transbay Terminal. The place is fairly crowded this late Friday afternoon, and, except for three women celebrating a birthday or anniversary of some sort, I am the only white in a roomful of young black workingmen watching the A's blow a 7–1 lead on the TV. Someone puts dance music on the jukebox, which competes with the baseball game and a loud fellow who declaims about how second basemen no longer know how to turn a double play. The fellow's wife telephones to ask him to come home. He shouts back to the bartender to tell her that he'll be home when he's good and ready, but I notice that at this moment four other guys pay their tabs and head out the door. Shortly, so does he.

Suddenly the floor moves, and all conversation stops. The jukebox carries on, but the announcer of the baseball game in Oakland says, "Whoa, what's that?" The floor moves again, and this time there is a sound, a rumble like someone rolling a keg in the basement. Around the bar, beer drinkers freeze in mid-guzzle. Only the three white women carry on oblivious to the disturbance. The announcer of the game clarifies, "Apparently we are having a bit of an earth tremor here."

Then the third wave hits, and it turns my stomach. The floor seems to drop a few inches and then shifts a sudden foot to the left and hangs trembling. My beer has spilled, and foam runs down my crotch. "Earthquake," says the bartender, and, as if in response to his invocation, the gross movement ceases and settles into a rumble like distant thunder. Even the tipsy white girls now have hushed and grabbed hold of the table. The jukebox has stopped, and everyone instinctively looks toward the TV for a word from the announcers. But there is none—just the picture of the field and dead air. The game has halted and the infielders have sat down cross-legged on the dirt.

The earthquake was 5.7 magnitude on the Richter scale and centered near the SP tracks between San Luis Obispo and San Jose. The northbound *Coast Starlight* is delayed two hours while track crews check the gauge between San Luis Obispo and Oakland. As a major delay on one train in the west tends to lead to even greater delays on others, nothing will be on time for the remainder of my journey.*

When I finally do board the train at Oakland, sleeping-car attendant Elwood Burwell has my bed ready and is full of talk about how earthquakes don't bother him; nothing does, since he likes his job so much. Before this he managed a laundry in L.A. He was an unhappy, restless man till he took his wife and two kids on a vacation by train to Oregon.

"That trip changed everything. Nothing seemed real at my old job anymore. I just wanted to chuck everything and work on the railroad. I don't suppose many people can understand that kind of an urge nowadays."

He put in his application and prayed for a year, but when the call came, he wasn't sure he should accept it. "What good is it to get the world and lose your family?" he asks rhetorically. He worried about the time away from home, but his wife encouraged him: "Life's too short not to do what you have to do." It worked. With two days off for every three-day run, "It's the deal of a lifetime. How many people have jobs where they can see the world and still be with their family for two straight days out of every five?"

Elwood sings a lot as he does his work in the sleeper. He has his coffeepot set up in the stairway vestibule where everyone can help himself. He has the complimentary wine and snack packs on the pillow when you board, instead of delivering them himself after you're settled

---

* Geologists have since identified this quake as one of the precursors to the great quake of '89. Incredibly that quake also interrupted an A's baseball game and Amtrak schedules all over the West!

in. There is less show and more go in his kind of service. While other attendants are fussing around with the basics that Elwood takes care of ahead of time, he is getting to know his passengers in amiable chats. He says, "So many guys with more experience than me make the job so much tougher on themselves because they think it has to be unpleasant work. I do it so I can have a good time, and that makes my passengers have a good time."

Elwood believes that the California life-style helped make it possible for his dream to come true. "Here a man changing his whole way of life at thirty-five is no big deal. I don't know, but I don't think people live that way back east. It's not cool to be dissatisfied enough to risk everything to try something new. But that's the California way."

Chapter Fifteen

─────────

Of Mice and Men

THE *COAST STARLIGHT* NORTH

I N any epic enterprise like railroading, there are times when things just don't work. The earthquake inaugurates a run of bad luck on the route between California and Montana that colors a tableau of the performance of men and their works amid adversity and mischance.

Since the *Coast Starlight* is two hours behind schedule because of the earthquake, the train is on a time-makeup routine. This means that station stops are supposed to be less than two minutes, and all freight trains are supposed to park on sidings to give us a highball through. The service chief assures me that we will make up much of our lost time by morning.

But it doesn't work that way. A woman on the train has had symptoms of a heart attack, so we stop at Sacramento for ten minutes while a doctor examines her and decides that she has only had an attack of hyperventilation. A boy wanders off to buy a candy bar at Marysville and the train backs up to retrieve him after pulling out. Another ten minutes lost. During this delay, the freight waiting on the siding for us to pass forty miles down the track at Chico is given the green light to come onto the main line ahead of us. We will follow it at thirty-five miles an hour for much of the night.

Just as I begin to experience that delightful feeling of settling in for an overnight run, the brakes squeal and the train decelerates sharply. I brace myself for the expected crash but instead hear the PA announcement explaining that, yes, that was an emergency stop, but we should not be alarmed because it is only a burst air hose.

Nothing hampered the progress of railroading like the inability to stop. Early trains relied on human muscle for braking; on passenger trains there would be a brakeman in every car. When the engineer called for brakes with short blasts on the whistle, the brakemen would scurry outside and physically horse the train to a stop by cranking manual brake wheels. On freights, the procedure was even more cumbersome as brakemen riding in the caboose had to scurry along the running boards atop the freight cars setting the brakes on each car one by one. It didn't work very well.

The tabloids loved the stories of train accidents and fed the public lurid details of passengers roasted in fires from the coal heating stoves of wrecked coaches, of steam engines exploding from head-on collisions quaintly known as "cornfield meets," and of passengers screaming to their deaths as runaway cars from a broken train careened down a mountainside or off open suspension bridges.

In 1869, George Westinghouse designed brakes powered by air pressure carried by hoses from pumps on the engine. In the initial design, the air pressure was used to clamp the brake shoes against the wheels. When the air pressure was released, springs lifted the shoes off the wheel. The flaw in this design appeared very quickly—a broken or punctured hose, a faulty valve, and there would be no brakes—and the design was reversed. Powerful springs clamp the shoes against the wheels, and the air pressure is used to hold them off the wheels when brakes are not called for. Now when there is a break in the hoses or some other loss of air pressure, the brakes literally spring into action and bring the train to a halt.

The invention found application fairly quickly on a few of the well-known short, fast passenger trains where the inability to stop could prove a severe embarrassment, but the railroads continued to rely on human muscle and sinew for others and for freight trains, where the costs of installing air brakes were considered unacceptable. Moreover, there was a remarkable assumption that the system simply wouldn't work on long, heavy freights.

Lorenzo Coffin, a prosperous farmer from Iowa, was appalled at the stories of brakemen who had lost their hands, limbs, and lives in their work atop and between the cars. Coffin made it his personal crusade to coerce the railroads into universally adopting the Westinghouse brake, as well as automatic couplers. Said Coffin, "My first job was to arouse the public to this awful wrong . . . that it was taken as a matter of course that railroad men of necessity be maimed and killed."

Regarded by the railroads as a fanatic, Coffin was thrown out of a lot of executives' offices over the next few years, so he turned to the press. In 1874, he recruited no less a voice than the Reverend Lyman Abbott, who wrote in *Harper's*, "So long as brakes cost more than trainmen we may expect the present sacrificial method of [braking and decoupling] to be continued."

It was not until 1886 that Coffin, as rail commissioner for Iowa, was able to prod the Master Car-Builders Association to a series of tests of the brakes on long heavy trains of the always innovative Burlington Railroad. The tests were a failure and Coffin was a crushed man, but Westinghouse himself had witnessed the tests and returned to his shops in Pittsburgh to refine his design.

In 1887 they tried again. According to an eyewitness, the "immense train rolled down the grade into Burlington at 40 miles per hour. . . . [At a signal, the brakes were applied] and the train came to a standstill within 500 feet and hardly a jar." Coffin, at sixty-five, cried openly as he watched.

But it wasn't until 1893, twenty-four years after Westinghouse's invention, that the Interstate Commerce Commission finally had national legislative authority to enforce the "Coffin Bill," which made air brakes mandatory safety equipment on all trains. Within a year, employee accidents were down a whopping 60 percent. The railroads discovered to their surprise that the brakes saved them money. Moreover, passenger accident rates declined to almost nothing. Those railroads such as the Burlington and the Pennsylvania that were known to have embraced the technology most wholeheartedly began to enjoy a competitive edge over those that had not. It became possible to increase train speeds radically, while railroad safety came to be a thing taken for granted. A do-gooder and government regulation in the gilded age, a cautionary tale for the post-1980s.

I get off to watch the repair. The assistant engineer from the engine and an assistant conductor from the last car walk the train with their flashlights and lanterns looking for the break. The pumps in the engine continue to run during the search, and it doesn't take long to find the burst hose, thanks to the loud hiss of escaping air. The hose flops about violently like a wounded snake until the conductor signals the engineer to cut the air pumps. Heavy tools materialize; a section of hose is yanked out and replaced with a spare. The air is pumped up, and I can see the brake shoes lifting off the wheels. The procedure has delayed us another twenty minutes.

In the morning we are two and a half hours behind schedule. The unfortunate bearer of this unwelcome news is Art Geary, the conductor whom I rode with on this route going south, though the reunion with a familiar face is some recompense. "Oh, yeah, when the earth moves, it's big trouble for railroads," he says.

By way of apology for the bad advice at Klamath Falls, he offers to show me just how effective moving earth can be in disrupting a railroad, and he takes me downstairs to the open window of the vestibule door as we wind through the breathtaking central Cascades.

The morning is warm and sunny and the air wafts in with the springtime scent of snowmelt on awakening mountain forest floors. Soon he directs my attention to an open stretch where the tall timber is interrupted by a series of sloping grassy downs. The Cascade region is volcanically young and active, and strange phenomena happen here that do not involve the pyrotechnics of fire and lava. Three years ago a track crew was working at this spot near Willamette Pass on a sunny spring morning when the melting snows had the ground supersaturated. There was no warning rumble or tangible earth movement, but the men noticed that the track they thought they had just lined straight was no longer true. They lined it again and sighted down the line. Where there was supposed to be a broad U shape, they saw an elongated W, and the bends were growing noticeably as they stared. They dropped their tools and started walking, felt the world slide sideways, and sprinted toward a rock outcropping. They clung there while the mountainside, track, trees, and earth quietly slipped down toward the creek in the canyon below. Only when it would have been too late for anyone still working out where they had been did the rumble commence.

When the Southern Pacific crews regraded and relaid the track through here a few weeks later, they discovered that the slope of the mountain had increased by a degree. No earthquake was ever recorded, but the earth here had unquestionably moved. "The mountain just breathed," says Art, "and everything came rolling down."

The view from the open window as we drift down through the canyons and slopes of the west side of the Cascade divide is varied and sensational. There are places where we can see the tracks behind us high above and those ahead of us far below. We cruise through dozens of tunnels, horseshoes, and cliff cuts, above pristine blue lakes and beneath tall forested pinnacles. In Salt Creek Canyon, Art points out the wrecked boxcars of a freight that just went over the edge because of bad track. Several high bridges over yawning rocky gulfs provoke an involuntary tightening of various muscles.

Bridges figure prominently in stories of train disasters in the days before the railroads became our safest mode of travel. They were often the last pieces of the route built and suffered from the twin pressures of the construction company's haste to meet deadlines and shortage of capital. Sometimes temporary bridgework intended to be used only during construction of a route was never replaced until a tragedy occurred during regular operation.

Railroad accidents were already a scandal during the 1850s, but it wasn't until after the Civil War, with a public attuned to moral crusades, that highly publicized disasters aroused effective public response. The "Angola Horror" became a model for the process.

Twenty-two miles west of Buffalo, New York, engineer Charles Carscadin drove the *New York Express* past Angola toward a bridge over Big Sisters Creek in fair weather at midday in 1867. Some of the passengers in the last two coaches decided to forego lunch in the forward dining car, intending to dine in Buffalo restaurants, since the train was due in at 1:30 P.M. The decision would cost them their lives.

A little past the Angola depot, the rear coach loosened an axle crossing a rough switch frog, misaligning the wheels so that they came off the track and bumped along the ties so noisily that some passengers moved up to the next forward coach. Crossing the bridge, the engineer had no hint of trouble in the rear, where the stricken coach had now dragged the car ahead of it off the rails too. Halfway across the bridge, the rear car broke loose and fell onto the rocks of the creek below; shortly the next car broke its coupling and fell too.

The train was nearly half a mile past the bridge by the time the engineer knew he had lost two crowded coaches. When he backed up to the bridge, passengers in the dining car were met with a grisly sight. Down in the ravine, the potbellied stoves had set the splintered wooden coaches ablaze, and the howls of the dying could be heard above the panting of the engine. Forty-nine died in the flames before a bucket brigade of surviving passengers could douse the wreck.

While some were working to save victims, others were engaged in working to aid the company in the impending investigation. Railroad employees spotted the switch frog where the trouble began and recognized that its shape and the nicks in it told the story of an improperly maintained piece of equipment. One employee heard the roadmaster shout, "Take out that rail and put in a new one." The investigation led to a consensus—the rear coach car was a compromise car, one of those with extra-wide wheels for use on roads of different gauges, and the public clamor forced the extinction of such cars. Thus the Angola Horror brought about one needed reform, though the issue of tampering with evidence never surfaced at the time.

At least the Angola bridge held. A series of highly publicized bridge disasters in the 1870s led eventually to regular bridge inspections, which turned up dozens of disasters waiting to happen. One of those that didn't wait struck again the ill-starred Lake Shore & Michigan Southern, providing it with its second lesson, and this time there could be no tampering with the evidence.

Trains normally slow down to cross suspect bridges, and surviving passengers testified that the *Pacific Express* did so noticeably as it approached the bridge over Ashtabula Creek in Ohio on December 29, 1876. Midway across the bridge, engineer Dan McGuire at first thought his engine was laboring overmuch, then it seemed that he was running uphill. Instinctively he opened the throttle wide, and his engine, the first of two, poured on the power—so much power that the coupling to the second engine broke. Looking back as his engine ran onto solid ground, McGuire saw a tragedy in sickening slow motion. The timbers of the bridge were slowly giving way as beam by beam snapped and the second engine and eleven cars rode almost gently down into the ravine, only tipping off the rails at the last moment. Then the fatal combination of coal stoves and wooden cars worked its curse upon the passengers of the *Pacific Express:* thirty-four were burned to death. The Ashtabula catastrophe bulled the momentum of the nation toward government regulation of public safety.

That momentum was maintained by a disaster on the Farmington River in Connecticut, where 110 years later another collapsing bridge on I-95 would send several automobile and truck drivers to their deaths and provoke a similar spasm of overdue inspections. The train was a special excursion carrying devout Christians home from a gospel performance by Dwight Moody and Ira Sankey at Hartford. Moody spoke of God's fatherly love, departing sharply from the traditional message of fire and brimstone that New Englanders had heard since the days of Cotton Mather. His audience departed on a heavily loaded train at 11:00 P.M., believing fire was not in their future.

Conductor Tom Elmore had noted that the Tariffville bridge across the Farmington River seemed shaky when the train crossed it earlier on the way to Hartford. Now when the two engines were halfway across he felt a sagging, and then the bridge just broke. Down went the two engines, dragging four coaches with them. The cars crashed through the ice of the river, and seventeen drowned.

The cumulative result of these and dozens of other disasters, frequently involving bridges, was growing public pressure for government regulation and inspection. Slowly a consensus grew that where private enterprise served public interests, a moral hand was needed to ensure public safety. Americans increasingly turned to government, that entity which their Revolution, Constitution, and instincts so profoundly distrusted, to empower that hand. In a sense, the unbridled free enterprise embodied in the railroads of the gilded age created the big government that is its nemesis in the twentieth century.

Today on the *Coast Starlight,* a half-dozen other passengers have started to gather around Art and me at the open window. It's against government rules for passengers to open the window, partly because of the possibility of eye injuries from flying stones and dust, partly because of the greater danger of opening the whole door unintentionally. A small child once stepped off the running *California Zephyr* when one of these doors was inadvertently left open, though fortunately the train was climbing slowly at the time and she wasn't hurt badly.

Art's rear brakeman has been hailing him on the radio about a passenger with a beard and a green shirt who keeps opening a window and hanging out. Despite Art's assurances that he's with me, the brakeman doesn't like it. Since it's part of the brakeman's job to check the condition of the length of the train from his rear post as it rounds curves, he feels responsible for me. He's worried about whose liability it is if I decide to sue over a cinder in the eye. So the show is over, the window is closed. I'm hungry for a nice stack of railroad French toast anyway.

My tablemate for brunch in the diner is art dealer Louis Montori, who carries on about how natural it feels to ride a train as opposed to his usual mode of flying. "You don't have to make a break with Mother Earth—there's no farewell to the ground. You just walk on, ride, and walk off."

He worries about airline safety in the age of deregulation. Worse, he speculates that someday we'll discover that all this flying we did in the later twentieth century had some terrible unexpected biological consequence like the Romans' declining IQ caused by the lead in their plumbing systems. "Maybe we'll wake up one day and wonder what made us all slowly become impotent or androgynous or Republican or something horrible like that."

He is riding this train because he is taking a John Constable painting to Seattle to be authenticated by expert Charles Rhymes. It's handier just to carry the painting onto the train than to arrange air freight.

Louis says that 50 percent of the "works" of John Constable, a nineteenth-century British landscape painter, were done by various family members, mostly his children. The fraud constituted one of the most successful scams in art history until Rhymes and his colleague Graham Reynolds broke it open in the last decade by measuring the height of the trees in all of the works. Some were consistently shorter than others and, with a few well-authenticated pieces, provided the yardstick for gauging which are genuine. John Constable was taller than any of his children. "Maybe the world just looked a little larger to the kids from their height perspective."

Whatever the explanation, the result is a boom in the value of authentic Constables. "He's hot right now, and if I've got a real one back there with my luggage, I can go to Acapulco for the rest of the year."

A Mrs. Miller, the prototypical spunky little old lady, has been listening to Louis's dissertation with interest in the next booth. At Eugene, she gets off the train to buy a paper in the station. On the way out of the diner, she says to no one in particular and everyone in general, "Now don't let 'em leave without me." Nonetheless, when the train, still trying to make up time, quickly pulls out of the station, she has not yet returned. No one recalls her parting admonition until it's too late.

Five miles out of the station, conductor Geary gets a call on the radio from the stationmaster. Mrs. Miller has been left behind and has hired a cab to try to catch the train at Portland, three stops down the line.

It will take some doing. The train is scheduled to do the 124 miles between Eugene and Portland in three hours. But since we are running fast to make up time, we may be in and out of Portland in little more than two and a half hours. The taxi is going to have to average nearly sixty miles an hour to make it.

At Albany, the stationmaster has worse news. His scanner has picked up a help call from the taxi driver. The cab has blown a tire and the cabby carries only a doughnut for replacement. Mrs. Miller is stranded somewhere on Interstate 5.

By now Louis and I have moved to the lounge car, where the word has spread and the saga of Mrs. Miller has become the premier topic of interest. Several passengers familiar with the railroad books of Paul Theroux recall the unfortunate Mr. Duffil and the fact that Theroux himself was duffiled in, of all places, Moscow. I relate my close scrape at Klamath Falls, but my story is disqualified because I had a companion—true duffiling, we decide, entails being cast adrift alone, far from home.

At Salem we learn that the duffiling of Mrs. Miller is an unfinished story. A trucker driving an eighteen-wheeler heard the cabby's distress call on his CB and picked up Mrs. Miller on the interstate. In a convoy with two other big trucks, he is currently defying speed limits and state bears in an eighty-mile-an-hour race with the train to Portland.

Now the afternoon margaritas and Molson's ales have begun to cast their rowdy spell in the lounge car, where a man initiates a bookmaking operation. Odds are three to one against Mrs. Miller, but two boys celebrating their graduation from high school suggest subversive action in her cause. If enough of us get off the train at Portland and wander around the station for a while, we might delay the train's departure till the trucker pulls in with Mrs. Miller. Louis Montori refines the plan by venturing that the action is more likely to be successful if the participants detrain from many different cars rather than all of us piling out of the nearest door to the lounge car. If we can get six or seven different car attendants signaling the conductor that they still have people on the ground, there will be more confusion and a longer delay.

I remember that Portland is the stop for a train crew change; Art Geary will be replaced by a new conductor. So I volunteer to stall the new man—Art will formally introduce me and my purpose on the train, and I'll hand him my letter of introduction from Amtrak and attempt to initiate an interview on the platform. The plan is ratified. A beery oath seals the pact: the lounge car eleven hereby conspire that this train will not leave Portland until Mrs. Miller is aboard.

The approach into Portland through the SP yards is slow, and hopes run high. We run through south Portland at considerably slower speed than on the trip south two days ago—is the engineer in on the conspiracy? It is Sunday, and traffic on the streets does not seem heavy.

At the Portland station, a large crowd of travelers returning to

Seattle waits to board. Good. I can see members of the lounge car eleven popping off the train up and down the platform. Good. Several engage their car attendants in conversations and lead them away from the train toward the station. Very good. Art Geary knows what's going on, and with a wink at me, he takes the new conductor aside to go over the manifest in greater than usual detail. Super. I hang nearby ready to pounce as soon as the new guy pulls away from Art.

But it isn't necessary. Cheers from several of the lounge car eleven announce Mrs. Miller's arrival. A big Roadway truck is parked out in front of the station flanked by two state cruisers with blue lights flashing. Mrs. Miller, the trucker, and two Oregon state troopers burst out of the station doors, and the cheer spreads to passengers not part of the conspiracy but aware of the story. Mrs. Miller is feisty: "I told my grandson I'd be at his wedding and I'm going to be there."

It has been a moment rare in the annals of railroading: passengers aboard a train already two and a half hours behind schedule conspiring for further delay. But the critical moment occurred just outside of south Portland when the state troopers hopped on the trucker's tail and lit up their blues. The trucker tried one last expedient, the honest appeal. He explained Mrs. Miller's predicament to the bears over the radio and asked for their help. They agreed to escort the rig to the station, but if there was no Mrs. Miller in the truck and no train waiting for her at the station, he was going to have to eat the book. Thus the truck actually made up the most critical time through the streets of Portland, with the flashing blue lights clearing the way, just as they might for an ambulance. Honesty had succeeded where conspiracy was surely doomed to fail.

After Portland I ride with Brian Beers, a Union Pacific brakeman who is deadheading back to his home in Centralia. Brian is a handsome young trainman whose name, he is convinced, has given rise to more nicknames than any other in the world: Bud, Brew, Bullet, Old Mill, Mole's Son, Hiney, Lowbrow, Schlitz, Hops, Malt, Barley, Tap, Keg, Mug, and Ralph, to name a few. But even though his run is done for the day, he can't indulge in his namesake beverage till he is off the train. Whenever trainmen are deadheading back home from a run, they are still officially at work. Rule G is king today, because of the highly publicized 1987 rail accident of the *Colonial* and the fact that the railroads are unabashedly looking for any pretext to let people go to reduce their padded work force. Brian is fairly young and low on the seniority ladder, so he is particularly careful. But even he can remember the golden years of the seventies before the big crackdown. "I'd be deadheading home on this train, meet a honey here in this bar car, and have a few. If I got lucky and she was going to Seattle, I'd stay on and get off with her there, show her a good time, have a good time myself." When they started enforcing Rule G during deadheading runs it was the end of all that, and anyway, Brian got married.

Two young men dressed like cowboys have joined us and advertise their own violation of Rule G. Kevin and Shannon are ranch hands returning from a few days off in California to their work on a spread near Coeur d'Alene, Idaho. They want to know if Brian and I would like to join them in their compartment for an afternoon toke.

"So this is what cowboys really do to unwind at the end of a hard day on the range," I venture after declining their offer.

"No, it's what we do on the train going home after getting lucky in San Fran," says Kevin. "Our boss would bust our heads if he ever caught us blowing dope on the ranch." Both agree that the train is a special place to get stoned—"lots of good stimulation, the tracks rattling by, the scenery, strangers to talk to, the whole nine yards."

"What if the engineer feels the same way?" Brian wonders, again conjuring up the memory of the recent *Colonial* crash: marijuana use by a Conrail engineer was implicated in his failure to heed signal lights that would have kept him and his freight engine off of the main line where the *Colonial* was bearing down at 120 miles an hour.

"He probably does. As long as he does it on his time off like us, that's okay. Ya gotta be responsible with your recreational drug use, ya see," says Kevin without a hint of humor. Echoing actor-Desperado Jim, he believes that once people learn to be less neurotic about drugs, beginning with repeal of "prohibition," most of the problems they cause will wither away. He collects bottles from old opium-bearing patent medicines of the nineteenth century as testimonial to what he calls "our national heritage of euphoria. It's as American as hot dogs and apple pie."

While the publicity connected with recent accidents involving drug-using transportation employees has created a sense that America is dealing with a new scourge, at least one of the most horrific train disasters from an earlier era can be ascribed to the same cause, though it wasn't fully recognized as such at the time.

The night of June 22, 1918, a Hagenbeck-Wallace Circus train left Michigan City for Hammond, where a show was scheduled for the following day. The fourteen flatcars, seven stock cars, and four sleepers carried the usual selection of circus beasts, clowns, aerialists, roustabouts, Hercules the Strong Man, the equestrienne Miss Rose Borland, and "100 Dancing Girls, Count Them." At 3:00 in the morning, circus manager Charles Dollmer was working late over the books while his performers slept when conductor R. W. Johnson stopped the train to check out a possible hotbox. He sent flagman Trimm back with his lantern to protect the rear of the train.

By 1918, the flagman was the third and final line of defense against a rear-end collision. First an oncoming engineer would see an automatic slow signal a few miles back down the line. The next signal would be a red one, calling for him to stop his train still far to the rear of the train halted ahead of him. The flagman, standing far enough to the rear of the disabled train to allow reasonable braking space, was the human fail-safe element in the otherwise automatic system.

An empty troop train left Michigan City twenty-seven minutes behind the circus train. The night was clear, and all automatic signals were functioning properly. The troop train steamed right past the caution signal and bore down on the red signal. Flagman Trimm could see the headlight down the line and the silhouette of the red signal, which the train now swept past without any sign of slowing. Instantly the terrified Trimm knew that something was hideously wrong and only he could set it right. Furiously he waved his lantern in the wide arcs calling for an emergency stop, but the headlight kept coming. As a last desperate expedient, Trimm lit a red fusee and hurled it at the cab as the engine hurtled past, but still its pace did not slacken.

Helplessly he watched for a few surreal moments until the mighty crack of impact roused him to run to a scene out of a madman's nightmare. With the wooden cars splintered to kindling for the kerosene lanterns, the circus blazed—the gaudy props and trappings of the big top bursting from the flaming wreckage, rising with the smoke into the night sky, and falling scattered all over the area. The sleeping cars carrying the hundred dancing girls were telescoped, trapping many of the occupants while the flames roasted a dozen of them alive and screaming. Rose Borland was killed in her sleep on impact; Hercules the Strong Man was crushed from the chest down and begged his rescuers to kill him. Several performing families were wiped out entirely. Joe Coyle, the famous clown, lost his wife and two small children, who rode in the berth just above him. The animals, many of which were in stock cars up front, fared only a little better.

There was no water at hand, and rescuers from the nearby town of Ivanhoe had to brave a continuing conflagration to save those they could. When morning came to Ivanhoe, the circus was up in smoke with sixty-eight dead and another hundred seriously maimed.

At the investigation, the engineer of the troop train, who had miraculously survived, vehemently denied that he had violated Rule G, and no one had ever known him to drink on the job. He did testify that he hadn't slept for twenty-four hours, had eaten two heavy meals, and had closed the cab windows because the wind had been high that night. He admitted that he had dozed off several times and had no recollection of passing the red signal or flagman Trimm and his red fusee.

Some element was still missing; an experienced engineer might doze past a caution signal, perhaps even past a red one, but no engineer with normal faculties could doze past a waving lantern or ignore a lit fusee tossed literally into his face. Further questioning revealed that the engineer complained of "kidney pains" and used patent-medicine "kidney pills" on occasion. Had he taken any that night? Yes, he had taken "some kidney pills," he testified.

Throughout the later nineteenth century, the patent-medicine industry flourished in America. The active ingredient in most concoctions was opium, usually mixed with alcohol. They were sold over the counter without a prescription, and they worked, at least on symptoms, because the opium tended to relieve pains and induce mild euphoria. By 1918, however, society was increasingly aware of the addictive potential of opium. Patent-medicine men, shocked by the relatively weak provisions of the Harrison Act of 1914, feared that stronger laws might be passed which would cripple their industry. They replaced opium in many of their products with a synthetic derivative discovered in 1898 and initially deemed to be less addicting and debilitating because its pain-killing potency was such that far smaller amounts were effective. Often an ingredient in "kidney pills," the new drug was called heroin.

The investigation of the circus wreck concluded only that side effects of medication regrettably contributed to the accident. No one ever mentioned drug abuse or addiction; no one ever called for monitoring of engineers' drug habits.

Long before prohibition, drug abuse was our national dirty little secret. One study estimated that perhaps half a million Americans were addicted, usually unknowingly, to patent medicines. In some circles it was even fashionable; hostesses provided dishes of heroin tablets for their guests right along with the mints and cigarettes. And, of course, the national "soft" drink, Coca-Cola, in its real "classic" formulation was an elixir of cocaine. Though the Great Circus Wreck

certainly confirms that unregulated drug use could have awful consequences, at least in 1918 the story was such a rarity that people didn't
even recognize it for what it was.

Beyond Kelso, Kevin and Shannon return to their compartment for
their afternoon recreation, and Brian points out the huge dunes made
of ash that washed down the Toutle River from Mount St. Helens after
its explosion. So much material accumulated here that the bulldozers
actually reshaped the contours of the valley with it. The plan was that
the rains would slowly wash the stuff into the river and out to sea, but
the ash is so fertile that vegetation is taking root and threatening to
make these mounds permanent. Apparently the earth-shaping partnership between man and nature is an unequal one.

A Burlington Northern freight passes, and Brian calls my attention
to the rear-end device that has replaced the cabooses. "Fred, we call
it—Fucking Rear-End Device. We hate it, the union hates it." Now
everyone rides up front in the engine cabs on freights that have
dropped the caboose. Fred does most of the things that a caboose crew
would do during normal running, such as indicate when the train has
cleared a slow-order bridge or when the train has passed a switch that it
needs to back through. Brian concedes that it probably is a more
efficient way of operating when things are going smoothly, but when
there's trouble, the trouble is bigger trouble without a crew in a rear-
end car. Fred is useless in a derailment or hotbox situation. Fred can't
set out warning fusees or torpedoes in case of an unscheduled stop.
Fred makes "the long walk back" twice as long before a surviving
accident victim can receive any help. Fred allows transients to take
over the rear half of the train. And of course Fred makes for less rested
and more unhappy train crews, who miss the comforts of the caboose.

But then Fred has no feelings and can better deal with some of the
tragedies that involve the rear end of freight trains. Brian recalls a
fellow who earned the ironic nickname of Luck—his was bad and he
brought it to the train crews he worked with.

Luck kicked a hobo out of a caboose one night and the guy laid a curse
on him. "You start bouncing hoboes and you're going to have trouble,"
the guy told him. He took it as a threat of vandalism or violence.

But the next night, Luck was hanging from the rear car of a cabooseless freight backing into a siding. With only a flashlight in hand he saw
a figure huddled between the rails. His desperate signals to the engineer were too late. The drunk Canadian sailor passed out on the tracks
was sliced in two.

A few weeks later, Luck was working with an old conductor who was nearing retirement. They were on the rear of a train kicking a reefer (refrigerator car) up a small grade past a crossing to its spot by a loading dock. Luck was on the car the reefer had just uncoupled from, and the old conductor was on the ground waiting for the drifting reefer at the crossing, where he would mount it and set its brake at the dock so it wouldn't roll back. Luck hollered a warning as he saw the veteran conductor inexplicably preparing to jump the oncoming car from the end rather than from the side, one of the most dangerous and forbidden rookie moves on the railroad. The conductor lost his grip and fell—the oncoming car split him in two, and then, reaching the end of its drift up the incline, rolled back and quartered him again before crashing into and derailing the car that Luck had just leaped from.

Luck was still in mourning for his conductor friend when he was riding in the cab of a cabooseless freight that struck a car full of partying teenagers at a crossing. He made the long walk back to find two of them dead in the tangle of twisted metal; a third died in his arms.

Luck was granted a leave of absence and has since returned to work, but Brian admits that when he was on a crew with Luck recently, he stayed hyperalert throughout the run. Afterward he breathed a sigh of relief and discovered that he had taken up nail-biting.

So far as Brian knows, Luck isn't recording his misadventures in memoirs as did Henry Clay French, a railroad man whose career spanned a lot of unlucky years between 1870 and 1930. Beginning at fourteen as a call boy, whose job it was to seek out train crews in their leisure haunts, French was soon working as a yardman in Kansas City. These were the days of the old link-and-pin couplings, which required yardmen to work between moving cars, removing and inserting the pins at great risk to fingers, hands, limbs, and life. Inspections of handholds were unheard-of, and broken ones were usually patched with wire or nails by hurried trainmen themselves—when there was time and a man on the spot with initiative. One night, French was working with his friend Jack Foster at this hazardous task by lantern light when Foster grabbed for a missing handhold and was caught between two boxcars. French recorded seeing the ribs pop through his friend's skin with a burst of black blood before Foster died there by the track.

French quit the Kansas City yards and became a brakeman for the Santa Fe. The night of his first run into Dodge City, he was attracted into the street by the noise of a dance hall. Two horsemen rode in, and a furtive figure, apparently expecting them, emerged from the shadows, and with guns in both hands, killed both riders right in their saddles. The gunman was Bat Masterson; the horsemen were nameless scourges upon the peace the Mastersons were sworn to keep in Dodge. Without history's hindsight, French only knew that he had walked into a place where men died with their feet in their stirrups.

He quickly moved on to become a conductor on the Lawrence, Leavenworth & Galveston, where he experienced his first head-on collision. French's orders listed the other train as canceled, but when it loomed out of a "whiteout" snowstorm, he learned not to put too much faith in orders. There was a terrible slaughter among the stock of French's cattle cars. He was impressed by the courage and resourcefulness of the cowboys, who traveled on the train with their herd, as they braved terrible fires to rescue or shoot animals being roasted alive, and afterward rounded up the terrified survivors with almost parental care.

Shortly thereafter one of French's trains encountered a man swinging from a noose beneath a bridge near Winfield, Kansas, and the omen heralded a series of five wrecks in five weeks. He quit his job as conductor for the lesser job of fireman; nobody ever blamed firemen when things went wrong. But during this stint in a diminished role he got the westering itch, and in 1883 he headed, along with a mass migration of other railroad men harking back to the pioneers of the forties, for Oregon.

With the Oregon Railroad & Navigation Company, French immediately found himself in the midst of a mutiny by Chinese laborers over the issue of the company's feeding them western-style food. He witnessed the breaking of the strike by a foreman wielding a pick handle as club. Broken bones and busted heads welcomed French to the northwest as deadly gunshots had to Kansas.

He soon found a job as conductor on a stretch of line whose construction had been opposed by a local rancher who hired some Indians to shoot at the construction gangs. The line had gotten laid through the subterfuge of a management invitation to the farmer for a conference in a saloon. During the truce of the conference, the track crews hastily threw the line together with little thought to impending inspections. When the federal inspectors rode over the new line on French's train, he entertained them heartily in the bar car with generous libations. When they reached the bad stretch, "most of the government inspectors didn't know whether they were on a train or a boat." The line was judged satisfactory. By the time derailments occurred, no one remembered how the line had been approved.

French went on to work for several other railroads, including the ill-fated Oregon Pacific. T. Egenden Hogg, no crazier than other visionary rail builders who realized their dreams in the heady years of transcontinental rail building, planned a road from Yaquina Bay on the Oregon coast to New York City. Taking a cue from the Bennetts' conquest of Stampede Pass, Hogg attempted to begin his railroad by building the section over the high Cascade pass first, without connecting rails at either end of the construction.

Packhorses moved the rudiments of rail-building up to the pass, but Hogg showed none of the organizational brilliance of the Bennetts. A few rails were laid in the pass, and these were eventually connected to the bay on the Pacific. But the line never got down the east side of the mountains, and French's work was confined to the western run to the bay.

According to French, the one distinction of the Oregon Pacific was its disregard of Rule G. At the western end, a man named One-Legged Jack Slavens ran a liquor barge anchored in the bay which slaked the insatiable thirst of OP railmen. Everyone from brakemen up to management brass worked in a continual haze of intoxication, which finally drove French to walk away from his train one day, leaving it steaming on a siding in Albany.

French worked for half a dozen more railroads before retiring from the Union Pacific in 1930, and despite his career of mischance, he had no regrets: "The life of a railroad man is the finest life there is."

After Brian Beers detrains in Centralia, the *Coast Starlight* enters a schizophrenic world. On the left, Puget Sound stretches out toward the pristine Olympic Mountains of the peninsula; on the right, expanses of automobiles fill the parking lots of Boeing. Seattle, gateway to Alaska, the Orient, and the stars, lies just ahead.

The day is clear and sunny for my visit, apparently a rare treat, as the waterfront park is jammed with pale sun worshippers. Among them are not a few just plain bums. Despite the futuristic monorail and Space Needle, the predominant impression I find here is again of the street derelicts, in greater numbers and visibility than even in San Francisco. The explanation for this phenomenon is partly that despite its northerly latitude Seattle has a very even mean temperature year-round, partly that the place is a world-class port offering the kind of work that desperate men can slip into and out of with ease, and partly that this is the terminus of four major rail routes heavily traveled by hoboes—the UP, and NP, the Milwaukee Road, and the Great

Northern. The name "Skid Road" originated here as a designation of the area along an old logging skidder that ran right down through the center of town to the water and served as shelter for many a lost soul.

Seattle's King Street Union Station, with its red brick clock tower patterned after St. Mark's in Venice, is my introduction to the world of James Hill and his Great Northern Railway, the fifth of the great transcontinentals and today one of the three railroads, along with the Burlington and the Northern Pacific, composing the massive empire of the Burlington Northern. My train, the *Empire Builder*, bound for Montana, Minneapolis, and Chicago, is delayed because today's connecting *Coast Starlight* is again late, because of earthquake aftershocks along its route. It looks like the string of bad luck is going to follow me as I turn the northwestern corner and head back east.

The hex is highlighted by the waiting crowd, which seems to have more than its share of infirmity. A young couple waits with a five-year-old hooked up to a portable oxygen tank. A middle-aged woman repeatedly steers her daft elderly father away from the women's room. Several passengers are on crutches, and it strikes me that this is one condition that would cause me to fly rather than attempt to ride the train.

There is also a good display of sociopathic T-shirts and caps printed with slogans like "I don't get mad, I get even," "Shit happens," and "Kiss my ass." For the first time I realize that I shouldn't be irritated by this fashion. I should be grateful that such people come with warning labels that allow the rest of us to steer clear of them. With this cheering thought I board the *Empire Builder* anticipating a good cruise through the Cascades to Montana.

But the train isn't going anywhere yet. Its engines have been delayed by servicing problems out in the yard. The stationmaster has taken the unusual step of allowing passengers to board before the engine arrives so as to minimize any delay once it gets here. The cars are all hooked up to ground power so that the air conditioning and lights and galley equipment can work.

By the time the *Empire Builder* starts rolling it is already an hour behind schedule, but the climb up the western slopes of the Washington Cascades is beautiful. I can feel the pressure in my ears as we wind through the densely forested canyon of the Skykomish River. The foliage here is varied, as it is back in New England, deciduous and evergreen trees intermingled. Overhead tower wicked, jagged peaks, more sharply vertical than any I have seen yet. The forests give way to talus slopes below sheer cliffs, and I am impressed by the size of some of the boulders whose paths down the mountainside are marked by ragged scars.

Near Barring, Washington, the canyon widens to a high valley cradling a huge gulf between opposing mountain-goat walls. High up, patches of snow glisten in the early-evening sun, while on the grassy valley floor horses graze sleepily along the tracks.

Here the *Empire Builder* comes to a halt. It is no station, though there is a two-lane highway and a little country general store that looks like a Swiss mountain chalet. A freight has derailed on the tracks a few miles ahead of us. We aren't going anywhere for some time.

I spot engineer Glen McNerney in his blue overalls and green polka-dotted cap walking back from the head unit with a disgusted look on his face. The conductor has gone over to the little store to make some calls. Glen says these kinds of things happen all too often on the BN: its huge empire, the largest in the world, is overextended. It just happens that Glen was delayed an hour on his last trip through here with the *Empire Builder*, and the cause of that delay is sitting on the siding right next to us. It's a piggyback flatcar, one wheel rusted bright orange. "Hotbox. It was red-hot. When it cools down it gets oxidized like that." Over his radio we can hear the frantic communications of the trainmen working to clear the wreckage from the track ahead of us. Glen whistles when he hears a reference to some cars standing on end. Rescue squads have been called; people have been hurt.

Folks from the store and a couple of nearby houses have gathered with some passengers along the right-of-way beside the stalled Superliner. The conductor returns from the store and shoos everyone from the train back inside. We're going to park on a siding a mile down the line.

When we get there, we stop just behind the caboose of an eastbound freight waiting for the mess to clear. Fifteen minutes later another freight pulls in behind us, its smoky exhaust drifting past our windows on the gentle west wind and fouling our air conditioning. The conductor explains that a westbound freight is waiting on the other side of the derailment to come through. And of course there is the freight that derailed. The derailment has wrecked one of the two main-line tracks through here, so all of these trains will have to be sorted out over one line. Rail gridlock.

To pass the time, a woman in my sleeping car has organized a little day-care setup in her bedroom. Kids from all over the train have congregated here to play games, sing songs, and have stories read to them. She reminds me of my wife, and for a moment, I experience a sudden rush of impatience at the delay. After all, we're sitting on tracks pointed toward home—and going nowhere.

At the snack bar, the attendant has sold out of cards as passengers try to forget the delay in games of bridge, poker, gin, and solitaire. The diner is crowded, with more people than usual taking the full dinner as the evening wears on. But there isn't the party atmosphere I have observed on other trains during delays. The train is quiet, the passengers resigned and subdued. A man playing solitaire says that's because this train carries a lot of repeat veteran passengers. They're used to it.

At dusk a freight rumbles by us in the opposite direction, the remnant of the train that derailed. Then the freight in front of us pulls out, and shortly we begin to move, right on its tail. But then we stop again and back onto another siding. A second westbound freight rolls past, and then finally we are on our way. It is 9:00. The defunct schedule calls for us to be at Wenatchee, seventy-five miles away, at 8:08. We are over three hours behind schedule.

As we pass the site of the derailment I am surprised at how little of the mess remains. Two piggyback flatcars lie upended just off the grade, one without its front truck. The work train with its lifting crane idles while workmen walk the stretch of damaged track. The modern concrete spring-loaded ties are all busted up for several hundred yards. The track looks new, and later the conductor tells me it is—$1 million worth of new high-speed track and ties just laid a few months ago in an attempt to combat the delays that plague this stretch of the BN line. But then there has always been trouble here on the western approach to the eight-mile-long Cascade Tunnel, the longest in the Americas and the second built by the Great Northern in its struggle with nature in these northerly mountains.

Rail historians in various regions of the country offer differing opinions as to which accident deserves to be called America's worst rail disaster. For pure horror, one can't ignore those involving the fires in wooden cars fallen off bridges, such as the Angola and Ashtabula catastrophes. Most bizarre might be the Great Circus Wreck. For human foolishness there is the Michigan Southern collision at the "nonexistent" crossing diamond near Chicago or the collision in Massachusetts of two trains on a road whose superintendent would have no truck with the new-fangled telegraphing of orders. Many agree that in terms of numbers of casualties, the head-on collision of two trains at Nashville, Tennessee, in 1918 tops the list with ninety-nine killed and

171 injured. But I cast my vote for the Wellington tragedy that befell the Great Northern along the line I am traveling now. With ninety-seven killed, it rivals the Nashville crash for lovers of statistics, and it stands alone when compared to other calamities whose cause lay totally beyond the realm of human prevention. As declared by the Supreme Court itself in suits that followed, this was an act of God.

By the early twentieth century, the Great Northern had had enough experience with the capriciousness of the Cascade winters that it had instituted some unique countermeasures. Huge steam-driven rotary plows preceded trains running through the region, where miles of the line might be buried under twenty feet or more of snow, and massive snowsheds protected stretches of track where the danger of avalanches was most severe. Electric helper engines hauled trains through tunnels, which were longer and more frequent than on other roads because they provided some respite to the line from the ravages of winter. The electrics allowed the road steam engines to bank their fires as they passed through the long tunnels, thus avoiding asphyxiation of crew and passengers.

The winter of 1909–10 ended with two weeks of continuous heavy, wet snowfall that taxed these systems to their limit. In the small hours of February 23, two passenger trains, the *Fast Mail* and a Spokane local, already running late because of the storm, headed up the east slope of the Cascades with orders to meet one of the rotary plows just below the eastern entrance to the old two-and-half-mile-long Cascade Tunnel. Arriving at the east portal station, the conductors learned that the plow had been trapped by a snowslide at Windy Point, well west of the tunnel. The trains carried no diners and no one knew how long they might be stalled, so the decision was made to lay over at Cascade Station, where there were a cook shack and some rudimentary amenities. If things turned bad, they could always retreat to Leavenworth farther down the east slope. Two nights later, with the storm still raging, plows had opened a segment of the line far enough west of the tunnel to allow the trains to proceed. Shortly after their departure from the east portal, an avalanche swept down on the tracks where they had been parked, wiping out the cook shack and closing the possibility of returning to Leavenworth.

By the time the trains reached Wellington, on the west side of the tunnel, the drifts and snowslides had closed the westward line once again. Underpaid track crews were overworked to exhaustion; many had quit and gotten out when they could.

Superintendent James O'Neill, aboard one of the trains, now directed matters himself. He tried parking the trains inside the tunnel to shelter them from the storm and protect them from a possible avalanche, but the fumes from the engines, which had to keep steam up to heat the cars and provide power, threatened to asphyxiate everyone aboard. He considered spotting the trains under a snowshed, but none was long enough to cover a whole train, and besides, snowsheds were located precisely in the places where avalanches were most likely to occur. The trains ended up steaming on a siding at Wellington beneath the forty-five-degree slope of a mountain denuded of most of its trees and topsoil by a forest fire the previous year.

A rotary plow struggled east from Scenic to the rescue, but the heavy snows and another avalanche cut it off from its coal supply before it reached Wellington and it was snowed under, its fires out, two days later. Now the passenger trains were truly trapped. The night of the 26th, a panic erupted on board when several passengers told stories of dreams and premonitions of impending disaster.

O'Neill and two brakemen set out to hike their way down the line to Scenic to get some kind of help. Their trek through blinding snow covered nine miles and one thousand vertical feet through bottomless drifts and down near-vertical slopes. On the 27th, five passengers followed in their snow-filled tracks, preferring the dangers of braving the storm on foot to huddling in helpless terror in the train at Wellington. On the 28th, another group, this time including a number of railroad employees, abandoned the stricken trains. Now panic reigned among those left behind, who took the departure of the trainmen as proof that they had been left, as it were, aboard a sinking ship.

That night the weather turned warm, the snow changed to rain, and hideous claps of thunder echoed up and down the ravine. At 1:45 in the morning of March 1, the sleepless passengers and remaining trainmen heard a clap of thunder followed by a different kind of rumble whose volume grew rather than diminished after the flash. It was the mountain—snow, fire-scarred tree trunks, boulders, and mud—coming down upon them with a fury that swept everything before it. Half a mile wide, the slide wiped both trains and two-thirds of the town of Wellington off the side of the mountain and into the ravine.

Because the slide contained boulders and tree trunks as well as snow and mud, it had a pulverizing effect on the passenger trains; even the heavy steel engines lay twisted, torn, and bent at the bottom of the ravine afterward. Thus only a handful survived to tell of the horror, and even these had to wait nine more days for rescue.

The first from the outside world to contact the survivors were rescue crews recruited by O'Neill after he had walked out to Scenic. They were not prepared for what they found, and so a pack trail was opened to bring in food, medical supplies, tools, and blasting powder. Even after the storm subsided, the rotary plows were useless in snow mixed with tree trunks and boulders. The line had to be blasted clear, and it wasn't until March 9 that the first train from the east made its way to Wellington. On the 12th the way was finally clear to Scenic and the west. For two weeks, the snows of the Cascades held the mighty Great Northern hostage. A new tunnel, the longest and most ambitious yet, would become the lasting memorial to the ninety-seven killed the night of the great slide.

The absolute helplessness of men and machines to prevent the Wellington tragedy spurred perhaps the most mammoth reconstruction effort undertaken by any railroad in American rail history. The Great Northern immediately set about building more snowsheds, but the ultimate solution would finally be a new line entirely and a second Cascade Tunnel, nearly eight miles long, which bypassed much of the avalanche-prone area and through which tonight's *Empire Builder* rumbles as I settle into my bunk to sleep.

The tunnel is so long that huge fans have been installed to blow fresh air through it from east to west. A monster garage door at the east portal remains closed until opened by a signal from the approaching train. Nonetheless, engine fumes percolate into my compartment as I drift off, and I sleep fitfully, dreaming of trains trapped in the tunnel, of derailments, of earthquakes and avalanches and collisions.

And then he is there again, outside in the sleeping-car corridor, gym bag in hand. He's even weaker now, and there are tears on his face— something I saw only once, back at the Lahey Clinic when he wished my younger brother well at the wedding he would not be fit enough to attend.

"Terry, are we going home now?"

Something has changed again. I thought I had left him "at home" by the mulberry tree in Bloomington.

"I don't know, Dad." All night long I wrestle with his question, only half asleep while the Superliner rushes eastward, toward New Hampshire.

Chapter Sixteen

Northwest Passage

THE *EMPIRE BUILDER*

In the morning, with the tunnel and 27,000 miles of my journey behind me, the eastbound *Empire Builder* climbs through the lakes and ski resorts of the Whitefish region on the western slope of the Montana Rockies. I experience a wash of conflicting feelings. On one hand, I am headed east for the final homecoming. I can feel the pull— every lake, every summit, every tree presents itself in mental comparison to images of home in New Hampshire. Every milepost marks one subtracted from the three thousand miles that separate me from my own landscape, family, and friends.

But these feelings are countered by anticipation of the adventure I saved till last. I began making tracks six months ago partly from an urge to flee the shopping malls, the interstates and airports, the fast-food chains, the condominium developments—symbols of a land with no past. Despite Cheyenne, Meridien, Bloomington, Barstow, Old Sacramento, I feel as though I still haven't found what I'm looking for— unfinished business in my personal midlife crisis. Finally the odyssey has led me to a place called Essex, Montana—one last shot at timelessness and communion.

Essex lies in the western valley of the mystery pass over the continental divide that Lewis and Clark never found. It can be reached only by the rail line of the old Great Northern and, in good weather, the two lanes of U.S. Route 2. Though the frontier officially closed near the turn of the century, I have harbored an American fantasy that there remain isolated little pockets of real frontier, probably located in the highest mountains, somewhere in the most northern reaches of the Rockies. I am approaching Essex on the *Empire Builder* with high hopes.

The *Empire Builder* follows the tracks of James Hill's Great Northern Railway, last and most unusual of the five great pioneer transcontinental roads (the Milwaukee Road was built under postpioneer conditions in the twentieth century). This was the renegade transcontinental, the only one built without any assistance or encouragement from the federal government. This was the route that supplanted, for all practical purposes, the old dream of the "most direct and practicable water communication across this continent, for the purposes of commerce," envisioned in Thomas Jefferson's instructions to Lewis and Clark—the Northwest Passage.

I'm sure I'm not the only map lover who was intrigued as a child by the wavy black line just below the Canadian border that represents the Great Northern, meandering in near-polar isolation far from the population centers of America. The more southerly Northern Pacific hits all the big towns, Bismarck, Billings, Bozeman, Butte, and Missoula. Between Minneapolis and Spokane the Great Northern serves far smaller and more remote-sounding places—Fargo, Devil's Lake, Wolf Point, Havre, Cut Bank, and Glacier. A junior high school history teacher once told me there really was a Northwest Passage, that Lewis and Clark just missed finding it, and that the Great Northern ran right through it.

A glance at a topographical map quickly confirms that the narrowest neck in the Rocky Mountain chain runs through northern Montana just south of the border. A closer look reveals a place called Marias Pass, just along the southern edge of Glacier National Park, where a scant forty miles separates the headwaters of the Missouri and Columbia tributaries. A few miles down the Flathead River west of the pass, Burlington Northern helper engines still wait at the tiny town of Essex to assist heavy trains over the hump, as they have done for nearly a century. In conversations with trainmen throughout the country, I have been told that this is the place where the past meets the present, where man and nature still confront each other on relatively equal terms, where the law of time stands suspended.

*   *   *

I have ridden trains through enough of the great western American mountain ranges to be amazed that historians feel compelled to explain Lewis and Clark's failure to find the Marias Pass. These mountains are so vast that it seems the odds against an early-nineteenth-century party's finding any one particular pass should be astronomical. That an explanation is necessary is testimony to the epic dimension of what they did accomplish.

On their westbound journey working up the Missouri through north-central Montana, Lewis and Clark came to a fork with north and south branches, the north muddy, the south clear. Here was a feature not mentioned by the Hidatsa Indians whose description of the route to the Pacific waters the expedition was using as a guide. A difference of opinion arose about which river the Hidatsas had described. Their men thought the north branch, since the Missouri had been marked by muddiness from the start. But Lewis and Clark thought the south, since the Indians had described a river that came from "shining mountains" over a falls. A scouting expedition down the south branch found Great Falls, and so the north branch was named Marias, for Lewis's cousin, Maria Wood, and abandoned while the party headed southwest. If Lewis and Clark had considered how, in the later words of Robert Frost, "way leads on to way," they might have checked out the Marias River before heading south, where they encountered the disappointment of Lolo Pass and the series of mountain ranges beyond it.

On the return trip, when the dream of an easy passage was pretty much dead, Lewis took a side expedition up the Marias to locate the northern boundary of the Louisiana Purchase, but a disastrous fight with Blackfeet Indians, resulting in the only loss of life through combat of the entire expedition, turned his party back before they reached the river's headwaters and the Marias Pass. Thus the pass that offered the easiest passage between the Missouri and Columbia tributary headwaters went unacknowledged for nearly eighty years. Of course, without rails the passage in the time of Lewis and Clark wouldn't have amounted to much anyway, though it was better than any they did find. Neither the Two Medicine River on the east nor the Flathead on the west is navigable by anything much larger than a canoe, and the portage over the mile-high pass itself is steep and frequented by fifteen-foot snows and unpredictable grizzly bears.

Yet the "mystery pass" was probably first seen by white men as early as 1810, when David Thompson's expedition reported on traders who claimed to have crossed the continental divide by a "wide defile of easy passage." Astonishingly, the pass appears correctly named though incorrectly located in some rare maps of the Oregon Historical Society, dated 1859. In 1864 the Montana legislature even incorporated a wagon-road company to build through it, but was thwarted from finding it by the continuing hostility of the Blackfeet Indians, who ferociously regarded the pass as the anchor to their homelands and thus opposed its exploitation. It wasn't until after the pacification of the Blackfeet that John Stevens, a surveyor for James Hill's Great Northern Railway, finally relocated the pass in 1889, establishing it as the key that would allow the fifth transcontinental to compete with the already established four.

As the train grinds up the Flathead Valley, simple painted signs in the shape of pointing hands identify the various glacier-draped peaks rising to the northeast. I catch glimpses of hunting cabins on the mountainsides and fishing camps down along the rushing river. Occasionally I can see an empty stretch of two-lane Highway 2, which roughly parallels the railroad through the passage. There are no billboards, no neon lights, no ranches, certainly no fast-food franchises and no local hangouts either. The last thirty miles into Essex are pure pristine forested frontier.

And so is Essex. The first sign of its approach is the rattle of the train passing over switches for the helper sidings, then around a bend I can see the helpers, two pairs of green BN Geeps (railroad slang for general-purpose diesel engines) pumping idling exhaust up above the treetops. On the right, the white clapboard structure that is the old Essex depot drifts by, and across the helper sidings to the left sits the Izaak Walton Inn, my destination.

The train slows to a stop a few hundred yards beyond the inn. There is no station, only a waiting van with the words "Walton Inn" painted on its side. There are only two passengers detraining, myself and a Japanese man named Lin. Frank Krshka, an elderly employee of the inn, greets us, exchanges some small talk with the train conductor, and then drives us the few yards along the track to the inn. "You're late," he says. "Three hours."

The half-timbered Tudor-style hotel sits across a broad well-maintained lawn from the half-dozen tracks of the helper engine facility. A gang of college-age young people are hard at work busting up an old concrete sidewalk leading down to the tracks. Neat stacks of new brick stand ready for laying.

On the other side of the tracks, the old depot today serves as an office for the BN. Up the hill behind it the old schoolhouse now houses the young employees of the hotel. Adjacent to the hotel on its side of the tracks are the fueling and maintenance facilities for the helper engines. Scattered around the encompassing woods, small cabins complete the town of Essex, year-round population seven.

The lobby of the hotel, all dark, cool, old knotty pine, has the look and feel of a north-country hunting club. Game and fish trophies hang from the walls but are overshadowed by railroad paraphernalia, paintings, and photographs; the place is as much a museum as it is a hotel. The dining room at the west end of the first floor is bright and businesslike, the hearty food and workmanlike ambience more diner than tourist restaurant.

The bar is downstairs, its walls lined with railroad gear and spectacular photographs of the railroad in moments of challenge and adversity. I am particularly intrigued by photos of two Amtrak derailments that occurred near here in 1980 and 1981—Superliner cars wrapped around a snowy curve in a sickening tilt, a few even down on their sides in the drifts. Beyond the bar a pool table and Ping-Pong table stand dust-covered now in the summer, but are well worn from long winter evenings.

The rooms at the inn are on the upper two floors. They are plain, spartan even, each furnished with a simple iron bed, a dresser, and a sink. Bathrooms are just down the hall. The window from my room overlooks the tracks, a cool breeze and the soothing grumble of the idling helper engines banishing any thought of air conditioning.

There is no pool, no tennis court, no workout room, no golf course. According to the hotel's brochure, the hiking, skiing, boating, hunting, and fishing opportunities in the "million acres of wilderness" make them unnecessary. And then of course there is the railroad, which built the place and is still its main attraction.

The name of the *Empire Builder* doesn't actually refer to the railroad, but to its builder, the one-eyed tyrannical genius from Canada, James Jerome Hill. History could have bestowed the moniker on Commodore Vanderbilt or Colonel Holiday or Collis Huntington, each of whom built his empire before Hill. Maybe Hill won the prize because he was the last, maybe because he played the game by such radical rules, maybe because he integrated the individual strengths of each of the other three—the business shrewdness of Vanderbilt, the visionary innovation of Holiday, the pile-driving force of Huntington.

But when Hill started he was just an Ontario farm boy with a fantasy of becoming a trader in the Orient. He itched westward to St. Paul in 1856 thinking he might join up with a team of fur-trappers and work his way to Puget Sound, where he could ship to China, but he got to St. Paul too late, and by the time new outfits set out a year later, nineteen-year-old Jim Hill was firmly entrenched in the local grain trade and learning the secrets that would underpin his empire.

There was the vast grain potential of the northern prairie extending well up into Canada, and there were the immigrants, drawn to the region in increasing numbers without any organized recruitment effort. He saw firsthand the difficulties encountered by railroads relying on wood for fuel in the vast treeless prairie. He noted the habit of business interests on both sides of the Canadian border of artificially and unnecessarily restricting their scope of operation to their side of the line. Finally, he calculated the relative returns when the river packet boats set high rates versus low rates. He learned that the carriers' business grew most rapidly with low rates, despite the low profit margins. Thus the famous Hill credo of charging what his railroad could bear rather than what the market would bear.

After the Civil War, Hill got his first chance to put what he had learned into practice. As an agent for the decrepit St. Paul & Pacific Railroad, he inventoried available sources of coal and set up his own company to supply it. He looked north, up the Red River and across the border, to Winnipeg, where he formed a crucial association with Hudson's Bay Company agent Norman Kittson. With Kittson he founded the Red River Transportation Company to carry traders and supplies across the border. On one of his journeys, according to legend, he met the governor of the Canadian province, Donald Smith, on a dogsled 150 miles from the nearest human habitation. Hill, Kittson, Smith, and George Stephen of the Bank of Montreal arranged to buy the struggling St. Paul & Pacific, and Hill took over the job of rebuilding and extending it northwestward to the Canadian border, where he revamped it as the St. Paul, Minneapolis & Manitoba.

Meanwhile rail fever was stirring in Canada. By the 1870s, Prime Minister John A. MacDonald saw a transcontinental railroad as the only hope for uniting the sprawling confederation and forestalling continuing expansionist urges of his muscular southern neighbor. If the rebel colonies could build several prosperous transcontinentals, why couldn't Canada, with the economic support of the greatest empire-building nation in the world, build one?

For starters, there was the "lesson" of the American crash of 1873, which took the Northern Pacific, its financiers, and half of Wall Street with it. Canada at the time was a nation of only four million people, while the United States had thirty million taxpayers when it undertook the first Pacific railroad. Britain's Parliament wouldn't touch the project. The Canadian government demurred unless it could act merely as a stimulant to private interests, who would have to guarantee that the project would ultimately cost the treasury not one penny.

Hill, Kittson, Smith, and Stephen formed the Canadian Pacific Syndicate, which provided that guarantee (soon forgotten), and a connection was built between the St. Paul, Minneapolis & Manitoba and a stretch of the new Canadian line, an international link which brought much-needed revenue to both fledgling transcontinentals. In the age of intense nationalism, these men were either throwbacks to the earlier age of international empire or prophets of the multinational corporate state of the later twentieth century.

But soon there was a parting of the ways. Frustrated at the Canadian government's insistence on an all-Canada line rather than his proposed link to eastern Canada via the Manitoba through U.S. territory south of Lake Superior, and newly awakened to the fact that the CP would become a natural competitor for his own transcontinental project, Hill resigned from the company and sold his stock in 1882. The CP would build on to the coast of British Columbia guided by Hill's legacy of insight into routes, his choice of managers for construction, and the continuing mutually profitable commerce over the Manitoba connection. Hill, at the age of forty-four, now focused on his American project.

By the 1880s the nation had four transcontinental railroads. There were the two roads "officially sanctioned" and heavily subsidized by the U.S. government, the Union/Central Pacific from Omaha to San Francisco and the Northern Pacific from Lake Superior to Puget Sound. There was Huntington's Southern Pacific route from California to New Orleans, built with only partial federal support but nonetheless a part of the government's grand design as the southern connection in the triad of lines across the continent. Holliday's Santa Fe was the first sport in that it didn't follow one latitude (it departs Chicago as a central route and reaches California as a southern route), it served intermediate territory where markets didn't yet exist and termini were already well connected to rivals, and it was never part of the government's grand design. Yet nonetheless it too received government subsidies and land grants. By the time Hill was in the field, the Crédit Mobilier scandal had killed the government goose. Some said there would never be a fifth transcontinental. But Hill meant to duplicate the Santa Fe's feat in the north without any government assistance whatsoever.

He did it with a formula of elegant simplicity. Without government deadlines, Hill never had to hurry his construction. Without government inspections, he could build to very rudimentary standards and improve upon them when commerce generated capital. For example, the initial Great Northern line was unique in that the rails were laid directly onto the ties with no plates in between. Because he was building through virtually unsettled territory, he had no routing imperatives but for what was most economical. Thus Hill built cheaply and eventually more substantially than any of the government-backed roads and demonstrated in the process the incredible financial waste of the earlier projects. The Great Northern, originally dubbed Hill's Folly, was and remains the only continental transportation system ever built in America as pure private enterprise.

As the line worked its way westward, he threw out scores of spurs to gather the harvest of the wheatlands his trains would help to populate. He set rates as low as the railroad could bear, further guaranteeing his firm grip on the territory. No railroad was ever so thorough in "occupying" the larger region through which it passed. Because the Northern Pacific had failed notoriously at this task, it hardly counted as a competitor as the Great Northern built westward through the latitude which belonged to the NP in the government's grand design. Hill's greater competitor was the Canadian Pacific, which he had helped set in motion, and which operated along lines he had set down.

Each major leap of the railroad terminated at a point guaranteed to generate immediate traffic. First there were the connections to Manitoba. Next the westering line branched away from its transcontinental route to Great Falls and Helena in Montana to tap the mining that was booming there.

Then there was the crossing of the Rocky Mountains. Following the traditional continental-divide crossing of Lewis and Clark, the Northern Pacific plunged into the mountains farther east than it had to and then ran northwest with them, almost perversely maximizing the length of the Rockies crossing. Hill aimed his line farther north at the narrowest neck of the great Rocky Mountain chain. No crossing had yet been found, but the peaks here were a few thousand feet lower than those farther south. Surely the legendary "mystery pass" would turn up. In the winter of 1889, Hill sent John Stevens to find it. He did so in forty-below-zero weather—the Marias Pass at an altitude of only 5,200 feet is the nation's lowest rail crossing of the continental divide north of the SP's desert crossing in New Mexico. Helper engines would be needed on the western slope; otherwise it was the cheapest crossing to build and maintain in America.

Finally the route had to tackle the Cascades, as rugged in this latitude as the Rockies and far worse for weather. Following his usual strategy, Hill initially built a cheap, hair-raising series of switchbacks over four-thousand-foot Stevens Pass without a tunnel. While this may seem tame compared to the DRG's "Giants' Ladder" switchbacks over the eleven-thousand-foot Corona Pass in Colorado, the running of transcontinental passenger trains over switchbacks at this latitude with its particularly severe winters could never be a routine matter. The first Cascade Tunnel, eliminating the need for switchbacks, was built in 1900 with revenue generated by the stopgap route.

In 1893, with the other transcontinentals floundering or crashing into receivership, the Great Northern reached Puget Sound so profitably that Hill was able to buy control of the rival Northern Pacific. The final key to his success was his grand traffic design. The Great Northern served country at its western end filled with trees and at its eastern end bereft of them. Throughout the late 1880s and early 1890s processions of lumber trains rolled eastward to supply the substantial midwestern buildings still the dominant feature of the region today. Returning to the west, Hill's trains carried grain and southern cotton bound for the Orient, where he had carefully cultivated a market for these commodities. His dream of becoming an Orient trader fulfilled, he entered the twentieth century to face his greatest challenge and opportunity.

Upon Collis Huntington's death in 1900, Union Pacific president Edward Henry Harriman acquired Huntington's interest in the Southern Pacific, thus becoming the second man, after Hill, to be master of two transcontinentals. Harriman had already established himself as a railroad savior by resuscitating the UP from the ravages of Crédit Mobilier. Now, with the Illinois Central also under his thumb, he set out to assemble the greatest American railroad empire yet. A showdown between the two titans developed when Harriman sought to buy control of the Burlington, the white-knight granger road that had extended to nearly transcontinental proportions through enlightened management and geographical good luck. To Harriman, it meant a connection of the UP to Chicago and, along with the UP, SP, and IC, a monstrous network of rails that could dominate, perhaps even monopolize, the entire nation west of the Appalachians.

But Hill too coveted the Burlington for its link between Montana and Chicago and for its network of rails into lumber-hungry Nebraska and Iowa. With the financial backing of no less than J. P. Morgan, Hill won the Burlington, but Harriman counterattacked by buying heavily into the Northern Pacific. Wall Street rocked as the two behemoths struggled, buying massively in both the Burlington and the NP through futures contracts. Panic ensued when money men realized that together Hill and Harriman had bought more NP stock for future delivery than existed. To pursue the conflict by demanding delivery would have, in the words of historian John Moody, "brought down Wall Street like a house of cards." The Hill and Harriman interests, with all Wall Street hanging on the outcome, sat down to palaver.

The upshot was the mammoth Northern Securities Company, bringing together all of the properties of both Hill and Harriman. By the time this supercorporation was declared a violation of the Sherman Antitrust Act, the parties had worked out a peace. Hill kept all three northern roads, the GN, NP, and Burlington. Harriman won concessions that the NP would not build into UP territory in Oregon and that the Burlington would not be extended into a sixth transcontinental. Today it smells an awful lot like victory for Hill, who retained control of the largest rail empire ever built in America and one which remains so, as the Burlington Northern, even in the megamerger years of recent decades. Upon retiring from running his railroad empire, Hill acknowledged, "Most men who have really lived have had, in some shape, their great adventure. This railway is mine."

Today on the front-porch swing of the Izaac Walton Inn, I watch a modern Burlington Northern freight slow to a stop out on the main line. Jim Hartzfeld, a stocky vacationer from Madison, Wisconsin, narrates the operation as two of the helper engines, which are always idling at the ready on the siding by the hotel, move onto the main line ahead of the freight and back up to couple on. He says that sometimes they hook onto the rear and push, and sometimes one or two hitch onto both ends, depending on the weight of the train and the distribution of the load. The strength of the coupling drawbars limits the number of engines that can pull from the front. Jim says he's never seen more than eight engines on the front end of a freight. Today's train, of moderate length, pulled in with four and now pulls out with six in a furious roar and a cloud of sooty black smoke, issuing primarily from the helper engines, which have built up carbon in the cylinders while idling. The load heading east on this train is not lumber, but Toyotas.

I ask Jim what vacationers do here. He says that Madison doesn't have much live railroading anymore; he is here for the trains. "Where else can you sit on the porch of your hotel and watch helper engines hitch onto a dozen passing freights a day with two Amtrak passenger trains and wilderness thrown in besides?" His wife, Alice, is a "mountain person," so here they find something for each of them. It's been their regular June vacation for five years.

Today Alice is hiking up Spring Hill, just opposite the hotel and so named because of dozens of mountainside springs that bubble from its rocks. Last year she found one, just a few hundred yards off the marked trail, which formed a pool near a high outcropping from which she could look down on the trains climbing the valley while soaking in the icy waters. She is trying to rediscover that pool today.

I hope she does. All day long the image of the pool looking down on the rails of the Northwest Passage haunts me. I just hope Alice Hartzfeld returns with enough daylight remaining for me to find it myself.

Jim introduces me to Larry and Linda Vielleux, who took over the Izaak Walton Inn in 1982. Larry shows me into his office, a large wainscoted room cluttered with railroad and innkeeping artifacts, photos, letters, and sporting trophies. Before him, the place was owned by old college friends of Larry, Sid Goodrich and his wife Millie, who had bought it in 1973.

Larry and Linda had farmed a place south of Havre for twenty years when things went bad on them in 1980; the farm didn't provide a living and the constant struggle was breaking up their family life. The day Larry decided to quit, Sid called from Essex. Larry told him he was quitting farming, and Sid said, "I knew that. That's why I called." His father had just had a heart attack and needed attention, so Sid proposed that Larry take over the inn. "Just give it a try for a year."

So Larry sold the farm, went into debt, headed west, and bought the inn. "Scared hell out of me going into debt like that without a farm under my feet. But we never looked back. This life saved our family, it really did." He's not getting rich, but the inn does provide a better living than the farm ever did. Traditionally the best business has been in the summer, because of the fishing, hiking, and white-water enthusiasts, but recently Larry has witnessed a boom in cross-country skiing. This past year, the winter season was better than the summer for the first time ever, and when he succeeded in persuading Amtrak to make a stop here, Larry knew that the inn's future was secure.

I ask about the photos of derailments downstairs in the bar. "You know, there's a fascination with stuff like that in these parts. People here take a kind of pride in the fact that these mountains can still raise hell with the railroad and the highway." The Amtrak derailments happened in the two years just preceding Larry's tenure. The passengers had to stay at the inn for two days before they could be evacuated, but some of them must have liked something about the experience. Several still return every year.

But Larry's favorite derailment story involves grizzly bears. Five carloads of corn grain went off the tracks one winter up near the pass and broke open. Hundreds of tons of corn lay along the track, and the railroad salvaged the little that wasn't spoiled and buried the rest. By spring Larry heard strange reports of groups of bears behaving oddly along that stretch. One train even hit a couple of them.

Bears don't usually forage in groups, and they certainly don't let themselves get hit by trains, having pretty good common sense about dealing with the few things in the mountains bigger than themselves. Then a track crew had a run-in with some that charged so recklessly that two had to be shot. Further investigation revealed that the bears had dug pits down into the now-fermented corn and gorged themselves, getting drunk in the process.

Word got out to tourists and campers in the area, who hiked out to see the drunken bears. When one of them got mauled on railroad property, the railroad realized it had a problem. So they dug up the corn and burned it. Today whenever there is a report of whiskey stolen from some camp, the conventional wisdom says it was kids—or maybe, just maybe . . .

Highway 2 is frequently closed by avalanches in the winter. Just this past December, Larry had to put up seventy-five stranded travelers when the hotel was already nearly booked. They had a meeting in the lobby of travelers and guests. "People were packed into every square inch of that room with the wind howling outside." They worked out a communal solution so that everyone had a place to lay his head. Strangers doubled up in beds, families shared rooms, kids curled up on sofas and chairs.

Some romances began that night, and at least one was consummated. "When we thought we had everyone settled, the rescue squad brought in a young newlywed couple who had been stalled in their car in a snowdrift. There was a cot available in a third-floor room with a little old lady. I was nervous about asking her to share her room with newlyweds, but she was game—'I'll just have to go down to the bar for a while.' " She stayed down till 2:00 A.M. talking to a reporter, who must have phoned his story out, and it hit the AP wire. "Next day I get a call from Sid Goodrich, who wanted to know what I was doing with his old hotel putting newlyweds up with old ladies."

Three summers ago an Amtrak engine of the *Empire Builder* struck a pile of rocks someone had built between the rails and ruptured its fuel tanks. It was a full train with three hundred people stranded all day with no power, no galley, no lights, no air conditioning, no toilets. Amtrak called Larry and said they needed all the beer he had and four hundred sandwiches. Larry delivered, and an Essex helper engine eventually retrieved the stricken train, which was parked on a siding in front of the hotel with the helper providing power for the day it took to investigate the incident and bring out new engines. "Now, that was the biggest crowd we ever had, but at least they had their own beds and diner."

Today Larry is host to the Navigators, a fundamentalist Christian youth group here for their annual ten-day retreat. These are the young people I have seen working on the sidewalk out front. They pay for their stay with labor, and this is part of the discipline of their calling. Their leader, whose title is Speaker, says he wants them so tired at the end of the day that they will fall into bed exhausted after study and devotion in the early evening. It looks like they will. They are fanatic workers; I have tried to find a shirker among them, someone I can identify with, and there isn't a one.

Next week the inn will host the annual outing of Project Hope, a Montana civic program for children with terminal illnesses. The weekend is funded entirely by private contributors, and the list of sponsors from the Glacier region is impressive: a tire warehouse, several lodges, a boat sales outfit, three banks, a rafting outfitter, a gas station, a bus tour company, Glacier National Park, Amtrak, and, of course, the Izaak Walton Inn. These children will raft in white water, picnic on mountaintops, ride trains, attend concerts, tour the glaciers, fish, swim, hike, and enjoy more exhilarating experiences in three days than some of us do in years. It's the best example yet of the generous spirit of the west that makes men who live so far apart such good neighbors.

The town of Essex was never a place for homesteaders. Nothing grows here but trees, and most of the Montana mining is in the mountains a hundred miles farther south. It is more akin to the frontier fur-trading forts in that it is merely an outpost in a far-flung empire. It was not populated by root-seeking settlers, whose progeny consumed the frontier, and whose works doomed it to domestication. Instead it housed agents of the railroad whose work helped sustain an economic enterprise which just happened to pass through here, just as the old fur company agents did. Its very existence was predicated on the assumption that the surroundings would remain hostile and the economic enterprise running through would always need this prop, this service maintenance, to keep the line open. It harks back to days when empire was a holding action, not a conquest.

As the construction of the Great Northern worked up from the east toward the newly discovered Marias Pass in 1889, employee Eugene McCarthy was sent ahead to scout out the valley on the western side for timber for rail ties. In this region, the railroad was dealing with wilderness as unknown as all of these mountains had been in the days of Lewis and Clark. McCarthy completed his survey of the forest along the proposed line but noticed that only one site looked promising for the construction camp the railroad would need when it built down the western slope of the continental divide. Seeing opportunity, he personally filed a "Declaration of Occupancy" for the site back at the railhead and then returned to his claim and began clearing a townsite. The railroad management was not amused, however, by this private initiative of one of its employees working on the railroad's time, and it threatened to sue. The nearest court being hundreds of miles away, one suspects that the railroad's response involved other more immediate gestures as well, because shortly a "compromise" emerged which gave the railroad its construction site.

McCarthyville quickly sprouted as the latest in the long tradition of hell-on-wheels western rail camps. By 1892, it had a population of over a thousand, which began to populate the new cemetery as the saloons, gambling halls, and attendant gunplay took their toll. Each spring the melting snows revealed what was called "lead residue," bodies fallen in winter confrontations.

McCarthyville's most notorious inhabitant was probably Slippery Bill Morrison, a well-educated lifelong bachelor from Massachusetts who, for a while, divided his time equally between work for the railroad and high-stakes gambling. He got his nickname from his uncanny ability to win big at cards and survive the consequences. One night he played till the small hours sitting on an old spike keg at a crate used for a table and cleaned everybody out, a very dangerous thing to do. Sure enough, on his way back to his cabin someone jumped him, clubbed him, and roughed him up, but to no purpose. He had no money on him. The next day, Slippery Bill quietly went back to the spike keg and removed the winnings he had stashed there during the game.

Morrison worked as a conductor on the railroad until his train smashed into a work train in 1903 and killed fifteen people. When he found out that the company would mount a major investigation into everything and everyone connected with the accident, he quit the railroad, thus taking himself beyond the reach of the company inquiry, and never went back.

Morrison lived to see the demise of McCarthyville, which was slowly abandoned as the completed railroad had no further need of the construction site. Nature reclaimed the place when high winds torched it with cinders from a bonfire of old railroad ties in 1921. No trace of it remains today, and the railroad has long since moved its maintenance operations a few miles down the Flathead Valley to Essex.

It was proximity to good rail-tie timber and the expanse of level land large enough for sprawling construction operations that had recommended McCarthyville to the railroad initially, but otherwise it was a god-awful place, high up the valley, exposed to howling winds. For its long-term service facility, the railroad didn't need space so much as shelter. The site that became Essex nestles in a relatively narrow stretch of the Flathead Valley where steep slopes and a sharp curve to the river keep out the fierce mountain winds. Here too was a rushing creek to supply water for the steam engines and power for any mills that might be needed, and just enough elongated flat space for a small series of sidings, coal chutes, and associated buildings.

All the railroad originally wanted out of Essex was a place to hitch on helper engines for the climb over the pass and a dormitory in winter for the crews needed to shovel out the tracks when weather combined with the steep grade to shut down the line. The town had a post office by 1898 and ten years later a small hotel and lunchroom. By World War I a pool hall, a barber shop, a general merchandise store, a schoolhouse (which still stands), a handful of houses and cabins, and a nearby sawmill were built to fill the needs of the small population of year-round rail employees and their families. But that was all; this was no boom town.

In the meantime the railroad became increasingly aware that it had stumbled upon a new kind of economic opportunity, unlike the usual traffic in agriculture or mining. As far back as 1883, Lieutenant John Van Ornsdale had written of the remarkable scenery of the glacier-draped peaks north of the "mystery pass" region and hoped that some-day these mountains could be set aside as a national park. The editor of *Field and Stream* magazine, George Bird Grinnell, frequently visited the region in the last decade of the nineteenth century, establishing a bond of trust with the Blackfeet Indians and a legacy as the "father of

Glacier Park." When the U.S. government offered to purchase the tract from the Blackfeet in 1891, they specifically requested Grinnell as negotiator. Within a decade, Grinnell along with other travel and nature writers, eagerly encouraged by the Great Northern, had established Glacier in the national consciousness as the "Crown of the Continent." In 1910, President Taft signed the bill establishing Glacier National Park.

This was no fourteen-hundred-square-mile preserve of garden-variety wilderness. The Glacier-Waterton region is the result of two unique, ancient geological cataclysms which shaped terrain to be found nowhere else in the United States. Millions of years ago this was a vast inland sea whose sediments hardened into layered rock. Then the great overthrust occurred, related to the events shaping much of the Rocky Mountain chain, but different here because the old sedimentary rocks were forced up over newer volcanic beds. The result is a mountain landscape seemingly turned upside down with striated limestone and shale crags towering over ten thousand feet in the air. The second shaping event was the glacial age, when the ice gouged out the V-shaped canyons into U-shapes, sculpting the characteristic Matterhorn silhouette of the peaks and cutting off higher ravines entirely so that they became the spectacular hanging valleys unique to the Glacier Park region. Nowhere else in the United States were mountains so high subjected to the radical effects of the glaciers. And, of course, nowhere else did a glacier leave so many remnants of itself behind, thus giving the region its name.

With the federal government lacking the funds to adequately develop the recreational opportunities of the park, the Great Northern stepped in to assist with the building of chalets, cabins, hotels, and finally the spectacular Going to the Sun Auto Road. Some who had opposed the establishment of the park on the grounds that it was merely a scheme by the GN to ensure that no rival railroad could run through a more northerly pass, saw the GN's financial involvement as proof of their suspicions. The GN did have a competitive ax to grind, but the fact that no decent passes existed north of Marias ruled out the issue of forestalling new competition. The real issue was old competition with the Northern Pacific, which, despite Hill's ownership of both roads, operated as a distinct railroad and had been galling GN management for years with its highly successful promotion of its branch line to Yellowstone. Now the GN had its "own" national park, and this one didn't require a change to a branch line: it bounded the GN's main line all the way from its eastern to its western entrance. Eventually Glacier Park would inspire the GN's famous mountain goat logo and its slogan "See America First."

Back at Essex, that first little hotel burned down and another, the Red Beanery, was erected. It too burned. Up until 1935, the railroad housed most of its employees, especially its snow shovelers and section men, in railcars parked on the sidings. But Great Northern president W. P. Kenney decided that this would no longer do for a railroad whose stock sold as high as any in the nation, and he authorized the expenditure of $28,690 for construction of a 32-by-88-foot two-story frame hotel with the latest in steam heating, electric lighting, a restaurant, and rooms sufficient "to accommodate six crews of five men . . . and three or four division officers . . . and the necessary hotel help." By 1937, the cost estimate had increased to $35,500 (and the dimensions to 32 by 100 feet) and the railroad began dragging its feet. In 1939, the Great Northern contracted with a private builder and hotel operator to finally construct the place for $40,000, now a magnificent 36-by-114-foot mountain resort with twenty-nine bedrooms, ten bathrooms, spacious lobby, dining room, kitchen, drying room, storeroom, and general store. It stands little changed today.

The reason for the sudden aggrandizement of the project was the anticipated opening of a middle entrance to Glacier National Park at Essex, but the intervention of World War II killed the idea, and Essex was left with a white elephant of a hotel which could not hope to make much of a profit.

But the "inn between" refused to go under. A series of proprietors have run it as a mom-and-pop operation frequented by a steady, if unspectacular, number of enthusiasts of fishing, hiking, wilderness photography, mountain climbing, and the railroad. Larry Vielleux doesn't fantasize about a lot of growth for Essex. The town never has needed it, and that's what's so special about it. He's confident of carrying on successfully the holding action against nature and the elements—and history.

By 4:00 in the afternoon, Alice Hartzfeld has returned from Spring Hill and gives me directions to the mystery spring. Just behind the old depot, the trail to the summit begins. It is marked by blazes. Maybe a quarter mile up, it crosses a small stream. Shortly beyond the stream on the right, I will see a huge boulder, "big as a house." Here I must leave the trail and bushwack along the downhill face of the boulder. From the boulder, if I follow the contour of the hill northwest, without climbing or descending, I will cross another small stream. Then I have only to follow the stream uphill to its source, which is the mystery spring itself.

It's a bit late in the afternoon to be setting out alone on an off-trail exploration, but the destination is not far up the hill and my train home leaves at 7:00 in the morning. This is my only chance.

I'm not sure why I'm doing this. Seeking my own small piece of the western dream? Looking for trail's end in my unfinished quest for the west? Testing my nerve? Establishing my credentials as a bona fide American? Ever since the ride on the *Pioneer* through Idaho and Oregon, I have been itching to set foot off the rails, off the trail, and find for myself one of those perfect spots spoken of by followers of the western dream. It's the romance of the quest I am after. I couldn't have picked a better place to finally go for it.

As I set out the first thought is of the grizzlies, five hundred of them, according to latest Glacier Park count, as compared to the hundred or so known to inhabit Yellowstone. Earlier in the day, I read the lowdown on bears in a local recreation guide. "Bears don't like surprises." Hikers are advised to sing, clap, whistle, make lots of noise. "Bears don't like to be challenged." In a bear encounter, one should avert the eyes, make no sudden movements, and back off slowly. "Bears like their space." A wide detour around a bear's turf is a good idea. "Bears can climb trees, but don't like to." The safest place near a disturbed bear is a branch at least twelve feet up in a tree. "Bears can run faster than people." If a bear charges and climbing a tree is not an option, one should curl up in a fetal position and play dead, protecting the stomach and head until the bear goes away.

This last advice really gives me pause, and three times I stop and consider giving up the quest with these words ringing in my ears. What does this mean? Does it mean "protecting the stomach and head until the furious bear tires of mauling me"? Or does it mean "protecting the stomach and head until the curious bear stops sniffing and wanders placidly off"? The distinction is critical.

My musings are interrupted by the sound of feminine voices and footsteps on the trail above. Two of the girls in the Navigators group lope down from a quick sprint to the summit after their day of labor. Shamed, but singing too loudly to be musical, I continue on.

By the time I reach the "house" boulder, the sun's glintings pierce the heavy forest from a very low angle over my shoulder, but I reassure myself that sunset comes late in this northern latitude and take the pioneer's step off the marked trail. Now with every step into murky ferns and bushes and talus rocks a new fear germinates—snakes. Do rattlers live this far north? I don't know. As the shadows lengthen, making it increasingly difficult to trace a level contour along the slope, the whole witch's brew of forest fears bursts upon me. Spiders? Tarantulas live in the desert, I think. But ticks carrying Rocky Mountain spotted fever don't. Scorpions? Desert creatures, I think. What about big cats? What about dangers that I never heard of?

The welcome splash of the stream breaks the bad spell. Following the waters of the brook uphill is less scary, though the mossed rocks are slippery and I begin to think it was pretty stupid to do this alone. From occasional breaks in the foliage I can see the hotel below; I keep climbing.

Then I am brought up short. There is a fork in the stream that Alice didn't mention. Am I following the wrong brook? And if not, which way to go? I try to apply the same kind of reasoning that Lewis and Clark used when they encountered the Marias River, even though I know it led them away from the better passage. In a situation like this, it isn't having the most rational plan that matters. It is simply having a plan.

I theorize that the stream coming from the pool would be larger. The stream to the right is larger, and through the trees up above I think I see more sky than above the smaller one to the left. With a reason for making one choice over the other, I climb up along the stream from the right.

My singing has kept me from seeing much wildlife. There were prairie dogs down near the start of the trail, and a large owl watched me pass the house boulder without blinking. Just beyond the fork in the stream, a weasel-like creature sits on a rock dipping his head in a strange gesture that seems laden with meaning. Is it a warning, a mating dance? The creature is not at all timid and stands his ground until I am just a few feet away and then scurries off in the brush.

Just when I am convinced that I'm lost, no pool having presented itself and the sinking sun casting dangerously long shadows up the slope of Mount St. Nicholas across the valley, I hear the sound of falling water. I come up over a rocky outcropping where the foliage opens out toward the gulf of the valley. A little waterfall spills from moss stalactites clinging to an overhanging ledge. But there is no pool. The water splatters on a boulder, runs down its sides, and continues on down the stream I have just climbed.

From the opening in the tree canopy I can look northwest up the Flathead Valley. There is the river, there the highway, and, yes, there are the tracks of the Great Northern. Across the way the late red sunlight glints off the peak of Mount St. Nicholas. I may be lost, there may be another clearing with a pool, but this one will do just fine.

Without bothering to take off my shirt or my sneakers, I climb up on the waterfall boulder, the icy splash on my head sending electric thrills to my very toes. The sweat and the tension of the climb wash away. Yellow butterflies flit in the clearing and hallucinogenic magenta wildflowers spark at its verge.

I had thought to watch the westbound *Empire Builder* come through the valley, but the declining sun and the probability that the train will be late force me to abandon this plan. And anyway the BN provides a satisfactory surrogate in the long freight that shortly rounds the curve at the end of the river. I can see the exhaust from its laboring engines conjuring up a blue cloud that drifts with the valley breeze, almost keeping up with the train itself. The top of my head is numb from the arctic waterfall, but I force myself to stay seated in its splash as the train approaches. I hear the deep rumble of the engines reverberating off the mountain walls and, as the engines pass just beneath me, the sandpaper rasp of the exhaust ripping the quiet sunset air.

For a moment the universe shifts. I imagine I can see all the way to Chicago, beyond to New York, up the inland rail route to Springfield, and even farther up Highway 10 to Keene and the rocky, forested New Hampshire hillside where I cleared the trees and built my house ten years ago and to Lake Sunapee where my father and mother finally retired from their travels for their golden years. From there I can look back west over the first Pacific railroad to San Francisco, across the southern deserts to New Orleans, up the Mississippi to Chicago, along the southern Piedmont to circle the heartland through Bloomington, out over the Santa Fe and the southern Rockies, across the deserts and into the strongholds of the mountain men, through the Cascades and over the Columbia, up and down the West Coast and back here to my rock above the valley of the Northwest Passage—the entire odyssey of the past six months, tangible; the map of America lifted off the page and imprinted in experience. Grenville Dodge and Gary Holtsoi, William Faulkner and Dan Stevens, Fred Harvey and Larry Vielleux, Brigham Young and Lori Olsen, Colonel Holliday and Fred Diehl, Harvey girls and Navigators, Jim Clyman and Kurt Ferguson, John Sutter and Sarah Webb, Lewis and Clark and all of those passengers who take the train to explore the continent—Frank Pindell and his son and his grandson—a tableau of American experience in a flow as continuous as the waterfall washing over my head.

Without realizing it, I was beginning to lose faith in my journey. Till now I had continued to feel a stranger in my own land, an alien observer of other people's stories in a passing drama where I was an interloper. But I too have participated deeply in the fundamental rite of the national heritage. It only required 27,000 miles of riding the rails and climbing a thousand feet to a place where the miles and years converged on a wet rock in the sky to realize that now I have a story to tell, that it is a story of America, that it was my own story all along.

My father walked away from his father's dream of the railroad to pursue his own dream to be somebody. He sent me to a good college and paid for all of it. I always thought he hoped I would follow him into medicine, but when I switched majors from science to literature, he uttered not a word of protest as long as I still made dean's list.

So I defied him in other ways. I threw myself into the generational combat of the sixties, using my college education not to be someone, but to rise above his cultural limitations. He was the quintessential American, but he never understood anything about America. I never forgave him for that, and I let him know it in a thousand gestures of rejection. Still he uttered not a word of protest. Now I see why. Since we would occasionally play tennis or go fishing or watch a football game, he probably considered himself lucky. He had seen it all before.

When the headaches and dizziness began, it was exciting finally to be able to beat him at tennis. It never occurred to me that something deadly was skewing the marvelous athletic coordination that had made him a whiz on the tennis court or in a baseball infield. When I saw him on my birthday in 1985, he tried to explain that he thought the "benign" brain tumor he was about to have removed at the Lahey Clinic was something more serious and that he was scared. I couldn't take his fear seriously.

He entered the Lahey Clinic that September. The first operation created complications. The Cardinals were in the World Series that year and I watched the games with him in his hospital room, but he could no longer even follow the action. There were more operations, and after each one he would ask, "Are we going home now?"

Then came the relapses and the systemic infections. In February, we watched our New England Patriots lose the Super Bowl. It was the last time I saw him conscious. After he died in March, the autopsy showed half a dozen strange malignant tumors in his nervous system. He was only fifty-nine. The next year I ran for mayor and then began making tracks.

The BN freight has disappeared into the eastern gloaming now, and I am numb to the water that holds me transfixed on my rock in the sky.

But now I know why I came all this distance. It fell to me to atone not only for myself, but for my father as well. That's why it had to be rails, why it had to be a story of America—a story that might reveal to men like me and my father something they need to know. I have my dream too. I was a teacher for seventeen years.

Down the mountain I slip and stumble, the light waning in the northwest. It's almost embarrassing how quickly I reach the valley and the tracks. My perch couldn't have been more than five hundred feet up.

The Navigators are now paired up in study teams all over the lawn. Their text is Peter I: how to keep the faith amid persecution. Crossing the lawn, I stop to listen to a conversation between one of the veterans and one of the rookies. The veteran is seeking information about the spiritual development of rookie's wayward partner. Rookie is loyal and boosts his absent partner. Veteran asks how goes the Peter. Rookie holds up the preprinted Navigators interpretation sheet and says, "I suppose you can get that out of it, but it doesn't say that." Veteran says you'll get the hang of it.

The two Navigators stare at my dripping wet clothes with question in their look. Turning and pointing to the mountain I have just descended, I remember Lori Olsen, "Let us find our own tablets," and so resist the urge to shake them by the ears and show them mine.

Inside, Frank Krshka says the weasel-like creature was probably a marmot. Larry is glad I didn't wait for the *Empire Builder*—it is two hours late. Alice Hartzfeld insists that her spot was a pool you could submerge your whole body in. I have apparently found my own place.

In the morning the Navigators are up at six-thirty reading Peter. Twenty-two-year-old Christina Beall wants to know if I accept Jesus as my personal savior. I can't say that I do, but I tell her about a man I know in Mississippi who quit his lifetime alcoholism when he asked Jesus for help.

My train is an hour and a half late, so Frank Krshka invites me to accompany him on his morning chore down to the river where he measures the water depth for the U.S. Forestry Service. Frank is a retired AM radio man: announcer, DJ, programmer, sales manager, general manager, and finally owner of several stations in Montana. He and his wife loved the mountains and "the slow life," so they bought a general merchandise store in the valley, but a serious heart attack and a four-way-bypass operation put an end to that. He just hung around and helped out at the Walton Inn until Larry Vielleux asked him to do it for pay.

Off Route 2 we drive down a dirt road into the dense riverside forest.

The pickup pushes its way through pine boughs that hang down a foot above the dirt and then stops. "From here we walk," says Frank. "You know what not to do if we meet the grizz?"

Down a muddy path through tall weeds sprouting fuzz blossoms that look like the lights on motorboats, we push our way. Suddenly the brush blows up in front of us. Something crashes toward us, and Frank turns toward me for a sickening moment with his hand on his heart. Bear lore and CPR strategies tangle in my head. A gray shape bounds past us and plunges into the brake beyond.

"Jackrabbit, a big one," gasps Frank. "Thought it was the grizz." He holds his chest, panting, and decides that the ticker will hold.

We measure the water depth from shore with binoculars. The concrete posts of the highway bridge are marked at two-foot intervals. Today the waters rush by just above the two-foot mark. We call it two and a half and head back to the hotel to make our report. "That's low," says Larry. I picture dust-blown farmers struggling somewhere in Kansas. Here at the source, it is the first time I have really thought about the drought that has struck the nation during my travels.

My train arrives an hour and a half late. As I board, the Navigators are already on hands and knees laying bricks for the new walk. Larry and Linda and their grandchildren wave to the train from their porch. The Hartzfelds are in the swing, he rapt in thoughts of the two thousand miles of rail ahead of the *Empire Builder*, she checking hiking maps for her day's challenge. Frank is in the parking lot pointing at a large deer that has stopped by to say hello. And the BN trainmen stand at the dining-room window just finishing their second cups of coffee. Their helper engines chug at idle on the sidings just as they always have. Somewhere up the slope of Spring Hill the water splashes down the sides of mystery rock—just as it always has—here at the place where all the rails lead, in a million acres of wilderness.

The climb to Marias Pass is wild and breathtaking. I spot elk, deer, mountain goats, and more marmots as the train winds up to the mile-high pass. The cliffs and peaks tower vertically enough that I realize I am looking at them through the glass in the roof of the lounge-observation car. As we roll through timber snowsheds intended to protect trains from avalanches, the scene conjures one last story I gathered from the library of local history last night at the inn.

While nature found dozens of ways to harass the "holding action" of the Great Northern in the Montana Rockies, none provided the railroad men with such total defeat as the avalanches. Here, as in the Cascades, the conditions are perfect for them—steep slopes with trees precariously rooted in shallow soil, and snow depths up to twenty feet in the valleys, perhaps over forty up on the cornices that hang, in late winter, like a guillotine's blade, hundreds, sometimes thousands of feet above the path of the railroad.

The winter of 1929, nineteen years after the disaster at Wellington, brought consistently cold and snowy weather from December right through March, and as the inhabitants of the valley watched the cornices growing on the ridges, a sense of dread loomed. They waited for the first big thaw that would bring it all down. There were no helicopter-riding avalanche dynamiters in those days, and a long spell without small avalanches guaranteed the big one.

In late March the thaw came suddenly. Section foreman Philip Tanas lived with his wife and two children in a small house on a steep slope high above the tracks near Singleshot. For two nights after the thaw began he lay awake listening to the mountain moan. Old-timers explain that in the days before avalanche management, this warning was caused by rocks and boulders worked loose by the flow of snowmelt creating slow-motion mud slides underneath the unbroken snow mass.

On Saturday, Tanas used his day off to get his family out to Kalispell. On his own now, he got involved in a card game that night and never made it back to his house. His R&R saved his life, for while he was thus engaged, the first break came, and his house was swept away. In the morning Tanas surveyed the tracks of the avalanche. It had been a fairly moderate one, erasing his house and the railroad's telegraph lines, but leaving the rails themselves passable. The great mass of the huge cornices still hung high in the warm morning sunlight. The mountain continued to growl that night.

Monday morning, mail train 27, the same run that had been one of the two swept away at Wellington in 1910, stopped short of the avalanche area to unload supplies to repair the telegraph lines. Tanas was there and advised the engineer, "Get outa here as quick as you can, because that whole mountain's going to come down. It's been growling all night." But the engineer felt confident that in these modern times, the railroad had covered all of the truly dangerous areas with snowsheds, and he wanted to get through. And so after a wait for the supplies to be unloaded, he blasted his whistle and pulled out. By then the sun was high and warm. Gusts of warm spring air puffed up the valley from the south.

In the meantime, Tanas and trackwalker Gus Mazios had hiked down the line to a point just beyond a snowshed checking to see that the tracks were clear. As the train emerged from the snowshed, section workers farther down the line shouted a warning and pointed high toward the cornices that had been hanging up there just a few moments before. They were gone now, and a huge white cloud was tearing down the mountainside. Without even looking up, Tanas and Mazios scrambled for the safety of the snowshed a few hundred feet away. Then they heard the thunder of the avalanche, knew they'd never make it, and leaped over the embankment. They were buried instantly. Their bodies weren't found for eight days.

As Tanas and Mazios jumped to their deaths, the train had just emerged from the snowshed. The slide lifted the rear seven cars off the tracks, like a wave lifting a string of surfers paddling out beyond the breakers, and swept them away. Somehow the engine and lead car broke free and powered through the far edge of the avalanche to the safety of another snowshed. The conductor, brakeman, and postal crew were in the lead car playing cards when the avalanche struck, which saved their lives, though after the investigation they were disciplined for not being at their posts in the rear car, where they would have died for sure.

Some were not so lucky. A mail clerk stuck his head out of a mail car's sliding door to see what was coming down, and the impact of the slide rolled the door shut, beheading him in an instant. A telegraph lineman clung to the top of his pole as the white tidal wave surged past till the pole snapped, carrying him over the side to his death. Others were injured but were later dug out of the snow below the line alive. The wreck could have been another Wellington, but for the fact that the train carried only a handful of passengers.

Rescue and wrecker trains from Essex had to plow through seventeen smaller avalanches to reach the site of the big one, where they found the crash sight brightly decorated with dozens of bolts of colored silk carried in a mail car that had broken in two. The tableau provided a reminder that the empire that stretched through the Northwest Passage even to the Orient still paid its dues when nature flexed her muscle.

Marias Pass itself is a wide green saddle, with little lakes scattered about the grassy downs, tall craggy glaciered peaks to the north, and older-looking forested mountains to the south. A statue on the left commemorates John Stevens's discovery of the passage in 1889, and an obelisk on the right marks the continental divide itself.

At the base of the eastern slope lies the Glacier Park Lodge, built by the railroad in 1913 of ancient trees, some as much as six hundred years old and forty inches in diameter. Today gaily clad vacationers play tennis and golf and splash in the pool here at the gateway to the passage the Blackfeet kept hidden for a century. This lodge is only some thirty miles from the Izaac Walton Inn, but with its parking lot filled with BMWs and Winnebagos it seems as if we have rolled a continent and a century away from Essex.

Beyond the lodge, the mountains end abruptly. There are no foothills. The train crosses a trestle over the Two Medicine River and wends out across low rolling plains, grazing land, the Blackfoot Indian Reservation.

I watch the mountains recede from the window of the corridor door of the last car as the rails roll out from underneath at seventy-five miles per hour. From the top of a slight rise I capture a last glimpse of the west, a glacier sparkling on a peak named for Slippery Bill Morrison. Then down the eastern slope of the rise the mountains fall below the horizon for good.

Thomas Jefferson sent Lewis and Clark to investigate a tract of land that he suspected would shape the nation's destiny. In 1893, Frederick Jackson Turner crystallized the theory that became dogmatic myth, that the experience of the vast frontier west forged an American culture totally different from its European forebears. America was a radical departure from the past that made the past itself, in American eyes, forever suspect.

President Ronald Reagan was the myth's most eloquent spokesman in the 1980s with his paradoxically nostalgic message of America as the western promise of a better future: ". . . a settler pushes west and sings his song, and the song echoes out forever and fills the unknowing air. It is the American sound: it is hopeful, bighearted, idealistic—daring, decent, and fair. That's our heritage, that's our song. We sing it still. For all our problems, our differences, we are together as of old. . . . In this blessed land there is always a better tomorrow."

In this view, the history of America is of the west overwhelming the stagnant eastern and European past. The only remnant of the past worthy of the myth is the dream of a better tomorrow. Ironically, this generates a national history which self-destructs, always turning its back on the heritage that might engender a sense of national continuity and community. Thus we plow under our prairie and clear-cut our forests, pave over our fields, tear down our great buildings, rip up the tracks of our railroads, and turn away from our fathers.

The one constant is the essentially unbroken tradition of European-style exploitation and empire—from the fur-trading companies to the railroads to the land developers, mall developers, airline conglomerates, and highway builders of the twentieth century. There is a school of modern western historians who use this point to debunk the Turner myth. In their view, the west didn't mold America, Americans motivated by the European habit of empire shaped the west. The problems of the new world don't spring from birth pangs of a new order, but from apoplexy in an old one which has never learned to see itself properly.

Riding the rails throughout the west today, one doesn't find a clear resolution to this debate. One can't just dismiss the Turner-Reagan thesis. There are things going on here—have been for two centuries—that constitute a radical new cast of the dice in the human condition. But neither can one deny the overwhelming continuity of an imperial conquest that reveals itself in the network of rails themselves as well as all of the contemporary images of economic exploitation that threaten to subdue the very spirit of the west. Did the west conquer America or did America conquer the west? Is the west the promise of a better future to come or the last graveyard of a past never properly apprehended? I think of the holding action of the railroad against the mountains and of the mountains against the railroad. Maybe it hasn't been settled yet.

Chapter Seventeen

——————

Way East

THE *EMPIRE BUILDER*, THE *BROADWAY LIMITED*, THE *BANKERS*

A few of the native westerners I met in my quest for the west used a unique idiom when referring to the east. Instead of the familiar "back east," Max and Bea MacLain, Lori Olsen, Kurt Ferguson, Sarah Webb, and others always said "way east." The etiology of the native easterner's phrase "out west" is clear. The preposition suggests escape, expanse, and space—the qualities that drive easterners out here. The meaning of "back east" is evident also—it's the place behind you, from which you came, upon which you may choose to turn your back, and to which you reserve the right to return if things don't work out.

But "way east" invites metaphysical speculation. It is far away, perhaps farther than "out west." It is alien and intimidating, suspect though possibly not relevant. And yet it might be the faraway place where all the buttons are pushed that make things happen as they do here, out west. Thus it's distrusted and remote enough that one doesn't know for sure what to make of it.

All day long the *Empire Builder* struggles eastward against the immensity of the Montana and Dakota high plains along the Milk and then the Missouri rivers. The drought has burned the crops and devastated the economies of the little communities which huddle against bends in the river. I don't know what these places—Shelby, Havre, Malta—look like in good times, but today they are scenes out of a pioneer woman's worst nightmare. The barren fields lie scorched and lifeless as if scourged by fire-breathing devils riding the puffy clouds that scud overhead without releasing their moisture. I picture the woman Beret in Rölvaag's *Giants in the Earth,* gazing at the treeless horizon, waiting for some unknown horrible disaster to loom up out of the vastness and swallow her utterly. "Nothing to hide behind," she said. It's no wonder that so many made the less-known trek in the other direction, back east, back toward the rivers and the settled haunts of men, having met the limits of the frontier spirit here on the dry northern prairie.

There is another less glorious chapter in the tale of James Hill's empire that unfolded in these high plains during the decades surrounding the turn of the century. Hill's railroad was not the first to misrepresent the climate and the agricultural potential of lands promoted for settlement. The Northern Pacific's Jay Cooke had earlier established a benchmark of infamy by distributing, throughout Europe, weather maps of the northern prairie with distorted isotherms suggesting far warmer temperatures and by advertising his eastern terminus, Duluth, as a place whose similar latitude guaranteed a climate like that of Paris. Hill's misrepresentation of the region turned more on the issue of aridity than temperature. His agents bombarded land-hungry Europeans with descriptions of perfect conditions for raising gold mines of wheat and other grains. Illustrations of successful farms in Illinois and Indiana were represented as being located in the Dakotas or Montana, where a much drier climate prevails. Elaborate theories were devised to demonstrate that rainfall on the northern prairie was actually increasing yearly, perhaps even as a result of the railroad itself. The oft-repeated phrase "Rain follows the plow" implied that the railroads' settlement of the land was changing the climate in a favorable direction. Propagandists argued that the electricity of the telegraph lines, the sounds of the locomotives, and the seeding of clouds with smoke contributed to ever-increasing rainfall. The railroad lobby forced even government scientists working on the Geological Survey to strike out all references to areas of semiaridity and instead use the term "semihumidity."

The terrible truth was that the rail and the plow were changing the environment to the opposite effect. First there were the grasshoppers, whose voraciousness increased exponentially to the amount of acreage cultivated. Then there was drought, naturally occurring in ten-year cycles, but made increasingly devastating because of the loss of plowed topsoil to the steady high-plains wind. The first disaster began in the late 1880s and continued till nearly 1900. When drought struck again between 1910 and 1919, homesteaders began heading east in greater numbers than those moving west. Fully 80 percent of the area settled by the GN was not suited to crop agriculture, and even the remaining fruitful land, which had initially yielded twenty-five bushels to the acre, yielded less than two and a half bushels by the end of World War I.

The distress and anger of plains farmers, with dozens of other grievances besides drought, brought to fruition a long-simmering political movement which, coinciding with the close of the frontier, sounded the death knell for the reality—if not the myth—of American frontier individualism. The Granger movement and public clamor for regulation of railroad safety in the 1870s had already established a slim precedent of government intrusion into the prerogatives of the railroad empire builders. The main issues for the grangers then had been the railroads' high rates, land monopolization, ability to make or break communities and properties, domination of state governments, and "public be damned attitude." Grangers proposed various specific forms of regulation, most of which failed to rein in the empire builders in the gilded age, but the principles of the movement succeeded in landmark Supreme Court decisions of 1877: *Peik* v. *Chicago & North Western*, and *Chicago, Burlington & Quincy* v. *Iowa*. In these cases the railroads contended that they were private businesses which the state had no right to regulate, that companies were protected by preexisting charters, that the Constitution forbade states from impairing contracts, that low regulated rates were confiscatory in leaving no room for profit, and that states couldn't regulate railroads because they crossed state lines. The Supreme Court rejected all these arguments (though some hedging occurred later concerning the issues of crossing state lines and confiscatory rates), establishing once and for all the states' right to regulate private enterprise when there is a clear public interest involved.

Now with the turn of the century, the Populist Party, building on these earlier gains, advocated radical extensions of government power and reform of the sources of government legitimacy to provide western settlers with guarantees of survival. The Populist platform called for direct election of senators, maintenance of monetary stability through the coinage of silver, reclamation of unsold and undeveloped railroad land, establishment of federal postal savings banks, a graduated income tax to reduce the economic leverage of the moneyed over the common man, government ownership of telegraph lines and the rail-roads themselves, limitation of the President's office to a single term, adoption of the secret ballot, government crop storage, and a program of federal agricultural loans and irrigation projects. Much of this pro-gram, of course, has since been adopted. Ironically, the most substan-tial inheritance of the nation from the frontier experience may be the death of frontier individualism itself—the transition, in the words of historian Frederick Merk, "from the old frontier individualism to the concept of the welfare state."

Taking the train way east is more to me now than a homecoming; it's a reenactment of another less mythologized epic American journey of rediscovery. Going west, the rail traveler can identify with the pioneers as a historical point of reference. Going east, I cast about in imagination for models. There were lots of pioneers who packed it in and headed back, defeated by blizzards, locusts, Indians, drought, economics, or simply an environment too barren for the human spirit. Some were done in by their lack of strength or fortitude; some fled because there was "nothing to hide behind."

The train passes within sight of the Bear Paw Mountains, where one eastward journey came to an end. It was here in 1877 that Chief Joseph of the Nez Percé Indians gave up his seventeen-hundred-mile running battle with the U.S. Cavalry. After the discovery of gold led to white renunciation of treaties guaranteeing the Nez Percé a substantial res-ervation in their native lands in Idaho, Chief Joseph led his tribe, with women and children in tow, fighting the white man all the way, to this spot, where he uttered legendary words of peace: "I want to have time to look for my children and see how many I can find. Maybe I shall find them among the dead. . . . I am tired, my heart is sick and sad. From where the sun now stands, I will fight no more forever."

In the past decade, the eastbound *Empire Builder* has become a favorite of Japanese on pilgrimage to the engine that jump-started their own fantastic economy, the U.S. northeast. Accustomed to their "bullet trains" at home, these modern eastbound pilgrims find Amtrak to be delightfully quaint, just as interstate-driving Americans do the narrow country roads of the Cotswolds in England. New York is almost always their destination, and from there they fly back home. The train route also satisfies their almost mystical fascination with the immensity of the American landscape.

Who else rides way east today? Mary Black, whom I met in a bar car between New Orleans and Chicago, is working the bar on this train now. "It's a lot longer and slower run than that high-speed rattletrap I met you on before. But nobody stabs teddy bears on this train. No crazies, nobody in a hurry, no Mardi Gras rowdies, just easy people looking to see the other side of the country mostly."

Today the *Empire Builder* convoys an advance party of the 116th Engineering Battalion of the National Guard from Idaho to Devil's Lake, North Dakota, where their unit will build some bridges. Someone forgot to assemble the vehicles needed for a standard convoy, so at the last minute they were all told to get on the train. It's a real treat to travel this way, though they express some disappointment about their fellow passengers. They had heard that the trains are frequented by available women. That hasn't turned out to be the case on this run, so they have dubbed it "the neuter commuter."

The smoking section of the bar car features a print of a railroad switch, and a discussion of railroad terms ensues. I point out the frog, the wedge-shaped piece of track located where one rail crosses over another, and wonder why it is called a frog. A sergeant suggests that it's where one track "jumps" another. Someone else suggests that in the Army it would be an acronym. Another suggestion is that it's a corruption of some foreign railroading word. But one guardsman insists that it looks like a frog. I wonder how he can see a frog in that wedge shape, and he asks me where I am from. I say New Hampshire. He says, "Well, there you go. You don't have frogs like that so far way east."

A National Park Service ranger from Montana is headed east to a conference in Washington. He takes on the 116th Regiment in an argument over environmental legislation. He holds his own concerning limiting of the antelope hunt (antelope are too few and too easy—their curiosity makes them approach rather than flee a noisy hunter in a blind), protecting grizzlies (the National Guard concedes that their demise would be a national loss, and they're harmless to everyone except those stupid enough to provoke a mauling), and tightening acid-rain controls (the National Guard likes to fish).

But the Guard stands its ground on wolf bounties and ATVs. They want to know who would feel less proud of America if it contained no wolves. One even suggests that a bounty war on wolves would further the cause of peace, giving natural-born fighting men a harmless or even beneficial campaign on which to vent their atavistic need for combat. And as for ATVs, the Guard wants to know what good are millions of square miles of western wilderness if you can't make use of them. And how can a few ATVs threaten the vast spaces which have been so resistant to conquest by man for so long anyway?

Ranger gamely tries to explain the environmental paradox of the west, that this landscape that seems so rugged, so tough, is actually among the most fragile in the world, therefore the most threatened by man's activities. The Guard doesn't buy it, and after a few more rounds of beer decides that what the west really needs is a bounty war on wolves by Guardsmen mounted on ATVs.

Another kind of regiment also rides the *Empire Builder* today. A Southern Baptist missionary group from Texas is crossing the upper midwest to witness for Jesus and proselytize for their denomination. It's a family affair with cute towheaded small boys, fetching teenage southern belles, and silver-shocked Norman Rockwell grandparents part of the hook. I haven't been able to get any of the evangelicals I've met in my travels to admit it, but I'm convinced that one basis of their pitch is that people who look so good must be on to something. So they really work at it and succeed. A mother and father playing hearts ask if I've considered that it might be God's hand. Since they are doing God's work, maybe his grace shines in their appearance.

No, I hadn't thought of that, but it touches a very original American creed. Our New England Puritans believed that you could not change through your works whether you were one of God's elect or not, but you could discern your predestined status before God in your material success. Thus the Puritans amassed wealth as proof that they were among the chosen. In glamour-conscious twentieth-century America, it is a small step from the Puritans' creed to belief that proof of being born again shows in physical beauty.

A young man from Portland is traveling to New York to perfect his skills and find his fortune as an auctioneer. "I coulda stayed in Portland if all I wanted was to sell off the junk in deceased old ladies' houses. But I wanta get into art and big-time antique collectibles. Ya gotta go east to do that." He's never been east of the Mississippi before and took the train to fill in one of his own geographical white spaces. "Ya got mountains and deserts out west, plains in the midwest, and cities along the east coast. What the hell is in between the plains and the cities?"

And then there are two boys who have just graduated from junior high school in Spokane and are traveling without their parents to Memphis to visit their grandmother as a graduation present. Their luggage consists mainly of a mammoth stash of candy bars, peanuts, and potato chips. In my trainwalk earlier, I have met two girls the same age riding alone on the train to visit the divorced father of one of them in Chicago. I trade this piece of intelligence to the two boys for one of their Snickers bars. Later I see the foursome giggling over burgers in the snack bar, still later sharing pizza slices and holding hands in front of the evening movie, and, near midnight, their two pairs of heads huddled together in the observation-car moonlight, starry-eyed and whispering, all thought of food now banished. For them the memory of riding a train way east is forever cast in glory.

Jim Hill himself relegated the passenger train to something less than glamorous status, declaring it to be "like the male teat—neither useful nor ornamental." He was not referring to the simple emigrant trains that brought settlers to build his empire; rather the expensive flagship trains like the New York Central's *20th Century Limited*, the Union Pacific's *Overland Limited*, the Santa Fe's *Chief*, the Southern Pacific's *Sunset Limited*, and the Northern Pacific's *North Coast Limited* provoked his disdain. In his day, Hill's entrant into this competition was the *Oriental Limited*, a slow (seventy-two hours between Chicago and Seattle), nondescript "luxury" train which thrived primarily because the competition, the NP's *North Coast Limited*, was even slower due to the NP's route through the Rocky Mountains.

But after Hill's retirement, there was a change of attitude in Great Northern management. Other railroads had succeeded in founding their identities on the fast wheels of big-name luxury passenger trains. Though the GN served virtually no population centers except at its termini, Glacier National Park attracted almost as many fares as a major city. The Puget Sound area was booming, and intercontinental travel to Asia increasingly flowed through Seattle. In 1929, in conjunction with the opening of the second Cascade Tunnel, the GN inaugurated the *Empire Builder*, a passenger train intended to rival the *20th Century Limited* and surpass any of the other western luxury trains. Initially carded at sixty-two hours, the route would shrink to forty-five by the end of World War II (today Amtrak's version is carded for forty-eight but rarely meets that schedule). The railroad kicked off its new service with a series of radio programs, "The Empire Builders," nationally broadcast in cooperation with NBC. The first four broadcasts featured an adventure drama of the Royal Canadian Mounted Police, a romance built around the inaugural run of the *Empire Builder*, a narrated tour of Glacier Park, and a fast-paced "day in the life of . . ." drama about the operations of a modern GN train-dispatching office.

All four presented the *Empire Builder* in a lead role as a manifestation of the future of civilization in the northwest.

In addition to the usual first-class amenities found on other great passenger trains, the *Empire Builder* featured a glass-canopied "Observation-Solarium Lounge" with carved walnut panels, parchment-shaded lamps, easy chairs, tapestries, writing desks, a buffet, and a mixologist ensconced in an early Tudor decor. Appointments in the heavyweight six-wheel-trucked sleepers, dining cars, and coaches throughout the train continued this level of opulence in a year that began with the promise of wealth within every man's reach. But after the crash, it appeared that Hill's animosity toward extravagant passenger trains might be vindicated. Eventually only a scaled-back and unprofitable *Empire Builder* continued to make the run between Chicago and Seattle until the 1940s, and the *Oriental Limited* was dropped from service entirely.

By World War II a new technology had begun to revolutionize passenger travel. In 1934, the Burlington ran its first diesel-powered streamliner from Denver to Chicago. In 1935 the Union Pacific inaugurated regular service on the diesel-powered streamliner *City of Portland* from Chicago to Portland. Aside from the novelty, the diesel trains, which could cross the continent without time-consuming engine changes, knocked twelve hours off the old steam-driven schedule. To businessmen, it meant an extra day for productive work. The time savings must have been analogous to that produced by the supersonic Concorde in recent years, and the sensational public response was just what the promoters of the Concorde hoped for and never really received.

The GN responded with air-conditioned semistreamlined luxury coaches but held back from fully adopting the new technology. A huge investment in the original *Empire Builder* had not yet paid for itself, and the rival NP and Milwaukee Road seemed in no hurry to take the plunge either. As if by "gentlemen's agreement" all three continued to make the Chicago-Seattle run with steam power on a schedule of about sixty hours. The UP could have the fast-trackers traveling to Portland. The real northwest business was Seattle.

World War II changed everything. With armies to be transported and a nation literally on the move, all transcontinental railroads had more passenger business than they could carry. The *Oriental Limited* was pressed back into service, and extra cars were added to all GN trains, including the *Empire Builder*. Diesels first appeared in GN passenger service at Essex as helpers to haul the unusually long passenger trains over Marias Pass. The old *Empire Builder* equipment was wearing out fast in 1943 when GN management ordered five complete new streamlined passenger trains from Pullman and diesels to power them. These trains were revolutionary in more respects than their engines. Lightweight, lower, longer, and sometimes featuring four-wheel instead of six-wheel trucks, these passenger cars heralded the trend that Maxwell Greene ascribes to "the socialist influence." Less glamorous than the old heavyweights, they were built for speed. Now the schedule from Chicago was cut to forty-five hours, and crowds turned out all along the route to watch the new *Empire Builder* burn up the prairie.

After the war, the *Empire Builder* showed itself to be particularly resistant to the forces bringing doom to many of the great passenger trains. Passenger traffic continued to increase and enabled the GN to institute innovations which still leave their mark on American rail travel today. The GN completely abandoned the old open-berth sleepers in favor of cars with private rooms and built the "slumber-coaches" still used on eastern Amtrak runs, which provide tiny private sleeping compartments at little more than the cost of a coach seat. Capitalizing on the magnificent scenery of the Rockies and Cascade crossings, GN developed the dome coaches, which proved so popular that many upscale passengers chose those accommodations over sleeping cars. Most significant, these new cars were not built by Pullman, but were Budd cars constructed around a stainless-steel center beam, which gave them the longevity that makes them the backbone of Amtrak's eastern Heritage fleet today.

The pre-Amtrak *Empire Builder* outlived the *20th Century Limited*, the *Broadway Limited*, and the *Overland*. When Amtrak assumed most of the nation's passenger routes in 1971, Burlington Northern management considered continuing the *Builder* in private service as the DRG did with its *California Zephyr* and the Southern did with its *Crescent*. The decision to turn the run and, more important, its equipment over to Amtrak was a major factor in Amtrak's eventual success. Today Amtrak's *Empire Builder* is equipped with the new double-decker Superliners, whose spectacular size and spaciousness seem especially well-suited to this route, but I'm looking forward to changing trains in Chicago, where the real *Empire Builder*'s old rock-solid cars still ply the tracks at ninety miles per hour.

Morning along miles and miles of Mississippi. Early fishermen hold up their catches to show off for the passing train while dredges struggle to deepen the channel of the rain-starved waterway. The drought is a boon to fishermen, decreasing the volume of the river and thus concentrating the fish. For everyone else it is a disaster. If it continues, even dredging won't keep the channel open, but when the crops fail, there won't be much to haul anyway. Burned corn stretches to the Minnesota horizon, where there is still no hint of rain.

The green hills, limestone bluffs, and blue lakes south of La Crosse, Wisconsin, contrast sharply with the predominant imagery of desolation I have watched for most of this ride, and I have plenty of time to appreciate them, because the train has problems here. The Soo Line bought this stretch of track from the Milwaukee Road a few years ago, and someone lost the records of track maintenance. The railroad had no idea how close the rails were to metal fatigue until several freight derailments highlighted the problem. Now the tracks between Minneapolis and Milwaukee are posted at ten miles an hour over numerous stretches where relining is being done. My destination way east begins to seem ever more remote as the service crew explains what will happen in Chicago, where many of us are going to miss eastern connections. At Milwaukee I take a long shot and give the conductor a message to relay ahead to Union Station requesting a ticket transfer and bedroom reservation on the *Broadway Limited* to New York, just in case I miss my intended connection with the earlier *Capitol Limited* to Washington.

In my sleeping car we are pampered during the slow run by the superlative attentions of sleeping-car attendant Sabrina Butler. Sabrina's coffeepot is always full, and she has it set up in the central vestibule where you can always get at it. She has also stocked the little vestibule with magazines, peppermint candies, fruit juices, and an ice chest. She shows no signs of fatigue, even though she has been on her feet in a moving train for most of two days. To Sabrina I award the "Making Tracks Commendation for Most Outstanding Sleeping-Car Attendant." It's a small gesture, since in the rush to find a train headed east out of Chicago Union Station, I forget to tip for the first time in my travels.

The *Empire Builder* arrives in Union Station at 7:30 P.M., three hours and twenty minutes late. My plan had been to take the *Capitol Limited* to Washington to meet some Amtrak officials before heading up the corridor home. Now my only concern is to get home by whatever route will get me there the fastest.

It's crazy in Union Station. Late commuters who know their way around sprint this way and that, jostling Amtrak riders who generally don't. The *California Zephyr* is also late, so a long line of passengers off both trains wait at the ticket windows to get seats on trains headed east. The crowd elbows for position and cranes its collective neck to read the overhead video departure board.

The *Capitol Limited* is gone, departed on time at 7:15. The *Lake Shore Limited* left for New York, Boston, and Springfield at 6:30. The slow *Cardinal* is just making last call and doesn't get into the northeast until late tomorrow night. It looks like I'll have to take my chances getting on the good old *Broadway Limited*, last train of the day headed east.

It must be ninety-five degrees in the station—I can feel the sweat gluing my shirt to my back. I have a headache; babies are crying everywhere; there is more diesel exhaust in here than I have ever seen before.

Just as I contemplate spending an unscheduled night in Chicago, a PA announcement calls a Perry Pandale to the Amtrak passenger service desk. Is it me? My long-shot message from Milwaukee? I give up my spot in line to answer the call.

The friendly agent at the desk has my transferred ticket and, telegraph be praised, a first-class roomette for me on the *Broadway Limited*. I can board now if I wish.

At the gates, an officious Amtrak employee insists the *Broadway* is not ready for boarding yet and won't let me through. But I can see train 40 on track 24. When the doors open for a baggage cart, I zip through. There's my sleeping car, second one up. I'm on it and in my room without a hitch. I crank up the air conditioning full blast and down comes the curtain, down comes the sink. Off with the sweaty clothes. Cold water, soap, splash, splash—relief. For fifteen minutes I have the *Broadway Limited* all to myself.

By the time boarding is announced, I am washed and refreshed and in my last change of clean clothes. It's time for reunions. My car attendant is J. R. Stokes, whom I met previously on the *Cardinal* through West Virginia, and the service chief is the woman I met on the *Crescent* to New Orleans, the former engineer. I can't believe my luck. I join them on the platform to greet the tired, sweaty, harried passengers who stream out of the gate trundling their baggage and baby carriages. "Good evening, welcome to the *Broadway Limited*."

My intent had been to meet every single passenger in my section of the train and zero in on those who are westerners heading east for the first time and thus continue the "way east" survey of my *Empire Builder* run. But as luck would have it, except for a group of young guys who are new Amtrak reservations employees riding in the last sleeping car as part of their training program, they are all easterners headed home like me. The trainees board with all the rowdiness of a fraternity and invite me to join them for "some serious partying" later in the evening.

The *Broadway Limited* races out of Chicago right on time. The last time I rode this train, it was crowded with people stranded by other modes of transportation in a February blizzard; tonight it is packed with those who missed other connections. The service chief makes the obligatory announcement about doubling up in the coach seats, and I settle into my spacious roomette seat with a full bowl in my pipe and puff with satisfaction. I like the feel of the old solid Heritage car, the closeness of the tracks, and the rattling speed of the prototypical eastern train. Now I can feel the miles ticking off and the sense of headlong motion toward home.

Shortly the thought of this being my last overnight train ride makes the invitation to party sound attractive. I head back to the last car just in time to encounter a dozen grumbling Amtrak trainees who have been evicted from their sleeping-car digs. The rooms are needed for paying passengers. They will have to camp out and sleep in the lounge car.

But in the double room two doors down from mine, two cheerful young women dressed in business suits are just cracking their complimentary bottles of wine. They ask me to join them. "What shall we toast?" asks one.

"How about the end of a thirty-thousand-mile train trip?" I suggest. "Cheers."

I have found my party. Doreen Keegan and Diane Shortelle work for an interior design firm in Stamford, Connecticut, and are returning from a convention in Chicago, where they have wined and dined and danced for three days. They took the train because Doreen has a phobia about flying, elevators, cliffs, high bridges, top bunks, and a million other things. They love it. No phones, no clients, no contractors—off the treadmill.

Several of the Amtrak trainees drift back, J. R. breaks out a dozen of the little bottles of wine, and by midnight we have a crowd of participants who spill out down the corridor and into my room. For the first time in thirty thousand miles, I tell more stories than I listen to. It all comes bursting forth in a stream that makes me hoarse by bedtime. It feels good; I have gotten off my treadmill.

Pennsylvania flies by in the morning, and I drink in the greenness like a man too long without water. Running through Horseshoe Curve, along the Juniata River, across the Susquehanna, down through the Amish country, and beside the Schuylkill into Philadelphia, the *Broadway Limited* accelerates eastward, without losing a tick on its schedule.

By now I have traveled enough to have developed a habit of looking ahead and scheming ways to smooth my passage through approaching connection points. This train ends at Penn Station in New York, and it's Friday afternoon: there is no worse place to be in space and time.* Since the train is on schedule, I could make a ten-minute connection to a corridor train in Philadelphia that runs through New York, Stamford, New Haven, and right up to Springfield before heading east to Boston.

Doreen and Diane had intended to catch a commuter train out of New York for Stamford that would involve not only the detested Penn Station but also a transfer to Grand Central, from which their commuter departs. As their travel agent I advise them to join me on the corridor train that will take them right through New York all the way to Stamford. They're game and promise that if it works as well as I say it will, I can have the remainder of their considerable stash of wine to take with me for the ride up to Springfield. Done.

The connection at Philly is a breeze. As the deep buzz of the 120-mile-an-hour corridor train to the northeast resonates in the bones, Doreen holds her breath and gasps, "Whoa, this is a little like flying." I tell her it's called humming.

Over the second glass of wine, Diane tells me about herself. She grew up in Minneapolis, and always knew she wanted to do interior design. When she took a trip to Europe, she decided to make her career way east.

At thirty-one, she's never married and never looked back. "There are windows on the East Coast," she says. "The city, the ocean, old New England upcountry where you live. Out west, unless you go all the way to the coast, there aren't so many opportunities." And then there is the action, mercantile, competitive, lucrative. "I did more living in my first year working in New York than I had done in my entire life in Minnesota."

And so it goes on the corridor train, whose name, significantly, is the *Bankers*. Conversation runs to fashion, business ventures, merchandising, taste, what will sell and how to push it. One woman is opening a boutique in Darien and needs to know the prime price tier to target. A

---

*Since this writing, renovations to Penn Station have been completed. It is less unpleasant than it was, but still a feeble shadow of its former glory.

man from Lancaster is going to New York to look for a good source for handbags in the garment district. Another man from Maryland boasts that with his connections in the garment district his dress shop is untouchable in Hagerstown. A western adherent to the myths about way east would find all of his preconceptions fulfilled.

No account of passenger railroading way east would be complete without some homage to the great station whose pitiful remnants I have been trying so hard to avoid. At least in choosing to ride through the underground level without disembarking I can experience a piece of it and imagine that above me the echoes of Americans on the move still resonate in the grand glass concourse and monumental rooms of what was once our greatest piece of rail architecture, New York's Penn Station.

Throughout the era during which America conquered a continent with her railroads, a strange irony persisted in the heart of the region where the works of man seemed most triumphant. Out west the Mississippi and Missouri rivers had been bridged, the mountains tamed, and the deserts crossed. But the mighty Pennsylvania Railroad, "the standard railroad of the world," was barred from entry into New York City by a river just a few hundred miles long. All PRR trains terminated at the dreadful Exchange Place Station in Jersey City, where passengers had to board ferries for the uncomfortable passage across the Hudson River to Manhattan's West Side, a crowded maelstrom of commercial activity which made further progress into the city a greater nightmare than the crossing.

As long as the obstacle remained, the PRR could never capitalize on its more direct route to Chicago in its mortal competition with the New York Central. Even its excellent connections through Washington to southern railroads serving New Orleans and Florida foundered on the shores of the Hudson, where the most opulent service began or ended with a frantic hassle.

For thirty years, railroad president Alexander Cassatt searched for a route into Gotham. By 1890 there was a plan on the drawing boards for a suspension bridge over the river, but the cost began at $50 million and ballooned to over $100 million by the turn of the century. It would have required a span greater than twice that of Roebling's Brooklyn Bridge and extraordinary height to clear the masts of the tall ships that plied the harbor. An early attempt to tunnel under the harbor for a commuter route had ended in disaster in 1880 when the soft mud of the river bottom gave way and a crew of sandhogs died.

Other tunnels had been rejected because passengers would be asphyxiated by engine smoke in tubes so long, but by the beginning of the new century two advances in technology turned the tide in their favor. One was the development of reliable electric railroad engine systems, the other the new "shield" method of tunneling, in which a huge cylinder enclosed the excavators and moved slowly forward as the cutting edge of the tubes progressed through the mud.

By 1901, the B&O had operated electric engines successfully for five years through its harbor tunnel in Baltimore, and Cassatt also visited the new Gare Quai d'Orsay in Paris, where electric engines brought passenger trains through tunnels under the Seine into the heart of the city. Soon other developments helped shape the grand design that would ultimately soar far beyond merely tunneling under the Hudson. The Long Island Rail Road faced a similar problem with the East River, and when its president, Austin Corbin, died in 1900, Cassatt quietly bought a controlling interest in the LIRR. Meanwhile, Charles McKim, the architect who had already left his classical mark on New York, visited the Baths of Caracalla in Rome. He was so impressed with the great vaulted ceilings and huge indoor expanses of space dedicated to public purposes that he made sketches which he kept as an inspiration for a great edifice he hoped he might be called upon to build. His opportunity would come sooner than he could have dreamed.

When Cassatt returned from Paris, he set anonymous agents of the PRR to the task of buying up huge swaths of real estate across Hackensack, Manhattan Island, and Queens. The grand design now emerged. The main line in New Jersey would split off from the route to Exchange Place and cross the Hackensack meadows with a new stop built specifically as a station for changing from steam to electric engines, Manhattan Transfer. Then two tracks would plunge under the granite of Bergen Hill and the mud of the Hudson in two tubes. At Manhattan the tracks would run underground straight across the island at 32nd Street, splitting into twenty-one tracks for the new station to be located at Eighth Avenue. Here Cassatt would engage McKim to build the monumental station whose combination of classical Roman and modern European design would symbolize not only the PRR's conquest of New York and the railroad's mastery of this continent, but indeed America's emergence as a crossroads of the world.

But the plan would not stop there. The tracks would continue toward Long Island in four tunnels under the East River and Queens to link up with the LIRR tracks at a massive new rail yard in Sunnyside. Thus Penn Station would also serve as the Manhattan terminus for the LIRR.

Finally, the line would turn north, climbing a monstrous ramp over Queens to cross the narrow neck of Long Island Sound at Hell Gate on a high bridge and link up with the New York, New Haven, and Hartford. Cassatt had devised a plan that would not only bring the PRR into New York, but would provide a route through it linking Boston and New England to PRR connections to all points of the country.

Throughout the first decade of the new century the work moved forward, to the fascination and delight of New Yorkers, who saw the project as confirmation that their city was destined to be the capital of the twentieth-century world. Huge chugging air compressors on both shores of the rivers maintained pressure in the tubes, which sandhogs entered through airlocks. As the great shields inched forward, the sandhogs shoveled tons of mud and rock into rail carts. Dynamite was used to blast through the rock of Bergen Hill, and on Manhattan itself, 32nd Street simply ceased to exist as the great cut for the tracks thirty-six feet down bisected the island from river to river.

Ironically the tunneling under the Hudson was almost uneventful, but elsewhere there was trouble. A pressure blowout under the East River drowned a sandhog crew; a tardy explosion of a dynamite charge on Manhattan leveled an entire block; sandhogs suffered the bends despite elaborate precautions, including one of the world's first decompression chambers; a forgotten underground stream at 6th Street flooded the cut.

By 1909 the tunnels were completed. Under the Hudson, elaborate measurements were taken before the final excavation to guarantee that the tubes would meet properly aligned. But the night before the official connection, enthusiastic sandhogs from New Jersey shoved a box of cigars through the last barrier of mud to their Manhattan counterparts. Under the East River, where there had been greater difficulty, an eight-inch pipe was pushed through the mud to connect the two tubes and equalize the air pressure in them before the final connection was made. The difference in air pressure was initially great enough that objects could be blown through it like cartridges in a pneumatic tube. A rag doll became the first lady to make the passage under the East River.

In the meantime a struggle that was prophetic of the future was shaping up over the building of the station itself. The directors of the PRR wanted to build a hotel over the station, thus eliminating the key element in McKim's design, the vast indoor space above his great rooms. But McKim prevailed, and in 1910 the public could finally enter what was at that time America's grandest building.

Penn Station occupied two full city blocks, from 31st to 33rd Street.

Its outer perimeter of Doric columns enclosed four of the largest rooms in the world: the formal dining room and its only slightly less cavernous café, the towering arcade with its rows of fashionable shops (America's first enclosed mall), the vast echoing chasm of the waiting room with its grand staircase, and finally the concourse. If the massive pink travertine of the first three chambers harked back to the glory of the Roman Baths of Caracalla, the concourse, built entirely of iron webbing and glass, pointed the way to the future. Through its granite deck, sunken below street level, the black wrought-iron stairs descended even farther to the level of the tracks and the trains. Above, the intricate lattices of iron and glass suggested the out-of-doors and the binding spell of distant travel. Except for the red signs identifying train gates, all was black and white—an interior which captured the essence of stark black-and-white photography.

For nearly fifty years Penn Station presided over the drama of America on the move. Scores of trains arrived and departed every day, but certain ones became stars: the first-class daylight *Congressional* to Washington, the *Cannon Ball* "jazz train" to Montauk by way of the LIRR, the *Florida Special* with its luxury through cars connecting with the Florida East Coast Railway all the way to Miami, the *Havana Special* connecting to a Seaboard run to the Florida Keys and a steamship for Cuba, the *Crescent* connecting with the Southern Railroad to New Orleans and steamships to Mexico and Panama, and, of course, the *Broadway Limited* to Chicago with through coaches all the way to L.A. and San Francisco on the Santa Fe's *El Capitan* and *Chief.* There were human stars too: Charlie Chaplin, Count Basie, Albert Einstein, Will Rogers, Eleanor Roosevelt, and the Duke of Windsor were among the regulars loyal to the Pennsylvania routes out of New York.

During the Depression, Penn Station was a shelter to the homeless, as its squalid successor is again today. Two world wars marched through its great rooms as thousands of GIs had to be transported to and from the troopships. Movies were shot there and politicians made speeches there.

But near the close of World War II the end of the line appeared on the horizon. In 1944 the Federal Highway Act was passed, appropriating the first $1.5 million for the building of a national highway system after the war. Boeing and McDonnell-Douglas had on the boards blueprints for civilian aircraft utilizing the great leaps in technology that had been generated by the war. In 1946, construction was begun on the New Jersey Turnpike from New York to Philadelphia. Airports would receive millions of dollars in federal aid and tax-exempt status while the railroads would continue to pay taxes on the lands under their tracks. Whether it was the claustrophobia posited by my train companion Maxwell Greene or, the more conventional theory, that cars and planes were heralds of the future while trains were conveyances of the past, the generation returning from war unquestionably turned its collective back on the railroad as a means of passenger transportation.

The PRR had plowed the profits of the war years into new equipment and rolling stock; the NYC used them to put its financial house in order. It didn't matter. Both faced dire financial straits by 1955, when the Pennsylvania secretly sold the air rights over Penn Station to future organizers of the third Madison Square Garden.

On July 21, 1961, the plan to tear down the aboveground station and build the new sports arena was announced, though there was some hedging about preserving the main waiting room and building the garden around it. Drawings of the new underground station were published—with surprisingly little public response, considering that they were remarkably true to the abomination that exists today. A small group of architects protested under the banner of AGBANY (Action Group for Better Architecture in New York), but their picketing was ignored by a city that three years later instituted the Landmarks Preservation Commission, which could have saved Penn Station.

The developers moved fast, using the standard twin bludgeons of increased tax revenue and progress to move a city that didn't need much convincing. The station was in disreputable shape, and its neighborhood had never developed the vitality the original planners had hoped for. The grand architecture of the building itself was now seen as a liability with its great distances, foreboding carriageways, labyrinthine passages, gloomy cavernous spaces, and the Victorian austerity of its seatless waiting room and separate men's and women's retiring rooms.

By 1966 it was gone—carted off as landfill for the vast New Jersey meadowlands. Madison Square Garden developer Irving Felt was photographed wielding a gold-plated wrench in a simulation of applying the final bolt to the last steel column of the frame for the sports arena that twenty years later would itself be slated for redevelopment because of competition from the new sports complexes out in those same Jersey meadowlands. It was just under a hundred years since the driving of the Golden Spike in 1869.

Like no structure since Roebling's Brooklyn Bridge, Penn Station symbolized a vision of a people's identity and destiny. Its architectural roots lay in that most American of the monuments of ancient Western civilization, the Roman public baths, built for the comfort of the people, in a style that ennobled them. Its greatest innovations, the concourse roof and the electrified train tunnels, were inventions of modern Europe carried out on an American scale. Its enclosed shops, services, and thoroughfares constituted a separate downtown Main Street amid the world's greatest city. And under its concourse people could board trains with through cars to all points of a continent without having to disembark at borders or the termini of individual railroads. It was nothing less than an edifice of union—integration—of history and space, time and place.

Across the New Jersey meadowlands the *Bankers* today flashes at over a hundred miles per hour past the old Manhattan Transfer, where steam locomotives were replaced with electrics for the plunge into the tunnel before the completion of the all-electric line to Washington in 1928. The train slows for the big turn to the east and then dives into the blackness of the tunnel under Bergen Hill and the Hudson River. Even at the reduced speed of sixty miles per hour, the loud ride through the tunnel surpasses the rush of a subway ride. You can feel the midpoint when the slight downhill slope levels out and then gives way to an uphill sensation.

The imminent arrival at Penn Station is signaled by a slowing of speed and a splash of daylight near Ninth Avenue before the passage under the post office and the conductor's announcing, "This station stop is Penn Station, New York."

At first the entrance into the station itself suggests a subway stop, with its fluorescent lighting, dirty concrete platforms, and posters advertising Broadway shows and cigarettes, but here are half a dozen Amtrak trains, including the *Silver Meteor* with its sleeper, lounge, and dining cars bound for Miami fourteen hundred miles away.

Sipping my third glass of wine, I watch the scramble of passengers detraining and the even more chaotic boarding of those bound for points northeast. There are still redcaps to assist passengers with their luggage, but otherwise a traveler from the era of Penn Station's greatness would not recognize the scene.

But the train pulls out right on time and slips under the East River; a few moments later we emerge into the Sunnyside Yards in Queens. Here the Long Island Rail Road peels off to the east while the Amtrak line makes a slow turn northward for the climb over the city streets to the heights of the Hell Gate Bridge spanning the East River. Since the bridge is several hundred feet high at its centerpoint, the grade on the ramp over Queens is nearly as striking as some of those over great mountain passes out west.

Down below it is Friday-afternoon rush hour. The streets are clogged. The neighborhoods of brownstone row houses evince the ebb and flow of life in the heart of the teeming city. Here we pass over a street where flowers bloom, tiny lawns are trimmed, and the laundry is hung to dry out back. Another street is all derelict autos, trash, and weeds, and the laundry is hung out front. Here the street corner is a grandstand behind a baseball-diamond backstop where fathers proudly watch their small boys play the American game; there the street corner is a line of men waiting to buy a bottle at a seedy package store. And as the train climbs to the bridge, the peaks of the Manhattan skyline rise above it all, purple and black before the sinking afternoon sun.

From the bridge itself, I can see jets taking off every five minutes from La Guardia. Commercial ships, fishing boats, and pleasure craft ply the waters below. Rush-hour traffic crawls along the parkways by both shores and over the half-dozen other bridges I can see from here. Out west, restless Americans built their transportation systems to conquer space; way east, in the crowded city, they built them to create space. From the top of Hell Gate Bridge I can see the mix of elements that make America in exact opposite proportions from those in the view from the mystery spring overlooking the Flathead Valley in Essex, Montana.

On the north shore of Hell Gate, the train turns east and rattles over the junction of the New York, New Haven & Hartford line from New York's other station, Grand Central. Ahead lies New England—New Haven, Hartford, and Springfield: home. We accelerate and race the autos on Interstate 95.

Out there it looks hot, and the drivers hunch over their wheels and sweat and curse the traffic. Inside the train it is cool, and the friendly chatter of passengers who were strangers when they boarded combines with the wine and the rhythm of Heine Marouche to lull me to a reverie of peace and ease as I anticipate my return to the placid New Hampshire summer. The spring trout will no longer be biting, but the smallmouth bass will provide just enough action in the long rose-skied evenings. On the Fourth of July my children will splash all day in the chilly waters off the dock at my mother's house on Lake Sunapee. My mother will soak in the warmth of her memories and the gentle New Hampshire summer sun while her children and their spouses play their father's games. If my children were on this train, they would ask, "Are we humming, Daddy?" Despite the loss of Penn Station and so much of the past, perhaps we will salvage something yet. At this moment, I would answer, "Yes, children, yes indeed, we are humming."

Epilogue

THE *CAPITOL LIMITED*

S I X months after my return home I went to Chicago to ride back east on the train I missed before, the *Capitol Limited*, to the newly renovated Union Station in Washington, D.C. Christmas was approaching, and through a snowy Indiana evening the train carried dozens of young mothers back to Valparaiso, Warsaw, and Fort Wayne after a day of shopping in Chicago. The "Shop Till You Drop Express," they called it, and it was a lively ride, with Christmas carols and eggnogs in the bar car. Two fellows from Atlanta who liked to call themselves the "rough riders" spun southern yarns for the Yankee belles, who returned their kindness with good, clean, wholesome flirtation.

In the morning I finally got to ride the tracks of the old Baltimore & Ohio. This was the nation's first regularly scheduled passenger run, and it was laid over the route of a turnpike in which George Washington once held stock. From the dome observation car, I saw the monument at Martinsburg commemorating the outbreak of the great strikes of 1877, the site at Harpers Ferry where John Brown declared the opening of hostilities for the Civil War, and the dozens of tunnels which bore through the wrinkles of the Appalachian Mountains. Approaching

Washington, I could judge our proximity by the size of the condominium developments that surround it like fortress ramparts. Finally we backed into Union Station, which in my previous travels had always been a place under renovation with temporary walkways and waiting areas not too much more pleasant than Penn Station in New York. Nothing in thirty-thousand miles of rail travel in America had prepared me for what I was to find.

From 1835, when the B&O laid its first tracks out of Washington, until the twentieth century, the railroad was a rather unwelcome nuisance in the capital. Both the B&O and the Pennsylvania seemed bent on suffocating the sylvan Mall of Pierre L'Enfant with stations, roundhouses, tracks, and smoke and drowning out parliamentary debate with bells and whistles, chugging engines, and banging couplings. In 1901 legislators had had enough and ordered the railroads to back off from the monumental heart of America's City Beautiful. The "Washington Plan" was in the wind, a scheme to extend the colossal architecture of the Capitol and White House with a memorial to Lincoln and other finishing touches that would complete the Mall cycle that we know today. Initially, dirty railroads were to have no part in it.

Architect Daniel Burnham was commissioned for the project and, in Rome, sketched the Baths of Diocletian at about the same time that Charles McKim was sketching the Baths of Caracalla. Returning through London, he met Pennsylvania president Alexander Cassatt, who was himself returning from Paris. Burnham suggested a "union station" for Washington serving both the Pennsy and the rival B&O, a station on a monumental scale that would make the railroad part of the Washington Plan rather than an eyesore beside it. Cassatt, while keeping his plans for New York to himself, agreed, provided that the government came through with a subsidy for the tunnel that would be needed to take trains under the Mall. Cassatt already had enough expensive tunneling in mind for his other project.

Thus Cassatt and the Pennsylvania Railroad came to have two architects simultaneously designing what were possibly the two greatest buildings in America. That Washington's Union Station never generated quite the same awe as New York's Penn Station may be due to its proximity to the Capitol, the White House, and the other monumental structures of the seat of American power. It was certainly built on the same colossal scale.

While the architecture of Penn Station was circumferential and vertical, as befits a building meant to establish its city as the center of things, Union Station's design was linear. Detraining, one crossed southwesterly through the huge glassed-over concourse, into the vaulted Main Hall with its high Constantinian arches and gold-leafed ceiling panels, and out under mammoth military statuary into the Plaza, which opened on lawns and gardens leading directly to the Mall and the Capitol. This was a gateway rather than a central square. Visitors to the new Rome were initiated through a succession of environments providing a proper transition from the earthiness of trackside to the grandeur of the Capitol dome. Outside, the marble cornices, the arched entries, the epic inscriptions, and the plaza fountains constituted a fitting monument to the Columbian spirit embodied in the railroad and the nation over which the capital presided.

The station's history since its opening in 1907 until the 1950s parallels that of Penn Station with the glamour of the great luxury passenger trains, the glitter of the rich and famous, the bustle and drama of two world wars, and the passage of countless Americans pursuing their birthright to travel. With its proximity to the Mall, its high profile in presidential inaugurations, and the establishment of the station's famous Savarin Restaurant and associated shops as a haunt of wellheeled Washingtonians who patronized the station even when they weren't catching a train, Union Station perhaps integrated itself into the community of the city in a way that Penn Station never did. This may be one reason for the very different fates of the two buildings. The other was the proximity of the moral force of democratic government.

Throughout the fifties, the Pennsy and B&O passenger service suffered the same setbacks that other railroads did. The competing auto and trucking industries boomed, and in Washington the other major cause of the railroad's decline was strikingly highlighted when the government built Washington's international airport. Meanwhile the railroads paid the highest tax of any commercial structure in the city on Union Station, whose construction they had financed themselves. By 1960, the railroads were looking into ways to rid themselves of the costly behemoth. Schemes included tearing it down and building an office tower, selling it to the Smithsonian, and donating it to the government in return for free use of a small corner of it as a scaled-down station. In 1964, a committee tagged the building as a landmark deserving preservation. Though the resolution had no force in law, it was not easy for private enterprise to demolish a National Landmark within the shadow of the Capitol.

Union Station's first attempted rebirth resulted in a miscarriage. Under Interior Secretary Stuart Udall, the National Visitors Center project was initiated in 1968. Union Station would be redeveloped as a center for initiating and educating visitors to the capital with exhibits and multimedia orientation presentations.

The project was a $30 million disaster highlighted by a carpeted Main Hall (with $20,000 worth of cigarette holes burned into it after an inaugural ball) with a pit in its center where visitors were treated to a slide show called PAVE (the Primary Audio-Visual Experience). Nobody went there. The roof leaked, and after hosting Ronald Reagan's inaugural in 1981, the place was closed.

But at least the Visitors Center project had made the building Congress's responsibility. A bipartisan crusade to revive Union Station was initiated by Democrat Patrick Moynihan and Republican Robert Stafford, with the enthusiastic support of the newly invigorated Amtrak corporation. Dozens of fast Amtrak trains in the corridor between Washington and Boston now carried a substantial percentage of the "shuttle" passenger traffic; three popular trains ran daily to the south Atlantic coast and Florida; the *Crescent* to New Orleans had made a comeback; two trains, the fast *Capitol Limited* and the heartland-cruising *Cardinal*, connected Washington with Chicago and the west; and scores of MARC commuter trains served closer points in Maryland and Virginia. A good railway station at the nation's capital actually made sense. Congress fixed the roof and with the Redevelopment Act of 1981 committed the government to a new vision of a station housing a modern shopping mall and entertainment centers along the lines of the highly successful Rouse waterfront projects in Boston and Baltimore. Secretary of Transportation Elizabeth Dole furthered the cause by finding funds during the lean Reagan years, and the project took off.

Today Union Station is one of the most exciting places in Washington. Besides rail passengers bound to and from the far corners of the nation, the place is thronged day and night with people who will never ride a train, but who come in on the subway from the condo complexes or who park in the towering parking garage out back and patronize the three levels of shops, restaurants, cinemas, nightclubs, and à la carte courts in the great vaulted halls. During my visit a particularly popular attraction was the Christmas model railroad occupying the entire west end of the refinished Main Hall. Another hot spot was Fat Tuesday's, featuring "the world's largest selection of frozen alcoholic beverages." And all of this, one of America's most fabulous shopping malls, is built inside Burnham's original building modeled on the ancient Baths of Diocletian.

Here finally is a work of man worthy of the land I have traveled, one that reconciles the past and the present, that promises a future not cast adrift in tawdry isolation from its roots, that fulfills Daniel Burhham's prophecy: "Union Station will never die, but long after we are gone, will be a living thing, asserting itself with growing insistency. Remember our sons and grandsons are going to do things that would stagger us."

The renaissance of Union Station has coincided with that of Amtrak as a whole. Gone are the days when shortsighted, demagogic politicians could point to half-empty trains and stations populated only by vagrants as evidence of the superfluity of national passenger railroads in America. Now Amtrak trains are always full and hundreds of travelers are turned away daily because there just isn't enough equipment to carry the people who want to ride. And this despite the fact that budget cuts during the Reagan era have stretched the system and its equipment to a point where delayed arrivals and equipment failures, the kiss of death for any passenger railroad, have increased recently for the first time since the desperate early years of the system.

Today Amtrak is the nation's sixth-largest carrier of intercity travelers, accounting for 17 percent of all passages in the markets which it serves. It is the largest single carrier in the critical northeast corridor, surpassing any of the shuttle airlines, where it takes 33 percent of the market for the New York–Washington connection and 70 percent for the intermediate cities of Baltimore, Philadelphia, and Wilmington. Though a majority of Americans have still not availed themselves of the rail-travel option, the gleaming silver cars with the red-white-and-blue logo have crept into the mass consciousness as advertisers as diverse as New England Telephone, Honda, Mercedes, Merrill Lynch, the *Boston Globe*, Budweiser, and Disney World have incorporated images of the trains in their TV spots. At least three television dramas and a pair of thriller novels have been set aboard Amtrak trains, and a dozen motion pictures have featured Amtrak cameos in the past few years.

Clearly something is afoot in the land. At Union Station I meet Amtrak spokesman Clifford Black, an urbane, impeccably dressed, articulate patrician who seems better suited for collegiate ivied halls than for the sooty business of participating in the management of a national passenger railroad. It turns out he was an English instructor for many years before striking out in a public relations partnership that led to his current Amtrak role. Over coffee and Danish in the popular à la carte court, he attributes "the Amtrak miracle" to several factors. First there are the fortuitous circumstances of Amtrak's inception and early years. The Rail Passenger Service Act of 1970 gave the corporation rights and privileges that amount to a kind of eminent domain over all of the nation's rails, and thus Amtrak has a statutory mandate till 1996 to perform its task of moving Americans over rails whose freight-oriented managers would otherwise have no incentive to cooperate. And Congress's capital layout for new railcars and engines and maintenance facilities in the early 1970s provided an investment momentum that helped carry the corporation through the hostile Reagan years. Lacking these foundations, the Canadian national passenger rail system, VIA, faces drastic cuts and possible dismemberment as of this writing. But most significant, he says, has been the management of President Graham Claytor, former president of the Southern Railroad, whose mission of improving service while reducing cost to the taxpayer has inspired employees to a level of corporate loyalty and productivity rare in American business. As a result, Amtrak runs over the greatest track mileage of any of the world's major national passenger railways and yet has the smallest percentage government subsidy of its operating budget.

Besides these blessings, Black believes that the Amtrak success story involves larger factors too. "Americans realize better than some of their leaders that the railroad built the country, and they don't wish to see it die." He tells the story of the hundreds of phone calls he receives from community leaders in small cities and towns across America pleading for rail service. "Mr. Black, you probably don't realize this," they usually begin, "but the railroad built Maple City. Our whole town is built around the yards and shops and businesses brought here by the railroad." Of course he realizes it. The railroad built just about all the cities west of the Appalachians. Waxing philosophical, Black says, "The great mixing bowl of our society needs the very graphic, physical bond provided by the railroads. That you can touch the steel of a rail in Hartford and feel yourself connected to every city in the land—Americans have a subliminal yearning for that. They're just not so sure how much they want to pay for it."*

While the unwillingness to pay the bills still haunts all political dialogue in Washington, Cliff Black sees paradoxical hope in the crises that loom in America's near future. "America is just coming to the frightening realization that the auto-based economy is quite literally choking the country." As it did briefly during the energy crisis of 1974, the nation will look again to the railroads when exhaust pollution darkens and warms the skies and pavement covers ever more of our land. Collapsing interstate bridges and broken airplanes will bring

---

* As this book goes to press, President Bush has just proposed elimination of Amtrak funding in his 1990 budget. Amtrak officials seem not terribly concerned.

increasing scrutiny of the government's discriminatory subsidy of the auto and aviation industries just as the rail disasters reformed its relationship with the railroads a century earlier. The trucking industry faces a crisis in a dwindling employee pool that will lead to higher costs, making railroads more competitive.

I ask Cliff Black about Amtrak's vision of passenger railroading's role in the future of America. "It begins with a penny-per-gallon fuel tax out of a Transportation Trust Fund that goes to support Amtrak. If we had that we wouldn't ever have to ask for further subsidy." The first capital expenditures always mentioned are the new fleet of Viewliners for the aging eastern trains, more locomotives and sleeping cars to accommodate the increasing demand for long-distance rail travel, the extension of the high-speed electrified northeast corridor all the way to Boston to better compete for the New England leg of metropolitan shuttle traffic, and the judicious addition of routes in growing sections of the country.

Beyond that, Black describes a vision of a "kinder, gentler" transportation system based less on mass use of foreign-oil-dependent, fuel-wasting, and air-polluting automobiles on multilane superhighways, less on the frantic pace of dangerously overcrowded air corridors, and more on a mix of high-speed, high-tech trains and high-comfort traditional long-distance trains. Officials speak of a balanced triad of transportation options in a vein reminiscent of the triad of nuclear defense that has kept the peace for over forty years. "Americans will never give up the freedom of the private automobile or the speed of the airplane," says Cliff Black. "But the time is ripe for a rediscovery of the third option, one that has been there all along, one that costs us less than either of the others, one that despite its rich association with America's past may be the nearly lost key to its future."

I think he's right, but the Amtrak miracle notwithstanding, not all of the experiences of riding a train in America today are pleasant. One sees quickly that many of the forces that still endanger the railroad are the same ones that endanger the health of the land as a whole. Outside the train the view is all too often a panorama of junk and trash that is not confined just to the old decaying urban corridors. From New England, where the stuff litters the fields like grotesque rocks, to the southwest, where little arroyos are clogged with auto hulks and discarded refrigerators, the detritus proclaims a society gone mad with disposable consumerism. Unintelligible and intimidating graffiti mars brick walls in small midwestern towns and desert western-dream burgs alike—inarticulate advertisements of a simmering rage that answers in counterpoint the "legitimate" neon and billboard graffiti selling liquor and cigarettes and cheap, fast cars. Sometimes the scene outside is overtly hostile: "rocking," throwing stones at the passing train, has become the latest form of juvenile delinquency, especially in trendy southern California.

Inside the train, any trip can be spoiled by malfunctioning toilets, lounge or dining cars missing because of equipment failures, inoperative air conditioning, missed connections, power failures, and surly, incompetent crews. Though not the norm, these horrors do happen, and if your $2,000 family vacation encounters them, you will remember the odd look the travel agent gave you when you said you wanted to go by train. What can we expect when we don't want to pay the taxes necessary to guarantee clean air and water; or build prisons so that criminals are not recycled back to the streets; or hire inspectors to ensure the safety of airplanes, automobiles, and food; or pay teachers, cops, and social workers enough to make sure that only the best people perform those critical jobs; or cancel a deficit that will rob our children of their shot at prosperity? Until the day comes when oil shortages or fatal air pollution force us out of our automobiles, how can we hope to see a national passenger railroad funded well enough that its equipment always works and all of its employees are top-notch when we still don't want to pay for the things necessary to our very survival?

Long rail trips throughout America today can present a view of a nation that is not well, that is infected with a terrible virus of greed, materialism, waste, shortsightedness, and delusion. There were times in my travels when I felt like a tardy grandchild finally visiting a beloved grandmother, shocked to see how ill she has fallen during my absence. More disturbing still, she doesn't know she is sick, convinced by quack doctors that she is enjoying a period of remarkably good health, if only she could taste her food, move her bowels, and escape the violent pains in her lungs, her stomach, and the back of her head. But the country has been sick before and recovered to greater vitality; she has survived a great depression and a civil war.

Fortunately, failing equipment and poor service are the exception on the trains of Amtrak today, and desultory vistas are balanced by the magnificence of the land that, from a train, still inspires with unfulfilled possibility. The energy and conscience and creative enterprise that nursed the nation back to vitality in previous eras of ill health abound. From Project Hope in Essex, Montana, to the rendezvous of the mountain men in Oregon, the restoration of old Sacramento and downtown Meridian, the development of Olvera Street in Los Angeles, the design and building of the Vietnam War Memorial, the good neighbors living in the vast spaces of the west, the continuing influx of energetic immigrants inspired by the American dream, the spontaneous generation of a good time among the occupants of a passenger railroad car, and the salvation by Congress of passenger railroading itself, the key seems always to be the acceptance of the necessity of community and generosity in a land of individualism and private opportunity. If these characteristics are the prescription for an ailing patient, then a transportation system which cannot generate profits but can simultaneously preserve our mobility and our environment, which will not let us escape one another and the impacts of our politics but can make us feel part of the great adventure of being Americans, may play a significant part in the prognosis for recovery.

And finally there is Union Station, where politicians, developers, contractors, civic groups, railroad men, and a curious and culture-hungry public have conspired to pull off a little miracle of substantial beauty and purpose. As I stroll around the bustling halls after my interview with Cliff Black, listening to the ringing of cash registers and the echoing calls for train arrivals and boardings, I come to see the station as more than just an economically viable monument in a city of monuments. I think it's an edifice of freedom just as important as the free press, free churches, or free enterprise.

In all times travelers have served as the eyes of great peoples. From those who became cultural symbols like Marco Polo, Magellan, Hudson, and Lewis and Clark to the lesser millions who have brought home their impressions of the other side of the hill to share with their neighbors, travelers have been agents of discovery, perspective, and progress toward what is done better somewhere else, and of pride in what is done well at home. If something is amiss in the land, they are the first to know it; if some fine awakening is abroad, they are the first to proclaim it. Travel provides a way to verify the claims of leaders; it inspires new visions of better possibilities. Travelers bring us closer to people we have never seen, and they give us a clearer picture of ourselves. They are nothing less than agents of truth. Freedom of travel has always been one of the keystones distinguishing free from totalitarian states. The loss of a form of travel that provides a unique perspective of the country would be a loss of something much more than transportation.

Today in America, the frontier is gone, the buffalo are gone, the mountain men are gone, the prairie is gone, the cotton plantations are gone, the neighborhood school is gone, the corner grocer is gone, the family farms and Main Street are going, and most people travel by air or interstate where they do not see how our land has changed; but the railroad remains, and at Union Station, a short walk away from the forums where men and women chart the future, seventy intercity passenger trains packed with steel-riders arrive and depart every day.

Selected Bibliography

The source upon which I have relied above all others is Stewart Holbrook's classic *Story of American Railroads* (New York: Crown, 1947). To a lesser extent, I have used John Moody's *The Railroad Builders* (New Haven: Yale, 1919) in much the same way. Essentially I returned to Holbrook or Moody whenever I could not find a satisfactory source dedicated to the specific railroad I was dealing with at the time.

Most of the material concerning the building of the first transcontinental railroad comes from Maury Klein's *Union Pacific* (New York: Doubleday, 1987).

My primary source for the Southern Pacific and Collis Huntington is David Lavender's *The Great Persuader* (New York: Doubleday, 1970).

Aside from Holbrook, much of the material on the folklore of the Illinois Central comes from Botkin and Harlow's *Treasury of Railroad Folklore* (New York: Bonanza, 1953).

The stories of the Santa Fe and Fred Harvey are from James Marshall, *Santa Fe* (New York: Random House, 1945).

Most of the material on the railroads' role in the development of the American west is gleaned from Frederick Merk's *History of the Westward Movement* (New York: Knopf, 1978), and David Lavender, *The Great West* (New York: American Heritage, 1965).

Much of the material on the mountain men, the Mormons, and the Salt Lake region is from Dale Morgan, *The Great Salt Lake* (New York: Bobbs Merrill, 1947).

The background on the northwest is largely from Stewart Holbrook's other marvelous book, *The Columbia* (New York: Rinehart, 1956).

The history of the Great Northern is garnered from Agnes Laut, *Romance of the Rails* (Hartford: McBride, 1929) and Dorothy Woods, *The Great Northern Railroad* (New York: Random House, 1949).

The local material concerning Bloomington, Illinois, and Essex, Montana, comes from Matejka and Koos, The McLean County Historical Society's *History of the C&A Shops* (Champaign: Univ. of Illinois, 1988) and Atkinson and Atkinson, *Izaak Walton Inn* (Hungry Horse News, 1985) respectively.

Finally, the stories of Penn Station and Union Station are taken primarily from Lorraine Diehl, *The Late, Great Penn Station* (New York: American Heritage, 1985) and Highsmith and Landphiar, *Union Station* (New York: Chelsea Publishing, 1988) respectively.

In addition, the following sources each have provided one or more stories for the book:

Rollo Walter Brown, *I Travel by Train* (East Norwalk: Appleton, 1939).

Ted Conover, *Rolling Nowhere* (New York: Viking, 1984).

Arthur Dubin, *Some Classic Trains* (Milwaukee: Kalmback, 1964).

Dayton Duncan, *Out West* (New York: Viking, 1987).

Hamilton Ellis, *Pictorial Encyclopedia of Railroads* (Hamlyn, 1976).

John Steele Gordon, *The Scarlet Woman of Wall Street* (New York: Weidenfeld & Nicolson, 1988).

Oliver Jensen, *Railroads in America* (New York: American Heritage, 1981).

Ludovic Kennedy, *Coast to Coast* (New York: Dutton, 1981).

Charlton Ogburn, *Railroads, the Great American Adventure* (Washington, D.C.: National Geographic, 1977).

Elizabeth Page, *Wagons West* (New York: Farrar & Rinehart, 1930).

Martin Page, *Lost Pleasures of the Great Trains* (New York: William Morrow, 1975).

Francis Parkman, *The Oregon Trail* (Uniontown: Heritage, 1943).

Joseph Field Smith, *Essentials of Church History* (Salt Lake City: Deseret Book Co., 1950).

James Ward, *Railroads and the Character of America* (Knoxville: Univ. of Tennessee, 1986).

John White, *North American Passenger Railroads* (Baltimore: Johns Hopkins, 1978).

Bill Yenne, *History of North American Railroads* (New York: Gallery Books, 1986).

Index

Index